NOV 3 0 1998			

The Psychology of Gender

Contributors

Betsy Jane Becker is Assistant Professor in the Department of Counseling, Educational Psychology, and Special Education at Michigan State University.

Alice H. Eagly is Professor of Psychological Sciences at Purdue University.

Irene Hanson Frieze is Professor of Psychology and Women's Studies at the University of Pittsburgh.

Amy G. Halberstadt is Assistant Professor of Psychology at Vassar College.

Judith A. Hall is Assistant Professor in the Department of Social Medicine and Health Policy at the Harvard School of Public Health.

Larry V. Hedges is Associate Professor in the Department of Education at the University of Chicago.

Janet Shibley Hyde is Professor of Psychology at Denison University.

Marcia C. Linn is Adjunct Professor at the Graduate School of Education and Principal Investigator at the Lawrence Hall of Science at the University of California at Berkeley.

Maureen C. McHugh is Assistant Professor of Psychology at Duquesne University.

Anne C. Petersen is Professor of Human Development in the Department of Individual and Family Studies at the Pennsylvania State University.

Bernard E. Whitley, Jr., is Assistant Professor of Psychological Sciences at Ball State University.

The Psychology of Gender

Advances through Meta-analysis

edited by
Janet Shibley Hyde and
Marcia C. Linn

The Johns Hopkins University Press

Baltimore and London

The Johns Hopkins University Press, 701 West 40th Street, Baltimore, Maryland 21211
The Johns Hopkins Press Ltd, London

The paper in this book is acid-free and meets the guidelines for
permanence and durability of the Committee on Production Guidelines
for Book Longevity of the Council on Library Resources.

Library of Congress Cataloging-in-Publication Data
Main entry under title:

The Psychology of gender.

   Includes bibliographies and index.
   1. Sex differences (Psychology) 2. Sex role—Psychological aspects. 3. Meta-
analysis. I. Hyde, Janet Shibley. II. Linn, Marcia C. [DNLM: 1. Identification
(Psychology). 2. Sex Factors. BF 692.2 P974]
BF692.2.P76   1986   155.3'3   85-19822
ISBN 0-8018-2974-7 (alk. paper)

Contents

Acknowledgments   vii

1 Introduction: Meta-analysis and the Psychology of Gender
Janet Shibley Hyde   1

2 Statistical Methods in the Meta-analysis of Research on Gender Differences
Larry V. Hedges and Betsy Jane Becker   14

3 Gender Differences in Aggression
Janet Shibley Hyde   51

4 A Meta-analysis of Gender Differences in Spatial Ability: Implications for Mathematics and Science Achievement
Marcia C. Linn and Anne C. Petersen   67

5 Assessing the Theoretical Models for Sex Differences in Causal Attributions of Success and Failure
Bernard E. Whitley, Jr., Maureen C. McHugh, and Irene Hanson Frieze   102

6 Smiling and Gazing
Judith A. Hall and Amy G. Halberstadt   136

7 Some Meta-analytic Approaches to Examining the Validity of Gender-Difference Research
Alice H. Eagly   159

8 Influence Again: An Examination of Reviews and Studies of Gender Differences in Social Influence
Betsy Jane Becker   178

9 Meta-analysis of Studies of Gender Differences: Implications and Future Directions
Marcia C. Linn   210

Appendixes
A. Studies Reviewed in Aggression   233
B. Studies Reviewed in Spatial Ability   248
C. Studies Reviewed in Attributions   255
D. Studies Reviewed in Smiling and Gazing   260
E. Studies Reviewed in Influenceability   269

Author Index   279
Subject Index   289

Acknowledgments

The research for chapter 2 was supported by the Spencer Foundation.

Chapter 4 is based in part on research supported by National Science Foundation grant SED-81-12631, by National Institute of Mental Health grant MH30252/38142, and by the Spencer Foundation.

The authors of chapter 5 would like to express their appreciation to Alice Eagly, Amy Halberstadt, Judith Hall, and Janet Hyde for their helpful comments on earlier drafts of the chapter.

The authors of chapter 6 are indebted to Larry Hedges and Theresa Pigott for conducting extensive analyses of the data, to Karen Littell for her assistance in conducting the study of situational correlates of effect size, and to the other authors of the present volume for their comments.

Preparation of chapter 7 was supported by National Science Foundation grant BNS-8216742. The author thanks Betsy Becker, Judith Hall, Janet Hyde, and Marcia Linn for their comments on a draft of the chapter.

Preparation of chapter 9 was supported in part by National Science Foundation grant SED-81-12631. The author greatly appreciates helpful comments from Janet Hyde and Alice Eagly.

Any opinions, findings and conclusions, or recommendations expressed in this book are those of the authors and do not necessarily reflect the views of the supporting agencies.

The Psychology of Gender

Introduction: Meta-analysis and the Psychology of Gender

Janet Shibley Hyde

Abstract

The literature on gender differences in psychological characteristics such as aggression, spatial ability, and patterns of causal attributions appears to be inconsistent and contradictory. The statistical technique of meta-analysis offers much promise for systematically integrating this diverse literature and suggesting substantive conclusions. Various methods of meta-analysis are reviewed historically. There are serious problems with the methods of vote counting and probability combining. The statistic d is the measure to be preferred. Methods of analyzing variation in d over studies have been developed and show great promise for detecting variables that moderate gender differences.

The following are quotations from Conclusions sections of some recent review articles in the *Psychological Bulletin*.

> The literature reveals findings that produce reasonable agreement, although there are a discouraging number of inconsistencies across studies examining the same variables. (Salmoni, Schmidt & Walter, 1984, p. 382)

> Widely varying incidence rates of postpartum depression have been reported in the literature. . . . Methodological and conceptual problems hinder the generalizability of the research. (Hopkins, Marcus & Campbell, 1984, p. 510)

> Many studies have methodological weaknesses. . . . More research is needed. (Jemmott & Locke, 1984, p. 78)

Reviewer's conclusions that studies in an area are inconsistent and poorly controlled and that more, better research is needed are so common that they are trite. In some cases, such conclusions are reached after a review of a hundred or more studies. One begins to wonder if there are ever enough studies on a given topic to reach any conclusions. Governmental agencies funding social science research, as well as the general public, are likely to share this concern. Too often social science research appears to consist of large masses of contradictory studies from which no consistent conclusions can be reached.

Research on psychological gender differences is no exception to this pattern. For example, Maccoby and Jacklin, in their well-known review (1974, p. 82), located studies of gender differences in verbal ability; of the 33 tests involving subjects 11 years of age or older, 12 showed females scoring higher, 19 found no significant gender difference, and 2 found males scoring higher. Maccoby and Jacklin concluded that females have greater verbal ability than males, beginning around age 11.

In the last decade, meta-analysis has emerged as a quantitative, systematic method for synthesizing the results from numerous studies on a given topic (Green & Hall, 1984). Therefore, it holds great promise for producing some substantial conclusions out of the apparently inconsistent literature on psychological gender differences. This book is devoted to demonstrating how meta-analysis can be applied to furthering our understanding of the psychology of gender.

The Narrative Review and Its Problems

The traditional method of literature reviewing in the social sciences might be termed a "narrative review." The reviewer locates as many studies as possible on a given topic, reads them, and attempts to discern trends in the outcomes. The reviewer may be testing a theory or hypothesis or may approach the review from a neutral position, trying to detect patterns in the studies.

There are a number of problems with the traditional narrative method of review. First, by attaching more importance to some studies than others, or perhaps because of personal biases, two different reviewers of the same set of studies may reach substantially different conclusions. Second, if the number of studies on a given topic is large—say, a hundred or more, as often happens in the literature on gender differences—the information quickly begins to exceed the human capacity to process it. Some reviewers deal with this situation by excluding studies that they feel contain methodological flaws, but this selection process, too, may be subject to reviewer bias and also discards a great deal of information. Others deal with the situation by using the method of vote counting; that is, the reviewer lists all of the studies and their outcomes—whether significant in the hypothesized direction, not significant, or significant in the opposite direction to the hypothesis—and then counts the "votes" favoring or discrediting the hypothesis. Vote counting can lead to erroneous conclusions, as I discuss later in this chapter. It also typically gives the impression that research outcomes are highly inconsistent. Third, even if the reviewer is able to reach the conclusion that there is some effect—whether it is the effect of psychotherapy, the predictive validity of a job-screening test, or the gender difference in aggression—the conclusion is not quantitative, and thus one still has no idea how large the effect is.

Modern meta-analysis techniques have been designed to overcome precisely these problems of narrative review.

Advances in Techniques of Meta-analysis

Meta-analysis has been defined as follows:

> Meta-analysis is the quantitative cumulation and analysis of descriptive statistics across studies. (Hunter, Schmidt & Jackson, 1982)

> Meta-analysis refers generally to the application of quantitative methods to the problem of combining evidence from different studies. (Hedges & Olkin, 1982)

> The approach to research integration referred to as "meta-analysis" is nothing more than the attitude of data analysis applied to quantitative summaries of individual experiments. (Glass, McGaw & Smith, 1981, p. 21)

What these definitions—by leaders in the development and articulation of meta-analytic techniques—have in common is an agreement on the twofold thrust of meta-analysis: the synthesis or integration of numerous studies on a single topic and a quantitative or statistical approach to that synthesis. These authors have advocated the estimation of effect size using statistics such as d and r. In so doing, meta-analysis avoids some of the criticisms of traditional methods of hypothesis testing and offers as an alternative the descriptive measures of the magnitude of effects.

Although methods of combining probabilities across studies were available as early as 1952 (Baker, 1952), it was not until the late 1970s that statistical methods for meta-analysis proliferated and came to be applied widely.

Vote Counting

One simple and seemingly logical advance over the narrative review is to list all of the studies that have been assembled and tabulate the number that show significant effects in the hypothesized direction, the number that show no significant effects, and the number that show significant effects in the direction opposite to the hypothesis. There are many criticisms of this method, but two of the most serious are that it can lead to false conclusions and that it creates the illusion of conflicting results when the results are actually not contradictory.

In order to explain the first criticism—that vote counting can lead to false conclusions—let us examine a hypothetical case. Suppose that Dr. Ian Powerhungry reviewed 60 studies on gender differences in aggression. Suppose further that each of those studies was based on 40 subjects (20 males and 20 females) and that all of the studies sampled from a population in which the true value of d was 0.50, that is, that the male and female means were one-half standard deviation apart. Thus we are assuming that the null hypothesis is false. Finally, assume that all of the studies used two-tailed t-tests and an α-level of 0.05 in deciding whether the gender difference was significant or not. How many of the 60 studies surveyed by Powerhungry will correctly report that there is a significant gender difference in aggression? Many people give the incorrect answer that 95 percent or 57 of the studies should show significant gender differences with males being more aggressive. However, this answer confuses Type I and Type II errors. When investigators set $\alpha = 0.05$, they are fixing the rate of Type I errors, that is, the rate of reaching false conclusions when the null hypothesis is true. However, in the review situation specified here, we have assumed that the null hypothesis is false. Thus, when we calculate an error rate, we are concerned with β, or the probability of a Type II error; that is, falsely overlooking significant effects. Simple power calculations show that the power of the t-tests specified above is only 0.33 (Cohen, 1969, p. 34), so that only 20 of the 60 studies will show males to be significantly more aggressive, and the remaining 40 studies will find no significant gender difference or an occasional significant finding of greater female aggression (even if there were 60 subjects per study, 30 males and 30 females, the power would rise only to 0.47, and still only a minority of studies would detect the true effect). Because fewer than half of the studies found males to be significantly more aggressive, Powerhungry concluded that there were no gender differences in aggression. His use of vote counting led to a false conclusion (we assumed that gender differences were significant, with $d = 0.50$). Thus one problem with vote counting is essentially this: it can lead to false conclusions because many studies in a review may have poor power and thus will fail to detect true effects.

In fact, the situation is so bad that in a set of studies with mean power less than 0.50, the probability of reaching a false conclusion using vote counting actually increases as the number of studies in the review grows larger (Hedges & Olkin, 1980).

Further, it is well to remember that if the null hypothesis is true (there are no gender differences) and investigators test at the 0.05 level of significance, then only 5 percent of the studies should show significant gender differences by chance. Thus if the reviewer finds even 30 percent or 50 percent of the studies having significant effects, that is far more than should occur if the null hypothesis is true.

The second criticism of vote-counting procedures raised above—that they create a false illusion of conflicting results—follows quickly from the first criticism and the example of Powerhungry. With 20 studies finding significant gender differences in aggression and 40 studies finding no significant differences, Powerhungry concluded that the results of different studies were highly contradictory. Because we know the way the statistics were set up, we know that the findings are not contradictory at all. All findings came from a sampling of a single population with consistent, significant gender differences and $d = 0.50$. The apparent inconsistency resulted from sampling variation in the statistic t (there would be sampling variation in d as well, but Powerhungry never got that far) and the poor power of the t-test for a sample size of 40, or even for a sample size of 60. Thus vote counting created the illusion that the results of the studies were contradictory when they were not. More recently developed methods of meta-analysis, to be discussed in a later section, allow the reviewer to test statistically whether there is significant variation in effect sizes across studies and thus to determine whether the studies have produced conflicting results.

Many reviews of psychological gender differences—the Maccoby and Jacklin review (1974) being a prime example—used vote-counting methods. Several of their conclusions of no gender differences closely resemble the one postulated earlier for Powerhungry. Thus some of their conclusions of no gender differences may have been false.

Probability-Combining Techniques

Rosenthal (1978) assembled a number of methods for combining probabilities from independent studies. The idea is that the probability levels (p-values) from all studies are combined into a single value to determine whether, over all studies, the effect reaches the 0.05 level of significance. (Actually, these methods test whether at least one study was of a population with a nonzero effect [Becker, personal communication]). The methods differ in exactly how one combines or weights the probabilities from the individual studies.

With the usual large number of studies and the resulting large number of subjects, these techniques tend to be very powerful, and the resulting p is almost always significant (Hunter, Schmidt & Jackson, 1982). The techniques by themselves are of limited usefulness because they tell the investigator only whether at least one study was of a population with a nonzero effect. They provide no estimate of the size of the effect.

In addition to his work on probability combining, Rosenthal (1979) has also developed a statistical analysis of the "file drawer problem." The file drawer problem assumes that scientists are more likely to publish results that attain statistical significance; that is, studies whose results are not significant are placed in the "file drawer," are never published, and thus can never be included in reviews or meta-analyses. If this phenomenon is a strong one, it could of course, lead to serious overestimation of the magnitude of effects, or even to the conclusion that a certain effect is significant, when in fact it is not. Using Rosenthal's technique (1979), one can take the combined p-value from the meta-analysis and then calculate the number of nonsignificant studies left in file drawers that would be required to reduce the p-level to nonsignificance. Typically the number turns out to be high—for example, 65,000 (Rosenthal & Rubin, 1978). It is ludicrous to think that there are 65,000 unpublished, nonsignificant studies on a topic lurking in file drawers, and so this computation gives one more confidence in the significance of the phenomenon being reviewed.

How serious is the file drawer problem in the literature on psychological gender differences? I tend to think it is not so serious a problem as it is in many other areas, for the following reason. In most areas of psychology, the phenomenon being reviewed would have been the primary variable in the studies reviewed. However, many studies report analyses of gender differences—whether significant or not—incidentally; some other variable was of primary interest. That is, in reviewing the outcome of psychotherapy , all of the studies in the sample were surely studies of psychotherapy outcome. One cannot imagine an incidental report of the outcome of psychotherapy. Gender differences, on the other hand, often are reported as an incidental analysis, and thus null findings can easily be reported when a study was published because of some other significant findings. Thus reviews of gender differences can more easily turn up published findings of no significant differences than would occur in most other areas.

Effect Size, *d*, for the Two-Group Design

In current meta-analysis, the most commonly used statistic is d, the measure originally devised by Cohen (1969) and advocated and developed by Glass, McGaw, and Smith (1981) in one of the basic texts on meta-analysis. Directed toward the two-group experimental design in which there is an experimental group and a control group, d is computed as the difference between the group means, divided by the pooled within-group standard deviation. (Glass and his colleagues originally defined d as the difference between group means divided by the standard deviation of the control group, but the use of the pooled within-group standard deviation yields a statistic with better properties [Hunter, Schmidt & Jackson, 1982]). The measure d indicates how far apart the group means are in standard deviation units. One advantage is that it is not inflated by large sample sizes, as is the statistic t. Further, unlike F, it can take on positive and negative values, reflecting experimental outcomes in the predicted direction or in the opposite direction.

The statistic d is readily applied to the analysis of gender differences; it becomes the difference between the mean for males and the mean for females, divided by the pooled within-group standard deviation. This computation of d, of course, can—and should—be done for any single study. Meta-analysis then cumulates d-values over many studies. As it turns out, a simple average of d's from many studies provides a biased estimate of the population value, so an alternative formula or a correction factor needs to be applied, as Hedges and Becker discuss in chapter 2.

Analysis of Variations in d

When one performs a meta-analysis, it quickly becomes apparent that the values of d one obtains vary substantially from one study to the next. What causes this variation? Hedges (1982a, 1982b) has developed analyses, the logic of which parallels traditional analysis of variance, that permit the investigator to explore the sources of variation in values of d over the studies being reviewed.

The first question is whether the variation in values of d can be attributed purely to random sampling variation. If the answer is yes, the investigator can stop and conclude that the set of studies has homogeneous effect sizes. If the answer is no—if there is significantly greater variation in d-values than would be expected by chance—then the investigator can proceed to a second step, analyzing this systematic variation. Essentially this can be regarded as a search for "moderator variables" that can explain the variation in effect sizes (Hunter, Schmidt & Jackson, 1982). These moderator variables can be chosen for theoretical reasons or simply on an empirical basis. For this reason, most current meta-analyses involve the coding of all studies for numerous other variables in addition to the effect size statistics. These potential moderator variables may be either discrete (categorical) or continuous (Hedges 1982a, 1982b; Rosenthal & Rubin, 1982). For example, in my analyses of gender differences in aggression (Chap. 3), studies were grouped into categories depending on whether the design was experimental or correlational, and age was included as a continuous variable. When the moderator variable is categorical, the goal is to develop categories of studies that have d-values that are significantly different from each other but that have internally homogenous d-values. Linn and Petersen's analyses of gender differences in spatial ability, reported in Chapter 4, are a good example. Three categories of spatial abilities were found, based on theoretical considerations in cognitive psychology, and the values of d were homogeneous within categories but differed significantly from one category to the next.

Effect Size and Meta-analysis in Correlational Studies

Researchers interested in the psychology of gender have used the techniques developed by Glass and by Hedges based on the two-group experimental design, which can be readily applied to males and females. It is worth noting that meta-analytic techniques have also been developed for correlational studies. They are summarized in a text by Hunter, Schmidt, and Jackson (1982). The statistic subjected to meta-analysis is r. The applications have mostly been in the area of industrial/organizational psychology. For example, when the issue is the validity of a test used to select employees, the statistic is the correlation between scores on the selection test and scores on some criterion measure of job performance. If there are a number of validity studies on this same selection test, they can be meta-analyzed. The values of r are averaged, weighted by the number of subjects in each study. Variation in r can then be analyzed for moderator variables.

I mention this other area of meta-analysis because it has, in some regards, progressed to greater sophistication. Industrial psychologists, for example, routinely correct their measures of effect size for attenuation and for restriction of range. That is, the correction for attenuation recognizes that unreliability of tests is a source of error variation in effect sizes, and thus effect sizes are limited in magnitude by test unreliability. Effect sizes (in this case, r) can be corrected (increased) to reflect the "true" effect size as if it could be measured with perfectly reliable tests. Similarly, restriction of range (which is common in industrial psychology because only those with high scores on the test are hired and thus provide data on the criterion measure of job performance) reduces the effect size r, and formulas are available to correct for it as well.

In the next stage of meta-analysis of psychological gender differences, we may want to begin applying some of these correction factors. It would be necessary to code studies for the reliability of the measures when doing the meta-analysis. I suspect that researchers will find many instances of only low to moderate reliability and, if corrections are applied, d-values may increase substantially. Investigators might also correct for restriction of range. For example, in an earlier review (Hyde, 1981), I noted that some of the studies on gender differences in verbal and quantitative ability were based on such restricted samples as Harvard freshmen or Berkeley freshmen. Clearly these subjects have already been highly selected for verbal and quantitative ability, and there is considerable restriction of range. If sufficient information is available in the original reports of research, the investigator can correct for this restriction of range.

I suspect, however, that corrections for restriction of range will not prove as satisfactory in the area of gender differences as they have in industrial psychology. For example, to simplify, does the admissions office select Berkeley males and females to be above a single cutoff score on the SAT verbal scale? Or does the admissions office select equal numbers of males and females, so that the cutoff score is different for males and females? Which policy is used in selection will affect the magnitude of the gender difference. In addition, of course, many other factors contribute to admissions policy—

and thus to restriction of range. Thus it seems doubtful whether a simple correction for restriction of range will ever allow one to estimate the value of d for the population as a whole based on a sample of Berkeley freshmen.

Advances in Reviews of Psychological Gender Differences

Reviews drawing conclusions about the nature of psychological gender differences first appeared several decades ago. The classic textbooks on differential psychology by Anne Anastasi (1958) and by Leona Tyler (1965) both contained chapters on sex differences. Both texts agreed that there are gender differences in verbal, spatial, and numerical abilities and in aggressiveness. Eleanor Maccoby's 1966 chapter reviewed sex differences in intellectual functioning, again concluding that there are gender differences in verbal, numerical, and spatial abilities. All of these reviews can be classified as narrative reviews.

By the early 1970s, the literature on psychological gender differences had become enormous, in part because of the flowering of the new field of the psychology of women. Trying to create order out of the chaos. Stanford psychologists Eleanor Maccoby and Carol Jacklin wrote *The Psychology of Sex Differences* (1974). They attempted a thorough review of research on gender differences in many domains, including cognitive abilities, perception, learning, memory, achievement motivation, self-concept, activity level, emotionality, and aggression. Sensitive to the tendency of researchers to publish significant findings and not to publish nonsignificant findings, they included in their review both published reports and unpublished studies such as dissertations and convention papers. In all, they reviewed over two thousand studies, most of them published between 1966 and 1973. On one hand, they concluded that the belief is unfounded that there are gender differences in the following domains: sociability, empathy, suggestability, self-esteem, learning of simple versus complex tasks, and achievement motivation. That is, the null hypothesis of no gender difference seemed most consistent with the data in those areas. On the other hand, they concluded that there were well-established gender differences in verbal ability, visual-spatial ability, mathematical ability, and aggressiveness. And they determined that the evidence was equivocal regarding gender differences in tactile sensitivity, fear and anxiety, activity level, competitiveness, dominance, compliance, and nurturance. Their method might be described as a combination of narrative review and vote counting.

Jeanne Block (1976) provided some important criticisms of Maccoby and Jacklin's methods and conclusions. She argued that they had a bias in favor of the null hypothesis of no gender differences. She was critical of their use of the vote-counting method. And she argued that they had been inconsistent in their decisions based on vote counting. For example, Maccoby and

Jacklin concluded that females are significantly better than males in verbal abilities when 28 percent of the studies found females scoring significantly higher; but they argued that the evidence regarding gender differences in dominance is equivocal when 36 percent of the studies found males to be more dominant (Block, 1976). These criticisms notwithstanding, we must recognize the Maccoby and Jacklin review as the intellectual foremother of many of the reviews in this volume.

In the late 1970s, statistical methods of meta-analysis were developed and these were quickly applied in the psychology of gender. The first meta-analysis of gender differences was Judith Hall's analysis (1978) of decoding nonverbal cues. She found significant gender differences, based on 75 studies, with females performing more accurately. In 1981, I reanalyzed the studies on verbal ability, mathematical ability, and visual-spatial ability assembled by Maccoby and Jacklin. As measures of effect size, I used both Glass's d (Glass, McGaw & Smith, 1981) and ω^2 (Hays, 1963). I found that the median value of d was .24 for verbal ability, .43 for quantitative ability, and .45 for spatial ability. The median values of ω^2 were .01 for verbal ability, .01 for quantitative ability, and .04 for spatial ability. Thus, although the gender differences are there, as Maccoby and Jacklin had concluded, they are not so large as many people would have assumed from the conclusion that they are "well established" (Hyde, 1981).

Similarly, Irene Frieze, Bernard Whitley, Barbara Hanusa, and Maureen McHugh (1982) reviewed studies on gender differences in causal attributions for success and failure. The values of d for gender differences were generally close to zero; for example, they were 0.09 to 0.19 for attributions of success to one's ability, depending on how researchers had worded the questions. Thus Frieze and her colleagues argued that "there are no strongly supported sex differences in attributions" (1982, p. 341), a conclusion that differed considerably from the impressions left by earlier narrative reviews.

Alice Eagly and Linda Carli (1981) reviewed social psychological research on gender differences in influenceability, using both probability-combining techniques developed by Rosenthal (1978) and d as an estimate of effect size. Again, the magnitude of the gender differences was small: the median value of d was 0.16 for persuasion studies and 0.32 for studies involving group pressure to conform. This review is also interesting because the authors made serious efforts to examine subcategories of studies—or moderator variables, to use a different terminology—for possible variations in d. They found that male researchers tended to find larger gender differences in influenceability than female researchers did: the mean effect size for studies authored by women was 0.01 to 0.02, whereas the mean effect size for studies authored by men was 0.21 to 0.34.

Marylee Taylor and Judith Hall (1982) applied meta-analysis in a novel way to test the assertion that androgyny is associated with mental health as assessed by measures of self-esteem. Cumulating data over the available studies, they concluded that it is not androgyny, but rather masculinity, that correlates with positive self-esteem.

These five meta-analytic reviews were based on the statistical methods available at the time. They used Glass's d as the measure of effect size and typically took some average (mean or median) of d-values over the studies. Often there was an effort to correlate d with features of the studies being reviewed. Since the publication of these studies, Hedges and others have developed more advanced statistical methods for meta-analysis that allow the reviewer to explore more precisely variations in d in the sample of studies being analyzed. All of the chapters in this volume make use of these state-of-the-art techniques and explore the questions they can answer in the psychology of gender.

Preview

The chapters in this volume provide novel and informative applications of meta-analysis to the pscyhology of gender. The topics span the breadth of research on gender differences, from cognitive abilities to aggression to conformity to nonverbal behaviors. In chapter 2, Larry Hedges and Betsy Becker provide an explanation of statistical methods in meta-analysis, designed for those who have no prior experience with meta-analysis. In chapter 3, I present my meta-analysis of studies of gender differences in aggression, investigating moderator variables such as age and method of measuring aggression. In chapter 4, Marcia Linn and Anne Petersen present their analysis of gender differences in spatial ability, concluding that there are three distinct kinds of spatial ability that show different patterns of gender differences. Bernard Whitley, Irene Frieze, and Maureen McHugh, in chapter 5, present their analysis of studies of causal attributions for success and failure; they conclude that the magnitude of the gender differences is close to zero. In chapter 6, Judith Hall and Amy Halberstadt present the results of their meta-analyses of studies of gender differences in smiling and gazing, concluding that females do indeed smile and gaze more. They go on to look at situational factors as moderators, contrasting three theoretical frameworks: warmth-affiliation, social tension, and dominance-status. Alice Eagly, in chapter 7, explores a novel application of meta-analysis; she suggests that it can test for construct validity and external validity in gender-differences research. In chapter 8, Betsy Becker discusses the results of her meta-analyses of studies of gender differences in influenceability and conformity. Finally, in chapter 9, Marcia Linn examines the implications for policy and for research of the meta-analyses presented in the book.

References

Anastasi, A. (1958). *Differential psychology* (3rd ed.). New York: Macmillan.

Baker, P. C. (1952). Combining tests of significance in cross-validation. *Educational and Psychological Measurement*, *12*, 300-306.

Block, J. H. (1976). Issues, problems, and pitfalls in assessing sex differences: A critical review of *The psychology of sex differences*. *Merrill-Palmer Quarterly*, *22*, 283-308.

Cohen, J. (1969). *Statistical power analysis for the behavioral sciences*. New York: Academic Press.

Eagly, A. H., & Carli, L. L. (1981). Sex of researchers and sex-typed communications as determinants of sex differences in influenceability: A meta-analysis of social influence studies. *Psychological Bulletin*, *90*, 1-20.

Frieze, I. H., Whitley, B. E., Hanusa, B. H., & McHugh, M. (1982). Assessing the theoretical models for sex differences in causal attributions for success and failure. *Sex Roles*, *8*, 333-344.

Glass, G. V., McGaw, B., & Smith, M. L. (1981). *Meta-analysis in social research*. Beverly Hills: Sage.

Green, B. F., & Hall, J. A. (1984). Quantitative methods for literature reviews. *Annual Review of Psychology*, *35*, 37-53.

Hall, J. A. (1978). Gender effects in decoding nonverbal cues. *Psychological Bulletin*, *85*, 845-857.

Hays, W. L. (1963). *Statistics*. New York: Holt, Rinehart & Winston.

Hedges, L. V. (1982*a*). Fitting categorical models to effect sizes from a series of experiments. *Journal of Educational Statistics*, *7*, 119-137.

Hedges, L. V. (1982*b*). Fitting continuous models to effect size data. *Journal of Educational Statistics*, *7*, 245-270.

Hedges, L. V. & Olkin, I. (1980). Vote-counting methods in research synthesis. *Psychological Bulletin*, *88*, 359-369.

Hedges, L. V. & Olkin, I. (1982). Analyses, reanalyses, and meta-analysis. *Contemporary Education Review*, *1*, 157-165.

Hopkins, J., Marcus, M., & Campbell, S. (1984). Postpartum depression: A critical review. *Psychological Bulletin*, *95*, 498-515.

Hunter, J. H., Schmidt, F. L., and Jackson, G. B. (1982). *Meta-analysis: Cumulating research findings across studies*. Beverly Hills: Sage.

Hyde, J. S. (1981). How large are cognitive gender differences? *American Psychologist*, *36*, 892-901.

Jemmott, J. B., & Locke, S. E. (1984). Psychosocial factors, immunologic mediation, and human susceptibility to infectious diseases: How much do we know? *Psychological Bulletin*, *95*, 78-108.

Maccoby, E. E. (1966). Sex differences in intellectual functioning. In E. E. Maccoby (ed.), *The development of sex differences*. Stanford: Stanford University Press.

Maccoby, E. E. & Jacklin, C. N. (1974). *The psychology of sex differences*. Stanford: Stanford University Press.

Rosenthal, R. (1978). Combining results of independent studies. *Psychological Bulletin*, *85*, 185-193.

Rosenthal, R. (1979). The "file drawer problem" and tolerance for null results. *Psychological Bulletin, 86*, 638–641.

Rosenthal, R. & Rubin, D. B. (1978). Interpersonal expectancy effects: The first 345 studies. *The Behavioral and Brain Sciences, 3*, 377–415.

Rosenthal, R., & Rubin, D. B. (1982). Comparing effect sizes of independent studies. *Psychological Bulletin, 92*, 500–504.

Salmoni, A. W., Schmidt, R. A., & Walter, C. B. (1984). Knowledge of results and motor learning: A review and critical reappraisal. *Psychological Bulletin, 95*, 355–386.

Taylor, M. C., & Hall, J. A. (1982). Psychological androgyny: Theories, methods, and conclusions. *Psychological Bulletin, 92*, 347–366.

Tyler, L. E. (1965). *The psychology of human differences*. New York: Appleton-Century-Crofts.

Statistical Methods in the Meta-analysis of Research on Gender Differences

Larry V. Hedges
Betsy Jane Becker

Abstract

This chapter is an introduction to statistical methods for meta-analysis. Methods are suggested for extracting estimates of effect size from the data given in research reports. The goals of statistical procedures for research synthesis are outlined. Conventional statistical methods are shown to be inadequate for research syntheses because these methods are conceptually too limited and because their assumptions are seriously violated. This suggests that special statistical methods are needed for meta-analysis. Basic statistical properties of effect size estimates are given and these properties are used to develop methods for combining effect size estimates and for testing the consistency of effect sizes across studies. Analogues to the analysis of variance and multiple regression analysis for effect sizes are then described. Finally, the importance of tests of consistency (homogeneity) of effect sizes in interpreting the results of a meta-analysis is discussed.

The accumulation of research evidence in many areas of the social sciences has outstripped most researchers' abilities to read and synthesize this evidence. In many cases, just identifying the (possibly hundreds of) relevant studies is a major undertaking. As the amount of research evidence has grown, so has the importance of comprehensive research reviews. Integrative reviews are attempts to synthesize large amounts of evidence in order to present easily understandable summaries of research literatures. Such integrative reviews serve as a crucial link that provides most scholars with access to the results of primary research studies on a given topic.

Perhaps as a result of the growing importance of integrative reviews, there has been a dramatic increase in the amount of scholarship devoted to the problems of methodology for research synthesis. The perspective of this work is that research reviews are part of the scientific process and therefore should be subject to standards of rigorous conduct that parallel the standards of primary research.

Much of the current scholarship concerning reviewing draws parallels between the methodological problems in primary research and in integrative reviews. It is common to think of primary research as following a series of steps that include selecting substantive research questions, operationalizing constructs, sampling, data analysis, interpretation, and reporting. The research reviewer must also follow each of these steps in an integrative review (Jackson, 1980). The sources of invalidity at each stage of a primary research project have parallels at each stage of a research review. In each case, the sampling method constrains generalizations that are permissable. The particular operationalizations of constructs that are chosen may involve subjective judgments that must be shown to be reliable and valid. Data analysis methods must be correct and must support the interpretations made by the investigator.

The recognition that reviewers face the same threats to the validity of their conclusions that primary researchers do, and that they must explicitly guard against these threats (Cooper, 1982), is a great step forward. A related and important perspective from primary research is that methods used in the study (or review) should be made explicit in the research report so that the methodology can be publicly evaluated, debated, or replicated (Fiske, 1983).

One of the most significant advances in methodology for conducting integrative reviews is meta-analysis (Glass, 1976), or the use of quantitative methods to summarize the results of research studies. In a typical meta-analysis, the results of each study are summarized by an index of effect size. The effect size indices may then be averaged to obtain an overall estimate of effect magnitude. Other statistical analyses can be performed to study the variation in the sizes of effects across studies.

Until recently, conventional statistical methods such as multiple regression analysis and the analysis of variance have been used to analyze effect size data in meta-analysis. The use of conventional statistical procedures for the analysis of effect size data initially seemed to be an innocuous extension of standard procedures to a new situation. However, recent research on statistical methods for meta-analysis has demonstrated that the use of conventional statistical procedures cannot be justified. Statistical procedures that have been designed specifically for meta-analysis are now available. These new procedures exploit the properties of effect sizes to provide analyses that avoid the difficulties of applying conventional statistical methods in meta-analysis.

This chapter introduces statistical methods in meta-analysis, including the new statistical methods that have recently been developed for the analysis of effect size data. The first section is a guide to extracting estimates of effect size from the data given in primary research reports. An analysis of the goals of statistical procedures for research synthesis follows, along with a demonstration that the application of conventional statistical methods in meta-analysis cannot accomplish some of these goals. We also show why special statistical methods are needed for effect size analyses. Next the basic statistical sampling properties of effect sizes are introduced. These properties are fundamental to the methods for combining estimates of effect sizes and for testing whether effect sizes are consistent across studies. Analogues to the analysis of variance and multiple regression analysis for effect sizes are then described. The importance of tests for the consistency (homogeneity) of effect sizes in interpreting the results of a meta-analysis is discussed next. We conclude with a discussion of the inferences and conclusions that can be based on analyses of effect size data. The implications of the use of these methods for reviewing and for research in general are explored.

Obtaining Estimates of Effect Size from Research Studies

The calculation of measures of study findings is an important early step in the meta-analysis process. After a domain of interest has been defined and a set of studies examining that domain has been collected, the reviewer must obtain a quantitative estimate of the size of the effect in each study. For example, one might want an index of the size of the gender difference in average performance on the outcome of interest in each study.

Many indices of differences in performance between the sexes have been used in quantitative reviews, and others can be imagined. Some of the more commonly used indices are the significance level, or p-value (e.g., Cooper, 1979), the percentage of nonoverlap of distributions (U) for the sexes (e.g., Eagly & Carli, 1981), ω^2, the "percentage of variance accounted for" measure (e.g., Hyde, 1981), and the point-biserial correlation of sex with the outcome variable (e.g., Steinkamp & Maehr, 1983).

The index used in the studies in this volume is the *effect size*, or standardized mean difference (Glass, 1976). There are several advantages to using the standardized mean difference as a measure of effect. It is both easy to interpret and understand and has the same interpretation across all studies in a collection (unlike the p-value). It is a directional measure, unlike the U and the ω^2 indices. Also it has a much simpler sampling distribution than either ω^2 or the point-biserial correlation, leading to straightforward analysis procedures.

The collection of effect size estimates must have three characteristics so that useful statistical inferences can be made. The estimates must represent the same construct, they must be independent, and they must estimate the same statistical parameter. The first two characteristics must be considered before effect sizes are calculated.

Assessment of whether all studies use measures of the same construct must be made by the reviewer and will involve determining whether the content of each test or scale represents ("samples") the variable or domain of interest. This process can be time consuming and often involves rather subjective judgments about similarities among tests and scales, many of which are not standardized and some of which may not even be available for inspection. It is wise to have several individuals judge the tests to ensure that they are reliably classified as measuring particular outcomes.

The issue of independence must also be considered before calculation begins. The more obvious kind of independence for estimates can be assured through their calculation; only one effect size of a given construct should be calculated for any one sample. Multiple measures of one construct from a single sample can be averaged or some other measure of central tendency can be used to represent them. When several outcome constructs are measured in many studies, separate statistical analyses are needed for the effect sizes representing each construct. This procedure was followed, for example, by Giaconia and Hedges (1982) in their investigation of the effects of open versus traditional education on many different kinds of educational outcomes.

More subtle kinds of interdependence among the effect sizes cannot always be "removed." For example, when a series of related studies is published by an individual or by a set of colleagues, they may be more alike than studies by other unassociated persons or groups. Similarly, the use of a particular test or scale in many studies may cause results to be more alike than if different tests were employed. This sort of interdependence can sometimes be signified with dummy variables. For example, the value "1" could be assigned to the studies from related authors (or using related tests) and "0" could be assigned otherwise. The coded categorical variable can be used to investigate the influence of the interdependence in effect size analyses. Glass, McGaw, and Smith (1981) discuss in more detail the coding of study features.

The choice of which statistical parameter to estimate is based on the substantive research questions the reviewer has formed and is constrained by the statistical designs of and the summary data presented in the primary research on the topic under review. The choice of a parameter will then guide the selection of an estimator or index. For example, suppose that the reviewer is interested in studying the extent to which there are differences between men and women in aggression. One study might report and examine the proportions of men and women in a sample who exhibit one or more aggressive behaviors. Another study might measure aggressiveness on a ratio or interval scale and thus would examine differences between the means for males and females on that outcome scale. These two studies provide estimates of different parameters.

The parameter most commonly estimated in meta-analyses is the population standardized mean difference δ. We define δ as the difference between the population means (μ^F and μ^M) divided by σ, the population standard deviation assumed common to both sexes. That is,

$$\delta = \frac{\mu^F - \mu^M}{\sigma}. \tag{1}$$

We use the Greek letter δ to indicate a population parameter defined by the population parameters μ^F, μ^M and σ of the observations of the study.

The choice of the direction of the sex difference is arbitrary, though it is usually convenient to subtract the mean that is expected to be smaller from the larger one (so that most of the effect size estimates will be positive).

Calculating Effect Sizes from Means and Standard Deviations

Glass suggested as an estimate of δ the sample statistic g, formed by replacing the parameters in (1) above by their sample estimators. Glass, McGaw, and Smith (1981) discuss the calculation of effect sizes. This is an elaboration of parts of their treatment, though some issues that they cover (e.g., calculation of effect sizes from nonparametric tests) are not dealt with here.

If a study reports means and standard deviations for males and females, an effect size g can be calculated as

$$g = \frac{\bar{Y}^F - \bar{Y}^M}{S}, \tag{2}$$

where $\bar{Y}^F$ and $\bar{Y}^M$ are the female and male sample means,

$$S^2 = \frac{(n^F - 1)S_F^2 + (n^M - 1)S_M^2}{n^F + n^M - 2}, \tag{3}$$

and n^F and n^M are the female and male sample sizes. S is the standard deviation estimated by pooling the within-group variances S_F^2 for females and S_M^2 for males.

If the study reports no subgroups within sexes, the means $\bar{Y}^F$ and $\bar{Y}^M$ will probably be reported. In that case, the calculation of g is straightforward. If means for subgroups are reported and the subgroups are equal in size, $\bar{Y}^F$ and $\bar{Y}^M$ can be calculated by simply averaging the subgroup means. If there are unequal sized subgroups, and the research report provides only subgroup means, the subgroup means must be weighted and averaged to get the proper means for the two sexes. For example:

$$\bar{Y}^M = \frac{n_{M1}\bar{Y}_{M1} + n_{M2}\bar{Y}_{M2} + n_{M3}\bar{Y}_{M3}}{n^M}, \tag{4}$$

where n_{M1} is the number of males in the first subgroup, etc., and $n^M = n_{M1} + n_{M2} + n_{M3}$ (i.e., n^M is the total number of males in the study).

In such cases, the standard deviations will have to be pooled to obtain the sum of squares about the mean that is common to all the males (or all females). We obtain the sum of squared scores for the ith subgroup within sex via

$$\sum_j Y_{ij}^2 = (n_i - 1)S_i^2 + n_i \bar{Y}_{Mi}^2 \tag{5}$$

and then obtain the sum of squares by summing across the groups and subtracting the mean squared term. This gives

$$(n^M - 1)S_M^2 = \sum_i \sum_j Y_{ij}^2 - n^M(\bar{Y}^M)^2. \tag{6}$$

The analogous procedure for females yields $(n^F - 1)S_F^2$. Then S_F^2 and S_M^2 can be used to calculate S via (3).

Calculating Effect Sizes from t-Statistics

If the study provides the values of a t-statistic, the effect size g can be obtained via

$$g = \sqrt{\frac{n^F + n^M}{n^F n^M}} \, t. \tag{7}$$

Calculating Effect Sizes from ANOVA Statistics

Similarly, estimates of g can be obtained from tests of the sex main effect from most analysis of variance (ANOVA) models. If F_{SEX} is the F-test for the between-sex effect in the one-way ANOVA, it will be equivalent to the square of the between-sex t-statistic and will have $n^F + n^M - 2$ degrees of freedom for error. From F_{SEX}, we can calculate an effect size estimate using

$$g = \pm \sqrt{\frac{n^F + n^M}{n^F n^M} F_{SEX}}, \tag{8}$$

where the sign is determined by the sign of the mean difference between gender groups.

If a multiway ANOVA presents many "between-group" effects for different factors, we create a new F-value with the appropriate error term by adding all between-group sums of squares besides that for the sex effect into the reported "error" or "within-group" sums of squares. It is important to add up sums of squares rather than mean squares. Sometimes the sums of squares (SS) are not reported and must be calculated from mean squares (MS) via $SS = df \times MS$, where df is the associated degrees of freedom.

We can calculate

$$F_{SEX} = \frac{SS_{SEX}}{SS_E \text{ (all but SEX)}/df_E} \tag{9}$$

and obtain g as in (8) above.

Calculation of Effect Sizes from Mixed-Model ANOVA Statistics

If a mixed model is presented, having some within- and some between-subject factors, we ignore all of the within-subject factors. We again pool sums of squares for between-subject factors (except those that involve interactions with within-subject variables). We follow the same procedure as in (9) to get the F_{SEX} that would have been reported in the one-way model.

Calculation of Effect Sizes from Correlations

If a study provides the correlation of the outcome variable (Y) with a dichotomous dummy variable representing group membership, we can obtain one form of an effect size estimate via

$$g' = \frac{\bar{Y}^F - \bar{Y}^M}{S_Y} = \sqrt{\frac{N(N-1)}{n^F n^M}}\, r, \tag{10}$$

where $N = n^M + n^F$, r is the point-biserial correlation (using a dummy variable with 0 = males, 1 = females, and S_Y is the (ungrouped) standard deviation for all subjects. Note that the effect size g estimated in (2) above had the within-group standard deviation S as denominator, whereas g' has the overall (ungrouped) standard deviation S_Y as a denominator. We can calculate g from g' if we have the value of S, via

$$g = \frac{S_Y}{S} g'.$$

If S is unavailable, we must realize that g' will be smaller than g, since in general S_Y is larger than S whenever $\bar{Y}^F$ and $\bar{Y}^M$ are markedly unequal.

Glass, McGaw, and Smith (1981) present formulas for translating between t and r and g and r, and many authors (e.g., Hall & Halbertstadt, Chap. 6) use the point-biserial r as the effect size estimate for analysis and interpretation. In fact, g and r are interchangeable when Glass's formulas are used to calculate them, and parallel analyses performed on the g's and r's (if transformed with Fisher's r-to-z formula) will produce equivalent results. However, we prefer not to report analyses in the r metric because the distribution of the standardized mean difference is approximately normal in large samples (and therefore is easily interpreted), whereas the distribution of r is nonnormal and skewed. The g estimates are also in a "difference" metric, which adds to their interpretability.

Problems Encountered in Estimating Effect Sizes

Use of Different Metrics

A problem that is commonly encountered when computing effect size estimates is that different authors use different and sometimes incompatible outcome metrics. Thus even when there are data to allow calculation of effect sizes, the same mean difference parameters may not be calculable for all studies. For example, some studies may use raw posttest scores, others change scores, and still others residual or analysis of covariance (ANCOVA) adjusted scores. The latter types of scores are most commonly found for research areas in which there are preexisting group differences that cannot be adjusted or controlled by random assignment or selection. This general problem of differing metrics for effect sizes is discussed by McGaw and Glass (1980).

In such cases, there are several practical approaches to obtaining estimates of effect size. Some research reports present data for calculating posttest effect sizes even though their analyses have been performed on change or residual scores. Similarly, we can sometimes use known or estimated values for pre-post correlations to create change-score effect sizes when insufficient sample data are presented. DerSimonian and Laird (1983) used this approach in obtaining estimates of the effects of coaching on SAT performance gains.

Even if it is impossible to compute all the estimates in a common metric, it may be sensible to compute for each study an estimate in the metric for which data are available and then look for differences in size of effect according to the particular metric used. Becker (chap. 8) did this in her examination of sex differences in social influence situations. She found significant variation in the magnitudes of sex differences that related to the metric used.

Insufficient Data for Effect Size Estimation

Another very common dilemma that arises in estimating effect sizes is that some studies report insufficient data to allow computation of effect size estimates. For example, one study may present means but not variances, another may present selected F-values rather than a complete ANOVA table, and another may present only p-values for such F-tests.

In some cases, effect size estimates can be obtained by substituting for the missing data (e.g., for the missing variances) values estimated from other studies with complete data on comparable measures. When only significant F-values are presented, we can sometimes still obtain proper estimates of S^2 by considering the sums of squares from the nonsignificant effects to be zero. Then if means are presented (which allows us to recover some between-group sum of squares), we can calculate the within-group and the other significant between-group sums of squares and proceed as discussed above.

Sometimes the values of test statistics are not given, but an exact significance level (e.g., $p = 0.31$) is given. In this case, it is possible in principle to use a table of critical values of the statistic to find the value of the test statistic that corresponds to the exact p-value. In practice, this can be rather difficult unless an extensive table of critical values of the test statistic is available. Often the exact significance level will not be given, and only a cutoff value such as $p < .05$ is given. Reviews have sometimes calculated "conservative" estimates of effect size by treating the cutoff value as the exact significance level (e.g., setting $p = .05$) and proceeding as described above. This procedure results in effect size estimates that are smaller in absolute magnitude than the true effect size. If the cutoff value is substantially larger than the exact significance level (e.g., a cutoff of $p < .05$ when $p = .001$), the resulting underestimate of effect size can be substantial.

Occasionally there is no way to obtain commensurate estimates and the study must be eliminated from the quantitative analysis of effect sizes. There is controversy concerning the best approach to reviewing studies for which effect sizes cannot be estimated. Often meta-analysts include studies with insufficient data for calculation of effect sizes by considering missing effect sizes to be zero. This is equivalent to assuming that all (or the average) of the studies with insufficient data find exactly no sex difference (or no treatment effect). This assumption may be justified, but there is no way to determine whether it is.

Substituting effect sizes equal to zero for all studies with inadequate data for effect size estimation is problematic for two reasons. First, the substitution of zero reduces the absolute magnitude of average effect size estimates. Some reviewers have argued that this produces a "conservative" estimate of effect magnitude.

Reduction in mean effect magnitude occurs for both the full set of studies and for subsets of the full collection, and each subset is likely to be influenced differently. Though it is almost certain that the sizes of mean effects would decrease (move toward zero) if the missing effect sizes were statistically insignificant, we do not always know the extent to which they would change (see Hedges, 1984). Also, if the data were missing for some other reason than failure to report statistically insignificant results, the true average effects might *not* be smaller than the estimates based on available data.

A second result of substituting zero effects for all missing data is an artificial change in the homogeneity of outcomes. Even if the true mean effect size for the gender difference were zero in the studies for which estimates are not available, we would expect a small amount of variation about that mean by chance. That variability would be artificially suppressed by the substitution of only zero. Thus the model of a single population effect size with value zero will erroneously appear to be very likely.

In some cases, the population sex difference may be truly nonzero, and in others the size of the true sex difference may relate to some varying study feature or features. In these cases, the addition of zero for studies in which effect sizes are not available would certainly distort estimates of average effect size and of relationships between effect size and study features. The addition of many zero effects may well artificially increase the heterogeneity of outcomes if the bulk of estimated effect sizes are not near zero.

Because we do not know the nature of the population parameters underlying our study results, we cannot determine what effect the addition of zero values to our set of study outcomes will have. To avoid introducing into the meta-analysis distortion such as that just described, one should not substitute zero effect sizes for studies with insufficient data to permit effect size estimation.

It may be that the studies with insufficient data for effect size estimation could be analyzed using methods like those suggested by Hedges and Olkin (1980, 1985) that are based on vote-counting estimation procedures. In some cases, one may also apply more general summary statistics like those described by Rosenthal (1978), which require the retrieval of only a significance level from each study.

Goals of Statistical Procedures in Research Synthesis

Before discussing specific statistical procedures for the quantitative synthesis of research, it is useful to consider what can be expected of a statistical analysis in the best possible situation. This is a kind of "thought experiment" that helps us to view seemingly novel statistical analyses in familiar ways.

Perhaps the simplest situation in which to synthesize research results is one in which the raw data from the several experiments is available and can be pooled directly. For example, suppose that we have a series of k experiments, each of which investigates a gender difference on a single outcome construct. This situation can be considered a special case of the more general two-group experimental situation. Assume that each study measures the normally distributed outcome variable using the same instrument and the same sampling plan so that the within-gender population variances of the outcome scores are identical. We can arbitrarily set the common within-group variances to the convenient value of one, although that is not essential.

The situation defined above is one in which the raw data from all of the individuals in all of the studies are directly comparable. Consequently, the outcome scores of all the individuals could be combined and analyzed in one large statistical analysis. In this situation, most social scientists would know how to proceed. The investigator would probably use the data from all individuals in one large 2 x k (two gender groups x k studies) analysis of variance (ANOVA). In our idealized case, the assumptions of ANOVA will be met exactly.

What will the investigator learn from this analysis of variance? There are three omnibus F-tests in the textbook analysis. The F-test for the main effect of studies is relatively uninteresting. It tests whether the average value of the outcome variable (averaged over both sexes) differs across studies. The other two F-tests are more important. The F-test for the gender factor tests whether one gender outperforms the other (on the average) across all k experiments. The F-test for the gender by studies interaction tests whether the difference between the sexes is consistent across studies.

The interpretation of the statistical analysis rests largely on these latter two tests. A large gender difference with a negligible interaction is easy to interpret: the gender difference is large and consistent across studies. If the interaction is not negligible, then interpretations become more complicated. An interaction suggests that the gender difference is larger in some studies than in others. Any blanket statements about the main effect must be qualified by the fact that sex differences vary significantly across studies.

If a significant interaction is found, most investigators would probably begin looking for reasons why the size of the gender difference varied across studies. Variation across studies in experimental procedure, conditions of measurement, or sample composition might figure in an explanation of variations in the effect. If a suitable explanatory variable were found, it might be entered into the statistical analysis as a (blocking) factor. The new statistical analysis would reveal (by an appropriate F-test) whether the new factor accounted for a significant amount of variation in the gender effect and whether variations in the size of the gender difference across studies within levels of the new factor remained substantial. That is, we can test whether a proposed explanatory factor succeeds in removing or "explaining" the variation in the size of the gender difference across studies. This test is conceptually analogous to the original test for the gender by studies interaction.

Thus, in the best possible case, where data from all studies can be combined directly, the statistical analysis can accomplish several objectives.

The analysis can

1. estimate (or test) the average size of the gender difference across all studies;
2. test the consistency of gender differences across studies (via the gender by studies interaction);
3. test the effect of explanatory variables (corresponding to differences among studies) that are used to help "explain" variations in the size of the difference between the sexes;
4. test the significance of variation in the gender main effect (or the size of the gender difference) across levels of the explanatory variables to determine if all variations in gender differences are essentially explained.

In evaluating statistical methods for research synthesis, it is useful to ask which objectives of the "best-case" analysis can be achieved in any proposed analysis. New statistical methods have been developed that provide all of the advantages of the best-case analysis for any meta-analysis. These methods permit the reviewer to answer essentially the same questions as if it were possible to directly combine the raw data from all studies. Conventional statistical procedures in meta-analysis fail to answer one or more of the questions that are of interest. Moreover, the use of some conventional analyses for effect size data frequently involves serious violations of the assumptions of these techniques. Thus conventional statistical procedures in meta-analysis are problematic for both statistical and conceptual reasons. We now turn to the specific problems of conventional statistical procedures in meta-analysis.

Conventional Analyses for Effect Size Data

Conventional analyses in research synthesis have been greatly influenced by the pioneering work of Glass (1976, 1978). He suggested combining the results of studies by first calculating an estimate of effect size g, which is the standardized difference between the experimental and control group means. In the context of the analysis of differences between the sexes, the difference between the means for males and females would replace the difference between experimental and control group means. The estimates of effect size from different studies are standardized, so they are, in effect, on the same scale. Consequently, the research synthesizer can combine these estimates across studies or treat the effect sizes as raw data for statistical analyses (analysis of variance or multiple linear regression) that relate characteristics of studies to treatment effects (Glass, McGaw & Smith, 1981).

Conceptual Problems with Conventional Analyses

Now compare the conventional analysis with the best-case analysis in which all of the raw data can be directly combined. In our idealized best case, the gender effect (mean difference between the sexes) corresponds directly to the effect size for the study. In the conventional analysis, the effect sizes can be averaged to obtain an estimate of the average size of the gender difference. Similarly, the effect of any particular explanatory variable can be tested by using that variable as a blocking factor in an analysis of variance (or as a predictor in a regression analysis) that uses the effect size as the dependent variable. Thus the conventional effect size analysis has two of the features of the best-case analysis.

The conventional analysis lacks two important features of the best-case analysis, however. First, it is impossible to directly test the consistency of effect sizes across studies in the conventional analysis. That is, there is no analogue in conventional effect size analyses to the test for gender by study interactions. The conventional analysis for testing systematic variation among k effect sizes has $k - 1$ degrees of freedom for systematic variation among effect sizes and one degree of freedom for the grand mean. No degrees of freedom remain for estimation of the error or nonsystematic variation. Second, it is consequently impossible to construct a test for whether the systematic variation in k effect sizes is larger than the nonsystematic variation exhibited by those effect sizes.

Note that it is possible, in the conventional analysis, to construct a test for differences among the average effect sizes of two or more groups of studies, as long as at least one of the groups contains two or more effect sizes. The multiple effect sizes within the group(s) serve as replicates from which an estimate of unsystematic variance is obtained. Then the test is constructed by comparing "systematic" variance among group mean effect sizes to the "unsystematic" variance of effect sizes within groups.

Such a test is conceptually and statistically perilous, however. How does the investigator know that the effect sizes only exhibit nonsystematic variability within the groups? If the investigator chooses the wrong groups, considerable systematic variance may be pooled into the estimate of the error variance. This was the essence of Presby's criticism (1978) of Glass's meta-analysis of psychotherapy outcome studies. She argued that Glass's analysis of differences among types of psychotherapy was flawed because he used overly broad categories of therapy—categories that included considerable systematic variation. The effect of including systematic variation in the estimates of error terms is well known to statisticians. It decreases the sensitivity (power) of the statistical test for systematic variation. The conceptual problem in the conventional analysis is that you can never know how much of the variation among effect sizes is systematic.

Precisely the same problem plagues an attempt to construct a test for the variation in effect sizes that remains after employing an explanatory variable. If the investigator tries to "explain" variation in effect sizes by grouping studies with similar characteristics (or using a linear predictor), there is no way to assess whether the remaining variation among the effect sizes is systematic or random.

Statistical Problems with Conventional Analyses

The analysis of effect sizes (or correlation coefficients or proportions) by using conventional statistical methods is also problematic for purely statistical reasons. Conventional statistical procedures (t-tests, ANOVA, multiple regression analysis) rely on parametric assumptions about the data that are not satisfied for effect size data. All of these procedures require that the unsystematic variance associated with every observation is the same (the so-called homoscedasticity assumption). That is, if we think of each observation as composed of a systematic part and an error part, then the errors for all observations must be equally variable. In the analysis of variance, we are accustomed to checking that within-cell variances are reasonably similar in value for all cells in the design. In regression analysis, we may check this assumption by determining whether the residual variance about the regression line is reasonably constant for all values of the predictor variable.

In the case of estimates of effect magnitude (either correlation coefficients, effect sizes, or proportions), the unsystematic variance of an observation can be calculated analytically. In fact, the unsystematic variance of estimates of effect size is proportional to $1/n$, where n is the sample size of the study on which the estimate is based. Therefore, if studies have different sample sizes, which is usually the case, the effect size estimates will have different error variances. If the sample sizes of the studies vary over a wide range, so will the error variances. In many meta-analyses, it is not unusual for the range of sample sizes to be on the order of 50 to 1. In such a case, the error variances are substantially heterogeneous.

A first reaction to this problem might be to recall that the effects of heterogeneity of variance on analysis of variance F-tests have been studied extensively (see, for example, Glass, Peckham, & Sanders, 1972). Also, heterogeneous variances have only small effects on the validity of the F-tests in a conventional analysis of variance. The situation in research synthesis is quite different from that in which robustness of F-tests is usually studied, however.

Studies of the effects of heterogeneity of variance in ANOVA usually assign a different variance to one or more groups in the design. Thus every observation in each group has the same variance, and there are at most three different variances in the entire experiment. In the case of research synthesis, the heterogeneity is usually more pronounced. Every observation (study) may have a different variance. Moreover, the range of variances studied in connection with the robustness of F-tests is usually rather limited, often less than five to one. The studies that have examined the effects of very wide ranges of variance have found that the F-test is not necessarily robust to substantial heterogeneity of variance. For example, Glass, Peckham, and Sanders (1972) reported that when the sample sizes of the groups are unequal, then the actual significance level of the F-test may be six times as large as the nominal significance level (0.30 instead of 0.05).

Thus the violation of the homogeneity-of-variance assumption of the analysis of variance and regression analysis is severe in research synthesis. This type of violation of the assumption has not been extensively studied. There is very little reason to believe that the usual robustness of the F-test will somehow prevail. The statistical problem of violation of this assumption combined with the potential problem of bias (reduction in statistical power) due to pooling of systematic variation into estimates of error variance raises severe questions about the validity of conventional statistical procedures in meta-analysis. There is no rigorously defensible argument for the use of conventional t-tests, analysis of variance, or regression analysis to analyze effect sizes or correlations.

Modern Statistical Methods for Effect Size Analyses

Modern statistical methods for the analysis of effect sizes overcome both the conceptual and the statistical problems that plague conventional statistical analyses. The new methods are designed specifically for effect size data, but they can be calculated from standard packaged statistical programs such as SAS or SPSS. The methods are derived from some basic properties of effect sizes, which are stated first. The systematic and unsystematic components of sample effect sizes are distinguished. Properties of the unsystematic (sampling) variation are discussed and used to construct statistical tests for the average effect size. Analogues to the analysis of variance and regression analysis for effect sizes are also presented.

Properties of Effect Sizes

We begin by focusing on the effect size or standardized mean difference for a single study. Glass (1976) defined the effect size as the difference between the experimental and control group means divided by the standard deviation of the control group. If there is no concrete reason to believe that the within-group variances differ, then the control group standard deviation may be replaced by a pooled within-group standard deviation defined as in (2). The pooled standard deviation has better statistical properties

(Hedges, 1981), and frequently it is the only standard deviation available when effect sizes must be derived from test statistics.

The effect size estimate g can be decomposed into a systematic part (reflecting a true or population treatment effect) and an unsystematic part (reflecting sampling error of the individual scores used to calculate the effect size). The systematic part of the effect size estimate is the population effect size defined in (1), namely,

$$\delta = (\mu^F - \mu^M)/\sigma,$$

where μ^F and μ^M are the population means of scores for females and males respectively and σ is the population standard deviation within the sex groups of the study. The unsystematic part of the effect size estimate g is the sampling error $\epsilon = g - \delta$. Thus the decomposition of g follows directly as

$$g = \delta + \epsilon.$$

This decomposition is analogous to the decomposition in test theory of observed scores into true score and error components.

This decomposition highlights an important feature of meta-analysis: all systematic relationships in meta-analysis are relationships involving δ, the population effect size. The sampling error ϵ is nonsystematic by definition and therefore does not have a systematic relationship to anything. The estimate of effect size g is useful only because it provides information about δ. Thus if a research synthesizer uses regression or analysis of variance to study the relationship between age of subjects and the gender-difference effect size, the systematic relationship is between the age of subjects and population effect size. This fundamental decomposition of the sample estimate of effect size into systematic and unsystematic components is essential in the statistical analysis of effect sizes.

The simplest statistical question in effect size analyses concerns the properties of g. Since g is of interest only because it provides information about δ, we need to know whether g is a good estimator of δ. The answer is that g is a slightly biased estimator of δ, tending to overestimate δ for small samples. A simple correction gives an unbiased estimator d of δ (Hedges, 1981). The unbiased estimator d is obtained by multiplying g by a constant that depends on the sample size in the study. That is,

$$d = c_n g = c_n (\bar{Y}^F - \bar{Y}^M)/S, \tag{11}$$

where the values of c_n are given to a very good approximation by

$$c_n = 1 - \frac{3}{4n^M + 4n^F - 9}. \tag{12}$$

Note that c_n is very near one for all but very small values of n^M and n^F. Consequently, g is almost unbiased except in very small samples. However, the correction for bias is easy to apply and the unbiased estimator has theoretical advantages. There is thus little reason not to use the bias correction routinely. The correction for bias is analogous to that for the sample estimate of the variance. The definition of the population variance has an n in the denominator. Using $n - 1$ in the denominator of the sample variance is equivalent to multiplying the population definition by the constant $n/(n - 1)$ to obtain an unbiased estimate. Although the factor $n/(n - 1)$ is near one except for very small samples, the unbiased estimator ($n - 1$ in the denominator) is usually used to estimate the variance. The discussion in the rest of this chapter uses the notation d for the estimator of effect size, and we assume that the bias correction has been used.

An understanding of the sampling properties of the estimator d of effect size is essential for the construction of statistical tests and estimation procedures for effect sizes. The sampling properties of d can be derived analytically for the case in which the assumptions of the t-test are met by the observations in a study. That is, if the t- or F-test used by the primary researcher is valid, the properties of the sampling error ϵ of the effect size are completely determined. Hedges (1981) showed that d is approximately normally distributed with mean δ and variance

$$v = \frac{n^M + n^F}{n^M n^F} + \frac{d^2}{2(n^M + n^F)} . \tag{13}$$

Alternatively, we could say that $\epsilon = d - \delta$ is normally distributed with mean zero and variance given in (13). If a study uses the same number of males and females, that is, $n^M = n^F = n$, then the variance (13) becomes

$$v = \frac{2}{n}(1 + \frac{d^2}{8}). \tag{14}$$

Note that the variance of d is completely determined by the sample sizes and the value of d. Consequently, it is possible to determine the sampling variance of d (or ϵ) from a single observation. The ability to determine the nonsystematic variance of d (the variance of ϵ) from a single observation of d is the key to modern statistical methods for meta-analysis. This relationship essentially permits the investigator to utilize all the degrees of freedom among different d-values for estimating systematic effects, while still providing a way to estimate the unsystematic variance needed to construct statistical tests.

The fact that the theoretical variance may be obtained from a single observation (effect size estimate) may seem unusual to some researchers, although most researchers are familiar with situations in which the variance of a single observation may be calculated from theoretical results. For example, most researchers are familiar with binomial theory in which the variance of a proportion p is given by $p(1 - p)/n$. Thus a single observed proportion enables the investigator to calculate a variance for the proportion. Similarly, most researchers are familiar with the fact that the z-transformed correlation has theoretical variance $1/(n - 3)$. In the cases of both proportions and z-transformed correlations, a single observation and the theoretical variance can be used to calculate a confidence level for the population parameter.

A single effect size estimate and the theoretical variance (13) can also be used to obtain a confidence interval for the population effect size. A $100(1 - \alpha)$ percent confidence interval for δ based on an effect size estimate d is given by

$$d - z_\alpha \sqrt{v} \le \delta \le d + z_\alpha \sqrt{v}, \tag{15}$$

where z_α is the 100α percent two-tailed critical value of the standard normal distribution and v is the variance of d given in (13).

Example 1. Consider a study in which the sample sizes are $n^M = 10$ and $n^F = 20$, the means for the two sexes are $\bar{Y}^F = 21.2$ and $\bar{Y}^M = 24.1$, and the pooled within-group standard deviation is 3.15. The (biased) standardized mean difference is

$$g = \frac{21.2 - 24.1}{3.15} = -0.921.$$

The correction factor c_n is

$$c_n = 1 - \frac{3}{4(10) + 4(20) - 9} = 0.973,$$

and the unbiased estimator d of the effect size is

$$d = (0.973)(-0.921) = -0.896.$$

The variance v of d is calculated from (13) as

$$v = \frac{10 + 20}{(10)(20)} + \frac{(-0.896)^2}{2(10 + 20)} = 0.1634$$

Hence a 95 percent confidence interval for δ based on d and v is

$$-0.896 - 1.96\sqrt{0.1634} \le \delta \le -0.896 + 1.96\sqrt{0.1634},$$

or

$$-1.688 \le \delta \le -0.104.$$

Combining Estimates of Effect Sizes from a Series of Studies

One of the first statistical questions that arises is how to combine estimates of effect size. Suppose that a series of k studies with sample sizes n_1^M, n_1^F, ... , n_k^M, n_k^F provide k independent effect size estimates (that is, effect size estimates based on independent samples) d_1, . . . , d_k. One way to combine the estimates is simply to take the average d. It can be shown, however, that the most precise combination is a weighted average that takes account of the variances v_1, . . . , v_k of d_1, . . . , d_k. This weighted average, denoted $d.$, is defined by

$$d. = \frac{\sum_{i=1}^{k} w_i d_i}{\sum_{i=1}^{k} w_i}, \tag{16}$$

where

$$w_i = 1/v_i = \frac{2(n_i^M + n_i^F)n_i^M n_i^F}{2(n_i^M + n_i^F)^2 + n_i^M n_i^F d_i^2}. \tag{17}$$

If all k studies share a common population effect size δ, the weighted mean $d.$ is approximately normally distributed with a mean δ and a variance of

$$v. = \frac{1}{\sum_{i=1}^{k} w_i} \tag{18}$$

Consequently, if it is reasonable to believe that a series of studies share a common effect size δ, then a $100(1 - \alpha)$ percent confidence interval for δ is given by

$$d. - z_\alpha \sqrt{v.} < \delta < d. + z_\alpha \sqrt{v.}, \tag{19}$$

where z_α is the 100α percent two-tailed critical value of the standard normal distribution. If the confidence interval does not include zero, or alternatively, if

$$| d./\sqrt{v.} | > z_\alpha \tag{20}$$

then the hypothesis that $\delta = 0$ is rejected at significance level α. Note that this test is conceptually a test for the "main effect" of sex across studies.

Example 2. Some effect size data from ten studies in Becker's analysis of gender differences on conformity (chap. 8) are given in table 2.1. The sample sizes (n_i^M and n_i^F), effect size estimate d_i, the sampling variance of the estimate v_i, the weight w_i given in (17) and $w_i d_i$ are given in the table for each study. Using the sums of the columns of w_i values and $w_i d_i$ values, we calculate the weighted average effect size estimate $d.$ using (16) as

$$d. = \frac{\sum\limits_{i=1}^{k} w_i d_i}{\sum\limits_{i=1}^{k} w_i} = \frac{35.120}{279.999} = 0.125.$$

The sum of the column of w_i values is used to calculate the sampling variance $v.$ of $d.$ via (18) as

$$v. = \frac{1}{\sum\limits_{i=1}^{k} w_i} = \frac{1}{279.999} = 0.00357.$$

The values of $d.$ and $v.$ are then used in (19) to construct a 95 percent confidence interval for the true (population) effect size δ via

$$0.165 - 1.96 \sqrt{0.00357} \leq \delta \leq 0.165 + 1.96 \sqrt{0.00357},$$

or

$$0.008 \leq \delta \leq 0.242.$$

Because the confidence interval does not include zero, the effect size δ is significantly different from zero at the 5 percent level of significance. Alternatively, we could have computed a test for the statistical significance of δ using (20), that is

$$\frac{d.}{\sqrt{v.}} = \frac{0.125}{\sqrt{0.00357}} = 2.092.$$

Table 2.1 Effect Size Data from Ten Studies of Gender Differences in Conformity

Study	n_i^M	n_i^F	d_i	v_i	w_i	$w_i d_i$	$w_i d_i^2$
1	70	71	−0.22	0.0285	35.036	−7.708	1.696
2	60	59	0.04	0.0336	29.742	1.190	0.048
3	77	114	−0.30	0.0220	45.466	−13.640	4.092
4	118	136	0.35	0.0161	62.233	21.782	7.624
5	32	32	0.62	0.0655	15.266	9.465	5.868
6	10	10	0.78	0.2152	4.647	3.624	2.827
7	45	45	0.39	0.0453	22.080	8.611	3.358
8	30	30	0.45	0.0684	14.630	6.583	2.962
9	40	40	0.36	0.0508	19.681	7.085	2.551
10	61	64	−0.06	0.0320	31.218	−1.873	0.112
Total					**279.999**	**35.120**	**31.138**

Note: Apparent inconsistencies between columns are due to rounding.

Because 2.092 exceeds 1.96, the 5 percent critical value of the standard normal distribution, we reject the hypothesis that $\delta = 0$ at the 5 percent ($\alpha = 0.05$) level of significance.

Testing Homogeneity of Effect Size

Combining estimates of effect size across studies is sensible if the studies have a common population effect size δ. In this case, the estimates of effect size differ only by unsystematic sampling error. If, on the other hand, studies do not share a common underlying effect size, then combining estimates of effect size across studies may be misleading. For example, if half of the studies have a large positive population effect size and half of the studies have a negative population effect size of equal magnitude, then the average of zero is not representative of the effect size in any of the studies. An obvious question is whether population effect sizes are relatively constant across studies. That is, how do we test for treatment by study interactions?

A test of homogeneity of effect size was given by Hedges (1982a) and independently by Rosenthal and Rubin (1982). The test involves computing

$$H_T = \sum_{i=1}^{k} w_i (d_i - d.)^2, \tag{21}$$

where $w_i = 1/v_i$ is the weight given in (17) and $d.$ is the weighted mean given in (16). The H_T statistic is simply the weighted sum of squares of the estimates $d_1, \ldots, d_k$ of effect size about the weighted mean $d.$. If all studies share a common effect size δ, then the statistic H_T has approximately a chi-square distribution with $(k - 1)$ degrees of freedom. If all studies do not have a common population effect size, then H_T will tend to be larger than expected under the condition of homogeneity. Thus the test for treatment by study interaction rejects homogeneity of effect size at significance level α if H_T exceeds the $100(1 - \alpha)$ percent critical value of the chi-square distribution with $(k - 1)$ degrees of freedom.

Although the defining formula (21) is useful to illustrate the intuitive nature of the H_T statistic, a computational formula is more useful for actually computing H_T values. Formula (21) is algebraically equivalent to the computational formula

$$H_T = \sum_{i=1}^{k} w_i d_i^2 - \frac{\left(\sum_{i=1}^{k} w_i d_i \right)^2}{\sum_{i=1}^{k} w_i}. \tag{22}$$

The advantage of (22) is that H_T can be computed from the sums across studies of three variables: w_i, $w_i d_i$, and $w_i d_i^2$. The weighted mean $d.$ and its variance $v.$ can also be computed from sums of w_i and $w_i d_i$. Consequently, any packaged computer program that computes sums or means can be used to obtain the components of H_T, $d.$, and $v.$ in a single run.

Example 3. Effect sizes from 10 studies reported in Becker's analysis of gender differences in conformity were reported in table 2.1. These effect sizes were used in example 2 to calculate the weighted average effect size estimate. Table 2.1 gives the sample sizes (n_i^M and n_i^F); the effect size estimate (d_i); the sampling variance v_i of the effect size; and the weight w_i, $w_i d_i$, and $w_i d_i^2$ for each study. The sums of the columns of w_i values, $w_i d_i$ values, and $w_i d_i^2$ are used to calculate the homogeneity statistic H_T via (22). This yields

$$H_T = \sum_{i=1}^{k} w_i d_i^2 - \frac{\left(\sum_{i=1}^{k} w_i d_i\right)^2}{\sum_{i=1}^{k} w_i} = 31.138 - \frac{(35.120)^2}{279.999} = 26.733.$$

We compare the value 26.733 with 16.9, the 95 percent critical value of the chi-square distribution with $k - 1 = 10 - 1 = 9$ degrees of freedom. Because 26.733 exceeds the critical value, we reject the hypothesis that all 10 studies have the same underlying (population) effect size. The studies do not, therefore, provide evidence of a gender difference of the same magnitude. Instead, at least some of them exhibit gender differences that are fundamentally different from the others. Consequently, any attempt to estimate or interpret the common "average" effect size may be misleading. The situation is analogous to finding a significant study by gender interaction, which makes the interpretation of the main effect of gender problematic.

An Analogue to Analysis of Variance for Effect Sizes

When effect sizes are not homogeneous across studies—that is, when treatment x study interactions are present—the research reviewer may want to explain variations in effect sizes by variations in characteristics of studies. One way to proceed is to group studies that share common characteristics that may influence effect size. The reviewer would seek to identify groupings so that the variability of effect sizes within groups is small.

A statistical procedure that permits this kind of analysis for effect sizes was introduced by Hedges (1982b). This analogue to the analysis of variance for effect sizes permits the reviewer to test the significance of variation between groups of effect sizes, and to test whether the remaining variation within groups of effect sizes is significant. Thus the reviewer can determine whether the grouping (explanatory) variable adequately explains the treatment by study interaction.

The analysis of variance for effect sizes involves partitioning the overall homogeneity statistic H_T given in (21) into independent homogeneity statistics, H_B and H_W, reflecting between-group and within-group homogeneity, respectively. These homogeneity statistics are related by the algebraic identity $H_T = H_B + H_W$, which is analogous to partitioning of sums of squares in the analysis of variance.

The between-group homogeneity statistic H_B is a weighted sum of squares of (weighted) group mean effect size estimates about the overall (weighted) mean effect size. That is

$$H_B = \Sigma w_{j.} (d_{j.} - d..)^2, \tag{23}$$

where $d..$ is the overall weighted mean across all studies ignoring groupings ($d..$ is the same as $d.$ in (16) above), $d_{j.}$ is the weighted mean of effect size estimates in the jth group, and $w_{j.} = 1/v_{j.}$ is the reciprocal of the variance of $d_{j.}$. Here the weighted means and their variances are calculated using (16) and (18). The between-group homogeneity statistic H_B is analogous to the F statistic for testing for between-group differences in a conventional analysis of variance.

When there are p groups, the statistic H_B has approximately a chi-square distribution with $(p - 1)$ degrees of freedom when there is no variation between group mean effect sizes. The test for variation in effect sizes between groups therefore consists of comparing H_B with the $100(1 - \alpha)$ percent critical value of the chi-square distribution with $(p - 1)$ degrees of freedom. If H_B exceeds the critical value, the variation between group mean effect sizes is significant at level α.

The within-group homogeneity statistic is just the sum of the homogeneity statistics (21) calculated for each of the p groups separately. That is

$$H_W = H_{W_1} + \cdots + H_{W_p}, \tag{24}$$

where $H_{W_1}, \ldots, H_{W_p}$ are the homogeneity statistics (21) calculated as if each group were an entire collection of studies. Whenever there is more than one study in a group, the within-group homogeneity statistic for the group can be used to provide a test of homogeneity of effect sizes within that group. If there is only one effect size estimate in a group, then $H_{W_i} = 0$ for that group. The total H_W provides an overall test of homogeneity of effect size within the groups of studies.

If there is a total of k studies divided into $p < k$ groups, then H_W has a chi-square distribution with $(k - p)$ degrees of freedom when the effect sizes are homogeneous within groups. The test for homogeneity of effect size within groups at significance level α consists of comparing H_W with the $100(1 - \alpha)$ percent critical value of the chi-sqaure distribution with $(k - p)$ degrees of freedom. The homogeneity of effect sizes within groups is rejected if H_W exceeds the critical value.

It is often convenient to summarize the fit statistics for the entire analysis in a table that is analogous to an analysis of variance summary table. Table

Table 2.2 Summary for Analogue to ANOVA for Effect Sizes

Source	Fit Statistic	df
Between Groups	H_B	$p - 1$
Within Groups		
Group 1	H_{W_1}	$k_1 - 1$
Group 2	H_{W_2}	$k_2 - 2$
.		
.		
.		
Group p	H_{W_p}	$k_p - 1$
Within-Group Total	H_W	$k - p$
Total	H_T	$k - 1$

2.2 exhibits all of the statistics with their respective degrees of freedom and reflects the fact that the between and within-group fit statistics add up to the total fit statistic H_T. The table also exhibits the within-group fit statistics for each group.

The easiest way to compute the statistics H_T, H_B, and H_W for the analogue to the analysis of variance for effect sizes involves the calculation of H_T and $H_{W_1}, H_{W_2}, \ldots, H_{W_p}$. Each of the H_{W_j} is essentially the homogeneity statistic H_T computed for a subset of studies. Consequently, the computational formula (22) can be used to compute H_T and $H_{W_1}, H_{W_2}, \ldots, H_{W_p}$. Then H_W is computed via $H_W = H_{W_1} + H_{W_2} + \cdots + H_{W_p}$. Finally, H_B is computed via the identity $H_B = H_T - H_W$.

First calculate or create the variables w_i, $w_i d_i$, and $w_i d_i^2$ for each study where w_i is the weight given in (17). Then calculate the sums of the three variables for each of the p groups of studies and across all studies. The sums for each group are then used to calculate the H_{W_j} for that group using (22). That is,

$$H_{W_j} = \sum_{\text{group } j} w_i d_i^2 - \frac{\left(\sum\limits_{\text{group } j} w_i d_i \right)^2}{\sum\limits_{\text{group } j} w_i}.$$

Use this process to calculate H_{W_j} for each group. The grand totals of w_i, $w_i d_i$, and $w_i d_i^2$ are used to calculate H_T.

Example 4. Returning to the 10 studies of gender differences in conformity, we study the relationship of the percentage of male authors and effect size using the analogue to the analysis of variance for effect sizes. Table 2.3 presents data from the studies including sample sizes (n_i^M and n_i^F), the effect size estimate (d_i), and the percentage of male authors. The calculated variables w_i, $w_i d_i$, and $w_i d_i^2$ are also given for each study. For the analysis, we group the studies into three groups:

1. studies in which 25 percent of the authors of the research report are male,
2. studies in which 50 percent of the authors of the research report are male,
3. studies in which 100 percent of the authors of the research report are male.

Sums of w_i, $w_i d_i$, and $w_i d_i^2$ for each group are also reported in table 2.3.

First, we calculate the within-group homogeneity statistics H_{W_j} for each group using the totals for each group given in table 2.3. For the group of two studies with 25 percent male authorship,

$$H_{W_1} = 1.743 - \frac{(-6.518)^2}{64.778} = 1.087.$$

The group of studies with 50 percent male authorship consists of a single study, so the within-group homogeneity statistic must be zero. To verify this fact, calculate

$$H_{W_2} = 4.092 - \frac{(-13.640)^2}{45.466} = 0.000.$$

Table 2.3 Data from Three Groups of Studies on Gender Differences in Conformity

Study	n_i^M	n_i^F	Male Authors (%)	Group	d_i	v_i	w_i	$w_i d_i$	$w_i d_i^2$
1	70	71	25	1	−0.22	0.0285	35.036	−7.708	1.696
2	60	59	25	1	0.04	0.0336	29.742	1.190	0.048
3	77	114	50	2	−0.30	0.0220	45.466	−13.640	4.092
4	118	136	100	3	0.35	0.0161	62.233	21.782	7.624
5	32	32	100	3	0.62	0.0655	15.266	9.465	5.868
6	10	10	100	3	0.78	0.2152	4.647	3.624	2.827
7	45	45	100	3	0.39	0.0453	22.080	8.611	3.358
8	30	30	100	3	0.45	0.0684	14.630	6.583	2.962
9	40	40	100	3	0.36	0.0508	19.681	7.085	2.551
10	61	64	100	3	−0.06	0.0320	31.218	−1.873	0.112
Total Group 1							66.778	−6.518	1.743
Total Group 2							45.466	−13.640	4.092
Total Group 3							169.755	55.278	25.303
Total all groups							**279.999**	**35.120**	**31.138**

Note: Apparent inconsistencies between columns are due to rounding.

For the group of seven studies with all (100 percent) male authorship,

$$H_{W_3} = 25.303 - \frac{(55.278)^2}{169.755} = 7.303.$$

Then calculate

$$H_W = 1.087 + 0.000 + 7.303 = 8.390.$$

Comparing 8.390 with 14.1, the 95 percent critical value of the chi-square distribution with $1 + 0 + 6 = 7$ degrees of freedom, we see that the homogeneity of effect size within groups of studies is not rejected.

Calculating the total homogeneity statistic H_T, we obtain

$$H_T = 31.138 - \frac{(35.120)^2}{279.999} = 26.733.$$

Using both H_T and H_W, we calculate H_B via

$$H_B = 26.733 - 8.390 = 18.343.$$

Comparing 18.343 with 5.99, the 95 percent critical value of the chi-square distribution with $p - 1 = 3 - 1 = 2$ degrees of freedom, we see that the between-group variation is significant at the $\alpha = 0.05$ level of significance. Hence the percentage of male authorship of these studies is significantly related to the effect size. The analysis is summarized in table 2.4.

Comparisons among Groups

Suppose that the reviewer "explains" the variations in effect sizes by finding that effect sizes are reasonably homogeneous within groups but differ between groups. If there are only two groups of studies, then a significant H_B statistic indicates that there is a significant difference between the population effect sizes of the groups. If there are more than two groups, then the

Table 2.4 Summary for Example 4

Source	Fit Statistic		df
Between Groups	15.030		2
Within Groups			
Group 1		6.118	1
Group 2		0.000	0
Group 3		7.553	6
Within-Group Total	13.671		7
Total	**28.701**		**9**

reviewer may want to explore differences among effect sizes for the different groups by using comparisons or contrasts analogous to the contrasts in analysis of variance.

Contrasts or comparisons are linear combinations of group mean effect sizes $d_1, \ldots, d_p$ of the form

$$c_1 d_1 + c_2 d_2 + \cdots + c_p d_p, \tag{25}$$

such that $c_1 + c_2 + \cdots + c_p = 0$. The reviewer explores differences among group mean effect sizes by choosing the constants $c_1, \ldots, c_p$ to reflect comparisons of interest. For example, to compare group one with group two the reviewer might specify $c_1 = 1, c_2 = -1, c_3 = \cdots = c_p = 0$. In this case, the contrast would be equivalent to $d_1 - d_2$. A test for the statistical significance of a planned or a priori contrast is derived from the fact that

$$z = \frac{c_1 d_1 + \cdots + c_p d_p}{\sqrt{c_1^2 v_1 + \cdots + c_p^2 v_p}} \tag{26}$$

has a standard normal distribution under the null hypothesis of no contrast effect (Hedges, 1982b). Alternatively, the planned contrast $c_1 d_1 + \cdots + c_p d_p$ could be tested by using the fact that

$$z^2 = \frac{(c_1 d_1 + \cdots + c_p d_p)^2}{c_1^2 v_1 + \cdots + c_p^2 v_p} \tag{27}$$

has the chi-square distribution with one degree of freedom under the null hypothesis of no contrast effect.

Example 5. Return to the 10 studies of gender differences in conformity. In example 4, the studies were grouped into three groups:

1. studies in which 25 percent of the authors are male,
2. studies in which 50 percent of the authors are male,
3. studies in which 100 percent of the authors are male.

The analysis demonstrated that the average effect sizes of the three groups of studies are significantly different. Suppose now that we wish to explore a priori contrasts among the effect sizes for these groups of studies. In particular, we will contrast group one with group two (studies in which 25 percent versus 50 of the authors are male). This contrast is defined by contrast coefficients $c_1 = 1.0$, $c_2 = -1.0$, and $c_3 = 0.0$. We will also contrast group three (studies with all or 100 percent male authorship) with the average of groups one and two. This second contrast is defined by contrast coefficients $c_1 = 1$, $c_2 = 1$, and $c_3 = -2$.

First compute the weighted mean effect size estimate for each group and the variance of this estimate. Using the sums given in table 2.3,

$$d_{1.} = \frac{-6.518}{64.778} = -0.101,$$

$$v_{1.} = \frac{1}{64.778} = 0.0154,$$

$$d_{2.} = \frac{-13.640}{45.466} = -0.300,$$

$$v_{2.} = \frac{1}{45.466} = 0.0220,$$

$$d_{3.} = \frac{55.278}{169.755} = 0.326,$$

$$v_{3.} = \frac{1}{169.755} = 0.0059.$$

The first contrast (group one versus group two) has the value

$$(1.0)(-0.101) + (-1.0)(-0.300) + (0.0)(0.326) = 0.199.$$

To test this contrast, we calculate

$$z^2 = \frac{[(1.0)(-0.101) + (-1.0)(-0.300) + (0.0)(0.326)]^2}{(1.0)^2(0.0.154) + (-1.0)^2(0.0220) + (0.0)^2(0.0059)} = 1.059.$$

Comparing the obtained value of z^2 with 3.84, the 95 percent critical value of the chi-square distribution with one degree of freedom, we see that the contrast is not significant at the $\alpha = 0.05$ level.

The second contrast (group three versus groups one and two) has the value

$$(1.0)(-0.101) + (1.0)(-0.300) + (-2.0)(0.326) = -1.053.$$

To test the significance of the second contrast, calculate

$$z^2 = \frac{[(1.0)(-0.101) + (1.0)(-0.300) + (-2.0)(0.326)]^2}{(1.0)^2(0.0154) + (1.0)^2(0.0220) + (-2.0)^2(0.0059)} = 18.177.$$

Because 18.177 exceeds 3.84, the second contrast is statistically significant at the $\alpha = 0.05$ level. Note that both of these significance tests relied on the fact that the contrasts were chosen a priori, that is, before looking at the data. Tests for post hoc or a posteriori contrasts are given in the next section.

Post Hoc or A Posteriori Comparisons

When the number of groups is large, a great many comparisons among groups are possible. The procedures given above for testing the significance of contrasts provide valid tests for the statistical significance of any one contrast that is selected before examining the data. When the contrasts to be tested are selected after examining the data (that is, are selected a posteriori), the nominal significance level of the testing procedures given above will be incorrect. In general, the probability of falsely rejecting the null hypothesis will exceed the apparent significance level of the test. This situation is analogous to the problem of post hoc testing of contrasts in the analysis of variance.

Several procedures are available to control the actual significance level of post hoc tests. One of the simplest procedures is an extension of the Scheffé method used for multiple comparisons in the analysis of variance. Adapting this procedure to the present context, each contrast among p groups is tested by comparing

$$z^2 = \frac{(c_1 d_1. + \cdots + c_p d_{p.})^2}{c_1^2 v_1. + \cdots + c_p^2 v_{p.}}$$

to the $100(1 - \alpha)$ percent critical value of the chi-square distribution with $p - 1$ (rather than one) degrees of freedom. Using this procedure, the probability that any contrast is falsely declared significant is less than α. This procedure has the advantage that it can also be used to obtain a simultaneous test for several contrasts. If each contrast is tested against the critical value given above, the chance that at least one contrast is falsely declared significant is less than α.

Example 6. Return to example 5, where two contrasts were tested under the assumption that the contrasts were a priori. Because the contrasts were planned a priori, each of the z^2 statistics were compared with 3.84, the 95 percent critical value of the chi-square distribution with one degree of freedom.

If the contrasts were not planned in advance (that is, were post hoc contrasts), then each of the z^2 statistics would be tested by comparing them with 5.99, the 95 percent critical value of the chi-square distribution with $3 - 1 = 2$ degrees of freedom. Note that in this case, the second contrast with a z^2 value of 18.177 would also be statistically significant at the $\alpha = 0.05$ level as a post hoc comparison.

An Analogue to Multiple Regression Analysis for Effect Sizes

In many research reviews, it is desirable to investigate the relationship of variations in one or more quantitative explanatory variables to variations in effect size. For example, Smith and Glass (1977) used conventional multiple regression analysis to determine the relationship between several coded characteristics of studies (e.g., type of therapy, duration of therapy, internal validity of the study) and effect size in their meta-analysis of psychotherapy outcome studies. The same method has been used in other meta-analyses such as those of the effects of class size (Glass & Smith, 1979; Smith & Glass, 1980). Conventional multiple regression analysis is inappropriate for use with effect sizes, but an alternative analysis provides an analogue to multiple regression analysis for effect sizes. This analysis essentially involves the use of a weighted regression procedure (Hedges, 1982c). It provides a way to estimate and test the relationship between several predictor variables and effect size. The analysis also provides a method of testing whether the regression model is adequately specified, that is, whether significant systematic variation in effect sizes remains unexplained by the data analysis model. In spite of the apparent complexity of these methods, the computational procedure can be explained quite easily without reference to complicated formulas.

Suppose that we have k independent effect size estimates $d_1, \ldots, d_k$ and p predictor variables $X_1, \ldots, X_p$ that are believed to be related to the effect sizes. That data analysis model is that the systematic part of the effect sizes (the population effect sizes) $\delta_1, \ldots, \delta_k$ are determined as a linear function of the values of the predictor variables $X_1, \ldots, X_p$. That is,

$$\delta_i = \beta_0 + \beta_1 x_{i1} + \cdots + \beta_p x_{ip},$$

where $\beta_0, \beta_1, \ldots, \beta_p$ are unknown regression coefficients and x_{ij} is the value of the jth predictor variable for the ith study. One object of the statistical analysis is to use the observed estimates of effect size $d_1, \ldots, d_k$ and the values of the predictor variables to estimate the relationship between $X_1, \ldots, X_p$ and the effect sizes (that is, to estimate the unknown regression coefficients). A second object of the analysis is to test whether the regression model is correctly specified, that is, whether significant systematic variation remains unexplained by the regression model.

The easiest way to compute the estimates of regression coefficients and the test for model specification is to use a packaged computer program (such as SAS Proc GLM or SPSS Regression) that can perform weighted regression analyses. It is possible to prove that the best estimate of the regression coefficients is obtained by using a weighted multiple regression of effect size estimates on the predictor variables, weighting each effect size by $w_i = 1/v_i$ given in (17). This is accomplished by creating a variable W whose value for each "case" or effect size equals the reciprocal of the variance of that effect size. The multiple regression is then run in the usual way except that the variable W is specified as the weighting variable (in SAS) or as a case weight (in SPSS or BMDP).

The output of the weighted regression analysis gives the estimates $\hat{\beta}_0$, $\hat{\beta}_1$, . . . , $\hat{\beta}_p$ of the regression coefficients directly. However, the standard errors and the t- or F-tests printed by the program are incorrect and should not be interpreted. The correct standard errors for $\hat{\beta}_0$, . . . , $\hat{\beta}_p$ can be obtained by dividing the standard error printed on the output by the square root of the residual or error mean square for the regression. That is,

$$S(\hat{\beta}_j) = SE(\hat{\beta}_j)/\sqrt{MS_E}, \tag{28}$$

where $S(\hat{\beta}_j)$ is the correct standard error of $\hat{\beta}_j$, $SE(\hat{\beta}_j)$ is the (incorrect) standard error of $\hat{\beta}_j$ printed by the program, and MS_E is the error or residual mean square for the regression. The correct test for the significance of $\hat{\beta}_j$ uses the fact that

$$z_j = \hat{\beta}_j/S(\hat{\beta}_j) \tag{29}$$

is approximately a standard normal variable if $\beta_j = 0$, where $S(\hat{\beta}_j)$ is the correct standard error of $\hat{\beta}_j$ given in (28). Consequently, if $|z_j|$ exceeds the 100α percent two-tailed critical value of the standard normal distribution, the hypothesis that $\beta_j = 0$ is rejected at the significance level α.

If the number k of studies exceeds $(p + 1)$, the number of predictors plus the intercept, then a test for model specification is possible. The test uses H_E, the (weighted) sum of squares about the regression line. This statistic is sometimes called the "residual" or "error" sum of squares on computer printouts. When the population effect sizes are completely determined by the predictor variables, that is, when the regression model is correctly specified, then the statistic H_E has a chi-square distribution with $(k - p - 1)$ degrees of freedom. Thus the test for model specification at significance level α involves comparing the error sum of squares H_E to the $100(1 - \alpha)$ percent critical value of the chi-square distribution with $(k - p - 1)$ degrees of freedom. The model specification is rejected if H_E exceeds the critical value. Thus the test for model specification is a test for greater than expected residual variation.

Note that some computer programs (such as SPSS Regression) print a weighted "degrees of freedom" for the error sum of squares. This weighted figure usually exceeds the total number of studies and is *not* equal to $k - p - 1$. Such large degrees-of-freedom figures do not indicate a malfunction in the program. The error degrees-of-freedom figure and the standard error of the estimated regression coefficients are incorrect for meta-analysis because the computer programs are adapted to facilitate computations in slightly different inference situations (such as those encountered with stratified survey data). Unfortunately, this adaptation results in the necessity for the minor corrections indicated above when using the programs for meta-analysis.

Example 7. Return once more to the 10 studies of gender differences in conformity examined earlier. Becker (chap. 8) hypothesizes that the number of stimulus items used in a study might be related to the effect size. This hypothesis can be examined by using a regression-like linear model. The sample sizes (n_i^M and n_i^F), the effect size estimate (d_i), the weight w_i, and the number of items (X_i) for each study are given in table 2.5. We use $\log(X_i)$ rather than X_i as a predictor of effect size in the linear model.

Running the regression using SAS Proc GLM, we obtain the regression coefficient estimates $\hat{\beta}_0 = -0.292$ for the intercept and $\hat{\beta}_1 = 0.197$ for the effect of $\log(X_i)$. The (incorrect) standard errors of $\hat{\beta}_0$ and $\hat{\beta}_1$ printed by the program are

$$SE(\hat{\beta}_0) = 0.0994,$$

$$SE(\hat{\beta}_1) = 0.0394,$$

and the mean square error is printed as

$$MS_E = 0.8113.$$

Consequently, the correct standard errors of $\hat{\beta}_0$ and $\hat{\beta}_1$ given by (28) are

$$S(\hat{\beta}_0) = SE(\hat{\beta}_0)/\sqrt{MS_E} = 0.0994/\sqrt{0.8113} = 0.110,$$

$$S(\hat{\beta}_1) = SE(\hat{\beta}_1)/\sqrt{MS_E} = 0.0394/\sqrt{0.8113} = 0.044.$$

The test statistics for each of these regression coefficients are

$$z_0 = \hat{\beta}_0/S(\hat{\beta}_0) = -0.292/0.110 = -2.654,$$

$$z_1 = \hat{\beta}_1/S(\hat{\beta}_1) = 0.197/0.044 = 4.477.$$

Table 2.5 Data from Ten Studies of Gender Differences in Conformity

Study	n_i^M	n_i^F	Items (N)	d_i	v_i	w_i
1	70	71	2	−0.22	0.0285	35.036
2	60	59	2	0.04	0.0336	29.742
3	77	114	2	−0.30	0.0220	45.466
4	118	136	38	0.35	0.0161	62.233
5	32	32	30	0.62	0.0655	15.266
6	10	10	45	0.78	0.2152	4.647
7	45	45	45	0.39	0.0453	22.080
8	30	30	45	0.45	0.0684	14.630
9	40	40	5	0.36	0.0508	19.681
10	61	64	5	−0.06	0.0320	31.218

Note: Apparent inconsistencies between v_i and w_i are due to rounding.

Since the absolute value of $z_1 = 4.477$ exceeds 1.96, the 95 percent critical value of the standard normal distribution, we conclude that the number of stimulus items is significantly related to effect size.

The error sum of squares from the printout which gives the test statistic for model specification is $H_E = 6.491$. Comparing 6.491 with 15.5, the 95 percent critical value of the chi-square distribution with $10 - (1 + 1) = 8$ degrees of freedom, we see the model specification cannot be rejected. Hence the model that the variations in effect sizes are simply a function of the number of stimulus items is consistent with the results of these 10 studies.

This analysis, along with the categorical model analysis of the same data given in example 6, illustrates the fact that more than one data analysis model may be consistent with the same data. This happens when the independent variables in the two models are highly correlated (as are percentage of male authors and number of stimulus items). Which model provides the best explanation? Statistical considerations alone cannot provide the answer. In situations where independent variables are highly correlated, the available data are not sufficient to distinguish among the competing models. Theoretical or methodological criteria must be used to interpret such results. In many cases, the interpretations will not provide sharp conclusions, but only evidence that is equivocal. In the present analysis, either a sociological variable (such as percentage of male authors) or a methodological variable (such as number of stimulus items) provides equally good explanations of variation among effect sizes. The explanation of results via the methodological variable provides a very plausible rival hypothesis to the social psychological explanation, which weakens the evidence for the substantive argument based on sex of researchers and sex-typed communication.

The Importance of Tests for Homogeneity and Model Specification

Some critics have argued that meta-analysis may lead to oversimplified conclusions about the effect of a treatment because it condenses the results of a series of studies into a few parameter estimates. For example, Presby (1978) argued that even when studies are grouped according to variations in the treatment, reviewers might reasonably disagree on the appropriate groupings. Grouping studies into overly broad categories and calculating a mean effect size for each category might serve to "wash out" real variations among treatments within the categories. Thus it would appear that variations in treatment were unrelated to effect size because the mean effect sizes for the categories did not differ. An obvious extension of this argument is that reviewers might reasonably disagree on explanatory variables that could be related to effect sizes. Hence failure to find variables that are systematically related to effect size in conventional analyses does not imply that the effect sizes are consistent across studies. It may only imply that the reviewer has examined the wrong explanatory variables.

A related criticism is that the studies in a collection may give fundamentally different answers (have different population effect sizes), perhaps because of the artifacts of a multitude of design flaws (Eysenck, 1978). Any analysis of the effect sizes is therefore an analysis of estimates that are influenced by a variety of factors other than the true magnitude of the effect of the treatment. Thus meta-analyses may be another case of "garbage in, garbage out." The argument underlying this criticism is that flaws in the design or execution of studies may influence effect sizes.

Both of these criticisms imply the existence of treatment by study interactions—interactions that make the average effect (main effect of treatment) difficult to interpret. The failure of conventional analyses to provide general tests for treatment by study interaction leaves their analyses vulnerable to criticisms such as those of Eysenck and Presby. Statistical tests of homogeneity of (within-group) effect size and tests for specification of categorical and multiple regression models can provide answers to such criticisms. More significantly, such tests provide concrete guidelines to the research reviewer about when the data have been adequately explained. In the simplest case, the reviewer summarizes the results of a series of studies by the average effect size estimate. Is this an oversimplification of the results of the studies? The test of homogeneity of effect size provides a method of empirically testing whether the variation in effect size estimates is greater than would be expected by chance alone. If the hypothesis of homogeneity is not rejected, the reviewer is in a strong position vis-à-vis the argument that studies exhibit real variability, which is obscured by coarse grouping. If the model of a single population effect size fits the data adequately, then a desire for parsimony suggests this model should be considered seriously.

Failure to reject the homogeneity of effect sizes from a series of studies does not necessarily disarm the criticism that the results of the studies are artifacts of design flaws. For example, if a series of studies all share the same flaw, consistent results across the series of studies may be an artifact of just that flaw. That is, the design flaw in all of the studies may act to make the effect sizes in the studies consistent and consistently wrong as an estimate of the treatment effect. On the other hand, the studies may not all have the same flaws. If a variety of different studies with different design flaws all yield consistent results, it may be implausible to explain the consistency of the results of a series of studies as the result of different artifacts all yielding the same bias. Thus the reviewer who finds consistency in research results and who knows the limitations of the individual studies is in a strong position against the "garbage in, garbage out" argument. It should be emphasized that careful examination of the individual research studies and some scrutiny of the attendant design problems is essential. Without such analysis of the studies, a single source of bias is a very real and plausible rival explanation for empirical consistency of research results.

When a reviewer explains the effects sizes from a series of studies via a model involving explanatory variables (e.g., the effect size varies according to grade level), tests of model specification play a role analogous to that of the test of homogeneity. It is difficult to argue that additional variables are needed to explain the variation in effect sizes if the specification test suggests that additional variables are not needed.

Evidence that the model is correctly specified does not necessarily mean that the artifacts of design flaws may be ignored. If all studies share a common design flaw, then the results of all of the studies may be biased to an unknown extent. If design flaws are correlated with explanatory variables, then the effects of those design flaws are confounded with the effects of the explanatory variables. It may be difficult or impossible to determine the real source of the effect. However, if several design flaws are uncorrelated with explanatory variables, and if simple models appear to be correctly specified, then it seems implausible that inferences drawn about the effect sizes are artifacts of biases due to design flaws.

Problems in Obtaining Well-Specified Models

It may seem unlikely that "messy" data from social science would be amenable to serious modeling of the type described in this chapter. The cynic might believe that model specification will always be rejected. Our experience with reanalyses of several meta-analyses and results of the studies in this volume suggest that the data from research studies in education and psychology are often consistent with relatively simple models.

It is rarely the case that an entire collection of effect sizes is homogeneous, however. Effect sizes calculated on different metrics (for example, raw posttest scores versus analysis-of-covariance-adjusted posttest scores) are rarely consistent with one another. Variations in experimental procedure sometimes must be used as explanatory variables. Even when all studies measure a common dependent variable such as conformity, different measurement procedures (requiring different cognitive tasks) are sometimes associated with variations in effect size. Perhaps the most significant explanatory variable in some types of studies is the degree of preexisting differences between the experimental and control groups. Well-controlled studies (for example, those with small pretest differences or those using random assignment) often provide effect sizes that are homogeneous or that conform to simple models. Poorly controlled studies rarely conform to simple models. Even when the average effect size for well-controlled studies may agree with that of poorly controlled studies, effect sizes from the latter group often exhibit much greater variability.

Tests of homogeneity of effect size and of model specification often force the investigator to pay closer attention to the effect size data and to the statistical analysis of the effect sizes. The results of such tests for models of interest frequently prompt the investigator to do further exploratory data analysis. The examination of studies that are apparent outliers can sometimes reveal explanatory variables (study classifications) associated with powerful effects. Sometimes examination of homogeneity statistics leads the investigator to discover inconsistencies (or outright errors) in calculations of effect sizes. In virtually all cases, more extensive examination of the available research studies and alternative data analysis models leads to greater insight about the phenomenon under study.

References

Cooper, H. M. (1979). Statistically combining independent studies: Meta-analysis of sex differences in conformity research. *Journal of Personality and Social Psychology, 37*, 131–146.

Cooper, H. M. (1982). Scientific guidelines for conducting integrative research reviews. *Review of Educational Research, 52*, 291–302.

DerSimonian, R., & Laird, N. M. (1983). Evaluating the effect of coaching on SAT scores: A meta-analysis of research. *Harvard Educational Review, 53*, 1–15.

Eagly, H. H., & Carli, L. L. (1981). Sex of researchers and sex-typed communications as determinants of sex differences in influenceability: A meta-analysis of social influence studies. *Psychological Bulletin, 90*, 1–20.

Eysenck, H. J. (1978). An exercise in mega-silliness. *American Psychologist, 33*, 517.

Fiske, D. W. (1983). The meta-analytic revolution in outcome research. *Journal of Consulting and Clinical Psychology, 51*, 65–70.

Giaconia, R. M. & Hedges, L. V. (1982). Identifying features of effective open education. *Review of Educational Research, 52*, 579–602.

Glass, G. V. (1976). Primary, secondary, and meta-analysis of research. *Educational Researcher, 5*, 3–8.

Glass, G. V. (1978). Integrating findings: The meta-analysis of research. In L. S. Shulman (ed.), *Review of research in education*, 5. Itasca, Il.: F. E. Peacock.

Glass, G. V., McGaw, B., & Smith, M. L. (1981). *Meta-analysis in social research*. Beverly Hills: Sage.

Glass, G. V., Peckham, P. D., & Sanders, J. R. (1972). Consequences of failure to meet assumptions underlying the fixed-effects analyses of variance and covariance. *Review of Educational Research, 42*, 237–288.

Glass, G. V., & Smith, M. L. (1979). Meta-analysis of research on the relationship of class-size and achievement. *Educational Evaluation and Policy Analysis, 1*, 2–16.

Hedges, L. V. (1981). Distribution theory for Glass's estimator of effect size and related estimators. *Journal of Educational Statistics, 6*, 107–128.

Hedges, L. V. (1982a). Estimation of effect size from a series of independent experiments. *Psychological Bulletin, 92*, 490-499.

Hedges, L. V. (1982b). Fitting categorical models to effect sizes from a series of experiments. *Journal of Educational Statistics, 7*, 119-137.

Hedges, L. V. (1982c). Fitting continuous models to effect size data. *Journal of Educational Statistics, 7*, 245-270.

Hedges, L. V. (1984). Estimation of effect size under nonrandom sampling: The effects of censoring studies yielding statistically insignificant mean differences. *Journal of Educational Statistics, 9*, 61-85.

Hedges, L. V. & Olkin, I. (1980). Vote-counting methods in research synthesis. *Psychological Bulletin, 88*, 359-369.

Hedges, L. V. & Olkin, I. (1985). *Statistical methods for meta-analysis*. New York: Academic Press.

Hyde, J. S. (1981). How large are cognitive gender differences? A meta-analysis using ω^2 and d. *American Psychologist, 36*, 892-901.

Jackson, G. B. (1980). Methods for integrative reviews. *Review of Educational Research, 50*, 438-460.

McGaw, B., & Glass, G. V. (1980). Choice of metric for effect size in meta-analysis. *American Educational Research Journal, 17*, 325-337.

Presby, S. (1978). Overly broad categories obscure important differences between therapies. *American Psychologist, 33*, 514-515.

Rosenthal, R. (1978). Combining results of independent studies. *Psychological Bulletin, 85*, 185-193.

Rosenthal, R., & Rubin, D. B. (1982). Comparing effect sizes of independent studies. *Psychological Bulletin, 92*, 500-504.

Smith, M. L., & Glass, G. V. (1977). Meta-analysis of psychotherapy outcome studies. *American Psychologist, 32*, 752-760.

Smith, M. L., & Glass, G. V. (1980). Meta-analysis of class size and its relationship to attitudes and instruction. *American Educational Research Journal, 17*, 419-433.

Steinkamp, M. W., & Maehr, M. L. (1983). Affect, ability, and science achievement: A quantitative synthesis of correlational research. *Review of Educational Research, 53*, 369-396.

Gender Differences in Aggression

3

Janet Shibley Hyde

Abstract

Gender differences in aggression are generally considered to be a reliable phenomenon. This chapter presents a meta-analysis of 143 studies of aggression, assessing the magnitude of the gender difference as well as factors that may be related to the magnitude of the difference. The effect size, d, was .50, averaged over 69 available values. Rosenthal's Z-test indicated that there were significant age trends in the effect size; studies of preschoolers found larger gender differences than studies of college students. Analyses using Hedges's homogeneity statistics indicated that there were significant variations in effect size depending on the kind of aggression measured (e.g., physical aggression, verbal aggression), the method of measurement (e.g., self-reports or direct observations), and the design (experimental versus naturalistic/correlational). Naturalistic/correlational studies tend to find larger gender differences than do experimental studies. For all categories of studies, effect sizes were positive, indicating that males were more aggressive than females for all types of aggression, all methods of measurement, and all designs, although effect sizes were generally small to moderate in magnitude. The implications of the results are discussed in terms of values—that is, whether the higher levels of aggression in males or the lower levels of aggression in females are to be valued.

Out of the massive research literature on psychological gender differences, a few behaviors have emerged as showing reliable gender differences. One of those is aggression. The greater aggressiveness of males, compared with females, is generally regarded as a consistent and large phenomenon. For example, Atkinson, Atkinson, and Hilgard, in their introductory psychology text, state "The one area in which observed sex differences are consistent with popular beliefs is aggression. Boys *are* more aggressive than girls, starting at about age 2 or 3" (1983, p. 91). Mussen, Conger, Kagan, and Huston express a similar view in their child development text: "Boys are more often aggressive than girls, a difference noted in most cultures around the world, at almost all ages, and in many animal species as well. Boys are especially prone to use physical aggression, but they also show more verbal aggression than girls do. . . . What accounts for such consistent sex differences?" (1984, p. 370).

Clearly these differences are thought to be important enough to be included in basic textbooks. And the consequences of this pattern of differences may be far-ranging; it has been proposed as an explanation for the lopsided gender ratio among children who are discipline problems in the schools, patterns of spouse abuse in adulthood, and the greater success (through aggressiveness) of men in the business world.

The major source that is generally cited as evidence for the textbook discussions is Maccoby and Jacklin's 1974 review. On the basis of a survey of 66 studies, they concluded that gender differences in aggression are "well established." Their review indicated that males are more aggressive both physically and verbally. They argued that the difference appears by age two or two and one-half and, although aggression generally declines with age, males are still more aggressive than females in the college years. Little research is available beyond that age level. Earlier reviews had reached similar conclusions (e.g., Terman & Tyler, 1954; Oetzel, 1966).

Meta-analysis first entered into the conclusions in 1980, when Tieger and Maccoby and Jacklin debated whether gender differences in aggression are caused by biological factors. Tieger (1980) argued against biological causation. One facet of his argument involved substantiating the point that gender differences in aggression are not present in very young children. To do so, he performed a meta-analysis, using probability-combining techniques (Rosenthal, 1978), of studies cited by Maccoby and Jacklin (1974) having subjects aged six or younger. The resulting weighted Z was not significant, leading Tieger to conclude that gender differences in aggression were not significant before six years of age.

In their rejoinder, Maccoby and Jacklin (1980) pointed out several flaws in Tieger's analysis. One was that he combined probabilities from dependent measures as though they were independent when he computed the Z statistic. They performed a reanalysis correcting this point and adding some additional studies, and found a highly significant gender difference in children six years of age and younger.

Both the Maccoby and Jacklin and Tieger analyses fall short in several ways. Both used probability-combining techniques in performing the meta-analysis. Such techniques yield only a final probability value or significance level, and thus they can answer only a yes-no question: Are gender differences in aggression, cumulated over many studies, in the predicted direction and significant or not? The sampling of studies in the 1974 Maccoby and

Jacklin review is now dated, and in their 1980 analysis, Maccoby and Jacklin admitted that their sampling of more recent studies was not systematic, potentially omitting many studies with null findings. Finally, both Tieger and Maccoby and Jacklin limited their analysis to studies in which the subjects were six years of age or younger; thus they provide no information regarding the pattern of gender differences in aggression over the life span.

Recognizing the limitations of previous reviews—and also being just plain curious to find out more about patterns of gender differences in aggression— I undertook a major meta-analysis of studies of gender differences in aggression (Hyde, 1984). I had several goals in doing that meta-analysis. I obtained an additional well-sampled group of recent studies to augment the sample in the 1974 review by Maccoby and Jacklin. I used statistics—specifically, d (see chap. 2) and ω^2 (Hyde, 1984)—that permitted an estimation of the magnitude of the gender difference (not just its existence or nonexistence as in the previous reviews). And finally, I analyzed the effects developmentally for all ages for which data were available.

Statistical methods in meta-analysis have proliferated in the last five years, increasing in elegance and in mathematical adequacy, as well as expanding the kinds of substantive questions that can be addressed. And so, before my 1984 review was even in print, the statistical methods used in it could be expanded and improved upon. My major goal in this chapter is to report the results of new analyses based on Hedges's homogeneity tests (1982a, 1982b, 1982c) applied to the same set of studies included in my 1984 review. Many of my conclusions in the 1984 article were tentative. By comparison, the results of the homogeneity tests permit much richer and firmer conclusions regarding such issues as whether the pattern of gender differences depends on the type of aggression measured (physical aggression, verbal aggression, etc.) or the method of measurement (direct observation, self-report, etc.). First I will describe the methods and results from my 1984 review; following that, I will discuss the results of the new analyses I have performed.

Method

The Sample of Studies

A total of 143 studies were included, derived from three sources. (1) Maccoby and Jacklin's table 7.1 (1974) yielded 63 studies. Studies with subjects not from the United States or Canada were eliminated; because gender roles vary cross-culturally, it seemed advisable to limit the assessment of the magnitude of gender differences to a single culture. (2) Maccoby and Jacklin's table 2 (1980) yielded further studies. (3) A recent sample of studies was obtained by searching the entire 1979, 1980, and 1981 volumes of *Psychological Abstracts* under the topics "aggressive behavior" and "aggressiveness."

Regarding the issue of sampling of studies in meta-analysis, Glass, McGaw, and Smith (1981) contend that it should be well-defined (in the sense that another investigator could "replicate" the sampling) and complete. They also cautioned against ignoring "hidden" studies such as dissertations, the quality of which may be equal to that of published studies but that may not be published because of null findings, although null findings should be included in a meta-analysis. The recent sample of studies I obtained through the *Psychological Abstracts* search meets Glass's criteria well. It is well defined, and it includes, not only published books and journal articles, but unpublished dissertations as well (see app. A).

In cases in which insufficient information for computation of effect size statistics was provided in the original article, a follow-up letter requesting further information was sent to the authors. Effect sizes were computed only when adequate information (e.q., means and standard deviations for males and females or a t-value for gender differences or an F-value or proportions used in a nonparametric test) was available; in no case did I convert a probability value (when only that was available) into an effect size.

Coding of the Studies

For each study, the following information was recorded: (1) All statistics on gender differences in the aggression measure(s), including means and standard deviations for males and females, t, F, or χ^2 and df; (2) the number of male and female subjects; (3) the mean age of the subjects (if the article reported no age but specified "undergraduates" or students in introductory psychology courses, the average age was set as 19; if data for several age groups were reported separately, these were recorded separately); (4) the nature of the design, whether experimental (aggression was manipulated or stimulated in some way) or naturalistic/correlational; (5) the method of measurement, whether direct observation, self-report, parental or teacher report, projective, peer report, or other; (6) the kind of aggression, whether physical, verbal, fantasy, rough-and-tumble play, willingness to shock or otherwise hurt, imitative, hostility scale, or other; and (7) the kind of sample, whether general classroom, families or individuals seeking therapy, or other.

Results

The results reported in my 1984 article were as follows. Including all 83 values available, the median value of d was 0.50. The median value of ω^2 was 0.05 over the 108 values available. However, this computation of the median included, in some cases, multiple dependent measures from a single study. Thus I performed a second computation, striving for more nearly independent data. Only one value per study was included; if there were three values, the middle one was used; if two values, the average of the two. The results were a median value of $d = 0.54$ (based on 62 values) and a median $\omega^2 = 0.06$ (based on 86 values). Thus the second computation, using independent values, did not yield substantially different results from the first computation with some dependencies in the data.

Effect Size as a Function of Features of the Studies

In my 1984 article, I also computed median effect sizes for various categories of studies. These results are shown in table 3.1. Notice first that many of these median effect sizes were not available because only four or fewer effect sizes were found in that category, too few for me to feel that computation was justified. Based on inspection of that table, I concluded "Gender differences are larger for naturalistic correlational studies than they are for experimental studies. Gender differences are larger when measured by direct observation, projective methods, or peer reports, and smaller when measured by self-reports, parent, or teacher reports. . . . It appears that physical aggression shows rather larger gender differences than other kinds, relative to the effect sizes computed over all studies" (Hyde, 1984, p. 729).

Table 3.1 Comparison of Median Effect Sizes According to Various Study Features

Feature	Effect Size	
	ω^2	d
1. Design		
Experimental	0.04	0.27
Naturalistic/correlational	0.07	0.54
2. Method of Measurement		
Direct observation	0.07	0.55
Self-report	0.02	0.25
Parent or teacher report	0.03	0.43
Projective	0.09	0.70
Peer report	0.09	0.63
3. Kind of Aggression		
Physical	0.07	0.72
Verbal	0.055	NA
Fantasy	NA	NA
Rough-and-tumble play	NA	NA
Willingness to shock, hurt	0.05	0.47
Imitative	0.08	0.30
Hostility scale	NA	NA
4. Date of Publication		
1966–1973	0.06	0.53
1978–1981	0.03	0.41

Source: Hyde (1984, p. 730)
Note: NA = not available; median could not be calculated because only four or fewer values were available.

Age Trends

I tested for age trends in effect sizes, that is, age trends in the magnitude of gender differences in aggression. For example, are gender differences small among preschoolers, increasing among older subjects (Tieger's hypothesis), or is the trend the reverse, gender differences becoming smaller with age, or are there no significant age trends in the magnitude of the gender differences? To test for the significance of age trends, I computed a Z statistic for a linear contrast, as developed by Rosenthal and Rubin (1982):

$$Z = \frac{\Sigma(\lambda d)}{[\Sigma(\lambda^2/w)]^{1/2}}$$

where λ is a contrast weight, d is the effect size statistic for the study, and $w = 2N/(8 + d^2)$. In testing for age trends λ was set equal to the average age of the children in the study minus the average of those ages over all studies.

The result was $Z = -2.00\, p < 0.05$, permitting the conclusion that there are significant age trends in the magnitude of the gender difference in aggression. Specifically, the negative Z-value indicates that the magnitude of the gender difference declines as the age of subjects increases. For studies with subjects' average age six or less, the median $\omega^2 = 0.07$ and $d = 0.58$. Looking only at studies of collge students, $\omega^2 = 0.01$ and $d = 0.27$. Thus gender differences in aggression are larger among preschoolers and are smaller among college students.

Analyses Using Homogeneity Statistics

As I noted earlier, newly developed statistical methods now permit me to do more precise analyses. Here I will report the results of new analyses using Hedges's homogeneity statistics (1982a, 1982b, 1982c), discussed in chapter 2. In computing average effect sizes, I used Hedges's d, which is an unbiased estimator of the population δ. I was also able to test for significant differences between d for various categories of studies, using a Z^2 statistic provided by Hedges (1982a); this analysis is analogous to a Scheffé post hoc test in the analysis of variance.

Based on 85 values, the average effect size for all studies was $d = 0.75$. Notice that this is higher than the median value of 0.50 that I reported previously. Statistically, d is a better estimator. It weights more heavily studies that have more "precise" estimates because they have large sample sizes. In effect, with this set of data, it weighted more heavily some studies that showed larger effect sizes.

In my recent sample of studies, I eliminated studies using clinical samples. However, the two sets of studies provided by Maccoby and Jacklin (1974, 1980) included some data based on clinical samples such as families seeking therapy. Because my goal is to estimate the value of d in the general population, it seems inappropriate to include studies based on clinical samples. Thus I did a reanalysis, eliminating all clinical samples and other selective samples and including only general samples such as those based on classrooms of children. After eliminating those samples, 69 values of d remained, with an average $d = 0.50$. Interestingly, this is identical to the median value of 0.50 that I had calculated previously. The clinical samples by themselves clearly showed larger gender differences ($d = 0.82$). Given the typical reasons for which boys and girls are taken for counseling—girls for withdrawn, fearful, anxious behavior, boys for aggression and hyperactivity—it is not surprising that gender differences are exaggerated in such special samples. In all of the analyses that follow, studies based on clinical samples and other select samples have been eliminated.

The next step was to test this pool of 69 values of d for homogeneity. The null hypothesis is that they are homogeneous, that is, that they can reasonably be viewed as values sampled from a single population with a population effect size δ, variations in effect size among the studies being due merely to sampling variation. If the null hypothesis is rejected, we must conclude that there is significant variation in effect sizes among the studies, most likely reflecting the fact that they have actually been drawn from two or more populations that have different population effect sizes. If that is the case, then the goal is to classify the studies by characteristics, such that the effect sizes

Table 3.2 Comparison of Effect Sizes According to Various Study Features, Using Hedges's, d

Feature	k	d
1. Design		
Experimental	27	0.29
Naturalistic/correlational	42	0.56
2. Method of Measurement		
Direct observation	42	0.51
Self-report	14	0.40
Parent or teacher report	8	0.48
Projective	1	0.83
Peer report	4	0.63
3. Kind of Aggression		
Mixed (physical + verbal)	16	0.43
Physical	26	0.60
Verbal	6	0.43
Fantasy	1	0.84
Willingness to shock, hurt	8	0.39
Imitative	5	0.49
Hostility scale	2	0.02
Other	5	0.43

Note: k = number of effect sizes from which d, a weighted estimator of the population δ, was calculated.

within categories are homogeneous. For all 69 values, the homogeneity statistic $H = 216.39$; the critical value for χ^2 (68) $= 90.53$. Thus we can conclude that the set of 69 values is not homogeneous.

The next step is to determine how the studies can be subdivided or categorized so that the effect sizes will be homogeneous within categories. The various categorizations listed in tables 3.1 and 3.2 were tried. The resulting homogeneity statistics are shown in table 3.3. The statistics there indicate that any of the three categorizations "works" in the sense that it results in significant differences in effect size between categories. However, the categorizations are not completely successful because, in general, there is still

Table 3.3 Homogeneity Statistics for Various Categorizations of Aggression Studies

Source	df^*	H	p^{**}	Mean Effect Size d
All studies	68	216.39	< .0001	0.50
Categorized by Design				
Between categories	1	27.99	< .0001	
Within categories	67	188.40	< .0001	
Experimental	26	72.61	< .0001	0.29
Naturalistic	41	115.79	< .0001	0.56
Categorized by Method of Measurement				
Between categories	4	16.35	< .0001	
Within categories	64	200.04	< .0001	
Direct observation	41	112.99	< .0001	0.51
Self-report	13	65.43	< .0001	0.40
Parent/teacher report	7	10.73	n.s.	0.48
Projective	0	0.00		0.83
Peer report	3	10.89	< .05	0.63
Categorized by Type of Aggression				
Between categories	7	36.59	< .0001	
Within categories	61	179.80	< .0001	
Mixed (physical + verbal)	15	27.48	< .05	0.43
Physical	25	87.03	< .0001	0.60
Verbal	5	29.50	< .0001	0.43
Fantasy	0	0.00		0.84
Willingness to shock	7	17.06	< .05	0.39
Imitative	4	5.69	n.s.	0.49
Hostility scale	1	7.74	< .05	0.02
Other	4	5.30	n.s.	0.43

$^*df$ for χ^2 test of significance of H
**Significance level of χ^2 test of significance of H

significant variation in effect sizes within categories of aggression studies. With such a large number of effect sizes, it is difficult to reduce within-category H statistics to nonsignificance because the significance tests are powerful; at least it can be said that any of the three categorizations shown in table 3.3 produces within-category statistics that are comparatively far smaller than the statistics for all studies pooled.

Using Hedges's Z^2 statistic (chap. 2, formula 27), I next tested for the significance of the difference of d-values for various categories of studies. The results indicated that the mean effect size of 0.56 for naturalistic/correlational studies is significantly larger than the mean effect size of 0.29 for experimental studies ($Z^2 = 27.24$, compared against a critical value of $\chi^2 = 3.84$ for 1 df). Studies based on direct observations had a mean effect size of 0.51, which was not significantly larger than the mean effect size of 0.40 for self-report studies ($Z^2 = 4.01$, compared against a critical value of $\chi^2 = 5.99$ with 2 df). Similarly, the mean effect size of 0.60 for physical aggression was not significantly larger than the mean effect size of 0.43 for verbal aggression ($Z^2 = 3.48$, compared against a critical value of $\chi^2 = 9.48$ with 4 df).

Substantively, then, I can conclude that gender differences in aggression are significantly larger in naturalistic/correlational studies than they are in experimental studies. However, studies based on direct observation do not find significantly larger gender differences in aggression than do studies based on self-report or other methods of measurement. And gender differences in physical aggression are not significantly larger than gender differences in verbal aggression.

Fitting a Continuous Model to the Effect Sizes

Hedges (1982c) has developed methods for fitting continuous models to effect size data. One or several variables can be entered as predictors of effect sizes in a regression-type approach. In applying this technique to the aggression data, I entered age, method of measurement, and type of aggression (using dummy variables to code these last two categorical variables) as predictors into the regression equation, with effect size, d, as the criterion. As I noted in my 1984 analysis of these studies, there tends to be a confounding of age, design, and type of aggression; that is, studies with preschoolers tend to be naturalistic studies of physical aggression based on direct observations, whereas studies of college students tend to be experimental studies using willingness to shock as a measure. Using the continuous model-fitting technique, I was able to enter age as a covariate, thereby partialing out its effects, and then look at the effects of method of measurement and kind of aggression in predicting effect size. The results indicated that method of measurement is a significant predictor of effect size ($H = 16.35$, $df = 4$). Type of aggression is also a significant predictor of effect size ($H = 28.86$, $df = 7$). Age and type of aggression also show a significant interaction in predicting effect sizes ($H = 20.15$, $df = 5$).

Elimination of an "Outlier" Study

In computing values of d and homogeneity statistics, "outlier" studies become obvious. The clearest case of that in this data set is Schuck's and my study (Hyde and Schuck, 1977). It produced $d = 3.13$, a value that far exceeds that of any other studies. Fortunately—yet ironically—because the study happens to be one of mine, I was able to analyze it to try to determine why it produced such an extraordinary effect size. Hedges has pointed out that all computations of d should be based on statistics computed from individual subjects. If some aggregate unit is used instead, the statistical effect is to reduce error (within-group) variance, thus inflating significance tests and the d-value (for an example, see White, 1982). That is precisely what occurred in our 1977 study. The data were naturalistic observations in preschool classrooms, and the unit of analysis in that statistical test was the classroom, not the individual child. That is, our numbers represented numbers of acts of aggression in a classroom per unit of time. The result is to reduce error variance and produce an inflated value of d. Some correction factors are available in situations such as this, but because of some peculiar features of the data, none of them could be applied in this particular case. Thus this study was eliminated with the clinical samples when the number of d-values was reduced to 69 in the analyses discussed earlier.

I think that there are two lessons to be learned from my experience with this one peculiar study. First, researchers undertaking the estimation of effect sizes and meta-analyses should exercise caution to ensure that d-values are based on statistics reflecting data for individuals, not aggregates. The problem of aggregate data may occur any time the classroom, rather than the individual, is the unit of analysis. Second, this case seems to me to provide some evidence for the validity of meta-analysis. That is, the homogeneity techniques quickly pointed out the deviance of this study, and reflection on the method of the study yielded a logical reason for the deviant effect size. The inappropriately calculated value could then be eliminated from computations.

Discussion

If I were able to cite a single value for the magnitude of the gender difference in aggression, it would be $d = 0.50$ (based on Hedges's d statistic averaged over 69 values). That is, the mean for males and the mean for females are approximately one-half standard deviation apart. However, the results of the homogeneity analyses indicate that this single value oversimplifies the results from a complex, nonhomogeneous set of effect sizes.

The analyses indicate that several factors are significant sources of variation in effect size: age, kind of aggression, method of measurement, and design. More specifically, gender differences in aggression tend to be larger among preschoolers and smaller among college students (Hyde, 1984). And naturalistic/correlational studies of aggression tend to find larger gender differences than do experimental studies.

How should the larger gender differences in naturalistic/correlational studies and the smaller gender difference in experimental studies be interpreted? The naturalistic studies are generally tapping "spontaneous" aggression, in the sense that an experimenter has not stimulated the aggressive behavior, although the behavior is still a result of years of gender-role socialization (and possibly hormonal effects as well). In the experimental—typically laboratory—studies, aggression is being stimulated in some way. Thus we may be seeing that gender differences are relatively larger when the aggression is spontaneous, but in the situation in which aggression is stimulated, the gender difference narrows. This might be interpreted as indicating that females are relatively low in spontaneous aggression, but the capacity for aggression is nonetheless present, so that females increase relative to males when the aggression is stimulated in an experimental situation, though males are still more aggressive. This conclusion is parallel to the results of the classic experiment by Bandura (1965) on the effects of imitation and reinforcement on gender differences in children's aggression. It may be that there are demand characteristics, to which females are more sensitive, in the laboratory experiment. The demand characteristics might imply that aggression is the desired behavior and might function much like the reinforcers in Bandura's experiment, increasing girls' aggression. Another possibility works from an assumption opposite to the previous one. In the laboratory experiment, there may be more inhibitions against aggression (an experimenter watching, etc.) than there are in naturalistic settings, which leads males to decrease their aggression. Further research will be needed to sort out which of these explanations is more accurate.

The results of the present analyses can be compared with some of Maccoby and Jacklin's more impressionistic conclusions (1974). Unlike some previous reviewers who had concluded that boys were more physically aggressive but girls were more verbally aggressive, Maccoby and Jacklin concluded that males show more aggression than females for both physical aggression and verbal aggression. The present analyses support this conclusion. Although the effect size is somewhat larger for physical aggression (0.60) than for verbal aggression (0.43), the difference is not significant, and both are fairly close to the overall effect size of 0.50. And, lest we lose the forest for the trees, the effect size for verbal aggression is still positive, indicating that males are more aggressive.

Maccoby and Jacklin also concluded that "boys consistently exhibit more aggression following exposure to a model" (1974, p. 229). Once again, the present analyses support this conclusion. For imitative aggression, the mean effect size is 0.49; it is thus similar in magnitude to the effect size for other measures of aggression.

Contributions of Meta-analysis to Understanding Gender Differences in Aggression

Since Maccoby and Jacklin's discursive 1974 review of gender differences in aggression, where has meta-analysis brought us? The historical development coincides with the development of more elegant and useful statistical techniques. The first meta-analyses, those by Tieger (1980) and Maccoby and Jacklin (1980), used probability-combining techniques to determine whether, when all studies of children six years of age or younger were combined, gender differences were statistically significant, with boys being more aggressive. My 1984 article went beyond those conclusions in two ways: (1) By using the effect size measures ω^2 and d, I was able to estimate the magnitude of gender differences in aggression; that is, the median d was 0.50 and the median ω^2 was 0.05. (2) I was able to test for the significance of age trends in the value of d (the magnitude of gender differences) using Rosenthal and Rubin's Z-test (1982). The trend, indeed, was significant, with gender differences being larger among preschoolers than among older subjects.

The third stage of meta-analysis is the one reported in this chapter, in which I used the homogeneity tests developed by Hedges (1982a, 1982b, 1982c). Several new findings emerged from these analyses. First, as an improvement over my computation of a median value of d, I was able to compute Hedges's unbiased estimator of the population δ. The original d was computed as 0.75, a value considerably higher than the median I had computed. However, once studies based on clinical samples and the one outlier study were eliminated, d was 0.50, identical to the median value I had calculated previously. Second, I found that the entire set of d-values (from which I had computed the median of 0.50) was actually nonhomogeneous, so that, in a sense, a single value misrepresents the complexity of the data, which probably fall into multiple categories of studies sharing different features. Third, I subdivided the entire set of studies into subsets of studies with different features (depending on design, method of measurement, and type of aggression, as shown in table 3.3), and I analyzed the homogeneity statistics resulting from those subdivisions. The subdivisions were not entirely successful in the sense that the H statistics were typically still significant (indicating significant nonhomogeneity) within the categories. However, they were successful in the sense that I was able to reduce the magnitude of the H statistics considerably compared with what H was for the entire set of studies pooled together. Further, the H statistics indicated that there was significant variation between categories, whether categorized by design (experimental versus naturalistic/correlational), by method of measurement, or by type of aggression. A significance test indicated that the mean effect size of 0.56 for naturalistic/correlational studies was significantly larger than the mean effect size of 0.29 for experimental studies.

In sum, then, meta-analysis tells us that the difference between the means for males and females in aggression is about 0.50 standard deviation, a difference that might be interpreted as moderate. However, the magnitude of the gender difference depends significantly on several features: the age of the subjects (gender differences are larger with younger subjects), whether the study was experimental or correlational (naturalistic/correlational studies produce larger gender differences), the type of aggression that is measured, and the method of measurement. I might also add that there was no subset of studies for which d is a negative value; that is, there are no types or measures of aggression on which females are more aggressive than males. None of these findings could have emerged solidly and objectively from the traditional discursive review.

One limitation of my analysis is that I failed to achieve homogeneity in some categories. This means that there are some other factors that influence the magnitude of the gender difference in aggression. It was beyond the scope of the present study to ascertain what those factors are. For example, it may be important to know whether the individual is tested in a group or alone (as occurs with the Buss shock measure). We will know more about gender and aggression when others sort out these factors, in meta-analysis and in primary research.

Applications and Implications

Perhaps the first thing that should be said here is that the present analyses have no implications regarding the causes—whether biological or environmental—of gender differences in aggression (Hyde, 1984). I have assessed the magnitude of the gender difference and found that the means for the distributions are one-half standard deviation apart, with some variations in the magnitude of the gender difference according to various features of the studies. This tells us nothing about sex hormones and gender-role socialization. Other studies with different designs will be needed to clarify those issues.

In discussing the implications of the results, the issues of values and interpretation are crucial. Are high levels of aggression or low levels of aggression—or perhaps intermediate levels—to be valued? Which level of aggression is more valuable to society? Which is more adaptive for the individual? Many popularized interpretations of the gender difference in aggression seem to value high levels of aggression; the argument is that it translates into everything from greater male proficiency in athletics to the greater success of men in the business world. In a scientific sense, of course, we lack data to support that claim directly. It would require, for example, research demonstrating that boys who are moderate to high in level of aggression as preschoolers are more successful in competitive careers in adulthood. It is possible that the correlations would be different—perhaps opposite in sign—for males and females. That is, aggression in the preschool years might correlate positively with career success for females, but negatively for males.

A feminist reinterpretation, however, is that the lower levels of aggression displayed by females are to be valued. In an era in which we are keenly aware of the threat of nuclear war, it seems more sane to value the control of aggression over the expression of aggression. Carol Gilligan (1982) has eloquently argued that theories of psychological development have focused on male qualities of individuation and separateness (and aggression?), while ignoring—and thereby implicitly devaluing—female qualities of relatedness and caring (and control of aggression?). Thus we might shift from regretting the lesser aggressiveness of females, viewing it as a lack of aggressiveness, to seeing it as a positive expression of empathy for others. Consistent with this approach, current theories of the evolution of the human species have shifted from the view that aggression and competitiveness were the distinctive human features to the view that cooperation in a peaceful social grouping was the distinctive element (e.g., Tanner, 1981; Rensberger, 1984).

What are the implications for the educational system? The answer in part relates to the issue of values. If we value the higher levels of aggressiveness in males, then schools should encourage aggression, competition, and assertion more in females. This might mean more emphasis on competitive athletics for girls, perhaps beginning in early elementary school, or perhaps even in the preschool years. In the academic classroom, it might mean encouraging reticent girls to speak up more forcefully in debates or to become more competitive about their success in mathematics courses.

If, on the other hand, we value the low level of aggressiveness of females, we might seek to reduce the level of aggressiveness in boys, while simultaneously encouraging peaceful cooperation for them. The research on promoting empathy and prosocial behavior is relevant here (e.g., Eisenberg-Berg & Mussen, 1977). We might want to deemphasize competitive sports in favor of cooperative sports or noncompetitive ones such as jogging. In the classroom, we would avoid competitively structured learning and work toward cooperatively structured learning (e.g., Aronson et al., 1978).

Which of these alternatives is chosen, of course, is a matter of values. What the psychologist can do is suggest alternatives that might otherwise be overlooked and examine the likely psychological consequences of following one or another alternative.

References

Aronson, E., Stephen, C., Sikes, J., Blaney, N., & Snapp, M. (1978). *The jigsaw classroom*. Beverly Hills: Sage.

Atkinson, R. L., Atkinson, R. C., & Hilgard, E. R. (1983). *Introduction to psychology* (8th ed.). New York: Harcourt Brace Jovanovich.

Bandura, A. (1965). Influence of model's reinforcement contingencies on the acquisition of imitative responses. *Journal of Personality and Social Psychology, 1*, 589-595.

Eisenberg-Berg, N., & Mussen, P. (1977). *Roots of caring, sharing, and helping*. San Francisco: Freeman.

Gilligan, C. (1982). *In a different voice: Psychological theory and women's development*. Cambridge: Harvard University Press.

Glass, G. V., McGaw, B., & Smith, M. L. (1981). *Meta-analysis in social research*. Beverly Hills: Sage.

Hedges, L. V. (1982a). Estimation of effect size from a series of independent experiments. *Psychological Bulletin, 92*, 490-499.

Hedges, L. V. (1982b). Fitting categorical models to effect sizes from a series of experiments. *Journal of Educational Statistics, 7*, 119-137.

Hedges, L. V. (1982c). Fitting continuous models to effect size data. *Journal of Educational Statistics, 7*, 245-270.

Hyde, J. S. (1984). How large are gender differences in aggression? A developmental meta-analysis. *Developmental Psychology, 20*, 722-736.

Hyde, J. S., & Schuck, J. R. (1977). The development of sex differences in aggression: A revised model. Paper presented at the meeting of the American Psychological Association, San Francisco, August 1977.

Maccoby, E. E., & Jacklin, C. N. (1974). *The psychology of sex differences*. Stanford: Stanford University Press.

Maccoby, E. E., & Jacklin, C. N. (1980). Sex differences in aggression: A rejoinder and reprise. *Child Development, 51*, 964-980.

Mussen, P. H., Conger, J. J., Kagan, J., & Huston, A. C. (1984). *Child development and personality* (6th ed.). New York: Harper & Row.

Oetzel, R. M. (1966). Annotated bibliography. In E. E. Maccoby (ed.), *The development of sex differences*. Stanford: Stanford University Press.

Rensberger, B. (1984). What made humans human? *New York Times Magazine*, April 8, 80-95.

Rosenthal, R. (1978). Combining results of independent studies. *Psychological Bulletin, 85*, 185-193.

Rosenthal, R., & Rubin, D. B. (1982). Comparing effect sizes of independent studies. *Psychological Bulletin, 92*, 500-504.

Tanner, N. M. (1981). *On becoming human*. Cambridge: Cambridge University Press.

Terman, L. M., & Tyler, L. E. (1954). Psychological sex differences. In L. Carmichael (ed.), *Manual of child psychology* (2nd ed.). New York: Wiley.

Tieger, T. (1980). On the biological basis of sex differences in aggression. *Child Development, 51*, 943–963.

White, K. B. (1982). The relation between socioeconomic status and academic achievement. *Psychological Bulletin, 91*, 461–481.

A Meta-analysis of Gender Differences in Spatial Ability: Implications for Mathematics and Science Achievement

Marcia C. Linn
Anne C. Petersen

4

Abstract

Many have hypothesized that gender differences in spatial ability form the basis for gender differences in mathematics and science achievement. To gain information about the plausibility of this hypothesis, this chapter compares data on the nature, magnitude, and age of first appearance of gender differences in spatial ability with data on mathematics achievement and science achievement. In addition, evidence for direct relationships between gender differences in spatial ability and gender differences in mathematics and science are examined. Results of several meta-analyses, as well as the results of national assessments of mathematics and science ability, are used to investigate these questions.

The review reveals inconsistent inferences about gender differences within spatial ability, aptitude in mathematics, and science achievement. Moreover, there is no apparent basis for inferring causal connections to explain the gender differences across these three areas. Evidence for direct relationships between gender differences in spatial ability and gender differences in mathematics and science is largely lacking. The role of affective and experiential factors in gender differences in each area are discussed.

Gender differences in spatial ability are commonly hypothesized to explain gender-related behavior in mathematics and science. For example, Benbow and Stanley, in their widely publicized article, said: "Sex differences in achievement and in attitude toward mathematics result from superior male mathematical ability which may, in turn, be related to greater male ability in spatial tasks" (1980, p. 1264). Meehan (1984) hypothesized that spatial ability may account for some of the gender differences observed in science performance. Fennema and Carpenter (1981) note that gender differences on items requiring "spatial" reasoning on the National Assessment of Educational Progress (NAEP) are large. Recently, these hypothesized relationships have been questioned by those who have performed, among other analyses, meta-analyses of gender differences in spatial ability (Chipman, Brush & Wilson, 1985; Linn & Petersen, 1985).

To examine this hypothesized linkage, this chapter provides (a) a comprehensive discussion of a meta-analysis of gender differences in spatial ability, and (b) a comparison of the nature, magnitude, and age of first occurrence of gender differences in spatial ability to the nature, magnitude, and age of first occurrence of gender differences in mathematics and science performance. This discussion draws on recent meta-analyses and large-scale investigations of gender differences in mathematics and science.

Of course, analysis of studies directly measuring these relationships would be the ideal approach for establishing links between gender differences in spatial ability and gender differences in mathematics and science achievement. A small number of studies, discussed below, directly examine these relationships. To test the causal hypothesis, however, longitudinal data are needed; few such studies exist. Given the paucity of studies directly testing the hypothesis that gender differences in spatial ability influence those in mathematics and science achievement, we have chosen to examine existing studies to see if the results are at least consistent with the hypothesis.

Part of the difficulty in establishing the hypothesized relationship is that constructs of spatial ability, mathematics achievement, and science achievement are relatively unspecified. Researchers have noted that each of these constructs lacks unity. Activities as disparate as perception of horizontality, location of simple figures within complex figures, and mental rotation of objects have all been referred to as measures of spatial ability. Exercises as varied as rapid arithmetic computation, reconstruction of geometric relationships, and solutions to algebra word problems have been used to measure mathematics achievement. Science achievement has been assessed with problems requiring conservation of quantity, questions about science-related information, such as the boiling temperature of water on the Celsius scale, and applications of propositional logic. Singular definitions of spatial ability, mathematics achievement, and science achievement are needed to afford consistent results.

Perhaps in part because of ambiguity about construct definitions, the existence and magnitude of gender differences in spatial ability, mathematics achievement, and science achievement vary widely from one investigation to another. An important question is whether there are consistent gender differences in each of these areas. Furthermore, when consistent differences are found, a second question is whether the differences are of sufficient magnitude to merit serious consideration.

There is considerable dispute concerning the age of first appearance of gender differences in mathematics, science, and spatial ability. In their landmark book on gender differences, Maccoby and Jacklin (1974) found some evidence for the emergence at adolescence of gender differences in both spatial ability and mathematics achievement. Subsequent investigations cast doubt on this assertion (Linn & Petersen, 1985; Newcombe, Bandura & Taylor, 1983). Recent studies, as well as meta-analyses of studies, provide a more detailed answer to the question about when in the life span gender differences in spatial ability, mathematics achievement, and science achievement can first be detected.

In summary, this chapter examines the plausibility of a linkage between gender differences in spatial ability and gender differences in mathematics and science achievement by assessing the nature, magnitude, and age of first occurrence of gender differences in each of these areas. This assessment is augmented by examination of the few direct investigations of the relationships between gender differences in spatial ability and gender differences in mathematics and science achievement. Finally, we discuss the implications of these relationships for the design of educational programs to serve all students.

Meta-analysis

Advances in meta-analysis procedures make this an advantageous tool for research synthesis (see chap. 2; Hedges, 1982a, 1982b). Meta-analysis offers a better approach for making valid inferences about groups of empirical studies than vote-counting methods, which are based on summing the number of studies with statistically significant results in each direction (e.g., Glass, 1976; Hedges & Olkin, 1980; Pillemar & Light, 1980). Meta-analysis, however, is not a panacea. The implications of a meta-analysis depend on the quality of the studies that go into it. For example, the research perspectives in a field influence what researchers study and constrain the possible outcomes from meta-analysis.

Advances in meta-analysis methods include procedures that allow researchers to adjust results based on the sample size in the study (using unbiased estimates of effect sizes). In addition, new procedures permit the test of homogeneity of effect sizes, that is, the test of whether each study is a replication of each other study. Lack of homogeneity of effect sizes indicates that there are interactions between the variable under investigation (in this case, sex) and characteristics of the research studies. These procedures increase the accuracy of conclusions from meta-analysis. As a result, it is likely that meta-analytic techniques will ultimately encourage progress in research. Research reviews that employ vote-counting methods or no quantitative consideration of studies are unlikely to provide direction for future research (see chaps. 1, 2, and 9 for further discussion). Our meta-analysis of gender differences in spatial ability (Linn & Petersen, 1985) used these new procedures, but they were not generally used in the meta-analyses of mathematics and science achievement reported in this chapter.

Gender Differences in Spatial Ability

As noted above, meta-analysis depends on the conceptualization, methodology, and quality of available primary analyses. The research perspectives that motivated those conducting primary analyses of spatial ability provide both the opportunities for and the limitations on possible inferences from meta-analysis. Thus a brief summary of the major perspectives that have had an impact on the present analysis is provided.

Four research perspectives have generated most studies of spatial ability: (a) the *differential* perspective, involving the analysis of spatial ability accomplishments of different populations (such as males and females); (b) the *psychometric* perspective, involving comparison of correlations between different spatial tasks to define "factors" in spatial ability; (c) the *cognitive* perspective, involving the identification of the processes used universally, albeit with quantitatively different efficiency, to solve a particular spatial ability task; and (d) the *strategic* perspective, involving identification of the qualitatively different strategies used by different respondents to solve a given spatial ability task. These four approaches illustrate the complexity of this field. The perspectives consider information at different levels of detail and take qualitatively different views. Given these different perspectives, it is easy to see how disparate measures of spatial ability would result.

To provide some cohesion to an analysis of spatial ability, and to make replication possible, we formed broad categories of spatial ability. The categories were labeled "spatial perception," "mental rotation," and "spatial visualization." These categories of spatial ability were selected after examination of factor-analytic, correlational, and process-oriented studies.

Spatial Perception

Spatial perception tests require subjects to locate the horizontal or the vertical in spite of distracting information. Verticality is measured, for example, by the rod-and-frame test (RFT), which requires subjects to place a rod vertically while viewing a frame oriented at 22 degrees (Witkin, Dyk & Paterson, 1962). Horizontality, which has recently been shown to relate to verticality (Liben, 1978; Linn & Kyllonen, 1981), is measured by water-level tasks that require subjects to draw or identify a horizontal line in a tilted bottle (e.g., DeAvila, Havassy, with Pascual-Leone, 1976; Harris, Hanley & Best, 1978; Inhelder & Piaget, 1958).

How are these tasks solved? A distinguishing feature of spatial perception performance is the use of kinesthetic cues for locating the horizontal or vertical (e.g., Linn & Kyllonen, 1981; Goodenough, Oltman & Cox, 1984; Sigman, Goodenough & Flannagan, 1978, 1979). For example, respondents to the RFT report that they rely on whether the position "feels" upright. The spatial perception tasks require respondents to locate the gravitational or retinal horizontal or vertical in spite of some distracting information (such as a tilted bottle or tilted frame). Thus efficient respondents attend to kinesthetic cues in spite of distracting information; others may use a strategy based on correcting for the distracting information.

Mental Rotation

Mental rotation is a dimension of spatial ability studied by Shepard and his colleagues (Shepard & Cooper, 1982; Shepard & Metzler, 1971). It involves the ability to rapidly and accurately rotate a two- or three-dimensional figure. They devised individually administered tasks to measure the speed of response to different amounts of rotation (Shepard & Metzler, 1971; Cooper & Shepard, 1973). Subsequently, Vandenberg (1971) modified the Shepard-Metzler mental rotations test for group administration. Other potential measures of this dimension are "flags and cards" from the French kit (French, Ekstrom & Price, 1963) and the Primary Mental Abilities-Space subtest (Thurstone & Thurstone, 1949).

Shepard and colleagues sought to substantiate an analogue process for mental rotation. They hypothesize that during a mental rotation, the respondent's mental processes pass through a series of intermediate states that have a one-to-one correspondence with the intermediate steps involved in rotating an object physically (Shepard & Cooper, 1982). Thus they infer a Gestalt-like mental rotation. Others challenge this view and suggest that mental rotation is subject to analytic processing strategies (e.g., Carpenter & Just, 1978; Just & Carpenter, 1976; Pylysyshyn, 1979, 1981).

Spatial Visualization

Spatial visualization refers to spatial ability tasks that require complicated, multistep analytic processing of spatially presented information. These tasks are quite distinct from both spatial perception and mental rotation tasks. In particular, compared to mental rotations, these tasks require analysis of the relationship between different spatial representations rather than a matching of those representations. Spatial visualization tasks include the embedded figures test, hidden figures, paper folding, the paper-form board, surface development, the spatial relations subtest of the Differential Aptitude Test, block design, and Guilford-Zimmerman spatial visualization. As many researchers have noted (Cattell, 1971; Guay & McDaniel, 1977; Shepard & Feng, 1972), an analytic strategy is required to solve these complex tasks. Mental rotation may or may not be an element of that strategy; spatial perception may sometimes play a rather small role.

Study Selection

Our meta-analysis included studies of spatial ability published since Maccoby and Jacklin's 1974 review and before June 1982. We examined journals likely to publish studies focused on spatial ability, as well as *Psychological Abstracts, Child Development Abstracts*, and the *Index Medicus*. Sources of studies included *Behavioral Genetics, Psychological Bulletin, Journal of Early Adolescence, Developmental Psychology*, and *Child Development*. In addition, papers presented at recent meetings of the American Educational Research Association, the American Psychological Association, and the Society for Research in Child Development were included. Inclusion of unpublished studies offsets, to some extent, the concern that available studies are biased toward significant effects while unpublished studies have nonsignificant findings (see app. B).

Initially we identified over 200 effect sizes; 172 entered the meta-analysis. Studies were eliminated because they: (a) had total samples of less than 40 respondents selected in a nonrandom fashion, for example, friends of the experimeter willing to spend 30 hours being tested (5 studies); (b) reported insufficient information to compute effect sizes (15 studies); or (c) had text presentations that did not coincide with the data reported in the tables (2 studies). Apparent typographical errors were clarified with the author when possible. Furthermore, to avoid dependence in the data, one effect size was randomly selected from studies that administered several measures from the same category of spatial ability to the same subjects, eliminating about 30 effect sizes.

Analysis Procedure

Following Hedges (1982*a*), we tested all 172 effect sizes to see if they could be from a uniform population; a lack of homogeneity was found, indicating that more than one kind of spatial ability was included. These effect sizes were then partitioned into the three categories described above. When homogeneity did not result for these categories, studies within a particular category of spatial ability were partitioned according to the age of the respondents (preadolescent: under 12; adolescent: 12–17; post adolescent: over 18) and again tested for homogeneity. Partitioning by age reflects both the differential tradition, because different age groups are hypothesized to have different levels of spatial ability, and the cognitive tradition, because tests of spatial ability can tap different processes at different points in development. If homogeneity was still not achieved, other partitions were investigated.

Results

As we report in greater detail elsewhere (Linn & Petersen, 1985), the results of this meta-analysis characterize the nature, magnitude, and age of first appearance of each of these three aspects of spatial ability.

Spatial Perception

For spatial perception, the 62 unbiased effect sizes were not homogeneous, and so they were partitioned by age. Results for each age group were acceptably homogeneous. The weighted average effect size for those 18 years of age and older was 0.64, significantly larger than the effect sizes for younger individuals (both were 0.37) and had confidence intervals that included zero. In addition, examination of significance tests for individual studies revealed gender differences on this dimension in students as young as 7 or 8 years old, the youngest groups for which data were available. Thus gender differences in spatial perception appear among young students and persist across the life span. An increase occurs after age 18, but no clear explanation for the increase was found.

Mental Rotation

The mental rotation aspect of spatial ability yielded 29 effect sizes; these were not homogeneous. Partitioning these effect sizes by age did not increase homogeneity. Rather, homogeneity could be achieved if the studies were subdivided by task. Considerably larger effect sizes were found for all age groups on the Vandenberg version of the Shepard-Metzler mental rotations test, averaging 0.94, than on the other measures of mental rotation, where the average was 0.26. This partition yielded homogeneity, or near homogeneity, for each group of effect sizes. Thus the effect size for the Vandenberg version of the Shepard-Metzler mental rotations test averaged close to one standard deviation, whereas the effect size for the Primary Mental Abilities–Space test and related measures averaged about one third of a standard deviation.

Gender differences on mental rotation tests occurred among the youngest respondents and were found across the life span. These tasks, however, are difficult for young children because they require high levels of concentration. Therefore, the Primary Mental Abilities–Space test was not used with respondents under age 10, and the Vandenberg version of the Shepard-Metzler test was not used among students younger than age 13. In summary, gender differences on mental rotation are found whenever it can be measured, but it has not been measured for children younger than age 10.

Spatial Visualization

Meta-analysis of the 81 effect sizes for spatial visualization revealed small effects that were homogeneous across the life span. The average effect size was about 0.13 of a standard deviation unit, with a confidence interval that included zero. Gender differences in spatial visualization do not change across the life span. Furthermore, these results are consistent with the findings of Maccoby and Jacklin (1974) in their examination of the embedded figures test.

Discussion

Homogeneous gender differences emerged for two of the three aspects of spatial ability identified in the meta-analysis, both favoring males. Gender differences occur on spatial perception, characterized by ability to disembed kinesthetic cues from visual cues. Gender differences occur on mental rotation, characterized by speed of angular rotation of a two- or three-dimensional figure. No gender differences are found for spatial visualization, which is characterized by a combination of both visual and nonvisual strategies.

Originally, diverse measures, such as those characterizing mental rotation, were combined. The statistical procedure of establishing homogeneity of effect sizes revealed that these tasks were not similar and motivated us to partition the tasks on underlying dimensions. The advantage of testing for homogeneity is well illustrated by this meta-analysis.

Of the gender differences in spatial ability that were observed, only those on the Vandenberg version of the Shepard-Metzler test were large. These, as mentioned above, were close to a standard deviation in magnitude. Other gender differences averaged close to one third of a standard deviation and can be viewed as small. For the largest category of spatial ability tests, those called "spatial visualization," no significant or meaningful gender differences were found.

The meta-analysis of spatial ability refutes the assertion that gender differences emerge in adolescence. Either gender differences did not emerge at all, as was found for spatial visualization, or they emerged at the earliest age the test could be used. For spatial perception, we discovered an increase in gender differences among those 18 years and older. However, many possible explanations, including a cohort effect among respondents included in studies since 1974, could account for this increase.

This meta-analysis represents a considerable advance in clarifying the nature of gender differences in spatial ability. Differences occur primarily on tasks where efficient solution requires rapid manipulation of symbolic information or on tasks that require recognition of the vertical or horizontal. Tasks that rely on symbolic information but require analytic strategies do not appear to yield gender differences.

Process-Based Explanations for Gender Differences in Spatial Ability

Some have proposed that gender differences in spatial ability result from different problem-solving processes used by males and females (e.g., Cooper, 1984). The processes of (a) acquiring strategies, (b) selecting a strategy, or (c) efficiently applying the strategy could each be the source of gender differences.

Differential acquisition of strategies could result if males are more likely than females to have experience with instruction or activities that develop the strategies. Some sort of biological constraint on the ability to profit from such experiences could also be involved.

Another explanation is based on the assumption that both males and females have acquired all the spatial strategies but select different strategies to solve the same problem. For example, mental rotation, based on analogy to the physical process, may be avoided by certain individuals because the procedure seems less reliable than an analytical feature-matching approach. Another factor governing selection of strategies could be previous experience in related areas such as art or engineering. If one has been instructed to use an analytic strategy with tasks that seem similar, less efficient processing will result. Cooper (1983) demonstrated that there are large individual differences in preference for visual strategies. However, no clear mechanism governing strategy selection has been identified.

Another explanation focuses on efficiency of strategy application. Kail, Carter, and Pellegrino (1979) hypothesize that some reasoners use an analogue strategy but rotate features of the object rather than the whole object. This strategy requires multiple rotations for complex figures and involves remembering the result of each rotation. This procedure is less efficient, under some task conditions, than rotation of the whole object. Acquisition of inefficient strategies may occur as a result of lack of relevant experiences or instruction or for other reasons.

Evidence supports the view that spatial visualization performance depends on awareness of the importance of selecting efficient processes used for each item (Lohman, 1979; Kyllonen, Lohman & Woltz, 1984; Snow & Lohman, 1984). In this sense, spatial visualization appears to resemble closely measures of general ability, especially general fluid ability (Snow et al., 1977). General fluid ability refers to ability to reason independent of verbal ability. Tests of reasoning about nonverbal information generally have pictorial presentations and include measures such as Raven's progressive matrices. In this view, general ability is seen as skill in selecting an appropriate strategy from one's repertoire, whether the repertoire includes spatial or verbal strategies.

For tasks involving selection among spatial strategies, it appears that the extent to which mental rotation of objects is required increases the magnitude of the gender difference. Sex differences in performance becomes more pronounced to the degree that a mental rotation strategy is required. Thus one mechanism governing gender differences in spatial ability may be a constraint on solution strategies. For tasks that rely strongly on an efficient mental rotation strategy, gender differences may be larger than for tasks where a variety of strategies have equal efficiency. Further research with tasks requiring greater or lesser reliance on this process would help to clarify the role of gender in spatial ability.

Biological Explanations for Gender Differences in Spatial Ability

Another set of explanations involves biological mechanisms for sex differences in spatial ability. A common hypothesis focuses on hormonal changes at puberty. Although many intriguing relationships between pubertal change and spatial performance have been proposed (e.g., Carey, Diamond & Woods, 1980; Newcombe, Bandura & Taylor, 1983; Petersen, 1983; Waber, 1976, 1977), they are inconsistently supported by research. Similarly, the meta-analysis results, showing no change in the magnitude of sex differences in spatial ability in early adolescence, contradict the hypothesized change with puberty.

Although the timing of maturation is no longer seen as a major factor in the development of sex differences in spatial ability, other biological influences, particularly genetic or prenatal endocrine influences, remain as potential hypotheses (see Crockett & Petersen, 1984, for a review). Some investigators (e.g., Bock & Kolakowski, 1973; Thomas, 1984) have argued that genetic factors influence the observed sex differences. Although there is ample evidence that spatial ability, like other cognitive abilities, is highly heritable (e.g., DeFries et al., 1976; Spuhler & Vandenberg, 1980), the usual Mendelian process of inheritance does not differentially distribute genes to males relative to females. The primary plausible genetic mechanism for sex differences is that a major gene governing spatial ability is carried on the X chromosome (Wittig & Petersen, 1979). Following the initial proposal of a major X-linked recessive gene for spatial ability (Bock & Kolakowski, 1973), subsequent research has failed to support the X-linked hypothesis (reviewed by Vandenberg & Kuse, 1979). Since this hypothesis has been examined primarily through statistical analysis of trait distributions and of relative correlations within females, it is possible that lack of confirmation is due to excessive measurement error and other error rather than to the absence of the mechanism.

The spatial ability meta-analysis reported above suggested that only two of the three spatial constructs show consistent sex differences. It is possible that the mixed results of studies examining the X-linked hypothesis might be due to variability in the types of measures used. Therefore, we reclassified the studies in terms of the constructs discussed in this paper. The reclassification did not, however, yield more consistent results. Some of the studies finding support for the X-linked hypothesis (e.g., Hartlage, 1970; Stafford, 1961) utilized a spatial visualization measure, a construct for which there was no consistent evidence for sex differences in our meta-analysis. Conversely, some of the studies failing to support the hypothesis measured mental rotation, a construct showing sex differences (e.g., McGee, 1978, 1979). Other studies produced mixed results on different constructs (Fralley, Eliot & Dayton, 1978; Goodenough et al., 1977; Walker, Krasnoff & Peaco, 1981; Yen, 1975). Two studies supporting the X-linked hypothesis did measure constructs for which there are consistent sex differences; mental rotation (Bock & Kolakowski, 1973) and spatial perception (Thomas & Jamison, 1981). Finally, there were studies not supporting the X-linked hypothesis that measured the constructs that here failed to show consistent sex differences (Corely et al., 1980). Given this lack of consistency, it seems clear that better measurement techniques are needed before consistent conclusions can be reached.

Prenatal hormones may contribute to observed sex differences in spatial ability. Just prior to and after birth, these hormones fluctuate to adult levels, with the related sex differences. There is some evidence that brain organization is affected by hormones at this time (Reinisch, Gandelman & Spiegel, 1979), although the mechanism linking hormones and brain organization to spatial ability is unexplained at present (Crockett & Petersen, 1984).

Our findings of prepubertal gender differences make it probable that to the extent that biological factors affect spatial ability, they arise early in development and interact with sex-typed experiences and sex-role expectations to produce the observed patterns of performance (e.g., Newcombe, Bandura & Taylor, 1983; Tobin-Richards & Petersen, 1981). Such effects will be much clearer if the different types of spatial ability are treated separately in subsequent studies and if multiple measures of the same spatial ability dimension are used to reduce measurement error.

Gender Differences in Mathematics Performance

The nature, magnitude, and age of first appearance of gender differences in mathematics achievement have recently been examined. Data stem primarily from large-scale national tests, including the National Assessment of Educational Progress (NAEP), the Scholastic Aptitude Test mathematics assessment (SAT-M), and the Project TALENT Survey. Because these tests are given to such a large sample of the population, meta-analysis has not been used, nor is it necessary. Typically, researchers do not report effect sizes for gender differences, but they can often be computed for the whole sample.

The nature of mathematics performance is generally subdivided into two categories: computation and problem solving. Further subdivision, on the basis of whether the problems require knowledge of geometry or not, has been used to examine the role of spatial ability. The supposition is that geometry, because of its relationship to spatial ability, might be more problematic for females than are other aspects of mathematics.

Results

Historically, as women have participated more equally in mathematics courses, differences in performance between males and females have diminished. Studies of data collected in the 1960s reveal differences on problem-solving items for males and females.

Steel and Wise (1979) analyzed data for the 1960 Project TALENT sample. For ninth graders, they found a statistically significant but very small (0.07 of a standard deviation) differences favoring males on this problem-solving test. Among twelfth graders, they found a difference of about 0.50 of a standard deviation favoring males. Results were similar for the 1963 and the 1969 survey. Thus gender differences in problem-solving performance appear to increase between ninth and twelfth grade, a period during which females tend to take fewer mathematics courses than males.

Large-scale examinations of mathematics performance at age 9, 13, and 17 were conducted in 1978 and 1979 by the National Assessment of Educational Progress (NAEP, 1979c, 1979d, 1983) and, in a related investigation, by Armstrong (1979). The 1978 NAEP study administered items to over seventy thousand 9, 13, and 17 year olds. In 1978, Armstrong surveyed about three thousand students at age 13 and at grade 12. The 1982 NAEP survey of over seventy thousand students replicated the earlier results.

In computation, NAEP data for age 9 and age 13 reveal that females outperformed males by about six percentage points; at age 17, males were about one percentage point above females. Thus females have an advantage in computation prior to age 17, and the difference at 17 is close to zero.

In problem solving, the NAEP data consistently reveal no significant differences between males and females at any age (Armstrong, 1979; NAEP, 1979c, 1979d). Slight nonsignificant differences arise among 17 year olds, but are eliminated if course preparation is considered (Armstrong, 1979). For example, Welch (1981) reports small effect sizes of 0.17 and 0.24 for two different NAEP tests administered to 17 year olds.

Many individual studies also assess mathematics ability. Maccoby and Jacklin (1974) categorized the existing studies and found an effect favoring males. Hyde (1981) conducted a meta-analysis using the same studies and found that the effect accounted for approximately 1 percent of the variance.

For studies of high-ability students, larger gender differences are expected on statistical grounds (Hyde, 1981). That is, if there are gender differences and if the standard deviations for the two groups are equal, studies of students at the high-ability extreme of the distribution will reveal larger gender differences than will studies of all students. For example, the Educational Testing Service reports that the difference between male and female performance on SAT-M (when the sex groups have similar standard deviations) is greater for students in the top tenth of their high school class than for the average: 67 points compared to 50 points. The finding that males perform better on problem-solving tests than females by about one-half a standard deviation at age 17 is also reported for the SAT-M. For example, the 1979–81 Admissions Testing Program of the College Board (ATP, 1979) indicates that on the SAT-M administered to high school seniors, males had an average of 493 and females had an average of 443. Benbow and Stanley (1984) reported a similar pattern of differences among the students whom they recruited for an accelerated mathematics program. Between 1972 and 1974, they recruited approximately 2,200 students. The average score of those students when recruited (at age 12 or 13) was about 547 for males and about 505 for females (about 42 points difference). When these students were in high school, the SAT-M was about 694 for males and about 645 for females (about 49 points difference).

Process Analysis

Recent process analysis of performance in mathematics sheds light on the gender differences. For example, Dougherty, Herbert, Edenhurt-Pape, and Small (1980) found that girls perform better on computation problems and boys perform better on estimation problems and on word problems with low computational demands. Furthermore, for the NAEP 1978 data, Fennema and Carpenter (1981) identified items with geometry content and measurement content. They reported that females were relatively less successful than males on both item types at ages 9, 13, and 17, and that differences increased with age. Similarly, Marshall (1983, 1984a, 1984b), analyzing the California Assessment Program, reports that in third and in sixth grade, females do far better on computation items and males do better on items where they are required to select the correct operation (among addition, subtraction, multiplication, and division) for solving a problem and on items requiring measurement. Looking at the specific pattern of errors in problem solving in a sixth-grade class, Marshall (1984b) found that in solving problems, males made significantly more errors in computation and in transcribing the problem while females made more errors in selecting the operation for the problem. In addition, females, more than males, indicated "I don't know" as an answer to problem-solving items, which suggests greater propensity for females to report uncertainty rather than make an educated guess. Those studying errors in computation (Brown & Van Lehn, 1980; Marshall, 1983; Riley, Greeno & Heller, 1983) find that males make the same errors as females but make them more frequently. No qualitative differences in performance have been found.

Similar findings are reported for problem solving. Studying problem solving in a class of sixth graders, Marshall (1984b) found that females make more errors, but they make the same types of errors that males make. No qualitative differences in the types of errors made by males and females have been identified.

In summary, gender differences in mathematics performance vary depending on the type of item administered. The magnitude of gender differences in mathematics achievement depends on the age of the participants, the year of testing, how selected the sample is, and whether problem solving or computation is studied. Differences favoring males of between 0.01 and 0.5 of a standard deviation, depending on whether a national sample or a college-bound sample is used and on whether the testing was recent or in 1960, are found on problem-solving among 17 year olds. Differences favoring males of 0.5 of a standard deviation are found among students who volunteer to take the SAT-M to qualify for advanced courses at age 12.

The age of first identification of gender differences in mathematics achievement depends on the aspect of mathematics being assessed. As noted, for computation, females outperform males starting at a very young age, but that advantage disappears by age 17. Males outperform females in certain aspects of problem solving after age 14, when course experience is not taken into consideration.

Discussion

Several explanations for this pattern of gender differences have been put forth. As mentioned at the outset, some authors hypothesize that gender differences in spatial ability are involved. No evidence for this view emerged, but we will postpone discussion of the hypothesis until the end of this chapter.

A second explanation concerns course taking and other mathematics experience. It is well known that females enroll in fewer mathematics courses than do males (Chipman, Brush & Wilson, 1985; Meece et al., 1982). Numerous investigations of the relationship between course enrollment and performance reveal that courses are the single most influential factor in achievement test performance (Chipman, Brush & Wilson, 1985). In addition, many studies document that even in the same mathematics classes, males' experiences differ from females' experiences, perhaps contributing to the differences in performance (e.g., NAEP, 1979c, 1979d).

Support for the experience hypothesis also comes from differences in out-of-school mathematics activities for males and females. The NAEP assessment of science for 1981–82 revealed large gender differences in out-of-school activities related to science and mathematics. For example, males were more likely to engage in measurement activities than were females (Hueftle, Rakow & Welch, 1983). The Lawrence Hall of Science reports much larger male than female enrollment in after-school mathematics classes. Newcombe, Bandura, and Taylor (1983), Petersen and Gitelson (in press), and Block and Block (1982) report gender-specific patterns in participation in out-of-school activities such as chess and mathematical games. Perhaps interest in these out-of-school mathematics activities is what differentiates high-scoring males from high-scoring females.

Interest in mathematics careers is greater for males than females and may influence mathematics course selection and mathematics performance. Gender differences in patterns of interest appear to be somewhat fundamental, strongly linked to sex-role stereotypes, and unlikely to change rapidly (e.g., Chipman, Brush & Wilson, 1985). These interests may be established among young children (e.g., Deaux, 1984), then reinforced by the media and by some teachers, school counselors, and parents (e.g. Parsons, Adler & Kaczala, 1982; Parsons, Kaczala & Meece, 1982). Although it is difficult to imagine that interest in mathematics does not influence mathematics learning, strong relationships between degree of interest and performance have not been established. Rather, interest seems to have an impact on career expectations and perception of one's own ability in mathematics. For example, females with the same ability as males assess their skills less favorably than do males (Chipman, Brush & Wilson, 1985; Stage et al., 1984). These factors, in turn, are correlated with mathematics performance.

A constellation of affective characteristics forms the third common explanation for gender differences in mathematics performance. These consist of attitudes about mathematics shaped by societal expectations for males and females. Some support can be found for the suggestion that females are less confident, more anxious, and more cautious when solving mathematics problems.

As Chipman, Brush, and Wilson (1985) suggest, these factors seem to overlap. Several studies report that if females and males of equal ability and with the same performance history are asked to indicate their likelihood of performing a problem correctly, males will be overconfident, while females will not be confident enough (e.g., Marshall, 1984b).

Other factors studied—such as attitudes among both males and females that mathematics is a male domain and stronger beliefs among males than among females that learning mathematics has career advantages—are negatively related to mathematics experience. For example, females who have taken many mathematics courses are more likely to believe that mathematics has career advantages for females than those who have taken few courses (Armstrong, 1979). Increased interest in careers involving mathematics among females has also occurred recently. These changes accompany great increases in the number of females majoring in mathematics and in engineering.

In summary, mathematics performance of males and females reflects differences in mathematics experience, expectations about mathematics performance, interest in mathematics careers, and caution in problem solving, among other factors. These dimensions do not have a uniform influence on all students, but rather are more pronounced for those with less mathematics experience. In addition, increases in female participation in mathematics courses and careers in recent years have accompanied increases in females' interest in mathematics. Considerably more change in course enrollment is required to ensure equitable access to mathematics-related careers and considerable effort is needed to ensure that females who receive training have the opportunity to use that training in traditionally male careers.

Gender Differences in Science Achievement

The magnitude, nature, and age of first appearance of gender differences in science achievement have been investigated in several meta-analyses (Steinkamp & Maehr, 1983; Meehan, 1984; Malone & Fleming, 1983). In addition, the National Assessment of Educational Progress assessed science achievement in 1969-70, 1972-73, 1976-77, and in 1981-82 (Hueftle, Rakow, & Welch, 1983; NAEP, 1978a, 1978b, 1979a, 1979b).

Measures of science achievement typically include two kinds of items. One type assesses information about science, including questions such as "What is evaporation?" The other aspect has been referred to as "scientific reasoning" and includes questions that ask students to design experiments and draw conclusions as well as questions about principles, such as conservation of liquid. Most assessments of science achievement have separated these two aspects of performance, although the vocabulary chosen to refer to each dimension varies from author to author.

The NAEP science assessments refer to information questions as "content" items and differentiate among biology, physical science, and earth science content. Reasoning tasks are called "inquiry" items by NAEP. In addition, NAEP has included science, technology, and society items in recent assessments. These items test understanding of the relationships between scientific advance and persistent social problems. This category also includes items assessing health and safety-related information and items requiring reasoning about social responsibility.

The NAEP 1976–77 and 1981–82 assessments revealed similar patterns of gender differences (NAEP, 1978*a*, 1978*b*, 1979*a*, 1979*b*). A slight, nonsignificant decline in overall scores during this period suggests that the well-publicized erosion of science knowledge characterizing NAEP results in the 1970s may be coming to an end. Given the similarities between recent assessments, this discussion will feature the 1981–82 assessment, which was administered to 18,000 13 and 17 year olds.

Overall, on science information, males scored about 5 percentage points higher than females at both age 13 and age 17. Although NAEP reports do not include information for computing effect sizes, a study of the 1977 assessment (de Benedictis et al., in press) revealed an average effect size for gender of 0.27 of a standard deviation. In addition, Welch (1981) reports effect sizes of 0.34 and 0.32 for two tests administered to 17 year olds. The largest differences were found for physical science items, the smallest for biology, with earth science in between. Interestingly, the physical science item used by Hueftler, Rakow, and Welch (1983) to illustrate this difference involved knowledge of where to place weights to stabilize a balance beam, which involved the computation of a ratio—an item often found in texts of mathematics problem solving.

The science, technology, and society cluster included science information items having to do with health and other topics. Females outperformed males in the health content area while males outperformed females in the environmental content areas. These results parallel the small gender differences in biology and larger differences in physical science discussed above. It appears that females are more likely to acquire biological and health knowledge as opposed to physical and earth science knowledge, a strong indication of the role of experience in science content learning.

Overall, on science reasoning, there were no significant gender differences at age 13 or 17. When items involve analytic processes and multistep reasoning but do not depend on specific science content, no gender differences arise. This finding, for analytic items, parallels the results for spatial visualization discussed earlier.

A study by de Benedictis, Delucchi, Harris, Linn, and Stage (in press) conducted a detailed analysis of gender differences in the 1977 NAEP science assessment for 17 year olds that augments these results. They found that items requiring knowledge of scientific vocabulary, such as "acceleration," "compound," "particle," and "velocity," yielded larger gender differences (an effect size of 0.4 favoring males) than items without such vocabulary.

Another interesting trend was identified in this study. Females were far more likely than males to use the response option of "I don't know." Overall, females used the "I don't know" response about 2 percent more often than did males; the average effect size was 0.24 of a standard deviation. This tendency is especially evident on difficult items in which females used the "I don't know" response 19 percent of the time whereas males used the "I don't know" response 13 percent of the time. Thus, among 17 year olds, females compared to males appeared to have a less specialized science vocabulary and to report less knowledge about science. These responses are consistent with the greater enrollment of males in science classes during high school (Hueftle, Rakow, & Welch, 1983).

Malone and Fleming (1983) conducted a meta-analysis of the relationship of gender to science information and science reasoning. They augmented published studies with 122 dissertations that examined these questions. Their data base included the NAEP 1977 results for science. Malone and Fleming computed effect sizes but did not assess homogeneity. In general, they found very small gender differences. For science information, the average effect size was 0.16 of a standard deviation unit, comparable to the 1982 NAEP finding. For science reasoning, the average effect size was 0.13 of a standard deviation unit, comparable to the nonsignificant differences reported by the 1982 NAEP. They also found an age-related trend, with larger gender differences at middle school than for older or younger students. Since this finding contradicts the NAEP results, more analysis is needed to understand it fully. Analyzing their data by content area revealed a pattern similar to that reported for NAEP: gender differences were larger for physical science than for chemistry and no differences were found for life sciences.

Steinkamp and Maehr (1983) examined the relationship between gender and science information (referred to as "achievement") and between gender and science reasoning (referred to as "cognitive ability"). They analyzed 66 studies, computing average correlations between gender and performance. They did not assess homogeneity. They found 15 studies that reported a relationship between gender and science information. The average correlation favored males and was 0.17, accounting for about 2 percent of the variance. They found 42 studies reporting data on gender and scientific reasoning with an average correlation favoring males of 0.13, accounting for about 1 percent of the variance. Thus a significant but small relationship between gender and performance was found for each aspect of science achievement. No analysis by age of subject was reported.

Meehan (1984) conducted a meta-analysis of scientific reasoning items classified as formal operations. Her analysis focused on students age 12 and older and included three categories of scientific reasoning: propositional reasoning, combinatorial reasoning, and proportional reasoning. Proportional reasoning, it should be noted, has a strong mathematics component and is often included in mathematics problem-solving exams. Meehan computed effect sizes using an effect size of zero for studies where no differences were found and no information concerning the actual effect size was available. Thus her results underestimated the actual effect sizes. For 64 studies of propositional logic, she found an effect size favoring males of 0.05 of a standard deviation unit. For 43 studies of combinatorial reasoning, she found an effect size favoring males of 0.05 of a standard deviation unit. For 53 studies of proportions, she found an effect size favoring males of 0.31. Thus she found small nonsignificant gender differences in propositional and combinatorial reasoning and larger differences for proportional reasoning. The effect size of about one-third of a standard deviation for proportional reasoning is smaller than the effect size of about half of a standard deviation characteristic of mathematics problem-solving items administered to 17 year olds, possibly because of the inclusion of effect sizes of zero for studies where the result was nonsignificant.

In summary, small but consistent gender differences in science information were detected, ranging from about 0.1 standard deviation to about 0.3 standard deviation, probably accounting for less than 5 percent of the variance. When patterns of gender differences in science information were examined, females were found to have more knowledge of health and males to have more knowledge of physical and earth science. For science reasoning, gender differences were detected when the items involved proportional reasoning, an aspect of mathematics problem solving.

A number of investigations have demonstrated the role of information about the particular science topic in scientific reasoning performance. Furthermore, they have shown that gender differences in science information may account for gender differences in scientific reasoning. For example, Peskin (1980) found that versions of scientific reasoning tasks involving science information likely to be studied by females were much easier for females than were versions involving science information likely to be known by males. In another example, Thomas (1984), using tasks developed by Linn (1983), found that proportional reasoning tasks involving balance beams were considerably more likely to yield gender differences than were proportional reasoning tasks involving "advertised specials" on groceries and clothing. Sinnott (1975) also found an interaction between task content and gender. More generally, recent research in scientific reasoning has clearly demonstrated the role of content and context in performance (Linn & Delucchi, 1983).

In summary, it seems that gender differences in science information account for gender differences in many reasoning tasks. Indeed, the gender differences in reasoning, when they occur, appear to reflect either knowledge of scientific information or proportional reasoning skill.

Discussion

The same three categories of explanations for the gender differences in mathematics achievement have been put forth to explain the gender differences in science achievement.

Spatial ability has been suggested as a factor in gender differences in science achievement (e.g., Meehan, 1984). It is clear that spatial ability correlates with science achievement (Linn & Pulos, 1982, 1983), but no evidence has been found to suggest that gender differences in spatial ability account for gender differences in scientific reasoning or scientific information. These issues will be discussed in the next section of this chapter.

The second category of explanations concerns science experience. It is well established that fewer females than males take advanced science courses and that course experience influences science achievement (e.g., Hueftle, Rakow & Welch, 1983; Linn & Pulos, 1983). Furthermore, many have demonstrated that females and males have different out-of-school experiences related to science (e.g., Kahle & Lakes, 1983; Block & Block, 1982; Hueftle, Rakow & Welch, 1983; NAEP, 1979b). Visits to science museums, science activities associated with scouting, and enrollment in out-of-school science classes are more likely for males than for females. These differences are well documented, and their relationship to gender differences in science achievement was strong in the study conducted by Linn and Pulos (1983). Further study of these relationships is needed.

The third explanation of gender differences in science achievement involves affective characteristics of males and females. As noted for mathematics, there is support for females displaying less confidence and greater caution than males in solving science items. This is reflected in their more frequent use of the "I don't know" response, even when an educated guess could be made (Wheeler & Harris, 1981; de Benedictis et al., in press). Support is also widespread for the notion that males are more confident about their science abilities than females. When males and females of equal ability perform the same problem, males express greater confidence than females (e.g., Chipman, Brush & Wilson, 1985; Linn, 1985).

Another well-documented affective difference between males and females has to do with altruism. Females have significantly higher scores than males in science responsibility items administered by NAEP (Hueftle, Rakow & Welch, 1983), primarily because of their greater reported willingness take part in socially responsible actions. Females have greater science knowledge about health and safety-related issues such as the effects of smoking and response to fires. These results are consistent with research on sex differences in empathy (e.g., Hoffman, 1977) and with the recent social-psychological theories of moral development put forth by Gilligan (1982). These theories emphasize that females are more caring and attuned to the feelings of others. These results also coincide with Hall's 1978 report of females' greater skill in decoding nonverbal cues and with Hall and Halberstadt's report of gender differences in eye contact with others (chap. 5).

As would be expected, males have significantly more positive attitudes than females about science classes and about careers in science (Chipman, Brush & Wilson, 1985). Consistent with the findings for mathematics, these beliefs are widespread and well established. Similarly, increased female participation in science courses and in science-related careers accompanies increasingly positive attitudes toward scientific careers on the part of female students. Thus, for 17 year olds, NAEP reports a decline between 1976 and 1981 in the gender differences in attitudes toward science careers (NAEP, 1979*b*).

The Relationship among Gender Differences in Mathematics, Science, and Spatial Ability

Examination of the nature, magnitude, and age of first appearance of gender differences in mathematics, science, and spatial ability fails to reveal a consistent pattern. This lack of cohesion raises serious doubts about the hypothesis that gender differences in spatial ability contribute to mathematics and science performance. Rather, the gender differences in mathematics and science interact idiosyncratically with experience and affective variables. The overlap of spatial ability, mathematics, and science achievement can best be attributed to the analytic ability required for all these tasks for which males and females have equal potential. Following a brief analysis of the lack of cohesion among gender differences in mathematics, science, and spatial abilities, we examine some of the research attempting to establish the gender relationships directly.

The Nature of Gender Differences in Mathematics, Science, and Spatial Ability

In general, examination of gender differences in spatial ability, mathematics, and science achievement reveals a lack of uniformity both within each domain and across the domains. In the spatial category, three separate aspects of ability were identified, and one of those aspects was further split into two separate components. Gender differences in spatial ability occur on fairly specific skills, one being the recognition of the horizontal or the vertical and the other being the rapid rotation of visually presented figures. Gender differences do not occur on spatial tasks that rely heavily on analytic combinations of complex information.

In mathematics achievement, at least two separate categories of behavior emerged: computation and problem solving. Further refinement of problem solving into specific subject matter areas such as measurement, geometry, and algebra, with correspondingly different magnitudes of gender differences, is partially supported by available data. Females outperform males in computation prior to age 17. Males outperform females on problem solving when course experience is not controlled for and when subjects are 14 or older.

Science achievement involves several components, including science information and science reasoning. Only science information consistently yields gender differences, with females less likely to have all the science information known to males. When science information is divided by content area, females excel in health knowledge while males excel in physical science knowledge. Gender differences in science reasoning occur primarily on tasks involving proportional reasoning. Proportional reasoning items, however, are also found in problem-solving tests for mathematics. On other aspects of scientific reasoning, gender differences are not consistently found. In addition, specific investigations of the role of science information in scientific reasoning reveal that often gender differences in reasoning performance are due, in part, to lack of science information.

Taken together, these investigations support a model of gender differences in mathematics, science, and spatial ability based on multiple interactions of analytic reasoning, course experience, factual knowledge, interest, and confidence. No clear main effects have emerged. In addition, rapidly changing levels of female participation in mathematics and science courses and careers are accompanying diminishing gender differences on all variables studied.

The Magnitude of Gender Differences in Spatial Ability in Mathematics and Science Achievement

In general, gender differences found for mathematics, science, and spatial ability are small relative to the larger gender differences in choice of careers in science, mathematics, and engineering. For example, 11 percent of engineering graduate students in 1982 were females (Vetter, 1983). The largest gender differences uncovered in these investigations are on the Vandenberg version of the Shepard-Metzler mental rotations test, an aspect of spatial ability revealing gender differences of close to a full standard deviation unit. The next largest gender differences are found in mathematics performance under certain conditions. Both the Project TALENT test given in 1960 and SAT-M tests given to high-ability students reveal gender differences in the neighborhood of half a standard deviation. The remaining investigations generally identified gender differences between one-tenth and one-third standard deviation in various aspects of spatial ability, mathematics, and science performance. When authors compute the percentage of variance accounted for by these effect sizes, they generally concur that between 1 and 5 percent of the variance is accounted for by gender. The Vandenberg version of the Shepard-Metzler figures is the only exception, where gender accounts for closer to 8 percent of the variance.

The Age of First Appearance of Gender Differences in Mathematics, Science, and Spatial Ability

Although many hypotheses concerning the first appearance of gender differences in all these areas during adolescence have been put forth, no evidence for this view was found. Gender differences in spatial ability tend to emerge either as soon as they are measurable or not at all. Gender differences in mathematics performance emerge early for computation (favoring females) and later for various aspects of problem solving (favoring males). For science information, studies reveal small differences at every age studied with the direction of the difference dependent on the content of the items.

Thus no evidence for the emergence of gender differences in any of these areas during adolescence is found. Furthermore, no evidence of rapid acceleration at adolescence or even for acceleration beyond adolescence is consistently observed. The one meta-analysis revealing a change at adolescence found the relationship curvilinear, increasing at adolescence and decreasing afterward (Steinkamp & Maehr, 1983). Since this finding was inconsistent with other large-scale studies, it cannot be seen as strong evidence for changes during adolescence.

Empirical Evidence Concerning Relationships among Mathematics, Science, and Spatial Ability

Given the lack of cohesion concerning the nature, magnitude, and age of first occurrence of gender differences in spatial ability, mathematics, and science achievement, strong relationships between the gender differences in one area and the gender differences in another seem unlikely. A number of empirical studies document this presumption.

It is important to distinguish between the general relationship between performance on one task and performance on another and the more specific relationship between the gender differences on one task and the gender differences on another. Mathematics, science, and spatial ability all share a common component of general ability. As summarized above and discussed by Lohman (1979), spatial visualization tasks closely resemble tasks referred to as fluid ability and, indeed, in many analyses cannot be separated from general ability. Thus it is not surprising that high correlations are found (a) between spatial ability and mathematics performance and (b) between spatial ability and science performance. Similar correlations are found between these measures and tests of vocabulary. These high correlations have no implications whatsoever for an overlap in the gender differences. Quite a different mechanism could account for the gender differences.

The best way to establish the role of spatial ability in mathematics and science performance would be through a longitudinal study. Petersen (1983) has conducted such a study and offers strong evidence supporting the importance of general ability in all three types of performance but no evidence for a single mechanism to account for gender differences in these three areas.

Linn and Pulos (1982, 1983) gathered data on over eight hundred students concerning the relationship between an aspect of scientific reasoning (proportional reasoning), an aspect of science information (volume displacement), and two aspects of spatial ability (spatial perception and spatial visualization). Hedges and Olkin (1980) synthesized the results of this study by testing a model for the correlations between scientific reasoning and spatial ability for males and females and for students in grades 7, 9, and 11 (a total of six correlations). Their analysis revealed that the correlations were different from zero as a group but that there were no sex or grade effects. Thus the correlations differed from zero, presumably, because of the effect of general ability; but neither the grade nor the sex of the student contributed to the pattern of correlations. In another analysis, Linn and Pulos (1982, 1983) used regression techniques to reach the same conclusion.

Recently, several researchers have reviewed the relationship between spatial ability and mathematics performance. These studies have been hampered by the fact that different researchers use different measures of spatial ability, which, as this paper reveals, do not necessarily measure a unitary characteristic. In general, however, those reviewing the relationship between spatial ability and mathematics achievement conclude that no clear evidence has been found for gender differences in spatial ability to explain gender differences in mathematics performance (Connor & Serbin, 1980; Chipman, Brush & Wilson, 1985; Petersen & Crockett, in press; Stage et al., in press; Wise, 1979).

Efforts to establish specific relationships between aspects of mathematics achievement likely to require spatial ability and measures of spatial performance have met with only limited success. Stallings (1979) found some relationship, but others have not. A major problem is that most studies employ measures of spatial visualization that, as our spatial ability analysis revealed, do not generally display gender differences.

It may be that more specific relationships between geometry tasks that require mental rotation and measures of mental rotations would yield consistency. Indeed, Fennema and Carpenter, in an analysis of the National Assessment of Education Progress data (1981), report that the single item having the highest gender difference is an item very similar to those on the Vandenberg version of the Shepard-Metzler mental rotations test. An important question is whether this ability is necessary for geometry, at least as it is commonly taught.

Another specific investigation by Burnett, Lane, and Dratt (1979) examined Rice University students' SAT-M scores and their spatial ability scores. These researchers found that for this group of students who have very high SAT-M scores, a relationship between gender differences in spatial ability and gender differences in mathematics performance could be documented. It would be useful to look more closely at the items in each test that revealed gender differences to ascertain whether phenomena such as the one described by Fennema and Carpenter (1981) account for this effect. As analysis continues, it appears that gender differences are found on items requiring single specialized strategies, often those requiring proportional reasoning or rapid rotation of objects, rather than on a range of tasks.

Efforts to show a specific relationship between gender differences in spatial ability and gender differences in science achievement have met with no success. For example, de Benedictis and colleagues (in press) attempted to identify items in the NAEP with high and low spatial visualization content and then to examine gender differences on those items. No pattern emerged. There were just as many gender differences on items appearing to require visualization skills as on items that did not appear to require those skills. Although correlations between spatial ability and science achievement are generally high, the explanatory value of spatial ability differences for gender differences in science has not been shown. Thus, in science, no general effect for spatial ability has emerged; but as discussed above, specific gender differences in science reasoning may reflect gender differences in science information.

Discussion

For spatial ability, mathematics achievement, and science achievement, gender differences, when they are found, do not reflect a common mechanism. Rather, it seems likely that many different factors contribute to the observed gender differences both as main effects and as the result of interactions. In fact, the main effect for spatial ability is generally small but might interact with affective or experience factors to appear larger in certain contexts.

In the section on spatial ability, general ability is described as the ability to select from among one's repertoire of strategies an appropriate one for a particular problem, consistent with Cooper (1984) and Snow and Lohman (1984). The aspect of spatial ability most closely aligned with this skill, spatial visualization, revealed no gender differences, just as tests of general ability reveal no gender differences (Maccoby & Jacklin, 1974). Females and males do not appear to differ in ability to select the best strategy. Rather, they may differ in the repertoire of strategies available to them. Tasks that require a single specialized strategy may reveal gender differences because the most efficient strategy is less well developed in females than in males. Speed of mental rotation is an example of such a strategy. One approach for responding to the observed pattern of gender differences is to help females gain specific skills to add to their repertoire for solving problems.

The Role of Instruction

Myriad training studies reveal that spatial abilities and other specific skills can be taught (e.g., Connor, Serbin & Schackman, 1977; Linn & Thier, 1975; Ben Haim, 1982). Numerous investigations of the role of course experience on performance in mathematics and science strongly support the notion that these courses have an impact on achievement. Thus one important way to respond to gender differences in spatial ability, mathematics achievement, and science achievement is to encourage males and females to participate equally in courses emphasizing these skills.

In spite of equal male and female participation in courses, however, studies reveal that gender differences in mathematics and science performance sometimes occur. Other factors, besides regularly organized courses, appear to contribute. One source of additional experience with mathematics and science is, of course, out-of-school or informal learning, as noted above. It seems likely that males more than females are exposed to instruction in mathematics and science outside of school. Of course, one cannot ascertain whether this differential exposure to mathematics and science course work results from societal expectations for males and females, from differential interests of males and females in mathematics and science, or from other sources. Nevertheless, it seems clear that course experience has an impact on performance and that additional courses are likely to be helpful.

There is no doubt that multiple skills can be used to solve the same problem. Studies of expertise reveal that even among highly talented individuals like chess masters, there are considerable individual differences in how tasks are performed. In only a few areas, mostly motor skills, do all experts use the same approach. For example, Gentner and Norman (1984) found that for the motor skill of typing, experts all behave similarly. Certain sports, such as speed skating, also reveal a remarkable convergence in performance. On the other hand, tasks such as chess playing and hardware design are characterized, not by convergence, but by divergence of expert performances. Thus females may use different strategies than males for certain specialized skills and still succeed equally on most tasks.

A variety of different mechanisms influence performance in mathematics, science, and spatial ability. Very specific skills contribute to performance on certain specific tasks like mental rotation or computing the proportions in a balance beam task. Rather than finding homogeneity in gender differences even within mathematics or science, we find considerable divergence across tasks. It seems likely that specific experiences and specific information are important in scientific and mathematical reasoning and that building up a store of these experiences is an important component of successful performance.

It has been well documented that expertise in areas such as chess playing requires a phenomenal number of hours of experience. The role of experience in mathematics and science performance is considerable as well. Differences may exist in degree of exposure to these experiences. Thus one important response to gender differences in mathematics and science performance is renewed efforts to provide both formal educational experiences and informal experiences equitably to males and females.

Currently, the most effective response to gender differences in mathematics, science, and spatial ability involves instruction to ensure that effective strategies are acquired (see Klein, 1984, for a discussion of exemplary programs). Effective educational programs provide experiences that contribute to expertise in mathematics and science. Given their slightly lower performance, females may benefit more than males from effective educational programs because such programs may be needed to remedy specific gaps in their knowledge; but exemplary educational programs will benefit all learners.

The Role of Affective Factors

Many affective factors have been put forth to explain gender differences in mathematics, science, and spatial ability. The lack of cohesion of these differences tends to cast doubt on any general mechanism. Rather, these factors may contribute to large interactions between gender and performance under selected conditions. As Deaux (1984) argues, societal expectations often interact with gender to make small effects larger.

One general notion is based on the lack of confidence displayed by females in problem solving. This idea was put forth to account for gender differences in mental rotations, in NAEP science performance, and in mathematics computation. The basic mechanism here is that females are more cautious, more careful in responding to test items, and therefore perform more slowly and are more likely to indicate that they do not know the answer when they are not sure about a question. Such caution may be realistic in that female respondents may have less information and therefore may simply be indicating a lack of knowledge. Alternatively, such caution may reflect a differential threshold for uncertainty, greater confidence among males, or greater willingness to verify responses to questions among females. This caution seems to reflect an unwillingness to be wrong in these situations—a response that may be reinforced by sex-role stereotypes of women as careful and as attentive to detail in the home or the office. Further research is needed to investigate the role of confidence and caution in mathematics and science performance.

An effective hypothesis supported by these data concerns interest in mathematics and science. It is well documented that females have less desire than males to engage in activities involving mathematics and science. It is not known whether this is a cause of, or a result of, gender differences in achievement. At any rate, attitudes are slowly becoming more similar for the sexes at the same time as course taking and career experiences of females are getting closer to those of males.

Another hypothesis to explain these findings concerns the role of societal expectations. Efforts have been made to show that female role models in areas where females rarely excel might contribute to improved performance of both males and females. Parsons, Adler, and Kaczala (1982) investigated the possible role of parental attitudes in gender differences in mathematics and found no consistent influence on students' performance but a strong influence on students' attitudes. Investigations of the role of school teachers and school counselors reveal similar mixed results. Some students report responding to these influences, others discount them. Efforts to implicate the media in building expectations for success in mathematics and science have been frequently put forth but infrequently supported (Deaux, 1985; Chipman, Brush & Wilson, 1985). It seems that interactions between societal expectations and performance arise and, at times, influence performance.

The Role of Biological Factors

Biological explanations have frequently been put forth to explain gender differences in mathematics, science, and spatial ability. Indeed, some have suggested that spatial ability differences might be biologically determined and provide the mechanism for a biological influence on mathematics and science. No evidence for that view can be found. The main biological explanation that remains for spatial ability concerns the role of prenatal hormones, although no empirical evidence for it has been found. Since this mechanism is set in place at birth, much opportunity to capitalize on interaction between possible biological factors and experience remains.

Implications

A single explanation for gender differences in mathematics performance, science performance, and spatial ability seems unlikely given the lack of a consistent pattern of gender differences in these areas. Indeed, the only hypothesis receiving any strong support is one based on differential experiences having impact on development of specific strategies.

An experience explanation, besides fitting the observed differences fairly well, also coincides with the success of programs to overcome gender differences. The area where greatest impact on gender differences has been and can be made is certainly in providing effective educational experiences for all students. If experience is a major contributor to the observed gender differences, then educational programs to provide more effective instruction in these areas are likely to be the best response.

References

Admissions Testing Program of the College Board (1979-81). *ATP guide for high schools and colleges*, Princeton, N.J.: Educational Testing Service.

Armstrong, J. M. (1979). *A national assessment of achievement and participation of women in mathematics*. Denver: Education Commission of the States (ERIC Document Reproduction Service No. ED 187562).

Benbow, C. P., & Stanley, J. C. (1980). Sex differences in mathematical ability: Fact or artifact? *Science, 210*, 1262-1264.

Benbow, C. P., & Stanley, J. C. (eds.) (1984). *Academic precocity: Aspects of its development*. Baltimore: Johns Hopkins University Press.

Ben-Haim, D. (1982). Spatial visualization: Sex differences, grade-level differences, and the effect of instruction on the performance of middle school boys and girls. *Dissertation Abstracts International, 43*, 2914A.

Block, J., & Block, J. (1982). *Cognitive Development from Childhood to Adolescence*. NIMH research grant MH16080. Manuscript.

Bock, R. D., & Kolakowski, D. (1973). Further evidence of sex-linked major-gene influence on human spatial visualizing ability. *American Journal of Human Genetics, 25*, 1-14.

Brown, J. S., & Van Lehn, K. (1980). Repair theory: A generative theory of bugs in procedural skills. *Cognitive Science, 4*, 379-426.

Burnett, S. A., Lane, D. M., & Dratt, L. M. (1979). Spatial visualization and sex differences in quantitative ability. *Intelligence, 3*, 345-354.

Carey, S. E., Diamond, R., & Woods, B. (1980). Development of face recognition— A maturational component? *Developmental Psychology, 16*, 257-269.

Carpenter, P. A., & Just, M. A. (1978). Eye fixations during mental rotation. In J. W. Senders, D. F. Fisher & R. A. Monty (eds.), *Eye movements and the higher psychological functions*. Hillsdale, N.J.: Erlbaum Associates.

Cattell, R. B. (1971). *Abilities: Their structure, growth, and action*, Boston: Houghton Mifflin.

Chipman, S. F., Brush, L., & Wilson, D. (eds.) (1985). *Women and mathematics: Balancing the equation*. New York: Erlbaum Associates.

Connor, J. M., & Serbin, L. A. (1980). *Mathematics, visual-spatial ability, and sex roles*. Binghamton, N.Y.: State University of New York (ERIC Document Reproduction Service No. ED 214798).

Connor, J. M., Serbin, L. A., & Schackman, M. (1977). Sex differences in response to training on a visual-spatial test. *Developmental Psychology, 13,* 293–295.

Cooper, L. A. (1983). *Spatial information processing: The nature of strategic variation.* Contribution to the symposium "Individual Differences in Spatial Ability and Information Processing," presented at the annual meeting of the American Educational Research Association, Montreal, April 12.

Cooper, L. A. (1984). *Strategic factors in complex spatial problem solving.* Paper presented at the Fifty-Sixth Annual Meeting of the Midwestern Psychological Association, Chicago, May 4.

Cooper, L. A. & Shepard, R. N. (1973). The time required to prepare for a rotated stimulus. *Memory and Cognition, 1,* 246–250.

Corely, R. P., DeFries, J. C., Kuse, A. R., & Vandenberg, S. G. (1980). Familial resemblance for the identical blocks test of spatial ability: No evidence for X-linkage. *Behavior Genetics, 10,* 211–215.

Crockett, L., & Petersen, A. C. (1984). Biology: Its role in gender-related educational experiences. In E. Fennema & J. Ayer (eds.), *Equity of equality: Women and education.* Chicago: NSSE and McCutchan.

Cronbach, L. J., & Meehl, P. E. (1955). Construct validity in psychological tests. *Psychological Bulletin, 52,* 281–302.

Deaux, K. K. (1984). From individual differences to social categories. *American Psychologist, 39,* 105–116.

Deaux, K. K. (1985). Sex and gender. *Annual Review of Psychology, 36,* 49–81.

DeAvila, E. A., & Havassy, B., with Pascual-Leone, J. (1976). *Mexican-American school children: A Neo-Piagetian analysis.* Washington D.C.: Georgetown University Press.

De Benedictis, T., Delucchi, K., Harris, A., Linn, M. C., & Stage, E. (in press). Sex differences in science: "I don't know". *Journal of Research in Science Teaching.*

DeFries, J. C., Ashton, G. C., Johnson, R. C., Kuse, A. R., McClaren, G. E., Mi, M. P., Rashad, M. N., Vandenberg, S. G., & Wilson, J. R. (1976). Parent-offspring resemblance for specific cognitive abilities in two ethnic groups. *Nature, 261,* 131–133.

Dougherty, K., Herbert, M., Edenhurt-Pape, M., & Small, A. (1980). *Sex-related differences in several aspects of mathematics achievement: Grades 2–5.* Manuscript. St. Louis: CERMEL.

Educational Testing Service (1979). *National Report: College-bound seniors.* Princeton, N.J.: Educational Testing Service.

Fennema, E. H., & Carpenter, T. P. (1981). Sex-related differences in mathematics: Results from national assessment. *The Mathematics Teacher, 74,* 554–559.

Fralley, J. S., Eliot, J., & Dayton, C. M. (1978). Further study of the X-linked recessive gene hypotheses for inheritance of spatial abilities. *Perceptual and Motor Skills, 47,* 1023–1029.

French, J. W., Ekstrom, R. B., & Price, L. A. (1963). *Manual for kit of reference tests for cognitive factors* (revised ed.). Princeton, N.J.: Educational Testing Service.

Gentner, D. R., & Norman, D. A. (1984). The typist's touch. *Psychology Today, 18,* 66–68.

Gilligan, C. (1982). *In a different voice: Psychological theory and women's development.* Cambridge: Harvard University Press.

Glass, G. V. (1976). Primary, secondary, and meta-analysis of research. *Educational Researcher, 5*, 3-8.

Goodenough, D. R., Gandini, E., Olkin, I., Pizzamiglio, L., Thayer, D., & Witkin, H. A. (1977). A study of X chromosome linkage with field dependence and spatial visualization. *Behavior Genetics, 7*, 373-413.

Goodenough, D. R., Oltman, P. K., & Cox, P. W. (1984). *The nature of individual differences in field dependence*. Princeton, N.J.: Educational Testing Service.

Guay, R. B., & McDaniel, E. D. (1977). The relationship of mathematical achievement and spatial abilities among elementary school children. *Journal of Research in Mathematics Education, 8*, 211-215.

Hall, J. A. (1978). Gender effects in decoding nonverbal cues. *Psychological Bulletin, 85*, 845-857.

Harris, L. J., Hanley, C., & Best, D. T. (1978). Conservation of horizontality: Sex differences in sixth graders and college students. In M. C. Smart & R. C. Smart (eds.), *Adolescents' development and relationships*. New York: Macmillan.

Hartlage, L. C. (1970). Sex-linked inheritance of spatial ability. *Perceptual and Motor Skills, 31*, 610.

Hedges, L. V., & Olkin, I. (1980). Vote-counting methods in research synthesis. *Psychological Bulletin, 88*, 359-369.

Hedges, L. V. (1982a). Estimation of effect size from a series of independent experiments. *Psychological Bulletin, 92*, 490-499.

Hedges, L. V. (1982b). Fitting categorical models to effect sizes from a series of experiments. *Journal of Educational Statistics, 7*, 119-137.

Hoffman, M. L. (1977). Sex differences in empathy and related behaviors. *Psychological Bulletin, 84*, 712-722.

Hueftle, S. J., Rakow, S. J., & Welch, W. W. (1983). *Images of science*. Minneapolis: University of Minnesota Press.

Hyde, J. S. (1981). How large are cognitive gender differences? *American Psychologist, 36*, 892-901.

Inhelder, B., & Piaget, J. (1958). *The growth of logical thinking from childhood to adolescence*. New York: Basic Books.

Just, M. A., & Carpenter, P. A. (1976). Eye fixations and cognitive processes. *Cognitive Psychology, 8*, 441-480.

Kahle, J. B., & Lakes, M. K. (1983). The myth of equality in science classrooms. *Journal of Research in Science Teaching, 20*, 131-140.

Kail, R., Carter, P., & Pellegrino, J. (1979). The locus of sex differences in spatial ability. *Perception and Psychophysics, 26*, 182-186.

Klein, S. S. (ed.) (1984). *Handbook for achieving sex equity through education*. Baltimore: Johns Hopkins University Press.

Kyllonen, P. C., Lohman, D. F., & Woltz, D. J. (1984). Componential modeling of alternative strategies for performing spatial tasks. *Journal of Educational Psychology, 76*, 1325-1345.

Liben, L. S. (1978). Performance on Piagetian spatial tasks as a function of sex, field dependence, and training. *Merrill-Palmer Quarterly, 24*, 97-110.

Linn, M. C. (1983). Content, context, and process in reasoning during adolescence: Selecting a model. *Journal of Early Adolescence, 3*, 63-82.

Linn, M. C., & Delucchi, K. (1983). *The water level: Influences of task features on gender differences in performance*. Berkeley: Lawrence Hall of Science, University of California.

Linn, M. C., & Kyllonen, P. (1981). The field dependency construct: Some, one, or none. *Journal of Educational Psychology, 73*, 261-273.

Linn, M. C., & Petersen, A. C. (1985). Emergence and characterization of sex differences in spatial ability: A meta-analysis. *Child Development, 56*, 1479-1498.

Linn, M. C., & Pulos, S. (1982). Aptitude and experience influences on proportional reasoning during adolescence: Focus on male-female differences. *Journal of Research in Mathematics Education, 14*, 30-46.

Linn, M. C., & Pulos, S. (1983). Male-Female differences in predicting displaced volume: Strategy usage, aptitude relationships, and experience influences. *Journal of Educational Psychology, 75*, 86-96.

Linn, M. C., & Thier, H. D. (1975). The effect of experiental science on development of logical thinking in children. *Journal of Research in Science Teaching, 12*, 49-62.

Loehlin, J. C., Sharan, S., & Jacoby, R. (1978). In pursuit of the "spatial gene": A family study. *Behavior Genetics, 8*, 27-41.

Lohman, D. F. (1979). *Spatial ability: A review and reanalysis of the correlational literature*. Technical Report No. 8. Stanford: Aptitude Research Project, School of Education, Stanford University (NTIS No. AD-A075972).

Maccoby, E. E., & Jacklin, C. N. (1974). *The psychology of sex differences*. Stanford: Stanford University Press.

Malone, M. R., & Fleming, M. L. (1983). The relationship of student characteristics and student performance in science as viewed by meta-analysis research. *Journal of Research in Science Teaching, 20*, 481-495.

Marshall, S. P. (1983). Sex differences in mathematical errors: An analysis of distractor choices. *Journal for Research in Mathematics Education, 14*, 325-336.

Marshall, S. P. (1984a). Sex differences in children's mathematics achievement: Solving computations and story problems. *Journal of Educational Psychology, 76*, 194-204.

Marshall, S. P. (1984b). Consistency of student errors in mathematical problem solving. Manuscript.

McGee, M. G. (1978). Intrafamilial correlations and heritability estimates for spatial ability in a Minnesota sample. *Behavior Genetics, 8*, 77-80.

McGee, M. G. (1979). Human spatial abilities: Psychometric studies and environmental, genetic, hormonal, and neurological influences. *Psychological Bulletin, 86*, 899-918.

Meece, J. L., Parsons, J. E., Kaczala, C., Goff, S. B., & Futterman, R. (1982). Sex differences in math achievement: Toward a model of achievement choice. *Psychological Bulletin, 91*, 324-348.

Meehan, A. M. (1984). A meta-analysis of sex differences in formal operational thought. *Child Development, 55*, 1110-1124.

Metzler, J. (1973). Chronometric studies of cognitive analogues of the rotation of three-dimensional objects. Doctoral dissertation, Stanford University.

National Assessment of Educational Progress (NAEP) (1978a). *Three national assessments of science: Changes in achievement, 1969-77*. Denver: Education Commission of the States.

NAEP (1978b). *Science achievement in the schools: A summary of results from the*

1976-77 national assessment of science. Denver: Education Commission of the States.

NAEP (1979a). *Three national assessments of science, 1969-77: Technical summary.* Denver: Education Commission of the States.

NAEP (1979b). *Attitudes toward science: A summary of results from the 1976-77 national assessment of science.* Denver: Education Commission of the States.

NAEP (1979c). *Mathematical application 1977-78 Assessment.* Denver: Education Commission of the States.

NAEP (1979d). *Mathematical knowledge and skills: Selected results from the second assessment of mathematics.* Denver: Education Commission of the States.

NAEP (1983). *The third national mathematics assessment: Results, trends, and issues.* Denver: Education Commission of the States.

Newcombe, N., Bandura, M., & Taylor, D. G. (1983). Sex differences in spatial ability and spatial activities. *Sex roles, 9,* 377-386.

Parsons, J. E., Adler, T. F., & Kaczala, C. (1982). Socialization of achievement attitudes and beliefs: Parental influences. *Child Development, 53,* 310-321.

Parsons, J. E., Kaczala, C., & Meece, J. (1982). Socialization of achievement attitudes and beliefs: Classroom influences. *Child Development, 53,* 322-339.

Peskin, J. (1980). Female performance and Inhelder and Piaget's tests of formal operation. *Genetic Psychology Monographs, 101,* 245-256.

Petersen, A. C. (1983). Pubertal change and cognition, In J. Brooks-Gunn & A. C. Petersen (eds.), *Girls at puberty: Biological and psychosocial perspectives.* New York: Plenum Press.

Petersen, A. C., & Crockett, L. S. (in press). Pubertal development and its relation to cognitive and psychosocial development in adolescent girls: Implications for parenting. In J. Lancaster and B. Hamburg (eds.). *School-age pregnancies and parenthood.* Hawthorne, N.Y.: Aldine Press.

Petersen, A. C., & Gitelson, I. B. (in press). *Toward understanding sex-related differences in cognitive performance.* New York: Academic Press.

Pillemer, D. B., & Light, R. J. (1980). Synthesizing outcomes: How to use research evidence from many studies. *Harvard Educational Review, 50,* 176-195.

Plomin, R., & Foch, T. T. (1982). Sex differences and individual differences. *Child Development 52,* 383-385.

Pylsyshyn, Z. W. (1979). The rate of "mental rotation" of images: A test of a holistic analogue hypothesis. *Memory and Cognition, 7,* 19-28.

Pylsyshyn, Z. W. (1981). The imagery debate: Analogue media versus tactic knowledge. *Psychological Review, 87,* 16-45.

Reinisch, J. M., Gandelman, R., & Spiegel, F. S. (1979). Prenatal influences on cognitive abilities: Data from experimental animals and human genetic and endocrine syndromes. In M. S. Wittig & A. C. Petersen (eds.), *Sex-related differences in cognitive functioning: Developmental issues.* New York: Academic Press.

Riley, M. S., Greeno, J. G., & Heller, J. I. (1983). Development of children's problem-solving ability in arithmetic. In H. Ginsberg (ed.) *The development of mathematical thinking.* New York: Academic Press.

Shepard, R. N. (1981). Psychophysical complementarity. In M. Kubovy & J. R. Pomerantz (eds.), *Perceptual organization.* Hillsdale, N.J.: Erlbaum Associates.

Shepard, R. N., & Cooper, L. A. (1982). *Mental images and their transformations*. Cambridge: Massachusetts Institute of Technology Press.

Shepard, R. N., & Feng, C. (1972). A chronometric study of mental paper-folding. *Cognitive Psychology, 3*, 228–243.

Shepard, R. N., & Hurwitz, S. (1981). Mental rotation in map reading: Discrimination of right and left turns. Manuscript.

Shepard, R. N., & Metzler, J. (1971). Mental rotation of three-dimensional objects. *Science, 171*, 701–703.

Sigman, E., Goodenough, D. R., & Flannagan, M. (1978). Subjective estimates of body tilt and the rod-and-frame test. *Perceptual and Motor Skills, 47*, 1051–1056.

Sigman, E., Goodenough, D. R., & Flannagan, M. (1979). Instructions, illusory self-tilt, and the rod-and-frame test. *Quarterly Journal of Experimental Psychology, 31*, 155–165.

Sinnott, J. D. (1975). Everyday thinking and Piagetian operativity in adults. *Human Development, 18*, 430–443.

Snow, R. E., & Lohman, D. F. (1984). Toward a theory of cognitive aptitude for learning from instruction. *Journal of Educational Psychology, 76*, 347–376.

Spuhler, K. P., & Vandenberg, S. G. (1980). Comparison of parent-offspring resemblance in specific cognitive abilities. *Behavior Genetics, 10*, 413–418.

Stafford, R. E. (1961). Sex differences in spatial visualization as evidence of sex-linked inheritance. *Perceptual and Motor Skills, 13*, 428.

Stage, E. K., Kreinberg, N., Eccles, J., & Becker, J. R. (1984). Increasing the participation and achievement of girls and women in mathematics, science, and engineering. In S. S. Klein (ed.), *Achieving sex equity through education*. Baltimore: Johns Hopkins University Press.

Stallings, J. (1979). *Factors influencing women's decisions to enroll in advanced mathematics courses*. Menlo Park, Calif.: SRI International (ERIC Document Reproduction Service No. ED 197 972).

Steel, L., & Wise, L. (1979). Origins of sex differences in high school math achievement and participation. Paper presented at the annual meeting of the American Educational Research Association, San Francisco, April 1979.

Steinkamp, M. W., & Maehr, M. L. (1983). Affect, ability, and science achievement: A quantitative synthesis of correlational research. *Review of Educational Research, 53*, 369–396.

Thomas, H., & Jamison, W. (1981). A test of the X-linked genetic hypothesis for sex differences on Piaget's water-level task. *Developmental Review, 1*, 274–283.

Thomas, S. J. (1984). Issues in assessing psychosocial development in adolescents. Paper presented at the annual meeting of the American Educational Research Association, New Orleans, April 1984.

Thurstone, L. L., & Thurstone, T. G. (1949). *Manual for the SRA primary mental abilities*. Chicago: Science Research Associates.

Tobin-Richards, M. H., & Petersen, A. C. (1981). Spatial and sex-appropriate activities: Spatial visual ability during adolescence. Paper presented at the annual meeting of the American Psychological Association, Los Angeles, August 1981.

Vandenberg, S. G. (1971). *A test of three-dimensional spatial visualization based on the Shepard-Metzler "mental rotation" study*. Boulder: University of Colorado.

Vandenberg, S. G., & Kuse, A. R. (1979). Spatial ability: A critical review of the sex-linked major gene hypothesis. In M. A. Wittig & A. C. Petersen (eds.), *Sex-related differences in cognitive functioning: Developmental issues*. New York: Academic Press.

Vetter, B. (1983). *Manpower Comments, 20*, 20.

Waber, D. P. (1976). Sex differences in cognition: A function of maturation rate? *Science, 192*, 572-574.

Waber, D. P. (1977). Sex differences in mental abilities, hemispheric lateralization, and rate of physical growth at adolescence. *Developmental Psychology, 13*, 29-38.

Walker, J. T., Krasnoff, A. G., & Peaco, D. (1981). Visual spatial perception in adolescents and their parents: The X-linked recessive hypothesis. *Behavior Genetics, 11*, 403-413.

Welch, W. (1981). Investigation of male-female differences in science performance. Paper presented at the annual meeting of the National Association for Research in Science Teaching, New York, April 1981.

Wheeler, R., & Harris, B. (1981). *Comparison of male and female performance on the AP physics test*. New York: College Entrance Examination Board.

Wise, L. (1979). *Origins and career consequences of sex differences in high school mathematics achievement*. Palo Alto: American Institutes for Research (ERIC Document Reproduction Service No. ED 180 846).

Witkin, H. A., Dyk, R. B., & Paterson, H. F. (1962). *Psychological differentiation*. New York: Wiley.

Wittig, M. A., & Petersen, A. C. (eds.) (1979). *Sex-related differences in cognitive functioning: Developmental issues*. New York: Academic Press.

Yen, W. M. (1975). Sex-linked major-gene influences on selected types of spatial performance. *Behavior Genetics, 5*, 281-298.

Assessing the Theoretical Models for Sex Differences in Causal Attributions of Success and Failure

5

Bernard E. Whitley, Jr.
Maureen C. McHugh
Irene Hanson Frieze

Abstract

Three basic models of attributional sex differences are reviewed: general externality, self-derogation, and low expectancy. Although all of the models predict that women are unlikely to attribute their success to ability, the models are quite different in their other predictions. A meta-analysis of 28 studies examining sex differences in success-failure attributions was conducted to determine which of these three models had the best empirical support. The use of two distinct wordings of attribution questions in the literature necessitated the assessment of the effects of attribution wording as well. Results indicated only two consistent sex differences: Men make stronger ability attributions than women regardless of the outcome and men attribute their successes and failures less to luck. Empirically, none of the models was well supported.

In the early 1970s, Weiner and his colleagues (1971) proposed an attributional theory of achievement motivation that has become the basis for much of the subsequent research on achievement attributions. The original theory viewed the individual's affective, cognitive, and behavioral reactions to an achievement-oriented success or failure as a function of the person's causal explanations for the event. These causal attributions were hypothesized to relate in systematic ways to feelings of pride and shame, to expectancies for one's future performance level, and to one's subsequent achievement behavior. Although modified and extended, the basic theoretical framework has received extensive empirical support (e.g., Frieze, 1980; Weiner, 1979).

In the time since this attributional model of achievement behavior was originally proposed, many researchers have utilized it as a means of explaining the differential achievement levels of men and women. The possibility that women and men might make systematically different attributions for their successes and failures was raised as an explanation for why women do not tend to achieve at the same levels as men in the work force, politics, or other fields traditionally associated with achievement in our society (Frieze, Parsons, et al., 1978).

This chapter first reviews this attributional framework and the various ways in which it has been applied as an explanation for differential achievement in women and men. Three different models have appeared in the literature. Each of these is briefly reviewed and is then tested through meta-analytic procedures. Results of these analyses are then discussed. Since none of the models is well supported empirically, possible methological considerations are presented along with suggestions for future research.

Attributions for Success and Failure

The original Weiner theory (Weiner et al., 1971) proposed four basic causes of achievement successes and failures: ability, effort, luck, and the ease or difficulty of the task. In spite of later work that indicated that these are only a few of the many attributions people make when given an opportunity to state their causal explanations in their own words (e.g., Frieze, 1976; Weiner, 1979), much of the research has continued to utilize the original four causal categories. Perhaps one reason for this is that these categories are easily classifiable into a convenient 2 x 2 system on the basis of whether they are internal or external to the person and in terms of their stability over time. Within this framework, ability and effort can be viewed as causes within the person, or internal attributions, while luck and task difficulty are outside of the person, or external attributions. Looking at the stability dimension, ability and the difficulty or ease of the task are viewed as relatively stable influences, and luck and effort as changeable or unstable.

As other causes, such as mood, fatigue, and the help of other people, were added to the theoretical model, the analysis was extended to three dimensions. In addition to internality and stability, a third dimension of controllability was added to the theoretical model (Weiner, 1979). "Controllability" is defined as the degree to which the primary actor in the situation can control the causal factors operating in the situation. For example, one has little control over ability (or mood, or fatigue) but a good deal of control over effort.

These dimensions are important because the theory predicts that they mediate the affective and cognitive consequences of the causal attribution. Theoretically, internal causes are expected to generate more affect, as are controllable causes. The model also predicts that unstable attributions will lead to the expectation of variability in future outcomes. These theoretical predictions have been supported by empirical data (e.g., Weiner et al., 1972; Weiner, 1979), although the support has not been completely consistent. This issue is addressed in more detail later in the chapter.

Attribution research within the achievement domain assumes that a success or failure is attributed to one or more causes on the basis of available information about the situation and the personal characteristics of the individual. Important situational variables include the nature of the task being done (e.g., an academic task like taking a test or writing a paper, a sports task like playing tennis, or some other type of achievement task), particular conditions operating at the time the performance occurs (such as the health of the person, noise levels, or other environmental factors), and the person's past history of performance on these types of tasks. Each of these situational factors will have an effect upon the attribution made (Frieze & Snyder, 1980). Many studies have in fact used ratings of these situational factors as synonomous with the causal explanations for an event (e.g., Bar-Tal & Frieze, 1977; Deaux & Farris, 1977; Pasquella, Mednick & Murray, 1981). Aside from this confusion of the situational precursors of the event with the post hoc explanation of the event, there has been little attention given by researchers to a systematic investigation of the relevant situational factors. Instead, there has been more interest in the attributional tendencies of various types of individuals. For example, some people are said to have an external locus of control (e.g., Phares, 1976). In attributional terms, this would mean that regardless of the situation, such people would attribute their successes and failures to external causes such as luck, fate, or other people. It has also been suggested (Frieze, 1980) that people with high achievement motivation have a general tendency to attribute their successes to their ability and effort (which would lead to high expectations for future performances and a good deal of pride) and their failures to lack of effort (which then results in greater striving in the future).

Methodological Issues in Assessing Causal Attributions

One of the difficulties in interpreting attributional research is that various researchers have used different techniques for assessing the causal attributions being made by people in achievement situations. Attributions have been measured using open-ended questions, Likert scales, and the percentage of causal influence assigned to various factors. In an empirical investigation that utilized all three techniques, Elig and Frieze (1979) found that these three measurement techniques yielded quite different results.

Attributional research is also inconsistent in the lists of causes used in these rating scales. The most commonly employed causal categories are those of ability, effort, luck and task difficulty originally described in the 1971 Weiner paper. As mentioned earlier, this list is hardly exhaustive. However, because these are the only consistent categories across studies, we have decided to use only these causes in the meta-analytic assessments described in this chapter.

Finally, a review of studies of causal attributions for success and failure indicates that attributional questions have generally been worded in one of two ways (Whitley & Frieze, 1985). The first style might be called *informational*. Questions worded in this style ask subjects about the extent to which they possess ability, effort, and luck relative to the task at hand, and the extent to which the task was easy or difficult. The subject is asked for general information about factors relevant to performance rather than whether or not these factors had any direct effect upon the outcome. It is quite possible for persons to believe that they have high ability on a task but that the task was so easy that this ability was irrelevant to the outcome. In such a case, the high rating on the ability question would not reflect the subjects' perceived causal influences in the situation.

The second style of wording is a more direct attributional question and is referred to here as *causal* wording. It asks the subjects about the extent to which various factors influenced, determined, or caused an outcome. As Arkin, Detchon, and Maruyama (1982) have demonstrated, the correlations of the two types of ratings for the same causal explanation may be quite low or even negative. Thus question wording may have a significant impact on the attributions elicited. In previous research, distinctions between these two wording forms have not been made, possibly because of an implicit assumption that they are equally valid and essentially interchangeable. Even though informational questions do not assess causal attributions, they were included in the meta-analysis because their authors intended them to be attributional studies and they were published as such. One purpose of our meta-analysis was to test the assumption that the wording forms have equivalent effects on the attributions they elicit.

Theories about Sex Differences in Attributions

In an attempt to apply the causal attribution research to sex differences in achievement, researchers have proposed several models of sex differences in patterns of causal attributions. The three most cited models (discussed in Frieze et al., 1982) are outlined here in terms of their predictions and the degree of empirical support each has received. In order to clarify the distinctions made by the three models, their major predictions are outlined in table 5.1.

General Externality

One of the first models proposed to explain the relative lack of female achievement suggested that women tend to be generally external in the attributions they make for success and failure (Feather, 1969; Simon & Feather, 1973). According to the attributional models discussed earlier, this would lead to a generally lower affect in women whether they do well or poorly.

Table 5.1 Predicted Attributions for Women According to Three Different Theoretical Models

	Theoretical Perspective		
	General Externality	Self-Derogation	Low Expectancy
Success			
Ability			x
Effort			x
Luck	x	x	
Task Ease	x	x	
Failure			
Low Ability		x	x
Lack of Effort		x	
Bad Luck	x		
Task Difficulty	x		x

There would be little pride in success or shame in failure. Women were believed to be less involved in achievement activities or in high performance for a number of reasons, including the fact that they were believed to be higher than men in both fear of success and fear of failure. Given this, their tendency would be to withdraw from achievement situations entirely. This withdrawal means that they do not see themselves as responsible for the outcomes they do receive, and thus they tend to make external attributions. Such external attributions in turn serve to maintain lack of involvement in future tasks. Task ease or luck attributions for success also protect against fears of success by taking away any responsibility for the success and decreasing possible feelings of shame for failure (Frieze, Parsons, et al., 1978; Simon & Feather, 1973).

Wiley, Crittenden, and Birg (1979) have also proposed an externality model from a sociological perspective. They argue that women and other low-status groups tend to have less control over their destinies than those of higher status, and that this lack of control causes them to attribute the outcomes they receive more to external factors.

Self-derogation

A second model takes a somewhat different perspective. In the self-derogation model, women are seen as attributing their success to external factors, but they are believed to attribute their failures to internal factors (e.g., Nicholls, 1975). This model of sex differences in attributions is based on the assumption that people attempt to maintain a set of consistent beliefs about themselves (e.g., Aronson & Mettee, 1968; Swann & Read, 1981). If women have low self-esteem, they are willing to believe only negative information about themselves; if they have high self-esteem, they are willing to believe only positive information about themselves, (e.g., Fitch, 1970). Since women typically have low self-esteem in achievement settings (Frieze, Parsons, et al., 1978), this need for consistency means that women accept negative information about themselves but discount positive information. Ickes and Layden (1978), Heilman and Kram (1978), and others use this type of explanation for assumed sex differences in attributions.

Low Expectancy

The third major viewpoint about sex differences in attributional patterns is related to the idea that women have generally low expectations about achievement situations. Attribution theorists have found generally that the initial expectations one brings to a task affect one's performance as well as the attributions made for the result of the performance. After the result of the performance is known, it is compared with the initial expectation. On the basis of both theory and empirical data, it has been found that expected outcomes are attributed more to stable factors; unexpected outcomes are attributed more to unstable causes. Thus initial expectancies are highly important to the attribution process (for more discussion of this issue, see Frieze, Fisher, et al., 1978; and Valle & Frieze, 1976).

Females generally do not expect to do as well as males when performing a large variety of academic, sports, motor skill, and other achievement-related tasks (Crandall, 1969; Lenney, 1977). Based on the general predictions of attribution theory, these low expectations would be expected to lead to unstable attributions for success and stable attributions for failure. This means that women with these negative beliefs about their own ability levels would tend to see their failures as being caused by stable factors such as lack of ability, and hence they would give up easily and blame themselves for failure. When successful, they would see the success as due to unstable causes such as unusually high effort and would not expect to continue to be successful. Such an attributional pattern would also result in a perpetuation of the initially low self-expectations since successful experiences are essentially discounted. Failures, on the other hand, reinforce the negative views of one's level of competence (Deaux, 1976; Frieze, Parsons, et al., 1978; Frieze, Fisher, et al., 1978; Jackaway, 1974).

Assessing the Theories about Sex Differences in Attributions

As our overview suggests, the three major theories make quite different predictions about what the sex differences in attributions will be. All three models predict that women will tend not to attribute their successes to their high ability. Other than this one similarity, however, the models differ in their predictions for sex differences in attributions for success and failure.

In order to assess which, if any, of these theories was best supported by the research literature, we conducted a meta-analysis of studies that addressed sex differences in ratings for causal attributions for success and failure (Frieze et al., 1982). The meta-analysis presented here is similar to this earlier analysis.

In deciding how to translate the three theoretical positions listed in table 5.1 into specific mathematical comparisons, we realized that each of the theories is somewhat ambiguous. Does saying that women make low attributions to ability for success and high attributions to ability for failure mean that a comparison should be made between success and failure within each sex? Or is the hypothesis really that women make less use of ability attributions for success than do men? Either comparison would fit the outlines of the theory. Since this ambiguity has not to our knowledge been dealt with or even acknowledged in other research, we decided to make both comparisons. Thus we conducted two meta-analyses of the attribution data. The first defined effect size in terms of male mean minus female mean and compared the mean effect sizes for success and failure conditions. It asks the question, Given that an outcome is a success or failure, do men's and women's attributions differ? The second meta-analysis defined effect size in terms of success mean minus failure mean and compared the mean effect sizes of women and men. It asks the question, Given that a person is a man or a woman, how do attributions for success differ from those for failure?

Summary

Three models have been proposed to explain sex differences in causal attributions for success and failure. One model holds that women tend to be generally external in their attributions; a second model holds that women attribute success to external factors and failure to internal factors; the third model holds that women have low expectations for success, resulting in unstable attributions for success and stable attributions for failure. Men are postulated by each model to show an opposite pattern. These models were compared in a meta-analysis that looked at the data in two ways. The first comparison focused on the magnitude of outcome differences within each sex; the second comparison focused on the magnitude of sex differences within outcome conditions.

Method

Selection of Studies

The studies employed in the meta-analysis are listed in appendix C. These studies were located through computerized searches of *Psychological Abstracts* and the *ERIC Index*, through reviews of programs of professional association meetings, and through informal professional networks. The studies were selected for analysis because (a) they dealt with actual, as opposed to hypothetical, and just completed, as opposed to retrospective, success and failure experiences; (b) they had the subjects attribute their outcomes to the causal categories of ability, effort, task, and luck; and (c) they used adults or adolescents as subjects. We established these criteria in order to identify a reasonably homogeneous set of studies for the meta-analysis. In addition, the first criterion excluded studies that might have been contaminated by speculative responses or memory lapses (cf. Ericsson & Simon, 1980; Fiske, 1980). The second criterion allowed us to focus on the four basic attributional categories. Thus studies that reported results by attributional dimension (e.g., ability and effort combined to form an internality dimension) without reporting the category means were not considered for inclusion in the meta-analysis. Although the use of dimensions can serve a heuristic purpose, we believe that limiting the meta-analysis to the four categories permitted a more detailed examination of sex differences. In addition, recent research (Meyer & Keolbl, 1982; Ronis, Hansen & O'Leary, 1983) has called the validity of constructing such dimensions into question. Finally, the age restriction was imposed to reduce variance due to developmental changes. Although that is an interesting question in itself, it is not at issue here.

The final sample consisted of 28 studies; 7 studies used informationally worded questions and 21 used causal questions. One informational question study (Deaux & Farris, 1977) included two experiments that were treated as independent studies in the analysis. The studies in the analysis included a total of 1,292 women and 1,401 men as subjects, most of whom were college students.

Procedure

Effect Size Measure

The measure of effect size used in this study was Hedges's (1981, 1982a) unbiased estimator g. To calculate g, we first calculated Cohen's (1977) effect size measure d, the difference of the two group means (outcome or sex, as appropriate) divided by their pooled standard deviation, and converted it to g by Hedges's formula. If group means or, more often, standard deviations were not reported, the following procedures, listed in order of preference, were used to estimate d: (a) if a test statistic (e.g., t, F, r) was reported, it was converted to d using the appropriate formula from Cohen; (b) if a p-value, but no test statistic, was reported, d was estimated from the tabled t-value for that p; (c) if the results of a study were reported as nonsignificant without a test statistic or p-value, d was assigned a value of zero (Cooper, 1979).

The handling of results reported as "nonsignificant" is a major problem in meta-analysis. We, like Cooper (1979), decided to use $d = 0$ in these cases because, being biased toward the null hypothesis, it provides the most conservative results. We believe that an alternative strategy of ignoring these studies (see, for example, chap. 8) biases the results too strongly in favor of the alternative hypothesis.

Statistical Analysis

For each comparision (success versus failure within each sex and sex differences within success and failure), the studies were grouped into four categories. For the success versus failure comparison, these groups were based on sex of subject and attributional question format (informational, causal); for the female versus male comparison, the bases were outcome (success, failure) and question format. Mean effect size, Hedges's homogeneity statistic (H), and Cohen's measure of nonoverlap (U) were calculated for each attributional category (ability, effort, task, luck) for each group (Hedges, 1982a; Cohen, 1977). H indicates the degree to which a set of effect sizes can be considered to have been drawn from the same population. A statistically significant H indicates that the effect sizes are more variable than would be expected by chance and suggests that there are study characteristics, such as methodology or subject sample, affecting the magnitude of the effect sizes. U indicates the degree to which two distributions of scores do not overlap. A U of 50 percent indicates complete overlap: the mean of one distribution exceeds 50 percent of the scores in the other distribution; that is, the means are equal. The greater the value of U, the less overlap there is in the distributions, making U a good indicator of the size of a difference in means. In addition, for each comparison, a 2 x 2 categorical model was fitted to the data (Hedges, 1982b), with ability, effort, task, and luck effect sizes as the dependent variables and grouping factors as independent variables. An ANOVA design was modeled by computing the orthogonal comparisons for the main effects of the independent variables and their interaction.

Results

Sex Differences within Outcomes

The mean effect sizes for sex differences are shown in table 5.2, and the effect sizes for each of the individual studies are listed in appendix C. For success, men made stronger attributions to ability than did women (mean $g = 0.13, p < .001$), whereas women made stronger attributions to luck (mean $g = -0.07, p < .05$). There were no differences for effort or task attributions. For failure, men made stronger attributions to ability (mean $g = 0.16, p < .001$) and effort (mean $g = 0.15, p < .001$), whereas women made stronger attributions to the task (mean $g = -0.08, p < .05$) and to luck (mean $g = -0.15, p < .001$).

Table 5.2 Mean Effect Sizes for Sex Differences

	Ability	Effort	Task	Luck
Success (n = 29)				
Mean g	0.13***	−0.04	−0.01	−0.07*
U	55.17	51.60	50.40	52.80
H	29.10	25.42	42.28*	156.67***
Failure (n = 29)				
Mean g	0.16***	0.15***	−0.08*	−0.15***
U	56.34	55.95	53.20	55.95
H	48.49**	72.15***	47.69**	82.85***

Note: Positive g indicates stronger attributions by men, negative g indicates stronger attributions by women.
*p < .05.　　**p < .01.　　***p < .001.

However, two points must be noted. First, in examining the U statistic, it can be seen that the statistically significant g's are small in an absolute sense. For the largest effect—failure attributions to ability—the average male attribution was larger than only 56.3 percent of the female attributions, a difference that Cohen (1977) characterizes as insignificant. Second, there is a large degree of heterogeneity in effect sizes as indicated by the H statistics, especially for failure. This heterogeneity suggests that there are study characteristics that have an impact on effect sizes in attribution studies. There were, however, too few studies to attempt a breakdown on characteristics other than question-wording style.

The results of the categorical analyses are shown in tables 5.3 through 5.6. In fitting the categorical model, significant between-class variation was found for attributions to ability, effort, and luck. For ability attributions,

Table 5.3 Analysis of Sex-Difference Effect Size Variance for Attributions to Ability

Source of Variation	df	H	p	Mean g	Standard Error	p
Between Classes	3	6.27	.10			
Within Classes	54	71.63	.05			
Success-causal	20	25.44	>.10	0.12	0.05	.01
Success-informational	7	3.34	>.80	0.17	0.08	.04
Failure-causal	20	28.77	.10	0.10	0.05	.04
Failure-informational	7	14.08	.05	0.35	0.09	.002
Total	**57**	**77.90**	**.02**			

Note: Positive g indicates stronger attributions by men, negative g indicates stronger attributions by women.

Table 5.4 Analysis of Sex-Difference Effect Size Variance for Attributions to Effort

Source of Variation	df	H	p	Mean g	Standard Error	p
Between Classes	3	12.93	.01			
Within Classes	54	94.62	< .001			
Success-causal	20	21.03	> .30	−0.03	0.05	.56
Success-informational	7	3.92	> .70	−0.09	0.08	.26
Failure-causal	20	57.76	< .001	0.11	0.05	.04
Failure-informational	7	11.91	> .10	0.27	0.09	.002
Total	**57**	**107.55**	**< .001**			

Note: Positive g indicates stronger attributions by men, negative g indicates stronger attributions by women.

Table 5.5 Analysis of Sex-Difference Effect Size Variance for Attributions to Task

Source of Variation	df	H	p	Mean g	Standard Error	p
Between Classes	3	1.94	> .50			
Within Classes	54	89.32	< .001			
Success-causal	20	26.66	> .10	−0.03	0.05	.52
Success-informational	7	14.88	< .05	0.04	0.08	.58
Failure-causal	20	43.58	< .01	−0.08	0.05	.10
Failure-informational	7	4.10	> .70	−0.07	0.09	.44
Total	**57**	**91.26**	**< .002**			

Note: Positive g indicates stronger attributions by men, negative g indicates stronger attributions by women.

Table 5.6 Analysis of Sex-Difference Effect Size Variance for Attributions to Luck

Source of Variation	df	H	p	Mean g	Standard Error	p
Between Classes	3	25.13	< .001			
Within Classes	54	215.78	< .001			
Success-causal	20	30.61	< .10	−0.13	0.05	.004
Success-informational	7	118.44	< .001	0.14	0.09	.11
Failure-causal	20	38.23	< .01	−0.25	0.05	.001
Failure-informational	7	28.50	< .001	0.17	0.09	.06
Total	**57**	**240.91**	**< .001**			

Note: Positive g indicates stronger attributions by men, negative g indicates stronger attributions by women.

$H = 6.27, p < .10$, with the mean effect size for informational wording $(0.25, p < .001)$ being larger than that for causal wording $(0.11, p = .001)$, $Z = 2.15, p = .02$. These results indicate that sex differences were larger when subjects were asked how much ability they had than when they were asked the extent to which ability caused the outcome.

For effort attributions, $H = 12.93, p < .01$, with the mean effect size for failure $(.15, p < .001)$ being larger and opposite in sign from that for success $(-0.04, ns)$, $Z = 3.58, p < .001$. These results indicate that men made stronger attributions to effort for failure, but that there was no sex difference for success. However, an outcome by wording interaction, $Z = 1.58$, $p = .06$, showed that the success-failure effect size difference was significant only for informational attributions, $p < .02$ (see table 5.4). Thus for failure, men are more likely than women to say that they did not try, but are not more likely to see effort as being more causal for success than for failure.

There were no categorical effects for task attributions $(H = 1.94, p > .50)$. For luck attributions $H = 25.13$ and $p < .001$, with the mean causal effect size being negative $(-0.18, p < .001)$ and the mean informational effect size being positive $(0.14, p = .02)$, $Z = 4.74, p < .001$. These results indicate that women tend to see luck as more causal than do men, but that men see themselves as having more luck (good or bad) than do women.

In sum, the first meta-analysis found that for success men make stronger attributions to ability and stronger informational (but not causal) attributions to luck, and women make stronger causal (but not informational) attributions to luck, with no sex differences in attributions to effort or the task. For failure, men make stronger attributions to ability and stronger informational (but not causal) attributions to effort, and women make stronger attributions to the task and stronger causal (but not informational) attributions to luck. Of the three models, these results best fit the externality model, especially for failure. However, two points must be noted. First, the fit is not very good, since no differences were found for success effort or task attributions. Second, the absolute size of the significant differences was small, with none reaching the criterion set by Cohen (1977) of 0.20 for a small effect size.

Outcome Differences within Sex

The mean effect sizes for outcome within sex are shown in table 5.7 and the effect sizes for the studies in appendix C. Both men and women showed the same pattern of results: attributions to ability, effort, and luck for success, and to the task for failure. With the exception of women's attributions to luck and men's to the task, all of the mean effect sizes fall into Cohen's small to medium range. There is, however, an extreme degree of heterogeneity of effect sizes, which was reduced to some degree by blocking on question wording (see tables 5.8 through 5.11).

Table 5.7   Mean Effect Sizes for Outcome Differences

	Ability	Effort	Task	Luck
Women (n = 29)				
Mean g	0.69*	0.56*	−0.34*	0.15*
U	75.48	71.20	63.28	52.80
H	278.06*	98.20*	287.15*	319.57*
Men (n = 29)				
Mean g	0.64*	0.35*	−0.18*	0.25*
U	74.00	63.65	57.12	59.85
H	232.66*	178.02*	256.08*	274.31*

Note: Positive g indicates stronger success attributions, negative g indicates stronger failure attributions.
*p < .001.

Table 5.8   Analysis of Outcome-Difference Effect Size Variance for Attributions to Ability

Source of Variation	df	H	p	Mean g	Standard Error	p
Between Classes	3	·179.79	< .001			
Within Classes	54	331.59	< .001			
Women-causal	20	103.21	< .001	0.46	0.05	< .001
Women-informational	7	67.01	< .001	1.64	0.10	< .001
Men-causal	20	85.97	< .001	0.44	0.05	< .001
Men-informational	7	75.40	< .001	1.32	0.09	< .001
Total	**57**	**511.38**	**< .001**			

Note: Positive g indicates stronger success attributions, negative g indicates stronger failure attributions.

Table 5.9   Analysis of Outcome-Difference Effect Size Variance for Attributions to Effort

Source of Variation	df	H	p	Mean g	Standard Error	p
Between Classes	3	13.63	< .01			
Within Classes	54	275.02	< .001			
Women-causal	20	84.50	< .001	0.56	0.05	< .001
Women-informational	7	13.67	< .10	0.57	0.09	< .001
Men-causal	20	162.45	< .001	0.38	0.05	< .001
Men-informational	7	14.40	< .05	0.27	0.08	< .001
Total	**57**	**288.65**	**< .001**			

Note: Positive g indicates stronger success attributions, negative g indicates stronger failure attributions.

Table 5.10 Analysis of Outcome-Difference Effect Size Variance for Attributions to Task

Source of Variation	df	H	p	Mean g	Standard Error	p
Between Classes	3	88.02	< .001			
Within Classes	54	461.85	< .001			
Women-causal	20	117.65	<.001	−0.17	0.05	<.001
Women-informational	7	113.71	<.001	−0.97	0.09	<.001
Men-causal	20	78.65	<.001	−0.06	0.05	.23
Men-informational	7	151.84	<.001	−0.56	0.09	<.001
Total	**57**	**549.87**	**<.001**			

Note: Positive g indicates stronger success attributions, negative g indicates stronger failure attributions.

Table 5.11 Analysis of Outcome-Difference Effect Size Variance for Attributions to Luck

Source of Variation	df	H	p	Mean g	Standard Error	p
Between Classes	3	219.31	< .001			
Within Classes	54	400.86	< .001			
Women-causal	20	78.66	<.001	−0.07	0.05	.14
Women-informational	7	147.82	<.001	1.00	0.10	<.001
Men-causal	20	68.56	<.001	0.01	0.05	.90
Men-informational	7	105.82	<.001	1.08	0.09	<.001
Total	**57**	**620.17**	**<.001**			

Note: Positive g indicates stronger success attributions, negative g indicates stronger failure attributions.

In fitting the categorical model, significant between-class variation was found for all four dependent variables. For ability, $H = 179.79$, $p < .001$, with significant contrasts for sex of subject ($Z = 2.34$, $p = .01$), question wording ($Z = 13.55$, $p < .001$), and the interaction ($Z = 1.97$, $p = .02$). Informational wording elicited a larger mean outcome effect (1.46, $p < .001$) than did causal wording (0.45, $p < .001$). The interaction indicated that women had a larger mean effect size than men for informational attributions (1.64 vs. 1.32, $p < .05$), but not for causal attributions (0.46 vs. 0.44, ns). Thus outcome affects the degree to which women perceive themselves as having ability to a greater extent than it does for men, but there is no sex difference in the degree to which outcome affects causal attributions to ability.

For effort, $H = 13.63$, $p < .01$, with a significant contrast for sex of subject, $Z = 3.44$, $p < .001$. Women's mean effect size (0.56) was larger than men's (0.35), indicating that both men and women attributed success to effort to a greater extent than they did failure, but women's tendency to do so was greater than men's.

For task attributions $H = 88.02, p < .001$, with significant contrasts for sex of subject ($Z = 3.57, p < .001$), question wording ($Z = 8.93, p < .001$), and the interaction ($Z = 2.06, p = .02$). Informational wording elicited a larger mean outcome effect ($-0.75, p < .001$) than did causal wording ($-0.11, p = .001$). The interaction indicated that women had a larger mean effect size than men for informational wording (-0.97 vs. $-0.56, p < .05$), but not for causal wording (-0.17 vs. $-0.06, ns$). Thus outcome affects the extent to which women perceive the task to be easy or difficult to a greater extent than it does for men, but there is no sex difference in the degree to which outcome affects causal attributions to the task.

For luck attributions, $H = 219.31, p < .001$. The mean informational effect size ($1.02, p < .001$) was larger than the mean causal effect size ($-0.03, ns$), $Z = 14.08, p < .001$. There were no effects for sex of subject or the interaction.

In sum, the second meta-analysis found that outcome has similar effects on men's and women's attributions. With the exception of attributions to effort, those sex differences that were found existed for informational, rather than causal attributions.

Discussion

The results of the meta-analyses were not supportive of any of the attributional analyses of sex differences in achievement. The first meta-analysis found that given a success outcome, men make stronger attributions to ability than do women, and women make stronger attributions to luck, with no differences for effort or task attributions. Given failure, men make significantly stronger attributions to ability and effort, and women to the task and luck. However, these effect sizes, while statistically significant, were quite small on an absolute scale. The second meta-analysis showed that men's and women's attributions for success as opposed to failure were quite similar: small to moderate effect sizes for all four attributional categories. Those sex differences that did emerge did so primarily for informational, rather than causal, attributions. Taken as a whole, these results indicate that while there are some small differences in the degree to which men and women make attributions, the overall pattern of attributions is the same for both sexes.

The results also showed that question wording has an important effect on the results of studies of attributions. The second meta-analysis indicated that informational questions elicited larger success-failure differences in attributions to ability, the task, and luck, and there were wording x sex interactions for attributions to ability and the task. Thus, while the subjects had a strong tendency to say that they had more ability and luck and an easier task after a success than after a failure, they were less likely to say that these factors were more causal to success than to failure.

Assessing Attributional Models for Explaining Sex Differences in Achievement

Challenging Existing Findings

As has been shown, sex differences in attributions for success and failure are not a major explanatory factor for differential achievement in women and men. In a recent issue of *Sex Roles*, inconsistencies in the data and the theories on sex differences in attributions were noted, and the idea that any of the explanatory theories were in any sense "established" was challenged (Frieze, Whitley et al., 1982; McHugh, Frieze & Hanusa, 1982). Although these models for sex differences in achievement attributions have received little empirical support, they have often been presented as established results based on extensive research (e.g., Arkes & Garske, 1981; Hyde & Rosenberg, 1980). It is misleading to present any of these models as validated, and even more problematic to present any one of the models as *the* model for understanding sex differences in achievement. The following sections discuss each of the three models in light of the results of these meta-analyses.

General Externality and the Differential Use of Luck

As mentioned earlier, the general externality model was originally proposed primarily to explain the apparently greater use by women of luck as an explanation for success and failure. This continues to surface as a consistent sex difference in attribution. Sohn (1982), for example, reports that the only "consequential relationship" between sex and attributions demonstrated by his effect size analysis was the greater use of luck by women to explain successful outcomes. Our meta-analysis found that women more often made luck attributions for both success and failure outcomes. Although these differences in luck attributions have been seen as supportive of the general externality model, the model actually implies more than this. General externality implies that women are also more likely than men to make attributions to task ease or difficulty. However, there is no support for this additional prediction in the studies reviewed here. Furthermore, there is no indication in the research literature that the attributions of women are more generally external than internal.

The view that women evidence a pattern of general externality has been challenged by Sweeney, Moreland, and Gruber (1982). In their replication of the often-cited Simon and Feather study (1973), they suggest that their findings (and those of Simon and Feather) might be better interpreted as indicating an internality pattern for men than an externality pattern for women. In support of this interpretation, they report that men, but not women, experienced more positive affect when they attributed their failure to lack of ability and lack of effort than when they attributed failure to external factors. This violates the assumptions of the general externality model, as well as the general predictions about affect made by the original Weiner model (Weiner, 1979; Weiner et al., 1971), although it is consistent with other research indicating that people feel better if they have some control over the causes of unfortunate events (e.g., Scheppele & Bart, 1983; Janoff-Bulman, 1979). The Sweeney, Moreland, and Gruber data may imply, however, that men have more need to feel this control than do women.

The general externality model further implies that women attribute their outcomes solely or primarily to luck. This is a misinterpretation of the actual data (McHugh, 1975). Luck ratings made by both sexes are generally lower than ratings of other causal attributions (Wong & Weiner, 1981), and lower percentages are typically assigned to luck than to other attribution measures when percentage measures are used (see McHugh, 1975). A similar pattern is seen in studies utilizing open-ended attribution measures where luck is infrequently cited by either men or women (Elig & Frieze, 1979; Parsons et al., 1982). Thus the conceptual significance of the differential use of luck attributions by men and women is unclear.

Interpretation of the greater use of luck by women is further complicated by the paradoxical data reported by Wong (1982). His research indicated that women gave higher ratings of luck than men for noncontingent outcomes on a finger maze task. At the same time, women also reported feeling more control of their outcomes in this situation, although outcomes were in reality not contingent upon performance. One possible explanation for this paradox is that women have a different conception of luck than men. For example, Wong suggests that whereas men tend to perceive externality and internality as opposing poles of a single dimension, women may have a two-dimensional view of locus of control and may see both internal and external causes as operating jointly to determine the outcome. Further research investigating women's and men's conceptions of luck might resolve this question.

It can be seen, then, that the general externality model can result in a misinterpretation of the types of attributions women make for success and failure and of how these differ from attributions made by men. Both men and women view internal factors as more important than external factors. In cases where men's and women's attributions do differ, there appears to be as much or more support for the conclusion that men evidence a general internality pattern as there is that women evidence a general externality pattern. The interpretation of such differences as externality in women suggests that the male attributional pattern was originally viewed as normative, since women exhibit externality relative to the more extreme internality of men. Further, the findings of Sweeney, Moreland and Gruber (1982) and Wong (1982) suggest that internal and external attributions may not have the same meaning or consequences for men and women.

The Self-Derogation Model

The self-derogation model also views women as making external attributions for their successes, but it predicts that they will attribute their failures to lack of ability. This model was not supported by our meta-analysis. We found that women more than men attributed both success and failure to luck, and that men made stronger ability attributions for failure.

The self-derogation model has been widely accepted. To a greater extent than the other models, self-derogation has profited from inconsistencies in the research literature. Women's greater use of luck (even when it occurs for both success and failure) is often cited as evidence for this model, and the failure to find sex differences in the use of task attributions has generally been ignored. Further, when women attribute failure to lack of ability, it is often viewed as self-derogation regardless of what attributions men make or how the women attribute success. Thus, even if only one aspect of the model is partially supported, authors may use the self-derogation model to explain their findings.

In addition to profiting from inconsistent applications, the self-derogation model may have come to be widely accepted because it is consistent with the general view of women within the achievement literature, which postulates that they have negative views of themselves and their abilities. Women's ratings of their abilities are low relative to men; it is interesting to note that this difference is defined as self-derogation in women rather than as self-enhancement in men.

The Low Expectancy Model

The findings that women make more luck attributions and lower estimates of their abilities have been viewed as supportive of the low expectancy model as well as the self-derogation model. The low expectancy model predicts that women will attribute success to unstable causes and failure to stable causes because they initially have low expectancies for success. Thus women should make luck and effort attributions for success. Just as women's greater use of luck to explain success cannot accurately be labeled "externality," neither can it be interpreted as indicating an unstable attributional pattern. Our meta-analysis found no sex differences for the use of effort to explain success, and again, women's use of luck is large only relative to men's. Women do not, as the low expectancy model predicts, characteristically attribute failure to low ability or other stable causes. On the contrary, men make more ability attributions for failure.

Perhaps the low expectancy model fails to predict women's attributional patterns because it is based on the finding that women have low expectancies for success. While women's expectancies for success tend to be lower than men's, this does not necessarily mean that they expect to fail. McHugh (1975), for example, has suggested that low expectancies are true for women only for tasks in which they have little direct experience. Given experience on a task, people tend to know how well they will do. However, given little experience, people may rely upon generalized expectancies or stereotypic assumptions. In general, women are not expected to be able to perform as well as men (e.g., Feldman-Summers & Kiesler, 1974). Thus McHugh suggests that the tendency to have low initial expectancies will be greatest for women who are performing unfamiliar tasks. Low expectancies have also been linked to the sex typing of the task. Several authors have suggested that women are especially likely to have low expectations for tasks that are viewed as masculine (e.g., Deaux, 1976; Frieze, Fisher et al., 1978; McHugh, 1975). Thus unstable attributions for success and stable attributions for failure might be characteristic of women only for certain tasks.

Summary

It is interesting to us that these models have received such enthusiastic support in spite of their weak empirical basis. One explanation for this may lie in the ambiguous predictions of the models discussed earlier. Such ambiguities may allow researchers with substantially different results to conclude that their data provide support for the same model.

Publication biases may also contribute to the acceptance of these models. The bias against publishing research that fails to find differences (Greenwald, 1975; McGuire, 1973) results in the publication of studies that do find sex differences, while studies that document sex similarities often remain unpublished (Frieze, Parsons et al., 1978; Maccoby & Jacklin, 1974). For this reason, it is important to reiterate that according to our analysis, the achievement attributions made by men and women are really quite similar; the few statistically significant differences found were of small magnitude. Sohn (1982) has reported a similar pattern of inconsequential (although statistically significant) differences in attributions to ability and luck.

A factor contributing to the widespread acceptance of these models may be their intuitive appeal. Conceptually, the theories seemed to make sense as an explanation for female achievement levels, and individuals may recall instances when their own or others' attributions seemed to fit the predicted patterns. Failure to find support for models does not mean that individual women do not show one or all of these patterns. For example, it is very likely that a woman with low expectancies for a particular task would make unstable attributions for success and stable attributions for failure. However, it is unlikely that all, or even most, women would consistently demonstrate such a pattern. However appealing the idea, it is not likely that a single model can be developed to explain or predict consistent dispositional attributional tendencies of all men or all women. The methodological and conceptual problems involved in attempting to establish such models are discussed in the next section.

When analyzed systematically, then, the existing research does not support any of the models of sex differences in attribution. Further, close examination suggests that all three models suffer from serious conceptual problems. Some of the problems discussed here were the ambiguity of predictions, the confusion between ratings relative to a fixed midpoint and relative to another group, acceptance of the male attributional pattern as normative, and the potential influence of situational factors. Thus it is essential, not only to examine established findings of sex differences in attribution more carefully, but also to be extremely cautious and thoughtful in interpreting such differences. Finally, it is important to bear in mind that regardless of whether sex differences are found or not, attributions may have different meanings and consequences for men and women.

Methodological Problems in Research on Sex Differences in Attribution

Situational Variables

Research context. The meta-analysis found that for causal attributions, considerable heterogeneity of effect sizes remained after the studies were blocked on question wording. Among the factors that could contribute to that heterogeneity is the context in which the research takes place. These contexts range from the traditional laboratory experiment in which the experimenter manipulates the subjects' success and failure experiences to natural experiments in which the subjects' outcomes are totally out of the control of the experimenter. Examples of the latter are classroom examinations and sports events.

Since real-life situations can have important consequences for subjects that are absent in laboratory experiments, patterns of attributions could be expected to differ in the two contexts. In fact, a meta-analysis by Whitley and Frieze (1985) found that outcome had a greater effect on task attributions in the natural than in the experimental context. These context differences probably derive from the more ego-involving quality of the tasks performed in the natural context. Thus even the small sex differences found in our meta-analysis may not be found in natural contexts. Furthermore, to the extent that men and women differ in their reactions to experimental versus natural tasks, the research context could lead to different attributions by each of the sexes. No research has been conducted on this question, however, and there were too few studies in this meta-analysis to allow us to block on research context.

Task domains. Task domains can be identified within research contexts and may represent another factor that contributes to the heterogeneity of effect sizes. Thus laboratory experiments have used cognitive tasks such as anagrams, motor coordination tasks, visual perception tasks, and social perception tasks. Natural experiments have included classroom examinations and sports events. The majority of laboratory experiments (69 percent) have used cognitive tasks, and the majority of the natural experiments (82 percent) have used academic tests (Whitley & Frieze, 1985). Studies of causal attributions have thus tended to ignore task domains that include a large part of human activity; these ignored domains could include some in which sex differences exist.

Future research could profitably focus on patterns of attributions across task domains for two reasons. First, tasks from some domains might be perceived to be more difficult or require more ability, effort, or luck for successful completion than others. These perceptions could effect attributions and could vary by sex. Cann and Pearce (1980) and Mitchell (1980), for example, have found that observers' attributions for an actor's performance can vary as a function of the actor's task. Other research has found that the task domain can exert an important effect on causal attributions (e.g., Frieze & Snyder, 1980; McGarvey et al., 1975). A taxonomy of task domains, scaled as to difficulty and the degree to which they require ability, effort, and luck to complete successfully, would assist in understanding how people perceive the causes of success and failure (see Frieze, Francis & Hanusa, 1983, for some preliminary work in this area).

The second implication of task domains is that certain individuals or groups might have different responses to different types of tasks. For example, men and women, might find certain tasks more ego involving, important, or familiar than other tasks (Frieze, Parsons, et al., 1978; Nicholls, 1975). There is a tendency for people to make more extreme attributions and to emphasize the role of ability relative to other attributions for tasks that are more important, ego involving, or unfamiliar (Luginbuhl, Crane & Kahan, 1975; Miller, 1976; Zaccaro & Lowe, 1980). Those sex differences that are found may be due to differential importance or familiarity. In fact, some 68 percent of all attribution studies use tasks from male-oriented task domains such as puzzle solving, motor coordination, and sports (Whitley & Frieze, 1985), which may be more familiar and be seen as more important and more ego-involving for males than females.

The obvious approach to disentangling the effects of sex of subject and sex relatedness of task domains is to include task domain as an independent variable in sex difference studies. A number of such studies have been conducted (see McHugh, Frieze & Hanusa, 1982, for a review); however, their results have been inconsistent. This inconsistency may be due at least in part to the variety of ways in which the sex relatedness of tasks has been operationalized. The manipulations have included telling subjects that success at an ambiguous task required either masculine or feminine sex-typed skills (e.g., McHugh, Fisher & Frieze, 1982), presenting false performance norms for each sex (e.g., Deaux & Farris, 1977), and using tasks judged to be sex typed (e.g., Croke, 1973). This variety of operational definitions indicates that there is no consensual definition of sex typing for a task domain, and so no effective research technology for determining the relation of sex typing of tasks to sex differences in attributions.

In summary, then, what is outwardly the same task may have different effects on men and women because it has a different meaning for each sex. This difference in meaning could be the result of differences in importance or ego involvement, familarity with the task, or beliefs about the sex appropriateness of the task. These dimensions are, of course, not independent, but correlated: a task that a person perceives to be sex appropriate will probably also be familiar and important.

Social context of the experiment. Subjects in an experiment do not, of course, act in isolation, but in a social context, any aspect of which could have differential effects on men's and women's attributions. The sex of the other participants in the experiment—the experimenter (e.g., Deaux & Farris, 1977) and other subjects (e.g., Heilman & Kram, 1978; Stephan, Rosenfield & Stephan, 1976)—could activate self-presentational motives that could affect the elicited attributions, as could public versus private reporting of expectancies, outcomes, and attributions (e.g., Diener & Dweck, 1980). Similarly, men and women could respond differently to different reward contingencies—individualistic, competitive, or cooperative—implicit or explicit in the experiment (e.g., McHugh, Fisher & Frieze, 1982). Unfortunately, the social context variables have not been investigated sufficiently, either as topics in themselves or in relation to sex differences in attributions, to allow an adequate assessment of their effects.

Summary. Given the variety of situational variables—research context, task domain, social context—that could elicit differential attributions from men and women, the heterogeneity of effect sizes found in the meta-analysis is not surprising. In addition, the characteristics of any one situation could combine additively, interact to reinforce each others' effects, or interact to suppress each others' effects. Unfortunately, the plethora of factors that may be active in even the most tightly controlled experiment makes it difficult to specify the effects and interactions of all the variables simultaneously. Compounding this difficulty is the fact that some variables, such as sex typing of the task, have received different operational definitions in different studies.

Personality and Motivation

An individual's enduring characteristics can affect attributions either independently or in conjunction with each other and with the characteristics of the situation. One approach that addresses this fact explores the effects of sex-role orientation to explain sex differences in attributions. However, as with the sex typing of tasks, this approach has met with mixed results. As with tasks, studies investigating the effects of the sex typing of persons have used a variety of operational definitions—psychological androgyny (e.g., Pasquella, Mednick & Murray, 1981), sex-role traditionality (e.g., Wiegers & Frieze, 1977), and attitudes toward women (e.g., Teglasi, 1978), among others. This multiplicity of definitions is to some extent unavoidable since the term "sex role" can have at least three different meanings (Angrist, 1969)—a position in society, a set of rules for interpersonal behavior, and a personality dimension—each of which could have separate effects on attributional patterns. In addition, sex role as a personality dimension might be confounded with other personality constructs, such as self-esteem (Whitley, 1982), making its independent effects difficult to assess. Other personality variables that have been examined in relation to attributions and sex differences in attribution include need for achievement (e.g., Bar-Tal & Frieze, 1977; Wiegers & Frieze, 1977), fear of success (e.g., O'Connell & Perez, 1982), locus of control (e.g., Viaene, 1979), self-esteem (e.g., Levine & Uleman, 1979), and authoritarianism (e.g., Goldberg & Evenbeck, 1976).

Although research that goes beyond physical gender in order to explain sex differences in attribution has great potential benefit, there are two problems facing any researcher interested in personality or motivational variables. First, the social context places constraints upon behavior that can diminish the effect of personality factors (e.g., Ekehammer & Magnusson, 1973; Mischel, 1968). In order to fully and reliably assess the effects of personality variables, one must sample an individual's behavior at a number of times and in a variety of situations (Epstein, 1979, 1980). Attribution research lacks such longitudinal behavior sampling. The second, and related, problem is that situational variables interact with personality variables to reinforce the effects of some factors and to suppress the effects of others (Cronbach, 1975). Levine, Gillman, and Reis (1982), for example, point out that their finding that achievement motivation was the personality variable that best predicted their subjects' attributions could be explained by the fact that the attributions referred to a competitive academic achievement task. For personality research to be useful in explaining attributional behavior, then, it must be longitudinal and take the experimental situation fully into account.

Measurement of General Attributional Tendencies

Research on sex differences in attributions is based on the assumption that the attributions made by men and women in one situation are representative of an enduring disposition to make certain types of attributions. However, most of the existing research involves the measurement of attributions in response to one or only a few outcomes on a single task in a particular context chosen by the experimenter. A number of studies have found that people do make different attributions for success and failure as well as for various types of situations (e.g., Frieze & Snyder, 1980). Thus the situational influences may be far more important determinants of attributions than personality characteristics or enduring dispositions toward one or another attribution.

Given the importance of the situational context, it is not at all clear how one would define an attributional disposition. It appears unlikely that there is an overriding tendency to always make a particular attribution. Even given an adequate conceptualization, research has not been well designed to find such dispositional effects. Limitations on tasks, settings, and number of measurements precludes a generalization across a range of situations. If one is interested in understanding the attributional dispositions of particular groups of people, one should assess their attributions in their most typical or most preferred environments on a large number of occasions. For example, Travis, Burnett-Doering and Reid (1982) asked their respondents to recall successes and failures that they had experienced in the courses of their lives. This approach does not allow the context to distort the usual attributional tendencies, although the possibility of memory errors can call the validity of the technique into question.

Alternatively, one might attempt to discern dispositional attributional tendencies by measuring causal attributions across a number of situations (Epstein, 1979, 1980). Such a strategy would make it less likely that the investigator would mistake situation-specific attributions for dispositional tendencies. To some extent, this goal of examining attributions across situations can be accomplished by meta-analysis. However, a meta-analysis is still limited by the types of situations utilized by the researchers whose work is published. Thus, although our results are more representative of cross-situational tendencies than are the results of a single study, they cannot be interpreted as *the* characteristic attributional patterns of men and women.

Toward Some Solutions

We have discussed a number of methodological and conceptual problems that are found in the research dealing with sex differences in attribution and attribution research in general. We would now like to discuss some approaches to solving those problems.

Replication

The root of our discussion is that oft-praised but rarely performed aspect of research, replication. Replication permits the assessment of the validity, reliability, and generalizability of a body of research (Campbell & Jackson, 1979). Validity can be conceptualized as a consistency of results across different operationalizations of the same construct (Campbell & Fiske, 1959). If what are intended to be minor variations in operational definitions, such as the wording of attributional questions, lead to major inconsistencies in study results, then the validity of the findings must be questioned. Such circumstances suggest that the researchers were not measuring what they had set out to measure. Conversely, different operational definitions might actually be reflecting different conceptual variables.

Another issue is the reliability of the data or the consistency of the results across studies. Even given identical operational definitions of constructs, variations in subject populations and research settings can lead to inconsistent results. Since reliability limits validity (e.g., Allen & Yen, 1979), we cannot have much faith in an inconsistent research literature. On the other hand, if study characteristics that systematically affect the results can be identified, reliability can be enhanced by taking those factors into account in designing research.

Finally, there is the question of generalizability, the applicability of the results of research conducted in one setting to new settings. If an effect is found to be valid and reliable in one setting, we may be tempted to assume that it is valid and reliable in other settings. However, the setting itself may have determined the results: thus it is necessary to repeat the study in other contexts. For example, we would want the effects found in laboratory settings to be demonstrated for natural settings (e.g., Whitley & Frieze, 1985).

Replication research, then, is a basic tool of science, providing indicators of the validity, reliability, and generalizability of theoretical constructs and principles. Unfortunately, replications are rarely carried out, or at least rarely published (Campbell & Jackson, 1979). Although there were sufficient studies that included an analysis of simple sex differences in attribution to allow us to conduct a meta-analysis, with few exceptions, variables that might interact with or more fully explain sex differences were tested only in one or a few studies, and the effects found were assumed to be valid, reliable, and general. Trite as it may sound, more research really is needed to determine the sources of sex differences in attributions.

Once a body of research concerned with a theory of sex differences in attribution is accumulated, we must have a means of critically, and preferably quantitatively, assessing its validity, reliability, and generalizability. Meta-analysis provides us with that means.

Meta-analysis

Meta-analysis has two contributions to make to replication research. First, as just mentioned, it provides a set of quantitative techniques for assessing the validity, reliability, and generalizability of research findings. The list of meta-analytic techniques is quite extensive (e.g., Cohen, 1977; Glass, McGaw & Smith, 1981; Hedges, 1982a, 1982b, 1982c, Hedges & Olkin, 1983; Hunter, Schmidt & Jackson, 1982; Rosenthal, 1978), and an appropriate set of techniques can be found for any body of research. Meta-analysis is, of course, not a panacea (e.g., Cook & Leviton, 1980), but it is an extremely useful method of summarizing and evaluating research. Consistency of effects within and across operational definitions of constructs argues in favor of reliability and validity, and differences between research settings could provide evidence of a lack of generalizability.

Second, if a body of research is found to be inconsistent, meta-analysis also provides the means of determining the sources of inconsistency. As discussed in the introductory section of this chapter, study characteristics can be correlated with effect sizes to determine possible sources of variation. Alternatively, possible sources of effect size variance can be identified and tested on an a priori basis as we did here with question wording. Once sources of effect size variance are identified, they themselves can be tested as independent variables in experiments (e.g., Cooper, Burger & Good, 1981). Meta-analysis is therefore not the terminus of research, but one step in a cycle of experimentation, replication, evaluation, and further experimentation.

Measurement

Before an investigator begins replication research, however, some thought must be given to measurement issues. Measurement is an important issue in attribution research because attributions and many of the factors hypothesized to affect them are latent variables—mental states or events that are not observable but that are presumed to exist because their effects are observable. Because they are not directly observable, latent variables must be measured indirectly, with psychometric instruments that constitute their operational definitions. Consequently, any structural or content characteristics of the measurement instruments that affect scores independently of the variable being measured introduce undesirable variance into research results (Loevinger, 1957).

Although this chapter has dealt with only one aspect of the measurement of attributions—question wording—a number of factors must be taken into consideration when deciding how to measure attributions. Researchers must first decide what they mean by "attribution" before setting out to measure it—are they interested in attributions as information, causes, or reasons? This analysis has focused on the information-cause distinction, but other researchers have pointed out that asking for a reason for an event is not the same as asking for its cause (Buss, 1978; Oresick, Sokol & Healey, 1980). A person's motives for asking attributional questions also determine the type of answer (Kruglanski et al., 1978), and the format of the questionnaire items used to elicit those latent attributions can affect how they are reported (Elig & Frieze, 1979).

Similarly, independent variables can be variously defined. Are sex roles, for example, to be defined at the anthropological, sociological, or psychological level (Angrist, 1969)? If psychological, which of the many possible assessment instruments (Whitley, 1983; 1985) is to be used? Even when scores on two instruments are highly correlated, they can have different relations to the same dependent variable (e.g., Whitley, 1983). In sum, researchers must take care to ensure that the content and structure of the instruments used as the operational definitions of attributions and independent variables are consistent with the conceptual definitions as formulated by the theory guiding their research (Cronbach & Meehl, 1955; Loevinger, 1957).

New Approaches to Understanding Women's Achievement

As noted earlier and in other papers (Frieze, Fisher et al., 1978; McHugh, Frieze & Hanusa, 1982), research on sex differences in attributions for success and failure has not provided the key to understanding women's achievement levels relative to men's. Yet we feel that the assessment of the theoretical models of sex differences in attributions presented here may ultimately contribute to our understanding of women's achievement.

It is important that the lack of supporting research for any of the models be recognized. We would hope that authors of textbooks on the psychology of women would refrain from discussing these models as though they were established fact. From the research to date, one would be forced to conclude that there is no sex difference in attributional tendencies sufficiently large to explain male and female achievement patterns. This does not mean that all research in this area should be abandoned.

Several directions for future research are suggested by this chapter. For example, researchers may wish to explore the meaning that ability and luck attributions have for each sex. Existing research has been based on the assumption that all individuals view the basic attributional factors and their underlying dimensions in similar ways. Exploration of individual interpretations of luck, ability, and other causal explanations may contribute to our understanding of the role of attributions in achievement as well as adding to our knowledge of achievement cognitions.

Another direction for research is the systematic assessment of attributional patterns across situations. More understanding of attributions in real-life settings is of special importance. Such studies would also help us to know how much various role responsibilities affect one's patterns of attributions. Perhaps the small differences that do exist in studies of sex differences in causal attributions are at least partially a function of the variations in life settings of males and females.

Our discussion should also alert researchers to various conceptual and methodological problems that have plagued research on sex differences in attributions. Many of these problems could potentially undermine the fruitfulness of alternative approaches to understanding sex differences in achievement. For example, McHugh (1984) recently suggested that sex differences in intrinsic motivation may help to explain more general sex differences in achievement behavior. Intrinsic motivation, like attributions, is typically studied in experimental situations using a limited set of tasks, which are frequently sex typed. These limitations must be overcome if this line of research is to be further pursued.

This chapter suggests that models developed in the future to explain sex differences in achievement should make unambiguous predictions about the responses of each sex without accepting the response pattern of either sex as normative. Second, the models should be examined in a variety of situations selected from many achievement domains. For each of these situations, the researcher should carefully evaluate the effects of the social context. Third, dispositional differences in addition to gender should be investigated as potential influences on behavior. Researchers should carefully design valid and reliable measures that can be used across several studies. And, eventually, meta-analytic techniques might be used to assess the consistency and significance of the reported results.

Based on these considerations, it does not appear fruitful to attempt to develop new attributional models for sex differences in achievement behavior. Even if we could generalize meaningfully across the group of all women and the group of all men, attributional differences would be highly specific to the task being evaluated. Further research that includes a person x situation perspective may be successful in generating a series of attributional models to explain some of the people, some of the time.

References

Allen, M. J., & Yen, W. M. (1979). *Introduction to measurement theory*. Monterey: Brooks/Cole.

Angrist, S. S. (1969). The study of sex roles. *Journal of Social Issues, 25*(1), 214-232.

Arkes, H. R., & Garske, J. P. (1981). *Psychological theories of motivation* (2nd ed.). Monterey: Brooks/Cole.

Arkin, R. M., Detchon, C. S., & Maruyama, G. M. (1982). Role of attribution, affect, and cognitive inference in test anxiety. *Journal of Personality and Social Psychology, 43*, 1111-1124.

Aronson, E. & Mettee, D. (1968). Dishonest behavior as a function of differential levels of self-esteem. *Journal of Personality and Social Psychology, 9*, 121-127.

Bar-Tal, D., & Frieze, I. H. (1977). Achievement motivation for males and females as a determinant of attributions for success and failure. *Sex Roles, 3*, 301-313.

Berg, P. A., & Hyde, J. S. (1976). *Gender and race differences in causal attributions in achievement situations.* Bowling Green: Bowling Green State University (ERIC Document Reproduction Service No. ED 138 865).

Breen, L. J., Vulcano, B., & Dyck, D. G. (1979). Observational learning and sex roles in learned helplessness. *Psychological Reports, 44*, 135-144.

Buss, A. R. (1978). Causes and reasons in attribution theory: A conceptual critique. *Journal of Personality and Social Psychology, 36*, 1311-1321.

Campbell, D. T., & Fiske, D. W. (1959). Convergent and discriminant validation by the multitrait-multimethod matrix. *Psychological Bulletin, 56*, 81-105.

Campbell, K. E., & Jackson, T. T. (1979). The role and need for replication research in social psychology. *Replications in Social Psychology, 1*, 3-14.

Cann, A., & Pearce, L. (1980). Attribution for performance on luck and skill tasks: Effects of outcome, sex of performer, and sex of subject. *Basic and Applied Social Psychology, 1*, 231-240.

Cohen, J. (1977). *Statistical power analysis for the behavioral sciences* (2nd ed.). New York: Academic Press.

Cook, T. D., & Leviton, L. C. (1980). Reviewing the literature: A comparison of traditional methods with meta-analysis. *Journal of Personality, 48*, 449-472.

Cooper, H. M. (1979). Combining the results of independent studies: A meta-analysis of sex differences in conformity research. *Journal of Personality and Social Psychology, 37*, 131-146.

Cooper, H. M., Burger, J., & Good, T. (1981). Gender differences in the academic locus of control of young children. *Journal of Personality and Social Psychology, 40*, 562-572.

Crandall, V. C. (1969). Sex differences in expectancy of intellectual and academic reinforcement. In C. P. Smith (ed.). *Achievement-related motives in children.* New York: Russell Sage.

Croke, J. H. (1973). Sex differences in causal attributions and expectancies for success as a function of the sex-role appropriateness of the task. Manuscript, Department of Psychology, University of California, Los Angeles.

Cronbach, L. J. (1975). Beyond the two disciplines of scientific psychology. *American psychologist, 30*, 116-127.

Cronbach, L. J., & Meehl, P. E. (1955). Construct validity in psychological tests. *Psychological Bulletin, 52*, 281-302.

Deaux, K. K. (1976). Sex: A perspective on the attribution process. In J. H. Harvey, W. Ickes & R. F. Kidd (eds.), *New directions in attribution research, 1*, Hillsdale, N.J.: Erlbaum Associates.

Deaux, K., & Farris, E. (1977). Attributing causes for one's own performance: The effects of sex, norms, and outcomes. *Journal of Research in Personality, 11*, 59-72.

Diener, C. I., & Dweck, C. S. (1980). An analysis of learned helplessness. Part 2: The processing of success. *Journal of Personality and Social Psychology, 39*, 940-952.

Ekehammer, B., & Magnussen, D. (1973). A method to study stressful situations. *Journal of Personality and Social Psychology, 27*, 176-179.

Elig, T. W., & Frieze, I. H. (1979). Measuring causal attributions for success and failure. *Journal of Personality and Social Psychology, 37*, 621-634.

Epstein, S. (1979). The stability of behavior. Part 1: On predicting most of the people much of the time. *Journal of Personality and Social Psychology, 37*, 1097-1126.

Epstein, S. (1980). The stability of behavior. Part 2: Implications for psychological research. *American Psychologist, 35*, 790-806.

Ericsson, K. A., & Simon, H. H. (1980). Verbal reports as data. *Psychological Review, 87*, 215-251.

Feather, N. T. (1969). Attribution of responsibility and valance of success and failure in relation to initial confidence and task performance. *Journal of Personality and Social Psychology, 13*, 129-144.

Feather, N. T., & Simon, J. G. (1972). Luck and the unexpected outcome: a field replication of laboratory findings. *Australian Journal of Psychology, 24*, 113-117.

Feather, N. T., & Simon, J. G. (1973). Fear of success and causal attributions for outcomes. *Journal of Personality, 41*, 525-542.

Feldman-Summers, S., & Kiesler, S. B. (1974). Those who are number two try harder: The effects of sex on attributions of causality. *Journal of Personality and Social Psychology, 30*, 846-855.

Fiske, D. W. (1980). When are verbal reports valid? *New Directions for Methodology of Social and Behavioral Science, 4*, 59-66.

Fitch, G. (1970). Effects of self-esteem, perceived performance, and choice on causal attribution. *Journal of Personality and Social Psychology, 16*, 311-315.

Forsythe, D. R., & Schlenker, B. R. (1977a). Attributing the causes of group performance: Effects of performance quality, task importance, and future testing. *Journal of Personality, 45*, 220-236.

Forsythe, D. R., & Schlenker, B. R. (1977b). Attributional egocentrism following performance of a competitive task. *Journal of Social Psychology, 102*, 215-222.

Frieze, I. H. (1976). Causal attributions and information seeking to explain success and failure. *Journal of Research in Personality, 10*, 293-305.

Frieze, I. H. (1980). Beliefs about success and failure in the classroom. In J. McMillan (ed.), *The social psychology of school learning*. New York: Academic Press.

Frieze, I. H., Fisher, J., Hanusa, B. H., McHugh, M. C., & Valle, V. A. (1978). Attribution of the causes of success and failure as internal and external barriers to achievement in women. In J. Sherman & F. Denmark (eds.), *Psychology of women: Future directions of research*. New York: Psychological Dimensions.

Frieze, I. H., Francis, W. R., & Hanusa, B. H. (1983). Defining success in classroom situations. In J. Levine & M. Wang (eds.), *Teacher and student perceptions: Implications for learning*. Hillsdale, N.J.: Erlbaum Associates.

Frieze, I. H., Parsons, J. E., Johnson, P., Ruble, D. N., & Zellman, G. (1978). *Women and sex roles: A social psychological perspective*. New York: Norton.

Frieze, I. H., & Snyder, H. N. (1980). Children's beliefs about the causes of success and failure in school settings. *Journal of Educational Psychology, 72,* 186-196.

Frieze, I. H., Whitley, B. E., Jr., Hanusa, B. H., & McHugh, M. C. (1982). Assessing the theoretical models for sex differences in causal attributions for success and failure. *Sex Roles, 8,* 333-343.

Glass, G. V., McGaw, B., & Smith, M. L. (1981). *Meta-analysis in social research.* Beverly Hills. Sage.

Goldberg, C., & Evenbeck, S. (1979). Causal attributions for success and failure as a function of authoritarianism and sex. *Perceptual and Motor Skills, 42,* 215-222.

Greenwald, A. G. (1975). Consequences of prejudice against the null hypothesis. *Psychological Bulletin, 82,* 1-20.

Griffen, B. O., Combs, A. L., Land, M. L., & Combs, N. H. (1981). Attributions of achievement for academic achievement: A field study. Paper presented at the meeting of the Midwestern Psychological Association, Detroit, May 1981 (ERIC Document Reproduction Service No. ED 205 884).

Hedges, L. V. (1981). Distribution theory for Glass's estimator of effect size and related measures. *Journal of Educational Statistics, 6,* 107-112.

Hedges, L. V. (1982*a*). Estimation of effect size from a series of independent studies. *Psychological Bulletin, 92,* 490-499.

Hedges, L. V. (1982*b*). Fitting categorical models to effect sizes from a series of experiments. *Journal of Educational Statistics, 7,* 119-137.

Hedges, L. V. (1982*c*). Fitting continuous models to effect size data. *Journal of Educational Statistics, 7,* 245-270.

Hedges, L. V. (1983). A random effects model for effect sizes. *Psychological Bulletin, 93,* 388-395.

Hedges, L. V., & Olkin, I. (1983). Clustering estimates of effect magnitude from independent studies. *Psychological Bulletin, 93,* 563-573.

Heilman, M. E., & Kram, K. E. (1978). Self-derogating behavior in women—fixed or flexible: The effects of coworker's sex. *Organizational Behavior and Human Performance, 22,* 497-507.

Hunter, J. E., Schmidt, F. L., & Jackson, G. B. (1982). *Meta-analysis: Cumulating research findings across studies.* Beverely Hills: Sage.

Hyde, J. S., & Rosenberg, B. G. (1980). *Half the human experience: The psychology of women* (2nd ed.). Lexington, Mass: Heath.

Ickes, W., & Layden, M. A. (1978). Attributional style. In J. H. Harvey, W. Ickes & R. F. Kidd (eds.), *New directions in attribution research, 2,* 121-152. Hillsdale, N.J.: Erlbaum Associates.

Jackaway, R. (1974). Sex differences in achievement motivation, behavior, and attributions about success and failure. Doctoral dissertation, State University of New York at Albany.

Janoff-Bulman, R. (1979). Characterological versus behavioral self-blame: Inquiries into depression and rape. *Journal of Personality and Social Psychology, 37,* 1798-1809.

Kruglanski, A. W., Hammel, I. Z., Maides, S. A., & Schwartz, J. M. (1978). Attribution theory as a special case of lay epistemology. In J. H. Harvey, W. J. Ickes & R. F. Kidd (eds.), *New directions in attribution research, 2,* 299-334. Hillsdale, N.J.: Erlbaum Associates.

Lenney, E. (1977). Women's self-confidence in achievement settings. *Psychological Bulletin, 84*, 1-13.

Levine, R. (1980). High need for achievement, superego severity, and causal attributions for success and failure (Doctoral dissertation, New York University, 1979). *Dissertation Abstracts International, 48*, 5410B.

Levine, R., Gillman, M. G., & Reis, H. (1982). Individual differences for sex differences in achievement attributions? *Sex Roles, 8*, 455-466.

Levine, R., & Uleman, J. (1979). Perceived locus of control, chronic, self-esteem, and attributions to success and failure. *Personality and Social Psychology Bulletin, 5*, 69-72.

Loevinger, J. (1957). Objective tests as instruments of psychological theory. *Psychological Reports, 3*, 635-694.

Luce, S. R. (1980). Sex differences in achievement attributions: Patterns and processes (Doctoral dissertation, Carlton University, 1979). *Dissertation Abstracts International, 40*, 5871B.

Luginbuhl, J., Crane, D., & Kahan, J. (1975). Causal attributions for success and failure. *Journal of Personality and Social Psychology, 31*, 86-93.

Maccoby, E. E., & Jacklin, C. N. (1974). *The psychology of sex differences*. Stanford: Stanford University Press.

McGarvey, W. E., Arkin, R. M., Kahan, J. P., & Miller, N. (1975). Causal attributions for success and failure: The role of stability. Paper presented at the annual meeting of the American Psychological Association, Chicago, August 1975.

McGuire, W. J. (1973). The yin and yang of progress in social psychology. *Journal of Personality and Social Psychology, 26*, 446-456.

McHugh, M. C. (1975). Sex differences in causal attributions: A critical review. Paper presented at the annual meeting of the Eastern Psychological Association, New York, April 1975.

McHugh, M. C. (1984). Sex differences in intrinsic motivation as a function of ambiguity of task feedback. Paper presented at the annual meeting of the Midwestern Psychological Association, Chicago, May 1984.

McHugh, M. C., Fisher, J. E., & Frieze, I. H. (1982). Effects of situational factors on the self-attributions of females and males. *Sex Roles, 8*, 389-394.

McHugh, M. C., Frieze, I. H., & Hanusa, B. H. (1982). Attributions and sex differences in achievement: Problems and new perspectives. *Sex Roles, 8*, 467-479.

McMahan, I. D. (1971). Sex differences in causal attributions for success and failure. Paper presented at the annual meeting of the Eastern Psychological Association, New York, April 1971.

Meerdink, G. B. (1980). The effects of psychological androgyny on attributions for success and failure (Doctoral dissertation, University of Toledo, 1980). *Dissertation Abstracts International, 41*, 1118B.

Meyer, J. P., & Koelbl, S. L. M. (1982). Students' test performances: Dimensionality of causal attributions. *Personality and Social Psychology Bulletin, 8*, 31-36.

Miller, D. T. (1976). Ego involvement and attributions for success and failure. *Journal of Personality and Social Psychology, 34*, 901-906.

Miller, D. T., & Porter, C. A. (1983). Self-blame in victims of violence. *Journal of Social Issues, 39*, 139-152.

Mischel, W. (1968). *Personality and assessment*. New York: Wiley.

Mitchell, M. E. (1980). The attribution of occupational achievement. Paper presented at the annual meeting of the Eastern Psychological Association, New York, April 1980.

Nicholls, J. G. (1975). Causal attributions and other achievement-related cognitions: Effects of task outcome, attainemt value, and sex. *Journal of Personality and Social Psychology, 31*, 379-389.

O'Connell, A. N., & Perez, S. (1982). Fear of success and causal attributions of success and failure in high school and college students. *Journal of Psychology, 111*, 141-151.

Oresick, R. J., Sokol, M., & Healy, J. M., Jr. (1980). Effects of question form on explanations of actions. Paper presented at the annual meeting of the American Psychological Association, Montreal, September 1980.

Parsons, J. E., Meece, J. L., Adler, T. F., & Kaczala, C. M. (1982). Sex differences in attributions and learned helplessness? *Sex Roles, 8*, 421-432.

Pasquella, M. J., Mednick, M. T., & Murray, S. R. (1981). Causal attributions of achievement outcomes: Sex-role identity, sex, and outcome comparisons. *Psychology of Women Quarterly, 5*, 586-590.

Phares, E. J. (1976). *Locus of control in personality*. Morristown, N.J.: General Learning Press.

Ronis, D. L., Hansen, R. D., & O'Leary, V. E. (1983). Understanding the meaning of achievement attributions: A test of derived locus and stability scores. *Journal of Personality and Social Psychology, 44*, 702-711.

Rosenthal, R. (1978). Combining results of independent studies. *Psychological Bulletin, 85*, 185-193.

Sasfy, J. H. (1975). Some relationships between causality for task participation and the causal attribution of task outcome (Doctoral dissertation, Pennsylvania State University, 1974). *Dissertation Abstracts International, 35*, 7134A-7135A.

Scheppele, K. L., & Bart, P. B. (1983). Through women's eyes: Defining danger in the wake of sexual assault. *Journal of Social Issues, 39*, 63-80.

Simon, J. G., & Feather, N. T. (1973). Causal attributions for success and failaure at university examinations. *Journal of Educational Psychology, 64*, 46-56.

Sohn, D. (1982). Sex differences in achievement self-attributions: An effect-size analysis. *Sex Roles, 8*, 345-358.

Stephan, W. G., Rosenfield, D., & Stephan, C. (1976). Egotism in males and females. *Journal of Personality and Social Psychology, 34*, 1161-1167.

Swann, W. B., & Read, S. J. (1981). Self-verification processes: How we sustain our self-conceptions. *Journal of Experimental Social Psychology, 17*, 351-372.

Sweeney, P. D., Moreland, R. L., & Gruber, K. L. (1982). Gender differences in external attributions for academic performance *Sex Roles, 8*, 358-374.

Teglasi, H. (1977). Influence of situational factors on causal attributions of college females. *Psychological Reports, 41*, 495-502.

Teglasi, H. (1978). Sex-role orientation, achievement motivation, and causal attributions of college females. *Sex Roles, 4*, 381-397.

Travis, C. B., Burnett-Doering, J., & Reid, P. T. (1982). The impact of sex, achievement domain, and conceptual orientation on causal attributions. *Sex Roles, 8*, 443-452.

Valle, V. A., & Frieze, I. H. (1976). Stability of causal attributions as a mediator in changing expectations for success. *Journal of Personality and Social Psychology, 33*, 73-79.

Viaene, N. (1979). The influence of expectancy for success, androgyny, and locus of control on sex differences in causal attributions for success and failure. Paper presented at the International Conference on Sex Role Stereotyping, Cardiff, July 1979.

Weiner, B. (1979). A theory of motivation for some classroom experiences. *Journal of Educational Psychology, 71*, 3-25.

Weiner, B., Frieze, I. H., Kukla, A., Reed, L., Rest, S., & Rosenbaum, R. M. (1971). *Perceiving the causes of success and failure*. Morristown, N.J.: General Learning Press.

Weiner, B., Heckhausen, H., Meyer, W., & Cook, R. E. (1972). Causal ascriptions and achievement behavior: Conceptual analysis of effort and reanalysis of locus of control. *Journal of Personality and Social Psychology, 21*, 239-248.

Whitley, B. E., Jr. (1983). Sex-role orientation and self-esteem: A critical meta-analytic review. *Journal of Personality and Social Psychology, 44*, 765-778.

Whitley, B. E., Jr. (1985). Sex-role orientation and psychological well-being: Two meta-analyses. *Sex Roles, 12*, 207-225.

Whitley, B. E., Jr., & Frieze, I. H. (1985). The effect of question wording style and research context on attributions for success and failure: A meta-analysis. Paper presented at the annual meeting of the Eastern Psychological Association, Boston.

Wiegers, R. M., & Frieze, I. H. (1977). Gender, female traditionality, achievement level, and cognitions of success and failure. *Psychology of Women Quarterly, 2*, 125-137.

Wiley, M. G., Crittenden, K. S., & Birg, L. D. (1979). Why a rejection? Causal attribution of a career achievement event. *Social Psychology Quarterly, 42*, 214-222.

Wong, P. T. P. (1982). Sex differences in performance attribution and contingency judgment. *Sex Roles, 8*, 381-388.

Wong, P. T. P., & Weiner, B. (1981). When people ask "why" questions, and the heuristics of attributional search. *Journal of Personality and Social Psychology, 40*, 650-663.

Zaccaro, S. J., & Lowe, C. A. (1980). Attributions for achievement behavior in a novel situation. Paper presented at the annual meeting of the American Psychological Association Meeting, Montreal, August 1980.

Smiling and Gazing

Judith A. Hall
Amy G. Halberstadt

Abstract

A meta-analysis of gender differences in nonverbal behavior indicates that adult females smile and gaze substantially more than adult males do. No gender differences appear in the limited data base for children's social smiling, but girls gaze at others more than boys do. An attempt to quantify situational aspects of the smiling and gazing studies produced reliable ratings of situational characteristics such as friendliness, comfort, and naturalness of task, as well as codes for subject age, location of study, subject's status, and unobtrusiveness of measurement, among others. Three hypotheses concerning situational determinants of the gender differences in smiling and gazing were addressed. These concerned warmth-affiliation, dominance-status, and social tension. For smiling, social tension emerged as the strongest predictor, warmth-affiliation had a weak but suggestive effect, and dominance-status was unrelated. For gazing, no hypothesis was strongly supported, though there were some significant results not related specifically to these three hypotheses. Although meta-analysis can dramatically advance our knowledge of overall gender differences in these nonverbal behaviors and how they relate to characteristics of the studies, important interpretational issues, such as psychological mechanisms and the exact patterns of male and female behavior, are not resolved by meta-analysis.

Our intuitions tell us that men and women behave differently in face-to-face encounters. They seem to have different interpersonal goals, inhibitions, tolerances for emotional engagement, and ways of expressing themselves. Though many of these differences have long seemed elusive, we now know that at least some of the difference between males' and females' social interaction involves measurable differences in nonverbal communication skill and expressive style.

Nonverbal gender differences have been studied for over sixty years, but research became especially abundant in the 1970s owing to the women's movement and the rise of nonverbal communication as a major direction within American social psychology. There now exists a very impressive descriptive literature on gender differences in over a dozen nonverbal skills and behaviors. These are documented by Hall (1984). This chapter summarizes the gender differences for smiling and gazing, two of the strongest nonverbal gender differences, and adds new analyses of the relationship of situational factors to gender differences in these two nonverbal behaviors.

Nonverbal gender differences have been found to be generally robust and of a magnitude that rivals or exceeds that of most other documented gender differences (Hall, 1984). Persistent findings indicate that females are superior to males in sending and judging the meanings of nonverbal cues, and that they have more expressive faces, smile and laugh more, gaze more, approach others more closely, touch others more, and exhibit fewer speech disturbances than males do. They are also gazed at more than males are, are approached more closely, and may receive more smiling as well. In sum, based on a literature of hundreds of studies, it appears that women occupy a more nonverbally conscious, positive, and interpersonally engaged world than men do.

Of course, generalizations such as these do not hold true under all conditions and situations, and some research has succeeded in qualifying the foregoing summary. To give just one example here, women's tendency to gaze more than men do seems not to occur when the distance separating the gazer from another is unusually large for a conversation; indeed, under such circumstances, women gaze less than men do (Aiello, 1972). Other studies that have varied the situations in which people were observed will be discussed later in this chapter.

Identifying such limiting, or moderating, factors in nonverbal gender differences may possibly help us in developing an understanding of the dynamics behind them. As is so often the case in social psychology, it is much easier to locate and describe differences than to decide on an appropriate interpretation of them. Explanation of any gender difference is well known to be difficult owing to our inability to manipulate gender and its many correlates. Many factors relating to cultural and personal history could be implicated in the nonverbal behavior of men and women.

Writers on nonverbal gender differences have found it easy to speculate on their possible determinants (e.g., Eakins & Eakins, 1978; Frieze & Ramsey, 1976; Hall, 1978, 1984; Henley, 1977). Though the level of theoretical commitment may be high in some quarters, the literature reveals a surprising paucity of efforts to put theoretical issues to test. Indeed, most empirical attention paid to nonverbal gender differences is noticeably atheoretical: gender effects are often secondary to an investigator's theoretical concerns and are examined simply on a routine basis.

It is to the lack of explanatory evidence that this chapter is addressed. We have chosen to concentrate on smiling and gazing, behaviors that show some of the most consistent gender differences and that have also stimulated considerable theoretical interest. Additional discussions of theoretical issues regarding these and other nonverbal gender differences can be found in the work of Hall (1984), Henley (1977), and Mayo and Henley (1981). In this chapter, we shall be concerned with the moderating effects of situational factors on the direction and magnitude of gender differences in smiling and gazing.

Explanations for the gender differences in smiling and gazing may be placed into three major categories. Various writers have mentioned these hypotheses, but only one hypothesis—that relating to dominance-status—has received any serious development (Henley, 1977). It is our impression that some writers would not consider the three to be separable hypotheses, and indeed there are ambiguities. However, we feel that much is to be gained by attempting to enforce certain analytical distinctions in examining this literature.

The warmth-affiliation hypothesis suggests that women smile and gaze more than men do because of their socioemotional orientation. They may take more pleasure in certain kinds of interpersonal interactions, they may feel more compelled to present themselves as pleasant, or they may take it to be their responsibility to make certain kinds of interactions pleasant for all concerned.

The dominance-status hypothesis suggests that women smile and gaze more than men do because they are socially weaker. Women may smile to ingratiate themselves with others whom they perceive to be more powerful, or with anyone for that matter, or they may display their social submissiveness by smiling to signal that they are harmless. Women may gaze more because their weak position requires them to be especially attentive to others' attitudes and behaviors; such attention would place the maximum amount of useful information at a woman's disposal and may also be ingratiating in itself.

Some discussions of the dominance-status hypothesis have drawn on evidence from subhuman primates (e.g., Henley, 1977). Ethologists have documented among primates a "fear grin" that is used by submissive or defensive individuals. However, it should be noted that such expressions are also used by more dominant monkeys toward less dominant ones as a positive gesture or sign of reassurance (Hinde, 1974). Thus the fear-submission function can be supplanted by a friendliness function, even at the subhuman level. Emphasizing the original function of a behavior pattern can obviously be misleading if its functions have expanded over time.

The social tension–nervousness hypothesis relates primarily to smiling, and suggests that women's greater smiling reflects attempts to mask or cope with social unease.

These hypotheses about overall nonverbal gender differences are not tested in the meta-analysis, because they require documentation of main effects that the meta-analysis does not address: first, that the nonverbal behaviors increase when the subject's situation is warmer, more anxious, or of lower dominance-status, and, second, that females are more often in situations that are warmer, more anxious, or of lower dominance-status. But if the nonverbal gender differences *vary* with characteristics of the situations (equivalent to a gender x situation interaction), it may suggest new avenues of thought about the psychology of those situations for males versus females, and ultimately about explanations. In this chapter, when we refer to "the warmth-affiliation hypothesis" (as well as for dominance-status and social tension), we mean the hypothesis stating that gender effects will be correlated with these situational factors.

It is important to recognize that the present meta-analysis can test hypotheses about the relationship of situational factors to gender differences, but it cannot actually put to rest any causal questions about those differences. Not only is meta-analysis generally unsuitable for causal analysis, because of its nonexperimental nature and the lack of information about groups' exact patterns of behavior across situations (this point is amplified later), but also this particular meta-analysis excludes the entire realm of individual differences from consideration. One can approach all three of the present hypotheses in terms of individual differences or traits rather than in terms of situations. The traits of affiliation, dominance-status, and social anxiety could interact with gender in the same way as their situational analogues do (see, for example, Frances, 1979). Though an analysis of traits is important, this is best done on a within-studies basis—that is, by comparing individuals who differ on the traits in question rather than by comparing the results of studies, as meta-analysis does. Most studies in the literature we examined offered little or no detail on the personal characteristics of the subjects, and in a number of studies nothing along these lines was known even to the investigators (see app. D for studies reviewed).

It is obvious that the causes of sex differences may not be mutually exclusive and, especially when viewed in a causal stream, can be virtually impossible to separate. Consider the possibility that women's tendency to smile more than men developed as an adaptive response at a time of extreme female subordination, but that, over time, women's smiling lost its meaning as a show of submission. Instead, smiling became an aspect of generalized gender-role expectations, with women expected to be (and expecting themselves to be) warmer and more expressive than men. The chief mechanisms for the development of the smiling gender difference within the lifetime of an individual would likely be same-gender modeling and internalization of gender-role norms. What we call *the* explanation of the gender difference in this hypothetical example depends on where in history we focus. Not only are very different mechanisms involved, but the indirect contribution of oppression cannot even be tested in this example since it occurred in the historical past. Thus in trying to explain a nonverbal gender difference, ambiguity will always remain. However, this pessimism is offset by our conviction that more explanatory efforts are needed and that meta-analysis is a useful tool for the development of interpretations.

In this chapter, we first describe gender differences in social smiling and gazing in children and adults. Second, we describe a meta-analytic study in which situational and interpersonal aspects of the original studies were coded or rated and then related to the gender-difference results. In this way, one can ascertain whether smiling and gazing gender differences can be predicted from knowledge of the circumstances and from the circumstances' inferred impact on the emotional and cognitive states of the people involved. To perform a meta-analysis by combining data retrieved from the original studies with new data, in this case, our ratings of the circumstances in which observation took place, is an exciting research approach whose use is well illustrated in the work of Eagly and Carli (1981) on task correlates of gender differences in persuasion and conformity.

Summary of Gender Differences

Smiling

In this chapter, we are interested chiefly in social smiling, and the study described later deals only with this kind of smiling. We shall briefly describe social laughing (or "smiling and laughing" when measured as one variable) as well as smiling and laughing observed in nonsocial situations, that is, when one does not have the opportunity to smile at another. Social smiling is given special consideration because the data base for social smiling is much better than it is for laughing.

As described further by Hall (1984), the studies reporting on gender differences in smiling (as well as gazing) were located principally via exhaustive searches of forty English-language journals and examination of published bibliographies. The data set summarized here is virtually identical with that summarized for these behaviors by Hall (1984).

Studies of social smiling were performed in both laboratory and field settings, with the former greatly predominating. Subjects rarely knew their nonverbal behavior was being observed, but they often knew they were in a research study of some sort. Dependent measures included total time devoted to smiling and frequency of smiling or of positive facial expression.

Table 6.1 shows results for children ages 2 through 12 and for adults, defined as college age and older. We know of no data reported separately for adolescents, for either smiling or gazing. Results are shown in several ways. The first, direction, is simply the direction of the result (whether males or females did more smiling), regardless of whether the result was significant and ignoring all studies where there was no difference at all or it was unknown.

The second, mean effect size, is the average d (Cohen, 1977). Each d was given a positive sign when females did more smiling and a negative sign when males did more. This index is unweighted with regard to sample sizes; a weighted version, d_w, is also discussed later (see Chapter 2 for further discussion of weighted and unweighted effect sizes). Other indices of effect size are available. One of these, the point-biserial correlation, was used by Hall in her 1984 summary of nonverbal gender differences, including smiling and gazing. The relationship between d and r is $d = 2r/\sqrt{1 - r^2}$.

Following Eagly and Carli (1981), both a minimum and a maximum effect size are given in table 6.1. The minimum is the average d considering all unknown results to be zero, and the maximum is the average d based only on those effect sizes that could be calculated. The minimum value is probably an underestimate because, given the obvious overall trends, the average unknown effect size is probably not zero but some positive value. The maximum value could be an overestimate because of the possibility that larger effects find their way into print more easily than smaller ones.

The third index in table 6.1 shows how many studies were significant favoring each gender, and the fourth index is the combined p (Stouffer

Table 6.1 Gender Differences in Subjects' Social Smiling

Outcome Measure	Children (20 studies)	Adults (24 studies)
Direction	47% (8/17) favor females (not significant)	95% (18/19) favor females ($p = 10^{-4}$)
Mean Effect Size (d)	between 0.00 (20 studies) and −0.04 (5 studies)	between 0.39 (24 studies) and 0.63 (15 studies)
Statistical Significance	10% (2/20) favor females significantly, none favors males significantly	50% (12/24) favor females significantly, none favors males significantly
Combined p	$p = .49$ (14 studies)	$p < 10^{-9}$ (20 studies)

Note: "Children" are ages 2–12. "Adults" are college age and older. "Direction" excludes results of "no difference" and unknown. For effect size, positive values indicate more female smiling. "Statistical significance" is based on all studies. "Combined p" excludes studies for which no statistical tests were reported or available. Results are two-tail.

method; Rosenthal, 1978), ignoring studies in which no statistical tests were reported and giving a z of zero to all results simply reported as "not significant." All results in table 6.1 are from independent samples of subjects. All tests of significance in this chapter are reported in two-tail form.

Table 6.1 indicates that there was virtually no evidence for a gender difference among children. More studies favored girls significantly than favored boys (10 percent versus none), but since only 2 of the entire group of 20 studies were significant, this is hardly a credible difference.

Among adults, however, the situation changes dramatically. All indices show that women engaged in more social smiling than men. When effect size is weighted according to its theoretical variance, that is, as a function of its sample size (see Chap. 2), the average effect size dropped to 0.42. The homogeneity test for studies of social smiling in adults was significant, indicating that there was significant variability among the effect sizes. The analyses reported in the second half of this chapter are an attempt to account for this nonrandom variation.

The age difference in table 6.1 is statistically significant; the correlation (r) between age, coded 0 for children and 1 for adults, and effect size (d) is 0.45.

Studies of social laughing included three kinds of dependent variables: laughing, smiling and laughing measured together as one variable, and a continuum that typically went from frown at one extreme, through smile, to laugh at the other extreme. There is overlap between the laughing studies and the smiling studies described earlier, since some studies reported both kinds of behavior.

For social laughing, the data are consistent with the preceding results in showing no gender difference among children and a strong one in adults. For children the average known effect size actually favored boys ($d = -0.54$, 5 results), though according to the direction index, girls showed more laughing (61 percent, or 11 of 18 results). There is some evidence that boys' laughter may predominate in the same-gender situation (i.e., when children are observed with others of their own gender). For adults there were only four studies, but all favored women and the average known effect size was $d = 0.77$ (4 results).

Studies of nonsocial smiling and nonsocial laughing are very few; they seem to show negligible gender differences, but even so those differences seem to favor females (Hall, 1984).

Gazing

Observations of children's gazing were done mainly in laboratory-based tasks and occasionally during play in school or laboratory. Studies of adults

Table 6.2 Gender Differences in Subjects' Gazing

Outcome Measure	Children (26 studies)	Adults (62 studies)
Direction	83% (15/18) favor females ($p = .004$)	84% (36/43) favor females ($p = 10^{-5}$)
Mean Effect Size (d)	between 0.18 (26 studies) and 0.43 (11 studies)	between 0.30 (62 studies) and 0.68 (30 studies)
Statistical Significance	19% (5/26) favor females significantly, none favors males significantly	34% (21/62) favor females significantly, 3% (2/62) favor males significantly
Combined p	$p = .006$ (25 studies)	$p < 10^{-9}$ (56 studies)

Note: Data and samples are coded as described in table 6.1.

were based mainly on laboratory interactions, such as interviews and conversations, and only occasionally on naturally occurring situations such as people passing on the sidewalk. Observation of nonverbal behavior was generally unobtrusive for both children and adults, though subjects frequently knew they were in a research study. The results in table 6.2 are based on total gazing or percentage of interaction spent in gazing whenever one of those was available; otherwise, they are based on whatever primary measure of gazing was used by the original authors, such as frequency of gazing or amount of mutual eye contact. All results in table 6.2 are independent of each other; there is, however, some overlap with the studies in table 6.1 because some studies reported results for both smiling and gazing.

Table 6.2 shows that among both children and adults (both as defined above), females gazed more than males do. In terms of the weighted effect size (d_w), the gender difference for children was 0.48 and for adults was 0.69. Though the proportions favoring females in direction were the same, the statistical significance for the gender difference in table 6.2 is more impressive for adults because of the larger number of studies. The difference between effect sizes for adults versus children was not significant: the correlation (r) between age, coded 0 for children and 1 for adults, and effect size (d) was 0.21.

Homogeneity tests revealed that for children's gazing, the effect sizes were acceptably homogeneous ($p > .05$), but for adults the effect sizes were not. This lack of homogeneity is addressed below.

Correlates of Gender Differences in Smiling and Gazing

In the preceding section, an overall description of the gender differences for smiling and gazing was given. The only correlate described so far has been age: there was a moderately strong positive age effect for smiling and a weaker positive age effect for gazing. But other correlates can be considered, each of which serves not only to describe the gender differences more exactly but also to guide our interpretations of them. Such correlates include subject and partner demographic characteristics, the participants' relationship to each other, and their situation.

The findings of nonhomogeneous effect sizes for gender differences in adults' smiling and gazing indicates that it may be possible to uncover factors that are correlated with effect size—that is, that account for the greater than chance level of variation in effect sizes. In this section, we present our study of situational correlates of effect size, based on the same literature analyzed above.

The meta-analytic approach to understanding situational correlates of gender differences is analogous to examining the impact of situational variables on the behavior of men versus women within a single study. Though not many studies have included such manipulations, there are enough to make a summary worthwhile. For smiling, the gender difference favoring females increased significantly when subjects were interacting rather than alone (Mackey, 1976), which fits the evidence compiled across studies described above, and when subjects were telling the truth rather than lying (Mehrabian, 1971a). There were no significant interactions of gender with the situational variable when subjects had high versus low expectations for the performance of a child confederate whom they were teaching (Chaikin and Derlega, 1978; Chaikin, Sigler & Derlega, 1974), or when subjects were trying to seek versus avoid approval (Rosenfeld, 1966).

For gazing, the gender difference favoring females increased when subjects were conversing rather than building with blocks together (Levine & Sutton-Smith, 1973), when subjects were close rather than far apart (Aiello, 1972, 1977a [two results], 1977b), and when subjects were concealing information in an interview (Exline, Gray & Schuette, 1965). On the other hand, the gazing gender difference did not vary significantly when the subject was with a friend versus a stranger (Foot, Chapman & Smith, 1977; Foot, Smith & Chapman, 1979; Russo, 1975 [$p < .10$]), when the other person smiled and laughed more versus less (Chapman & Chapman, 1974), when the other person was warm rather than cold (Wittig & Skolnick, 1978), when the subject was answering upsetting versus ordinary questions (Cherulnik, 1979), when the subject was under more versus less stress (Slane et al., 1980 [two results]), when the subject was in a more versus less competitive task (Exline, 1963; Foddy, 1978), when the subject was made more versus less dependent on an experimenter (Nevill, 1974), or when the subject was of lower versus equal status relative to the other person (Wittig & Skolnick, 1978). Thus the gazing gender difference seems unusually resistant to a range of situational manipulations that tapped all three factors of positive affect, status, and social tension. Later in this chapter, we shall compare these results with those of our between-studies analysis.

Method

Data Set

The data set consisted of the studies included in tables 6.1 and 6.2 that reported on the direction or effect size of the gender-difference result, with the exception that studies of children's smiling were not included because there were only five effect sizes. There were 20 smiling studies and 61 gazing studies. In appendix D, the age group and behavior category (smiling or gazing) are indicated for each study.

A research assistant photocopied and assembled the methods descriptions from each of the studies, eradicating the identification of the author and study.

Independent Variables

The present authors coded and rated each description of methods independently, blind to the identification of the studies and their results. We recognized a few of the studies from their method, but we did not recall any study's exact results.

The following variables were coded or rated whenever pertinent information was available. (Race and socioeconomic status were also coded but were unfortunately not reported in the majority of studies. These variables are not discussed.) Given in parentheses are the levels for the coded variables or the nature of the rating scale used for rated variables. The final entries are the frequencies of occurrence for each level of all coded variables.

A. Attributes of Subjects
   1. Subject age (1 = nursery school or younger; 2 = elementary school; 3 = high school; 4 = college; 5 = older). Frequencies for smiling, 0, 0, 0, 16, 4; for gazing, 6, 12, 0, 38, 5.
B. Attributes of Other Person
   1. Other's gender (1 = female; 2 = male; 3 = female and male; 4 = same gender; 5 = opposite gender). The category "female and male" refers almost exclusively to studies in which other's gender was a between-subject variable and results were reported as a main effect across both female and male others. Frequencies for smiling, 1, 5, 6, 4, 3; for gazing, 11, 6, 18, 19, 6.
   2. Other's age (coded as in A.1). Frequencies for smiling, 0, 3, 0, 13, 4; for gazing, 1, 10, 0, 39, 11.

3. Other's identity (1 = peer; 2 = confederate "peer"; 3 = interviewer; 4 = experimenter). Frequencies for smiling, 8, 2, 1, 0; for gazing, 24, 12, 12, 5.

4. Other's nonverbal programming (1 = no; 2 = yes). Nonverbal programming means that any aspect of the other's nonverbal behavior was prearranged, such as amount of gazing or distance from subject. Frequencies for smiling, 12, 8; for gazing, 30, 31.

C. Relational Variables
   1. Acquaintanceship (1 = strangers; 2 = just met; 3 = slightly acquainted; 4 = well acquainted; 5 = intimate). Frequencies for smiling, 10, 6, 0, 0, 1; for gazing, 14, 25, 9, 1, 4.
   2. Status (1 = subject is lower than other; 2 = both are same; 3 = subject is higher than other). Status refers to roles in the particular interaction and never to age alone. Frequencies for smiling, 0, 12, 6; for gazing, 20, 34, 3.
   3. Participants are allowed interpersonal interaction, defined as verbal give-and-take (1 = no; 2 = yes). Frequencies for smiling, 6, 14; for gazing, 13, 48.

D. Setting Variables
   1. Location (1 = laboratory; 2 = field). Frequencies for smiling, 18, 2; for gazing, 57, 3.
   2. Unobtrusiveness of observation (1 = subjects know observation of nonverbal behavior is occurring and why; 2 = subjects know observation is occurring but not what is being observed or why; 3 = subjects know they are being studied but do not know they are being observed; 4 = subjects think study will begin later [waiting-period observation]; 5 = subjects do not know they are involved in research of any sort). Frequencies for smiling, 0, 7, 6, 3, 3; for gazing, 1, 21, 25, 6, 8.
   3. Situation/task feels natural or familiar (nine-point scale from unusual to natural).
   4. Situation promotes comfortable feelings (nine-point scale from nervous to comfortable).
   5. Situation promotes friendly feelings (nine-point scale from unfriendly to friendly).
   6. Situation promotes competitive feelings (nine-point scale from cooperative to competitive).
   7. Situation has socioemotional emphasis (nine-point scale from low to high).
   8. Situation has goal orientation (nine-point scale from low to high).
   9. Task is cognitively difficult (nine-point scale from easy to complex).

Agreement between us for the nine-point ratings was as follows: natural, $r = 0.66$; comfortable, $r = 0.59$; friendly, $r = 0.46$; competitive, $r = 0.30$; socioemotional emphasis, $r = 0.58$; goal orientation, $r = 0.61$; complex, $r = 0.61$. Since both of us rated all studies and our ratings were averaged, the reliability of the mean ratings was higher than indicated by these correlations. These effective reliabilities were achieved by applying the Spearman-Brown prophecy formula to the average interrater correlations given above (Rosenthal & Rosnow, 1984). The reliabilities were: natural, 0.80; comfortable, 0.74; friendly, 0.63; competitive, 0.46; socioemotional emphasis, 0.73; goal orientation, 0.76; complex, 0.76.

For all the coded variables listed above, which are much more objective in nature, inconsistencies between us were resolved by Hall, who reread the methods descriptions and arbitrated the differences. In most such instances, inconsistencies were mistakes rather than differences in judgment.

Dependent Variables

Results were expressed in three ways: (1) Direction was coded 0 if males did more smiling or gazing and 1 if females did more. One study that showed exactly equal means was excluded for the direction index but not for the remaining outcome indices. (2) The first index of effect size was d, defined as the difference between male and female means divided by their common within-group standard deviation. This index was used in correlational analyses. The second index of effect size was d_w, described earlier. This was used in regression analyses. Results were pooled over experimental conditions within studies, if there were any, before being entered into the meta-analysis.

Results

It was possible to cluster the predictor variables in correspondence with two of the three hypotheses outlined above. Acquaintanceship, friendliness, and socioemotional emphasis will be called the warmth-affiliation cluster (median intercorrelation $= 0.36$, $p < .01$). Location (laboratory versus field), nervous-comfortable setting, and unusual-natural setting will be called the low social-tension cluster (median intercorrelation $= 0.62$, $p < .001$). These two clusters were unrelated to each other ($r = -0.09$). Subject's status was positively correlated with the warmth-affiliation cluster ($r = 0.27$, $p = .04$), indicating that the situation was judged to be "warmer" for the subject who was in a higher-status role. Status was uncorrelated with the low social-tension cluster ($r = 0.06$).

The first analysis in which effect sizes were predicted by the situational variables was a simple correlation matrix between smiling and gazing outcome measures (direction and d) and the predictors. All variables that showed a p of less than .10 for either outcome measure are shown in table 6.3.

First we shall discuss age effects. The smiling gender difference tends to decrease between the college-age level and the "older" category of subjects (which was still generally under age 30). Since it was demonstrated earlier that the smiling gender difference increases dramatically between childhood and college age, this negative relationship suggests that there is a curvilinear relationship such that the smiling gender difference is greatest in the college-age group. This interpretation is exactly consistent with Adams and Kirkevold's 1978 finding of a curvilinear gender difference for combined social and nonsocial smiling over a wide span of ages in restaurants. In our data, the average known effect size for college samples is $d = 0.70$ (11 results) and for older samples is $d = 0.41$ (4 results).

For gazing—though the correlation of .20 between subject age and effect size suggests a weak linear increase over the categories of nursery school, elementary school, college, and older—the relationship appears slightly

Table 6.3 Correlations of Smiling and Gazing Gender Differences with Predictors

Predictor Variable	Smiling		Gazing	
	Direction	ES	Direction	ES
Subject age (high = older)	0.10(19)	−0.50[+](15)	−0.00(61)	0.20(41)
Acquaintanceship (1 = strangers; 5 = intimate)	0.16(16)	0.49[+](14)	−0.21(53)	−0.09(39)
Friendliness of situation (1 = low; 9 = high)	0.41[+](19)	0.07(15)	0.27*(61)	0.08(41)
Socioemotional emphasis (1 = low; 9 = high)	−0.02(18)	0.12(15)	0.31*(58)	0.18(39)
Warmth-affiliation cluster[a]	0.18(16)	0.21(14)	0.30*(50)	0.12(37)
Location (1 = lab; 2 = field)	0.06(19)	−0.74**(15)	−0.12(60)	−0.14(41)
Comfortableness of situation (1 = nervous; 9 = comfortable)	0.09(19)	−0.45[+](15)	0.05(61)	−0.02(41)
Naturalness of task (1 = unusual; 9 = natural)	−0.03(19)	−0.62*(15)	0.06(61)	0.05(41)
Low social-tension cluster[a]	0.03(19)	−0.56*(15)	0.04(60)	0.01(41)
Interpersonal interaction (1 = no; 2 = yes)	0.39[+](19)	0.63**(15)	0.31*(61)	0.58***(41)

Note: ES stands for effect size (unweighted d). Direction is coded 0 if males were higher, 1 if females were higher. ES has a negative sign if males were higher, a positive sign if females were higher. Smiling data are for college and older samples; gazing data are for all age groups. N is in parentheses. See text for complete description of coding categories.
[a] Each cluster is the mean of the preceding three variables.
[+] $p \leq .10$.   *$p \leq .05$.   **$p \leq .01$.   ***$p \leq .001$.

curvilinear as well. Again the largest gender difference is among college students. The average known effect sizes (d) are nursery school, 0.34 (4 results); elementary school, 0.47 (7 results); college, 0.70 (26 results); and older, 0.54 (4 results).

For gazing, correlations of subjects' and partners' ages with effect size and direction were recomputed for only college students and older samples, in order to establish comparability with the smiling correlations, which were based on these two age groups. The relationships with subject age were nonsignificantly negative, as suggested by the mean effect sizes reported above that showed a larger gender difference for college than older samples. Further, the correlation between partner age and gazing effect size was significant, $r(28) = -0.38$, $p < .05$, indicating that women's tendency to gaze more than men was greater when the other person was of college age than when the other person was older (these are the only two age groups of others represented in this subsample).

It is perhaps not surprising to find the smiling and gazing gender differences peaking toward the end of adolescence, given that gender-role conformity is probably strong around that age. Since gender-role conformity among high school students should be as strong or stronger still, we hypothesize that the gender differences would be largest of all among high school students. It is unfortunate that no data for social smiling and gazing in these adolescents are available.

One may wonder if in our data set the relationship between age and size of effect is influenced by the other independent variables. For example, college students are more likely to be studied in laboratory settings, whereas adults are more likely to be studied in field settings ($r(69) = 0.37$, $p < .001$), and students are less likely than adults to know their partner prior to the study ($r(59) = 0.33$, $p < .01$). Since location and acquaintanceship are also associated with effect size (as shown in table 6.3), they may also account for the relationship between age and effect size. However, partial correlations of age and effect size controlling for acquaintanceship, location, and several other variables for college student and older samples indicated very little change in the strength and significance of the age–effect size relationship for both smiling and gazing.

Now we turn to the results pertaining to the three hypotheses presented earlier that deal with situational moderating factors in the gender differences. Table 6.3 shows that the warmth-affiliation hypothesis is supported in the correlations of acquaintanceship and friendliness with the smiling gender difference, and the correlations of friendliness and socioemotional emphasis with the gazing gender difference. The warmth-affiliation cluster, a composite variable, is positively associated with the gender differences but significantly so only for gazing direction. When only the college and older samples are considered for gazing, the correlations for friendliness and socioemotional status are smaller and nonsignificant, though still positive.

The social tension–nervousness hypothesis is supported in the correlations for location, comfort, and naturalness with the smiling effect size. The low social-tension cluster, which is a composite of these three variables, is significantly correlated as well.

The dominance-status hypothesis was tested by three variables; little support was obtained. Most central to the dominance-status hypothesis is the subject status variable—whether the subject was lower, equal to, or higher than the other in role status. If smiling and gazing gender differences were most pronounced when subjects were lower in status, it would suggest that low status has a motivational significance that is very different for males versus females. As the frequencies given earlier showed, for smiling there were no instances of subjects being of lower status, and for gazing there were very few instances of subjects being of higher status. Consequently, there are in effect only two levels of status available for each nonverbal behavior (equal versus higher for smiling, lower versus equal for gazing). The correlations for direction and effect size, for both smiling and gazing, gave no support to the dominance-status hypothesis. Conceivably, the hypothesis would receive better support if the status differences were larger or more salient than was probably the case in these studies.

The dominance-status hypothesis would also have predicted that sex differences would be different when subjects were with interviewers or experimenters—persons of authority—than with real or supposed peers. However, the identity of the other, whether peer, confederate "peer," interviewer, or experimenter, had no significant effect on the sizes of the sex differences.

Some authors have viewed relative age as a status variable within an interaction (e.g., Henley, 1977). Relative age was calculated by combining the information on subjects' and others' ages. (Recall that relative age was not used as a criterion for coding subjects' status.) Subjects were coded as younger than, same as, or older than the other person, and this variable was then correlated with smiling and gazing effect sizes. The results showed a nonsignificant negative relationship for smiling, $r(16) = -0.18$, and a significant positive relationship for gazing, $r(39) = 0.40$, $p = .01$. For gazing, there were no instances in which subjects were older, so this significant correlation indicates that the gender difference was smaller when the subject was younger than when the subject was the same age as the other person.

Interestingly, as table 6.3 shows, the variable called interpersonal interaction had the most consistent relationships to the smiling and gazing gender differences, although it was not designated a priori as an operationalization of any of the three hypotheses under review. Studies that observed active interaction between participants found larger differences favoring females than did studies in which participants had a passive or highly constrained relationship to each other. The latter group includes situations in which people pass on the sidewalk, listen together to funny stories through headphones, or deliver a monologue to someone. The correlations between the gazing gender difference and this variable remain significant and of similar magnitude even when only college and older subjects are considered. One should recall in interpreting these correlations that "noninteractive" does not mean "alone"; studies of subjects who were alone (not considered in the present analysis) show gender differences in smiling that are probably smaller still (see Hall, 1984).

The second kind of prediction analysis used weighted effect size (d_w) in a series of bivariate and multiple regressions. For details on how such analyses are carried out, readers should consult chapter 2. Table 6.4 shows the results for the bivariate regressions; these are analogous to the correlations in table 6.3 and are based on the same studies. Because more results were significant as a consequence of employing a more powerful data-analytic strategy, the criterion for inclusion in the table was $p < .05$ instead of $p < .10$.

Table 6.4 reveals a pattern that is similar to that in table 6.3, but the regression coefficients are often more significant than those found with the conventional method. The results for subject's age are similar to those found before and merit no further discussion. Only two of the three variables identified as the warmth-affiliation cluster were significant in the re-

Table 6.4 Standardized Regression Coefficients for Predictors of Smiling and Gazing Effect Sizes

Predictor Variable	Effect Size	
	Smiling	Gazing
Subject age (high = older)	−0.75***	0.16+
Acquaintanceship (1 = strangers; 5 = intimate)	0.42	−0.18*
Socioemotional emphasis (1 = low; 9 = high)	−0.15	0.19*
Location (1 = lab; 2 = field)	−0.87***	−0.10
Comfortableness of situation (1 = nervous; 9 = comfortable)	−0.79***	−0.12
Naturalness of task (1 = unusual; 9 = natural)	−0.81***	−0.11
Low social-tension cluster	−0.81***	−0.12
Competition (1 = low; 9 = high)	0.65***	0.01
Goal orientation (1 = low; 9 = high)	0.51**	0.03
Task difficulty (1 = easy; 9 = complex)	0.58**	0.01
Unobtrusiveness of observation (1 = obtrusive; 5 = unobtrusive)	−0.77***	0.03
Other's programming (1 = no; 2 = yes)	−0.65***	−0.23**
Subject status (1 = lower; 3 = higher)	−0.40	0.23**
Interpersonal interaction (1 = no; 2 = yes)	0.80***	0.55***

Note: Effect size is weighted d and is coded as described as in table 6.3. Samples are the same as in table 6.3. See text for complete description of coding categories.
+$p \le .10$.   *$p \le .05$.   **$p \le .01$.   ***$p \le .001$.

gressions, and these were acquaintanceship and socioemotional emphasis. For smiling, the evidence regarding the warmth-affiliation cluster was weaker than it was with the conventional analysis. For gazing, the coefficients were significant but not consistent in direction; the gender difference was larger for less well acquainted dyads and in situations with a greater socioemotional emphasis.

The variables that make up the low social-tension cluster emerged, by contrast, as potent predictors in the regressions. As was the case in the conventional analysis, all three variables in this cluster were strong predictors of the smiling gender differences, as was their composite. As before, none predicted the gazing gender difference significantly, though the relationships were in the same direction.

The next five variables in table 6.4 were not in table 6.3 because their relationships with the outcome measures were too weak to meet the $p < .10$ criterion of table 6.3. The greater statistical power of the weighted regression analysis brought these relationships into significance. The pattern of results for these variables suggests that perhaps they can be seen as aspects of social tension. The gender difference for smiling was significantly larger when the situation was more competitive, had more of a goal orientation, and was more difficult. These relationships may indicate that females experience more awkwardness with such tasks, conceivably because of the tasks' "masculine" connotations.

Other interpretations are possible, however. The effect-size data may reflect no change in females' smiling as a function of task, but may instead reflect a reduction in male smiling. Males may take more competitive, goal-oriented, and difficult tasks more seriously—perhaps because of ego involvement and the desire not to lose—and they therefore may lose what cheerfulness they would otherwise display.

Finally, it is possible that heightened relative levels of female smiling in such situations reflect the appeasement function mentioned earlier when the dominance-status hypothesis was presented. Females may feel the need to apologize facially for daring to compete and to strive on goal-oriented and difficult tasks. Determining which of these possibilities is closest to the truth is probably impossible in the context of meta-analysis, which deals only with relative male-female differences. What are needed are individual studies that manipulate these variables internally; this would allow crucial comparisons of the male and female means across conditions.

For the next variable in table 6.4, unobtrusiveness of observation, the gender difference in smiling increased when observation was more obtrusive. Again, some kind of self-consciousness or tension could explain this. The next variable, other's programming, tells whether the other person in the dyad was programmed to control his or her nonverbal behavior while with the subject. For both smiling and gazing, the gender difference was significantly larger when the other was not programmed. Possibly, an unprogrammed other is perceived as spontaneous and warm while a programmed other seems stiff and cold. The unprogrammed other may therefore stimulate a "friendly interaction" mind set that affects women's nonverbal behavior more positively than men's.

Subject's status, which did not appear in table 6.3, again did not predict the smiling difference significantly (not even at $p < .10$), but it did predict that for gazing. The gender difference increased when the subject was of higher status than the other. This result is consistent with that described earlier for relative age correlated with the gazing effect size in the conventional analysis. Finally, the interpersonal interaction variable showed a strong relationship to both gender differences, just as it did earlier.

In addition to these bivariate regressions, weighted multiple regressions were performed. A number of different models were tested. The simplest included subject's age, whether the subject engaged in active interpersonal interaction with the other, and the two clusters called warmth-affiliation and low social tension. These regressions permitted a test of whether the model fits the data—that is, whether or not there is a significant amount of residual variance after the predictors have been entered (see chap. 2).

For smiling, R^2 was 0.68, and the model specification test was far from significant, which indicates that the model did fit the data very well. This indicates that additional predictors are not necessary to account for the smiling gender differences. It does not, however, mean that we have located all the important predictors, since conceivably another prediction model could fit the data as well. For gazing, R^2 was 0.38, and the specification test was significant, indicating that the model did not fit. None of the gazing models that were tried did fit, which reflects the fact that most predictors bore a weak relationship to gazing gender differences.

In sum, the regression analyses based on weighted effect sizes yielded more significant results than did the conventional approach. We would conclude, based on all our analyses, that the social-tension hypothesis received strong support for smiling; the warmth-affiliation hypothesis received weak support for smiling and mixed support for gazing; and the dominance-status hypothesis received some support for gazing.

Unpredicted were the strong effects of more involved interpersonal interaction on both gender differences. This could reflect warmth-affiliation but also, in the present literature, it could reflect social tension since the interactive situations were likely to be laboratory studies (i.e., higher on social tension). The results for the interpersonal interaction variable are, unfortunately, not very revealing since we have yet to identify what it is about such interchange that promotes relatively higher levels of smiling and gazing for females. Perhaps for males the more involved face-to-face situation arouses conflict for the male gender role or feelings of confrontation, and they respond by reducing their levels of smiling and gazing, or at least by not increasing them as much as females are willing to do.

Since relatively little of the variation in gazing gender differences was accounted for in the meta-analysis, it is clearly possible that other situational factors besides those we quantified should be sought. One factor that is known to influence gazing gender differences is interpersonal distance, as mentioned earlier. One reversal of the usual gender difference occurred when subjects were conversing at an awkwardly great distance (Aiello, 1972). Another reversal (Fromme & Beam, 1974) suggests, however, that too-close distances may similarly disrupt the usual pattern; in that study, subjects were observed while approaching a confederate, and the average interpersonal distance achieved was only slightly over two feet. It remains for further research to uncover factors that can account better for the gazing effects.

Discussion

In overall magnitude, the smiling and gazing gender differences are, at least for adults, above 0.60 in standard deviation units—in the range that Cohen (1977) calls visible to the naked eye. Though only some 10 percent of variation in smiling or gazing is accounted for by gender, these differences are actually on the large side compared to other gender differences documented in this volume and by Hall (1984). Of the mean effect sizes for gender differences located by Hall for 47 cognitive and social-personality variables (excluding nonverbal behaviors), only 4 percent were of the magnitude $d > 0.60$, and only 19 percent were as large as $d = 0.50$.

Many of the larger effect sizes reviewed by Hall seem to tap a socioemotional dimension on which women are farther toward the positive end than men. Such variables included smiling, gazing, distance approached, making socioemotional contributions in small groups, self-ratings of empathy, low aggression, and self-related femininity (expressiveness and communion). Gender stereotypes that were supported to a considerably weaker or negligible degree included persuasion and conformity, attributions for performance, self-esteem, neuroticism, achievement motivation and values, and fear of success. It would seem, then, that with the exception of some cognitive skills, the most striking gender differences documented so far reflect differences in positive socioemotional orientation.

The fact that, in this chapter, relatively more smiling in women was strongly associated with apparent social tension may seem to challenge the interpretation of smiling as a socioemotional behavior. But smiling in response to tension is not necessarily an expression of tension, but may instead be an attempt to be cheerful in spite of it. Indeed, it may reflect the subject's effort to ease the other person's discomfort. Viewed in this way, smiling loses none of its socioemotional character.

The fact that the bulk of the studies reviewed in this chapter showed more female smiling and gazing probably indicates that most situations studied had the minimum qualities required to stimulate males' and females' different behavior patterns. Most studies involved friendly, but possibly nervous, interaction, especially interaction that was legitimate (for example, following an introduction by a third party) and risk-free (such as interactions in social psychology experiments). Investigators may thus have made most of their observations in the very kinds of situations that maximize the nonverbal gender differences. Almost all of these situations may have exceeded some kind of threshold on factors that elicit nonverbal gender differences; it is possible that after such a threshold is exceeded, minor variations in mood or task demands have little effect. This may be especially true for gazing in the college and older group, where the only strong predictor was the sheer fact of face-to-face interchange.

Interestingly, the results of within-study manipulations described earlier support this suggested threshold effect. The kinds of factors that predicted smiling and gazing gender differences in such studies were, by and large, consistent with our between-studies results. But for gazing, a relatively large number of studies that manipulated such factors failed to alter the gender differences significantly. This agrees with our relative paucity of significant situational predictors for the gazing gender difference. Quite possibly, in the individual studies where situational factors were experimentally manipulated, the impact of the manipulated stress, status, dependency, and so forth was trivial compared to the fact that the basic situation may already have been high enough on triggering factors to bring about the usual gender differences.

It is therefore apparent that a full understanding of the impact of situations and of the external validity of the overall gender differences is not possible until a broader spectrum of situations is tapped. If the situations studied are reasonably representative of those confronting people in everyday life, then the overall nonverbal gender differences are not biased. But if interactions in everyday life are actually less involved, less tense, or less friendly on the average, then the literature overestimates the magnitude of these gender differences. In view of the fact that only 5 to 10 percent of the studies included in this meta-analysis were done in field locations, and those tended to involve strangers, we should be cautious indeed about the generality of the differences obtained. Future investigators should attempt to include a representative array of situations, especially those involving familiar people in natural settings.

Although the present meta-analysis uncovered reliable predictors of gender differences, there is still ambiguity about what are the exact patterns of male and female behavior and what are the exact psychological mechanisms. Let us assume, for the moment, that women smile especially much, relative to men, when the situation promotes warmth and affiliation. We still do not know whether in such circumstances women genuinely feel more pleasant than men do or instead respond to gender-role demands by forcing themselves to act pleasant regardless of their actual feelings. Moreover, the difference between genuine and forced warmth is a subtle one that may be impossible to make on the basis of either observation or self-reports.

At any rate, the suggestion that expressive style or norms of expression rather than underlying "true" states may account for the nonverbal gender differences receives some support in the case of social tension and nervousness. It may well be that similar overall levels of nervousness produce dramatically different nonverbal behavior in men and women. Women may be less concerned about hiding their anxiety in social situations; we know that they are slightly more willing to admit to general as well as social anxiety (Hall, 1984), and they are known to be less concerned with monitoring their own social behavior (Rosenthal & DePaulo, 1979), particularly their facial expression (Buck, 1979). Men may succeed in ridding their faces of signs of "unmanly" nervousness, which is probably not hard to do since the face seems to be the most controllable nonverbal channel (Zuckerman, DePaulo & Rosenthal, 1981). But men may reveal their nervousness in other ways; the research shows they have more fidgety bodies and they make more speech errors (Hall, 1984), both of which can be seen as expressions of anxiety. Thus it may be that social tension makes women appear more cheerful and men more awkward than they would ordinarily be.

An alternative interpretation, suggested earlier, would be that women are motivated to neutralize tense situations and to try to rescue all parties from the talons of social awkwardness. In this case, their smiling would not express their own anxiety but rather would be a prosocial response to their awareness of the situation's tension. Again, women would not be more anxious than men, but would respond to the situation differently. Subtle, but altogether crucial, differences in interpretation such as we have been making are clearly beyond the capacities of a meta-analysis done on the existing literature base.

The approach we have taken to exploring smiling and gazing gender differences is to quantify social psychological aspects of the circumstances in which subjects' behavior was observed. The correlations we found represent evidence for moderating factors—that is, factors that are associated with changes in the size or frequency of occurrence of the gender differences. Such a procedure is not equivalent to formally testing a causal hypothesis; no correlational study can be. At best, it provides direction for future efforts by indicating which variables have the most promise as causal factors.

References

Adams, R. M., & Kirkevold, B. (1978). Looking, smiling, laughing, and moving in restaurants: Sex and age differences. *Environmental Psychology and Nonverbal Behavior, 3,* 117-121.

Aiello, J. R. (1972). A test of equilibrium theory: Visual interaction in relation to orientation, distance and sex of interactants. *Psychonomic Science, 27,* 335-336.

Aiello, J. R. (1977a). A further look at equilibrium theory: Visual interaction as a function of interpersonal distance. *Environmental Psychology and Nonverbal Behavior, 1,* 122-140.

Aiello, J. R. (1977b). Visual interaction at extended distances. *Personality and Social Psychology Bulletin, 3,* 83-86.

Buck, R. (1979). Individual differences in nonverbal sending accuracy and electrodermal responding: The externalizing-internalizing dimension. In R. Rosenthal (ed.), *Skill in nonverbal communication: Individual differences.* Cambridge, Mass: Oelgeschlager, Gunn & Hain.

Chaikin, A. L., & Derlega, V. J. (1978). Nonverbal mediators of expectancy effects in black and white children. *Journal of Applied Social Psychology, 8,* 117-125.

Chaikin, A. L., Sigler, E., & Derlega, V. J. (1974). Nonverbal mediators of teacher expectancy effects. *Journal of Personality and Social Psychology, 30,* 144-149.

Chapman, A. J., & Chapman, W. A. (1974). Responsiveness to humor: Its dependency upon a companion's humorous smiling and laughter. *Journal of Psychology, 88,* 245-252.

Cherulnik, P. D. (1979). Sex differences in the expression of emotion in a structured social encounter. *Sex Roles, 5,* 413-424.

Cohen, J. (1977). *Statistical power analysis for the behavioral sciences.* New York: Academic Press.

Eagly, A. H., & Carli, L. L. (1981). Sex of researchers and sex-typed communications as determinants of sex differences in influenceability. *Psychological Bulletin, 90,* 1-20.

Eakins, B. W., & Eakins, R. G. (1978). *Sex differences in human communication.* Boston: Houghton Mifflin.

Exline, R. V. (1963). Explorations in the process of person perception: Visual interaction in relation to competition, sex, and need for affiliation. *Journal of Personality, 31,* 1-20.

Exline, R., Gray, D., & Schuette, D. (1965). Visual behavior in a dyad as affected by interview content and sex of respondent. *Journal of Personality and Social Psychology, 1,* 201-209.

Foddy, M. (1978). Patterns of gaze in cooperative and competitive negotiation. *Human Relations, 31,* 925-938.

Foot, H. C., Chapman, A. J., & Smith, J. R. (1977). Friendship and social responsiveness in boys and girls. *Journal of Personality and Social Psychology, 35,* 401-411.

Foot, H. C., Smith, J. R., & Chapman, A. J. (1979). Non-verbal expressions of intimacy in children. In M. Cook & G. Wilson (eds.), *Love and attraction.* Oxford: Pergamon.

Frances, S. J. (1979). Sex differences in nonverbal behavior. *Sex Roles, 5,* 519-535.

Frieze, I. H., & Ramsey, S. J. (1976). Nonverbal maintenance of traditional sex roles. *Journal of Social Issues, 32*, 133–141.

Fromme, D. K., & Beam, D. C. (1974). Dominance and sex differences in nonverbal responses to differential eye contact. *Journal of Research in Personality, 8*, 76–87.

Hall, J. A. (1978). Gender effects in decoding nonverbal cues. *Psychological Bulletin, 85*, 845–857.

Hall, J. A. (1984). *Nonverbal sex differences: Communication accuracy and expressive style*. Baltimore: Johns Hopkins University Press.

Henley, N. M. (1977). *Body politics: Power, sex, and nonverbal communication*. Englewood Cliffs: Prentice-Hall.

Hinde, R. A. (1974). *Biological bases of human social behaviour*. New York: McGraw-Hill.

Levine, M. H., & Sutton-Smith, B. (1973). Effects of age, sex, and task on visual behavior during dyadic interaction. *Developmental Psychology, 9*, 400–405.

Mackey, W. C. (1976). Parameters of the smile as a social signal. *Journal of Genetic Psychology, 129*, 125–130.

Mayo, C., & Henley, N. M. (eds.) (1981). *Gender and nonverbal behavior*. New York: Springer-Verlag.

Mehrabian, A. (1971a). Nonverbal betrayal of feeling. *Journal of Experimental Research in Personality, 5*, 64–73.

Mehrabian, A. (1971b). Verbal and nonverbal interaction of strangers in a waiting situation. *Journal of Experimental Research in Personality, 5*, 127–138.

Nevill, D. (1974). Experimental manipulation of dependency motivation and its effects on eye contact and measures of field dependency. *Journal of Personality and Social Psychology, 29*, 72–79.

Rosenfeld, H. M. (1966). Approval-seeking and approval-inducing functions of verbal and nonverbal responses in the dyad. *Journal of Personality and Social Psychology, 4*, 597–605.

Rosenthal, R. (1978). Combining results of independent studies. *Psychological Bulletin, 85*, 185–193.

Rosenthal, R., & DePaulo, B. M. (1979). Sex differences in accommodation in nonverbal communication. In R. Rosenthal (ed.), *Skill in nonverbal communication: Individual differences*. Cambridge, Mass.: Oelgeschlager, Gunn & Hain.

Rosenthal, R., & Rosnow, R. L. (1984). *Essentials of behavioral research: Methods and data analysis*. New York: McGraw-Hill.

Russo, N. F. (1975). Eye contact, interpersonal distance, and the equilibrium theory. *Journal of Personality and Social Psychology, 31*, 497–502.

Slane, S., Dragan, W., Crandall, C. J., & Payne, P. (1980). Stress effects on the nonverbal behavior of repressors and sensitizers. *Journal of Psychology, 106*, 101–109.

Wittig, M. A., & Skolnick, P. (1978). Status versus warmth as determinants of sex differences in personal space. *Sex Roles, 4*, 493–503.

Zuckerman, M., DePaulo, B. M., & Rosenthal, R. (1981). Verbal and nonverbal communication of deception. In L. Berkowitz (ed.), *Advances in experimental social psychology*. Vol. 14. New York: Academic Press.

Some Meta-analytic approaches to Examining the Validity of Gender-Difference Research
Alice H. Eagly

Abstract

In the feminist critical scholarship of the 1970s, a number of important criticisms were directed toward research on psychological gender differences. In this chapter, these criticisms are summarized and restated in terms of possible threats to the construct validity and external validity of generalizations about gender differences. Then the capacity of meta-analytic reviews to evaluate these threats to validity is discussed. A number of methods for assessing the possible invalidity of gender-difference findings are illustrated.

Critics of research on psychological gender differences have often claimed that this research typically suffers from biases that prevent it from providing an accurate description of the differences and similarities between women and men. One of the most detailed critiques of this research is found in Carolyn Sherif's "Bias in Psychology" (1979), written from a feminist perspective. Sherif criticized research on gender differences as exemplifying the narrow research paradigms characteristic of mainstream psychology. According to Sherif, investigators of gender differences usually examine behavior in contrived and carefully controlled laboratory contexts and, as a consequence, deal only with "selectively chosen data" (1979, p. 108). She argued that the findings of such research are not only frequently unrepresentative of daily life but also vulnerable to researchers' biases, which often include implicit sexism.

Parlee's review of scholarly work on the psychology of women (1979) provided a similar critique of research on psychological gender differences. Parlee maintained that the research area has relied excessively on the laboratory experiment and other controlled methods of investigation that remove behavior from its natural social context. She argued that findings about gender differences, because they are stripped of their natural context, are misleading and cannot form the basis of valid generalizations about women and men. She also claimed that research on gender differences reflects an outdated "trait approach" to psychology and, as a consequence, does "not take into account even aspects of the immediate environment which have been demonstrated to influence behavior" (1979, p. 124).

In agreement with these critics, it must be acknowledged that gender-difference research, like other psychological research, is vulnerable to bias because of the many decisions that researchers make in designing experimental settings and choosing stimulus materials. As Sherif noted, "The test of 'truth' in any specific social situation is hazardous in that researchers' bias (pro or con) can enter at any step: in defining the task or test, in setting up the situation, in selecting the particular behaviors that are to be recorded and assessed" (1979, p. 123). Because decisions about how to conduct research are often not regulated by explicit rules but are loosely guided by traditions and intuitions, researchers' own attitudes and beliefs are likely to influence many of their choices.

Gender-difference research may be particularly vulnerable to some biases because researchers, as carriers of their society's culture, tend to have an elaborated set of beliefs about the nature of women and men. As Sherif and other critics have claimed, investigators' assumptions about gender and about the nature of research affect their choices of settings, tasks, and stimulus materials. As Gilligan (1982) has argued in relation to research on moral development, researchers' choices may have favored the interests, competence, and world view of men, with the result that the gender differences that are documented in research often tend to reflect unfavorably on women. Indeed, Bernard stated that scientists' demonstrations of gender differences have acted as "battle weapons against women" by portraying them as inferior and justifying their low status (1976, p. 13). Similarly, Shields (1975) maintained that early research on differences between women and men largely served to justify men's dominant status in society.

These critiques of gender-differences research should be examined with care. Sherif, Bernard, Shields, Parlee, and many other social scientists (e.g., Block, 1976; Grady, 1981; Kaplan & Sedney, 1980; Mednick, 1978; Vaughter, 1976) writing in the context of the new feminist critical scholarship of the 1970s, mounted a noteworthy challenge to the study of gender differences. They believed that "sex-differences" research was part of the traditional and out-dated scholarship that needed to be swept aside or, at the least, revised substantially. They maintained that gender-difference research had very serious conceptual and methodological shortcomings and that its findings should not be given much weight as a basis of knowledge about gender.

Acceptance of this negative assessment of gender-differences research could have serious scientific consequences. It would encourage scholars to discard the efforts of generations of researchers who have collectively amassed a large quantity of data. Much of this data was recorded in quantitative form and gathered with increasingly more sophisticated efforts to attain precision in measurement and freedom from many kinds of methodological biases and artifacts.

The political consequences of discrediting gender-difference findings might also be substantial, although the nature of these consequences would depend on the social climate. As scholars analyzing the history of gender-difference research have noted (e.g., Rosenberg, 1982; Shields, 1975, 1982), at a relatively early point in the scientific study of gender differences, some researchers approached their endeavor from essentially a feminist standpoint. Female researchers such as Helen Bradford Thompson (1903) and Leta Stetter Hollingsworth (1914) were notably successful in demonstrating that female and male behavior is not extremely different. Yet because of the attitudes and beliefs that scientists and other people held about women, these researchers were not particularly successful in overturning established scientific beliefs in substantial psychological gender differences, particularly belief in women's intellectual inferiority. The notion that women are intellectually inferior had especially important political consequences: It once formed a basis for widespread opposition to admitting women students to universities as well as for other forms of gender inequality (see Rosenberg, 1982).

Although the view of Bernard (1976), Shields (1975), and other writers that the findings of gender-difference research have helped prolong women's inferior status may be generally accurate for much of the period prior to the 1970s, this view is inaccurate for most of the research published subsequent to 1970 as well as for the work of early feminist scholars such as Thompson and Hollingsworth. In recent years, many investigators have reported the absence or small magnitude of gender differences (e.g., Deaux, 1984; Hyde, 1981; Maccoby & Jacklin, 1974), and as a consequence, newer findings concerning gender differences, particularly gender differences in cognitive abilities, are rarely cited today in support of sex-segregated education. In general, because the minimal differences that have been reported by many more investigators in recent years have been accepted much more widely in scientific circles and by the public, gender-difference research has probably furthered the cause of gender equality in the modern period.

Certainly the proper role of gender-difference findings in relation to social policy is an issue of considerable interest and complexity. In any event, should gender-difference research be dismissed on account of the modern feminist critiques, it is likely that decisions about education and the allocation of other resources between women and men would be influenced less and less by the findings of scientific research. Whether research findings ought to have some influence depends largely on their validity. Social policy can usefully be informed by research that presents a correct and objective portrayal of women and men.

As the authors of other chapters in this volume have noted, meta-analysis constitutes a methodological revolution in the study of gender differences because it provides explicit and statistically grounded methods of drawing conclusions from the large numbers of studies that have been conducted in the various areas of gender-difference research. By systematically aggregating the findings of such studies, the practitioners of meta-analysis usually accept the idea that most individual studies meet acceptable standards of validity (although meta-analysts sometimes may assess aspects of studies' validity). Meta-analysts also accept the idea that the collective research endeavor is cumulative and generally valid. Yet unless the recent challenges to gender-difference research can be either discounted or satisfactorily resolved through meta-analytic innovations or other methods, this new scholarship may represent merely a novel and more systematic treatment of findings that are fundamentally flawed.

Before deciding how to regard the feminist critiques of gender-difference research, psychologists ought to examine the claims of bias in terms of the specific validity issues that they imply. In this chapter, these validity issues will be discussed primarily in terms of the concepts of construct validity and external validity (generalizability). This chapter is not intended to defend or apologize for research on psychological gender differences, nor is it intended to reinforce the recent feminist challenges. Instead, the feminist critique is taken seriously, although it has been translated into the more conceptually elaborated vocabulary that has developed in psychology to discuss validity issues. This vocabulary is familiar to most psychologists and is commonly used in methodological discussions in psychology. Then meta-analytic innovations are evaluated as possible methods for assessing the threats to validity noted in the feminist critique.

Threats to the Validity of Gender-Difference Research

In its broadest sense, validity refers to the truth of a proposition: A valid proposition or statement is one that is true, and an invalid proposition or statement is one that is false. Yet because truth and falsity cannot be established in an absolute sense in any scientific field, validity must be understood in terms of what is tentatively or approximately true or false in the context of the knowledge that is currently available. Thus, in judging the validity of propositions about gender differences and similarities, one is attempting to discern their approximate truth or falsity. The claims that gender-difference research in a given domain is biased or misleading can best be interpreted as meaning that the generalizations that this research yields are largely false.

In a recent analysis, Cook and Campbell (1979) considered several types of validity. Their discussion of two of these types, construct validity and external validity, synthesized a number of earlier discussions of validity (e.g., Campbell & Fiske, 1959; Campbell & Stanley, 1966; Cronbach, 1971; Cronbach & Meehl, 1955) and proved helpful in delineating the kinds of bias that have been suggested in the recent critiques of gender-difference research.

Construct Validity

First and foremost, the feminist critique of the gender-difference literature raises the issue of construct validity, which refers to the approximate validity with which generalizations can be made about higher-order constructs on the basis of research operations. The particular aspect of construct validity that is a major focus of the critique is the extent of correspondence between the constructs on which females and males are compared and the operational definitions of these constructs. Researchers desire to draw conclusions about gender differences in terms of general constructs such as empathy and verbal ability rather than in terms of particular behaviors or responses to test items. If the claim is correct that gender-difference research is based on narrow and contrived laboratory research paradigms and on ability and personality tests of limited scope, generalizations about differences between women and men would tend to lack construct validity because of inadequate operationalization of dependent variable constructs. In Cook and Campbell's terms (1979), gender-difference research would suffer from "construct underrepresentation." In contrast, statements about gender differences would be construct valid to the extent that the classes of behaviors they concern have been investigated with operations that adequately represent their conceptual definitions.

The possible dangers of construct underrepresentation can be illustrated in relation to aggression. Aggression is usually defined as behavior that is intended to injure some person or object (e.g., Berkowitz, 1962). To study aggression, investigators have often utilized the Buss paradigm (1963), in which a "teacher" believes that he or she is delivering electric shock to punish a "learner's" errors (see Frodi, Macaulay & Thome, 1977, and chap. 1). If researchers had utilized only this method for eliciting aggression, the construct validity of aggression in the research literature would be in question because this single operational definition would fail to represent the range of behaviors inherent in the aggression construct. In Cook and Campbell's terms, aggression research would suffer from a "mono-operation bias." Indeed, many research areas in psychology have relied mainly on one or relatively few operational definitions and, as a result, probably have decreased construct validity.

Relying on a single method of measuring aggression would be problematic because it would very likely contain irrelevant and extraneous sources of variation—"surplus construct irrelevancies" in the Cook and Campbell terminology. For example, the tendency to deliver relatively strong shock in the Buss paradigm might reflect, not only aggression, but also (a) the subject's desire to be a good teacher, and (b) his or her confidence in dealing with electricity. Men and women might differ in these tendencies as well as in aggressiveness. Therefore, gender differences in the shock-delivery response likely reflect gender differences in a complex package of variables rather than merely in aggressiveness. Consequently, a conclusion about a gender difference in aggression is likely to lack construct validity to the extent that it is based exclusively or primarily on response in the Buss situation. In general, because it is very unlikely that any one operational definition can represent a construct such as aggression in pure form, adequate construct validity is achieved only when investigators have utilized at least several different operations to define a construct (Campbell & Fiske, 1959).

Finally, it should be noted that gender (or sex), the independent variable of interest in gender-difference research, cannot be said to have perfect construct validity. Ordinarily, gender is operationally defined by having research participants indicate whether they are male or female or by having observers in field studies classify research participants based on obvious external indicators of gender. The presence in the population of individuals whose sex chromosomes or gonads are not congruent with their socially identified gender or their personal gender identity raises questions about the sufficiency of any single operational definition, even in relation to conceptual definitions of gender as a socially constructed dichotomy (see Kessler & McKenna, 1978).

External Validity

According to Cook and Campbell (1979, p. 39), external validity is the approximate validity with which conclusions can be drawn about the generalizability of a relationship to and across populations. For example, with respect to generalizations to new populations, consider a researcher who studies gender differences in achievement motivation among tenth graders at a particular high school in Minneapolis. External validity in part concerns the extent to which the findings of such a study can be generalized to the target population about which this researcher desires to draw conclusions (e.g., American adolescents). Generalizability across populations in this example might concern the extent to which a gender difference that is valid for American adolescents generalizes to younger and older people and to people in other cultures.

The external validity problems that are extremely common in psychological research also trouble gender-difference research. As far as generalizability to and across populations of people is concerned, difficulties arise because it is relatively rare that studies have utilized systematic samples of respondents representative of the target populations about which conclusions are drawn. Research is based primarily on accidental, volunteer samples of college students or, somewhat less often, on less haphazard samples of children who participate at school. Yet investigators often draw general conclusions about differences in the attributes of women and men or girls and boys and are thereby generalizing from such samples of respondents to the general adult or child population.

Similar issues arise with respect to the settings and occasions utilized in research. Settings are commonly the psychological laboratory in research on social behavior and structured test situations in research on personality and abilities. Occasions are most commonly single encounters with strangers or infrequently administered tests. Yet investigators usually desire to generalize to behaviors and abilities manifested in a wide range of natural settings on a variety of types of occasions. The use of limited samples of settings and occasions in research makes it difficult to ensure that conclusions about gender differences are externally valid.

The Validity of Meta-analytic Generalizations about Gender Differences

Meta-analysis and Construct Validity

As a general rule, the construct validity of a gender-difference finding that was established through a meta-analytic aggregation of studies is greater than that of a finding established in a single study. This superiority stems from the derivation of the meta-analytic generalization from a set of studies, which most often have utilized differing operational definitions of the dependent variable of interest. Ideally, differing operationalizations of a variable are contaminated by quite different irrelevant sources of variation. Consequently, when findings are aggregated, the extraneous and nongeneralizable aspects of these operational definitions tend to cancel one another, if they are not widely shared across the studies. Therefore, meta-analytic conclusions about gender differences potentially have more satisfactory construct validity than conclusions based on a single operationalization.

It is only in the ideal case, however, that all irrelevant or extraneous determinants of the outcomes of individual studies would cancel one another when studies are aggregated. When a substantial proportion of studies share a particular extraneous feature that affects study outcomes, the sum of the individual study biases would not be zero (Cook & Leviton, 1980). For example, if it were true in studies of gender differences that the content of most stimulus materials tends to be more interesting or familiar to men than to women, aggregating across studies would not remove this bias. The conclusion that gender affects the behavioral tendency or trait of interest could be invalid even in the context of the stimulus materials that were used in the research because they would constitute a biased sample of the stimulus materials relevant to defining the construct supposedly affected by gender. In other words, the resulting conclusion about a gender difference would probably be invalid to some extent because of "construct underrepresentation" of the dependent variable and the associated "surplus construct irrelevancy." As a consequence, gender differences in response to the biased sample of stimulus materials could reflect a true gender difference in the attribute under investigation or differential interest in or familiarity with the stimulus materials (or both the true gender difference and the differential interest/familiarity factor).

As already noted, one of the major claims by critics of gender-difference research is that studies in this area do tend to share various extraneous features that bias study outcomes. For example, several writers have claimed that in the social influence literature, the content of the influence inductions typical of past experiments is more compatible with men's than women's expertise and interests (e.g., Baron & Byrne, 1977; Eagly, 1978; Jones, Hendrick & Epstein, 1979). As discussed later in this chapter, the demonstrated tendency for women to be more easily influenced than men was ascribed to a tendency for people to be influenced by materials unfamiliar or uninteresting to their own sex (and not to a true difference in how readily women and men are influenced).

A possible threat to construct validity has also been discussed in relation to research on gender differences in cognitive abilities. Dwyer (1979) noted that items in tests of mathematical ability tend to be set in contexts that are more familiar to males than females and therefore favor strong performance by males. According to this criticism, the typical test of mathematical ability underrepresents the construct of mathematical ability and is contaminated by an irrelevant variable that may account for the observed gender difference.

Dwyer also noted that, in contrast, on verbal tests, on which females have usually performed better than males, test developers have typically included items set in contexts more familiar to males than females, such as items with science content. This effort to "balance" potential sex bias in verbal tests that favor females, when coupled with the omission of a comparable effort to balance mathematical tests that favor males, may reflect an implicit sexism on the part of test developers.

Meta-analysis and External Validity

The external validity of meta-analytic conclusions about gender differences also should usually be greater than that of conclusions based on single studies. This superior external validity arises from the fact that the samples of persons, settings, and occasions on which these conclusions are based are considerably broader than those of a single study. Thus a single study of gender differences in verbal ability may be based on a sample of California college students, whereas a meta-analysis of gender differences in verbal ability would include samples of respondents from varying locations, of varying ages, socioeconomic statuses, and the like. Although the total sample of respondents included in the meta-analysis may not be fully representative of the population to which investigators wish to generalize, it is at least considerably wider than that of typical single studies. Yet serious lack of representativeness, which could occur, for example, with extreme reliance on college-student samples, would compromise the external validity of meta-analytic findings.

Similar points can be made about the settings and occasions of studies on which meta-analytic conclusions are based. Single studies have one or few settings and one or few occasions, whereas the set of studies synthesized in a meta-analytic review generally represents a large variety of settings and occasions. Whether these settings and occasions constitute a biased or representative sample of those that occur in daily life is an important question. Nevertheless, they constitute a broader sample than single studies and therefore would typically allow conclusions that are more externally valid.

Designing Meta-analyses to Address Concerns about the Possible Invalidity of Gender-Difference Research

The issues of whether gender-difference research in a given domain has adequate construct validity and whether the findings are generalizable are extremely broad. In any one meta-analysis, it would not be possible to address all aspects of these validity issues. Yet in any research area, there are usually particular variants of these broad validity issues that have been raised or that should be raised, in view of the types of studies that have been conducted. Within a meta-analysis, it is often possible for a reviewer to incorporate explicit tests of specific hypotheses about invalidity as well as to demonstrate sensitivity to the broader implications of the construct and external validity issues. In a well-designed meta-analysis, an investigator can take some important steps toward assessing the extent to which existing gender-difference findings provide valid descriptions of human behavior.

Classifying Studies by Attributes Relevant to Construct
and External Validity

To evaluate whether an aspect of behavior has been examined with adequate construct validity, a reviewer should examine the extent of correspondence between the construct in question and its operational definitions. A given construct, such as spatial ability, has been operationally defined in terms of behaviors elicited by certain stimuli, such as paper-and-pencil and other types of tests (see chap. 4). In general terms, the reviewer should examine abstract definitions of the construct in question (e.g., spatial ability) and then evaluate whether the operations that have been used to define this construct represent it adequately. To ensure breadth in the review, preferably more than one conceptual definition would be considered. A wide variety of operational definitions, if they are available, would be evaluated (see Glass, McGaw & Smith, 1981), although clearly faulty operationalizations should be excluded (Wortman, 1983).

As a preliminary approach, a researcher might attempt to speak to the construct validity issued by cataloging the ways in which the construct of interest has been operationally defined. Verbal ability, for example, has been operationally defined in the research literature in terms of certain tests. The wider the variety of tests and the more completely and purely they represent the construct of verbal skills, the greater would be the construct validity of any meta-analytic generalization about gender differences in verbal ability. Therefore, a reviewer can usefully catalog the operational definitions that have been employed, present a table with frequency distributions of these various types of operational definitions, and evaluate the extent to which these definitions are representative of the construct of interest.

The classification of studies with respect to their attributes is also important in relation to possible threats to external validity. To evaluate external validity, the meta-analyst should examine the distributions of persons, settings, and times utilized in the research literature and relate these distributions to the target populations of persons, settings, and times to which investigators have generalized. For example, with respect to persons, investigators usually desire to generalize to all women and men or possibly to female and males in a particular age range or in a particular culture. If the types of persons utilized in the research literature are considerably narrower than this target population, adequate external validity is not assured. In fact, classification of the types of subjects used in the research literature very commonly reveals a large proportion of college-student samples. Settings may be primarily research laboratories, and occasions primarily single-occasion interactions with strangers or structured stimulus materials. Should coding of the available studies reveal such skewed distributions of persons, settings, or occasions, the possibility of external invalidity from these sources should be evaluated by the meta-analyst.

Although it would often be possible to code studies in a relatively objective way to describe their attributes, sometimes objective coding cannot easily be achieved. For example, in gender-difference meta-analyses, it is often important to determine whether stimulus materials are "sex typed" in the sense of being more familiar to or liked by one sex rather than the other. The reviewer's own classification of the stimulus materials may lack adequate reliability (Stock, et al., 1982). Under such circumstances, it is wise to increase reliability by utilizing a panel of judges who rate the stimulus materials on relevant attributes. Sometimes sex-typing scores can be constructed from the differences between male and female judges' ratings of stimuli (e.g., Eagly & Carli, 1981).

Examination of the operational definitions of constructs and of the subjects, settings, and occasions used in research studies will invariably reveal failures to represent constructs adequately and to sample subjects, settings, and occasions in a manner representative of natural settings. As a collective enterprise carried out by many investigators, research in a given area has never been designed to systematically sample natural settings in an ecologically valid manner. Furthermore, it is typical that a small number of research paradigms become exceedingly popular because they enable investigators to test certain theories or to generate provocative findings. As a consequence, research, like other human endeavors, has certain faddish aspects, and research paradigms of a particular type often become extremely popular for a period of years. This concentration on a few research paradigms invariably raises validity issues for the individual who desires to present general conclusions based on an integrative review.

Testing for Interactions between Study Attributes and Subject Sex

Reviewers should not necessarily become discouraged if they encounter skewed distributions of research paradigms and of subjects, settings, and occasions. Under many circumstances, these limitations are not consequential because, even though the effect of interest varies in magnitude across studies, it can be shown to be relatively unaffected by variation in these aspects of research (see Glass, McGaw & Smith, 1981, 158–63). Less commonly (see, chap. 5), the findings in a domain are sufficiently homogeneous that the gender-difference effects from the studies (or a subgroup of the studies) can be assumed to be sampled from the same population, despite variation between studies in designs, subject populations, and settings (see Hedges, 1982a).

For example, if a particular behavior, such as aggression, has been studied primarily in laboratory settings with college-student subjects, the reviewer shuld evaluate whether reliance on this type of setting and this class of respondents has compromised the validity of gender-difference findings. This question might first be addressed by examining the homogeneity of the aggression findings (Hedges, 1982a). If the gender differences are homogeneous, despite some variation in the studies' settings and subject populations, these attributes of studies have little impact on study outcomes. Assuming that the hypothesis of homogeneity is rejected, the relation between these attributes of the studies and their gender-difference outcomes should be examined empirically. Described in analysis-of-variance terminology, sex x study-attribute interactions would be examined (see Light & Pillemer, 1984, pp. 156–159). Within a meta-analysis, such relations can often be evaluated via Hedges's tests (1982a) of categorical models or the similar procedures proposed by Rosenthal and Rubin (1982). If study attributes are continuous rather than categorical, Hedges's continuous model procedures (1982b) can be utilized. In general, studies would be classified by (or measured on) the attribute in question, and the effect of the attribute on the gender-difference finding would be evaluated on a between-study basis. In addition, the investigator should search for any within-study tests of the impact of the attribute on the gender difference (see Green & Hall, 1984).

Some examples may clarify this suggested examination of sex x study-attribute interactions. Consider the quite common situation in psychological research that most studies have been conducted in laboratory settings, although some studies have been conducted in the field. Under such circumstances, the relation between settings (laboratory vs. field) and the size of the gender difference should be examined. If the gender difference is unrelated to the setting of the research, it is unlikely that the preponderance of laboratory settings has compromised the external validity of the findings.

Similarly, if most studies were conducted with college-student subjects but some were conducted with respondents older and younger than college students, the gender-difference effect of interest can be related to respondents' age. If no relation is demonstrated, then it is unlikely that the concentration on college students has damaged the external validity of the findings. However, if the effect is significant only among college students, its external validity should be questioned.

Studies can also be classified by research paradigm in order to address the threat to construct validity that stems from the popularity of relatively few operational definitions. If type of research paradigm has no impact on the size of gender differences, then at least this aspect of threats to construct validity is not likely to be consequential in relation to the gender difference in question. However, if the finding occurs only in certain research paradigms (perhaps those believed or demonstrated to be "sex typed" in some sense), the overall gender effect produced by the meta-analysis may indeed be construct invalid.

In some meta-analyses, it may not be possible to relate some aspects of research paradigms or certain characteristics of the subjects, settings, and occasions to the findings of interest because the available studies have entirely (or almost entirely) omitted certain variants (see Light & Pillemer, 1984, p. 41). For example, social behaviors such as social influence (e.g., Eagly & Carli, 1981) and nonverbal decoding (e.g., Hall, 1978) have been studied almost exclusively in the context of either short-term interactions with strangers or structured exposures to stimulus materials such as videotaped presentations. Therefore, one cannot examine whether gender differences in these behaviors vary depending on the depth or length of acquaintance with other people, because close and long-term relationships have rarely been examined. Because gender differences in these social behaviors may well depend on these aspects of relationships, this source of potential invalidity cannot be discounted within the context of meta-analyses on these particular behaviors. Yet other social behaviors, such as touching (Stier & Hall, 1984), have been studied in a variety of role relationships.

In summary, some threats to validity can be examined in a meta-analysis by coding studies on attributes that are relevant to invalidity or by obtaining judgments of the status of studies on these attributes. The distribution of the studies in terms of these attributes can be usefully evaluated. More importantly, the relation of these study attributes to the gender-difference effect of interest should be examined. In the absence of a significant relation between these attributes and the effect, even a very skewed distribution of study attributes is probably of little consequence in relation to validity. Given a significant relation between a study attribute and a gender-difference effect, interpretation should focus on this sex x study-attribute interaction. It might be noted that this focus, which is common in meta-analytic studies, runs counter to Parlee's claim (1979) that gender-difference research reflects a trait approach to psychology and ignores the impact of situational variables.

Most certainly reviewers of gender-difference literature should search for possible construct and external invalidity when a particular threat to construct or external validity has already been proposed by critics of gender-difference research. Ordinarily, such a threat can be framed as a hypothesis and tested within a meta-analysis in a straightforward way. Yet a reviewer sensitive to validity issues will no doubt generate additional hypotheses concerning threats to validity and incorporate tests of these hypotheses in the design of meta-analyses.

Illustrations of Meta-analytic Tests of the Validity of Gender-Difference Research

The use of meta-analytic techniques for examining possible invalidity in gender-difference research will be illustrated briefly by describing a few aspects of Eagly and Carli's meta-analysis (1981) of gender differences in how easily people are influenced and Eagly and Crowley's meta-analysis (in press) of gender differences in helping behavior.

Social Influence Meta-analysis

In a meta-analysis of gender differences in social influence, Eagly and Carli (1981) were concerned about several aspects of validity, in particular about a possible threat to construct validity from influence inductions that disproportionately included masculine content. This meta-analysis, which examined a sample of 148 persuasion and conformity studies that had reported a test for gender difference, documented a relatively small overall tendency for women to be more easily influenced than men (see chap. 8).

It would be incautious to conclude that women are more influenceable than men merely on the basis of a mean gender-difference effect that differed significantly from zero (no effect). Even though drawing a conclusion on the basis of a large number of studies is probably substantially more valid than drawing conclusions on the basis of a single study or a small set of studies, numerous questions can be raised about the validity of the conclusion that women are more easily influenced than men.

A criticism had already gained widespread acceptance prior to the planning of the Eagly and Carli review. This criticism was based in part on conformity research by Sistrunk and McDavid (1971) showing that women are easily influenced on masculine topics and men on feminine topics. According to this criticism, the influence inductions used in conformity and persuasion experiments lack adequate construct validity because they favored the interests and expertise of men more often than women. By this logic, women appeared to be more readily influenced than men in the typical study merely because they were less interested in and informed about the particular topics on which the researchers had chosen to attempt to exert influence.

This biased stimulus-material artifact constitutes a specific hypothesis about a threat to construct validity. In designing a meta-analytic test of the hypothesis, Eagly and Carli rejected the method of obtaining ratings (either their own or expert judges') of how sex typed the stimulus materials were in the various studies. Such a method would be faulty because, in an era of intense concern about sex typing, even expert judges might have difficulty in making valid judgments. Therefore, Eagly and Carli had a large group of undergraduate students rate each of the topics employed in the persuasion experiments in the sample according to how interested and knowledgeable they considered themselves. From these ratings, they calculated sex-typing scores by subtracting the mean of females' judgments from the mean of males' judgments for each topic. For example, on the topic "characteristics of the game of football," men reported themselves considerably more interested and knowledgeable than women reported themselves. On the topic "benefits and problems of day-care centers," women reported themselves considerably more interested and knowledgeable than men reported themselves. These gender-difference scores constituted measures of the degree to which the topics used in the persuasion studies were sex typed. Similar measures could not be generated for conformity studies because information on topics was very often incomplete.

On a correlational basis, there was a small tendency for greater persuasibility in the female direction to be associated with more masculine topics on the basis of both the interest and knowledge ratings. However, sex-typed topics did not account for the overall tendency for women to be more persuasible than men because, summed over all of the topics used in the persuasion studies, the mean difference in males' and females' ratings of the topics was very small and in fact tended slightly to favor the interests of women. In other words, the meta-analysis obtained no support for the claim that researchers selected a disproportionate number of male-oriented topics. Thus an explicit meta-analytic test did not support the hypothesis that the construct validity of the conclusion that women are more easily influenced than men is compromised by a preponderance of masculine stimulus materials in the research. For further discussion of the determinants of the magnitude of the gender differences in this sampling of studies, see chapter 8.

Helping Behavior Meta-analysis

Eagly and Crowley (in press) implemented similar methods in a meta-analysis of gender differences in helping behavior. The sample consisted of 172 studies, which were predominantly field experiments. Although the reported gender differences proved to be very heterogeneous, the meta-analysis documented a small overall tendency for men to be more helpful than women.

As in the social influence meta-analysis, it is risky to conclude on the basis of a mean effect that differs significantly from zero that there is a true gender difference. Numerous questions can be raised about threats to validity. For example, one possible threat to construct validity is a variant of the criticism of biased stimulus materials considered in relation to social influence. According to this argument, the helping literature, because it has focused on helping that occurs in encounters with strangers, contains a disproportionate number of situations that elicit the chivalrous acts and heroic interventions that may be favored by men. Because the literature has not focused on helping that occurs in close or long-term relationships, it may have under-represented the acts of kindness and service to others that may be favored by women. Furthermore, the possibility should be considered that the helping acts examined in studies have disproportionately required specific skills and interests that are "masculine" (e.g., changing a flat tire).

Several approaches were utilized to examine various classes of threats to validity. One of these approaches involved having undergraduate respondents rate each of the helping behaviors employed in the studies used in the meta-analysis according to (a) how competent the respondent would be to provide the help, (b) how comfortable the respondent would feel in providing the help, and (c) how much danger the respondent would probably face if he or she provided the help. From these ratings, sex-typing scores were calculated by subtracting the mean of the female respondents' judgments from the mean of the male respondents' judgments for each behavior and dividing by the standard deviation. On a correlational basis, the tendency for men to engage in a helping behavior more often than women in the studies was significantly associated with the tendencies for the male (vs. female) respondents to rate themselves as (a) more competent, (b) more comfortable, and (c) facing less danger in relation to the behavior.

To evaluate the potential threats to validity posed by these demonstrated effects of gender differences in competence, comfort, and danger, it is relevant to know whether the helping literature as a whole has tended to utilize situations in which one sex or the other feels particularly competent, comfortable, or vulnerable. Thus, to determine whether helping behaviors that are sex typed have been disproportionately examined, the mean gender differences in the respondents' ratings of competence, comfort, and vulnerability to danger were summed over the entire sample of helping behaviors used in the studies. The aggregate competence and comfort scores were very close to the zero difference that indicated no gender difference in the ratings, but women reported that they would face significantly more danger from helping than men reported. It is possible, then, that the overall tendency for men to be somewhat more helpful than women in the studies that are available may be at least in part due to the tendency for the literature to have included a disproportionate number of situations in which women feel that helping might be dangerous to them and in which men feel less threatened.

Whether the tendency for women to feel more threatened than men by the helping opportunities that have been used in research actually constitutes a bias or artifact raises the external validity issue of the representativeness of these helping behaviors relative to the natural settings to which researchers wish to generalize. Although there is no simple answer to this question in terms of the information at hand, it is striking that the entire social psychological literature on helping behavior is concerned with helping in the context of short-term interactions with strangers. Women's helping may be displayed primarily in close or long-term relationships (within the family, for example). Helping in such contexts is unlikely to be threatening to women, whereas helping in the context of interactions with strangers appears often to pose some potential danger to women. Therefore, it is likely that there are serious threats to both the construct validity and the external validity of any conclusion that men are generally more helpful than women.

Conclusion

Because of the limited scope of this chapter, it does not offer any generalizations about the overall validity of gender-difference research. Rather, it proposes meta-analytic methods for examining threats to the validity of this research. The intent of this presentation is to sensitize reviewers of gender-difference studies to validity questions and to encourage straightforward tests of hypotheses about validity. By examining validity issues, meta-analysts can address, not only the specific challenges that have been directed toward gender-difference research, but also some of the well-known criticisms of meta-analysis as consisting merely of mindless aggregation of findings (e.g., Eysenck, 1978).

The feminist critiques of gender-difference research have raised important questions. Some of the statements contained in these critiques are extravagant and constitute unwarranted generalizations about the research. For example, some areas of research on gender differences in social behavior are inconsistent with both (a) Sherif's claim (1979) that gender-difference research is based on narrow laboratory paradigms, and (b) Parlee's claim (1979) that gender-difference research reflects a "trait approach" that neglects the impact of situational variables. Yet underlying these and other criticisms are the general issues of serious threats to construct validity and external validity. These issues should not be ignored by scholars who continue to investigate psychological gender differences. If the new meta-analytic scholarship on gender differences is to deserve attention as a basis for knowledge about gender, the now well-known feminist critiques of this research area will have to be addressed. They should be addressed in terms of the increasingly more sophisticated methods provided within the developing technology of meta-analysis.

References

Baron, R. A., & Byrne, D. (1977). *Social psychology: Understanding human interaction* (2nd ed.). Boston: Allyn & Bacon.

Berkowitz, L. (1962). *Aggression: A social psychological analysis*. New York: McGraw-Hill.

Bernard, J. (1976). *Sex differences: An overview* (Module 26). New York: MSS Modular Publications.

Block, J. H. (1976). Issues, problems, and pitfalls in assessing sex differences: A critical review of *The Psychology of Sex Differences*. *Merrill-Palmer Quarterly, 22,* 283–308.

Buss, A. H. (1963). Physical aggression in relation to different frustrations. *Journal of Abnormal and Social Psychology, 67,* 1–7.

Campbell, D. T., & Fiske, D. W. (1959). Convergent and discriminant validation by the multitrait-multimethod matrix. *Psychological Bulletin, 56,* 81–105.

Campbell, D. T., & Stanley, J. C. (1966). *Experimental and quasi-experimental research designs.* Chicago: Rand McNally.

Cook, T. D., & Campbell, D. T. (1979). *Quasi-experimentation: Design and analysis issues for field settings.* Chicago: Rand McNally.

Cook, T. D., & Leviton, L. C. (1980). Reviewing the literature: A comparison of traditional methods with meta-analysis. *Journal of Personality, 48,* 449–472.

Cronbach, L. J. (1971). Test validation. In R. L. Thorndike (ed.), *Educational measurement* (2nd ed.). Washington, DC: American Council on Education.

Cronbach, L. J., & Meehl, P. E. (1955). Construct validity in psychological tests. *Psychological Bulletin, 52,* 281–302.

Deaux, K. K. (1984). From individual differences to social categories: Analysis of a decade's research on gender. *American Psychologist, 39,* 105–116.

Dwyer, C. A. (1979). The role of tests and their construction in producing apparent sex-related differences. In M. A. Wittig & A. C. Petersen (eds.), *Sex-related differences in cognitive functioning: Developmental issues.* New York: Academic Press.

Eagly, A. H. (1978). Sex differences in influenceability. *Psychological Bulletin, 85,* 86–116.

Eagly, A. H., & Carli, L. L. (1981). Sex of researchers and sex-typed communications as determinants of sex differences in influenceability: A meta-analysis of social influence studies. *Psychological Bulletin, 90,* 1–20.

Eagly, A. H., & Crowley, M. (in press). Gender and helping behavior: A meta-analytic review of the social psychological literature. *Psychological Bulletin.*

Eysenck, H. J. (1978). An exercise in mega-silliness. *American Psychologist, 33,* 517.

Frodi, A., Macaulay, J., & Thome, P. R. (1977). Are women always less aggressive than men? A review of the experimental literature. *Psychological Bulletin, 84,* 634–660.

Gilligan, C. (1982). *In a different voice: Psychological theory and women's development.* Cambridge: Harvard University Press.

Glass, G. V., McGaw, B., & Smith, M. L. (1981). *Meta-analysis in social research.* Beverly Hills: Sage.

Grady, K. E. (1981). Sex bias in research design. *Psychology of Women Quarterly, 5,* 628–636.

Green, B. F., & Hall, J. A. (1984). Quantitative methods for literature reviews. *Annual Review of Psychology, 35,* 37–53.

Hall, J. A. (1978). Gender effects in decoding nonverbal cues. *Psychological Bulletin, 85,* 845–875.

Hedges, L. V. (1982a). Fitting categorical models to effect sizes from a series of experiments. *Journal of Educational Statistics, 7,* 119–137.

Hedges, L. V. (1982b). Fitting continuous models to effect size data. *Journal of Educational Statistics, 7,* 245-270.

Hollingsworth, L. S. (1914). Variability as related to sex differences in achievement. *American Journal of Sociology, 19,* 510-530.

Hyde, J. S. (1981). How large are cognitive gender differences? A meta-analysis using ω^2 and *d*. *American Psychologist, 36,* 892-901.

Jones, R. A., Hendrick, C., & Epstein, Y. M. (1979). *Introduction to social psychology.* Sunderland, Mass.: Sinauer Associates.

Kaplan, A. G., & Sedney, M. A. (1980). *Psychology and sex roles: An androgynous perspective.* Boston: Little, Brown.

Kessler, S. J., & McKenna, W. (1978). *Gender: An ethnomethodological approach.* New York: Wiley.

Light, R. J., & Pillemer, D. B. (1984). *Summing up: The science of reviewing research.* Cambridge: Harvard University Press.

Maccoby, E. E., & Jacklin, C. N. (1974). *The psychology of sex differences.* Stanford: Stanford University Press.

Mednick, M. T. S. (1978). Psychology of women: Research issues and trends. *Annals of the New York Academy of Sciences, 309,* 77-92.

Parlee, M. R. (1979). Psychology and women. *Signs: Journal of Women in Culture and Society, 5,* 121-133.

Rosenberg, R. (1982). *Beyond separate spheres: Intellectual roots of modern feminism.* New Haven: Yale University Press.

Rosenthal, R., & Rubin, D. B. (1982). Comparing effect sizes of independent studies. *Psychological Bulletin, 92,* 500-504.

Sherif, C. W. (1979). Bias in psychology. In J. A. Sherman & E. T. Beck (eds.), *The prism of sex: Essays in the sociology of knowledge.* Madison: University of Wisconsin Press.

Shields, S. A. (1975). Functionalism, Darwinism, and the psychology of women: A study in social myth. *American Psychologist, 30,* 739-754.

Shields, S. A. (1982). The variability hypothesis: The history of a biological model of sex differences in intelligence. *Signs: Journal of Women in Culture and Society, 7,* 769-797.

Sistrunk, F., & McDavid, J. W. (1971). Sex variable in conformity behavior. *Journal of Personality and Social Psychology, 17,* 200-207.

Stier, D. S., & Hall, J. A. (1984). Gender differences in touch: An empirical and theoretical review. *Journal of Personality and Social Psychology, 47,* 440-459.

Stock, W. A., Okun, M. A., Haring, M. J., Miller, W., Kinney, C., & Ceurvorst, R. W. (1982). Rigor in data synthesis: A case study of reliability in meta-analysis. *Educational Researcher, 11,* 10-20.

Thompson, H. B. (1903). *The mental traits of sex.* Chicago: University of Chicago Press.

Vaughter, R. M. (1976). Review essay: Psychology. *Signs: Journal of Women in Culture and Society, 2,* 120-146.

Wortman, P. M. (1983). Evaluation research: A methodological perspective. *Annual Review of Psychology, 34,* 223-260.

Influence Again: An Examination of Reviews and Studies of Gender Differences in Social Influence

Betsy Jane Becker

Abstract

In this chapter, I first examine four recent quantitative reviews of the literature on gender differences in social influence. I criticize their findings in light of the summaries used in each, taking special note of differences in the study conclusions. I then reanalyze results from 78 studies of gender differences in social influence that provide sufficient information for calculation of an estimate of the size of the gender difference.

My results differ from those of the earlier reviews in that the size of the gender difference is related to characteristics of the subjects and the outcome measure used. However, outcome measure characteristics were confounded with other study features so that single simple explanations could not be adopted.

For thirty or more years, researchers have studied factors that moderate social influence situations. One much-investigated aspect of the social influence situation is the sex of those being influenced. Some early studies suggested that women were more easily influenced than men, upholding the popular stereotype of women as being the more compliant and even gullible sex (see, e.g., Janis & Field, 1959; Tuddenham, 1958).

Maccoby and Jacklin (1974) did the first quantitative review of the literature on gender differences in influenceability, examining 47 studies. Several other investigators have reviewed studies of gender differences in social influence since Maccoby and Jacklin. These authors have augmented the collection of studies and have also used increasingly sophisticated quantitative techniques in their reviews.

In this chapter, I examine these reviews and some of the original studies of social influence, this time using more informative and rigorous statistical methods for analyzing variability in study outcomes. I compare the methodologies and the conclusions of the past reviews to my own. Some new insights into both gender differences in influenceability and quantitative research synthesis techniques are gained (see app. E).

I describe in the first section the studies of social influence, and in the second section, I describe the summary methods used in past reviews, clarifying their strengths and weaknesses. In the third section, I examine four major reviews of the literature on gender differences in social influence, presenting the conclusions of each review, qualified by an analysis of the methods used to derive the conclusions. The fourth and fifth sections present the methodology I use in reexamining some of the original studies of social influence and the results of the reanalysis. Finally, I discuss my results and their relationship to results of earlier reviews.

Studying Social Influence

Studies of many kinds of social influence are found in the social psychology literature. They range from simple examinations of attitude change (Kirkpatrick, 1936) to elaborate experiments like Milgram's classic obedience study of willingness to administer electric shocks to other subjects (1963). I examine two of the many social influence paradigms: the studies of persuasion and of conformity. Other prominent designs such as role playing, spontaneous imitation, and suggestibility research are not considered.

Persuasion and conformity studies provide a good subject for a critical examination of quantitative reviewing methods because they exhibit both good and bad features common to many research areas. Because the studies are numerous and because their results are not obviously consistent, biases associated with narrative review techniques (e.g., selective sampling and interpretation) are potentially serious. On the other hand, this inconsistency of results provides an opportunity to illustrate the use of quantitative review strategies for examining variability in the outcomes of studies. The many aspects of the social influence situation that have been investigated (i.e., other than sex of subjects) suggest plausible explanations of this variability in outcomes.

Another positive feature of this research area is that the studies of gender differences in persuasion and conformity should not be affected much by publication bias (the tendency not to publish results that are statistically insignificant). Because other features of the social influence setting have often been of primary research interest, reports of gender differences have been incidental to the main thrust of the research. The sex of the subject was sometimes included as a blocking factor to reduce between-subject variability. Results for the sex factor thus were published whether significant or not because of their minor role. (There are still many studies, however, that did not include the sex factor in the study design.)

The social influence studies are not totally free of the problem of reporting bias, the tendency not to report exact values of sample statistics that represent statistically insignificant effects in a published report. Reporting bias is a serious problem in this literature (as is shown below) and can influence the outcomes of a quantitative review.

Studies of Persuasion and Conformity

The important characteristics of persuasion and conformity research are now presented. Eagly (1978) described this research more fully.

In both persuasion studies and conformity studies, subjects are "informed" that an agent or source (which may be either a group or an individual) holds a particular position—often an opinion or belief. However, the two kinds of studies differ in the ways that the subjects are influenced.

Persuasion Studies

In persuasion studies, an argument or series of arguments supporting the agent's position is presented. Features of the agent, the agent's argument, and how they both interact with the sex of the subject have been studied in detail.

One commonly studied factor is the sex of the agent presenting the persuasive arguments. Burgoon, Jones, and Stewart (1975) and Morelock (1980) included this factor in their study designs. Using an analysis of covariance design, Burgoon and his colleagues found significantly different degrees of conformity for male and female subjects (females showed greater attitude changes), but found no interaction of sex of the agent with sex of the subject. Morelock, on the other hand, did find a significant two-way interaction, such that a persuasive message attributed to same-sex agents caused greater attitude change than a message from agents of the opposite sex.

Morelock also investigated the importance of the sex-role relevance of the topic of the persuasive argument in the influence situation. Again, she found an interaction with the sex of the subject, such that subjects showed greater attitude change on items classified as being more relevant to the opposite sex.

Typically, the dependent measure in the persuasion study is a scale that measures the subject's position with reference to the presented argument (an opinion scale). For example, when the persuasion message argued for the usefulness of tetanus inoculation, the outcome was a scale concerning intent to obtain inoculation (Leventhal, Jones & Trembly, 1966). Pretest-posttest designs have been used in persuasion studies to assess attitude change (e.g., Janis & Field, 1959; Scheidel, 1963).

Conformity Studies

In conformity studies, no argument is presented, but rather confederates (real or fictitious) of the experimenter act as agents and, by their responses, support a particular position (to which the subject may conform). The position is typically an unusual attitude or an incorrect response to a task. The extent of each subject's deviation from correct, average, or his or her own prior opinion or responses to the task is taken as a measure of conformity.

Many conformity studies use what Eagly (1978) has called the "group pressure paradigm." Some group pressure studies involve face-to-face interaction with people, and others use simulated group situations. The responses of other "subjects" are communicated to each true subject via a visual or auditory presentation. (See Crutchfield, 1955, for a detailed description of the visual-display equipment that has come to be called the "Crutchfield apparatus.")

Asch (1956) originated a very familiar paradigm for group pressure studies. Subjects are typically presented with a perceptual stimulus and are asked to make a judgment about it. For example, one might view a set of three parallel lines of unequal length and then be asked to indicate the shortest line. Attitudinal items, more ambiguous stimuli such as moving dot patterns, and other tasks are also used. Subjects make their responses publicly and believe that they are hearing the responses of other subjects, but the other subjects are in fact confederates of the experimenter. Usually the confederates' responses are planned to differ considerably from those of the true subjects. In the line-length example, all the confederates may state that the middle-length line is the shortest. Typical outcome measures are counts of items on which the subject agrees with the confederates' discrepant responses and numbers of errors made by the subject in attempting to conform.

Many features of the conformity situation and subjects have been studied. Costanzo and Shaw (1966) and Klein (1972) investigated age differences in influenceability, as well as the interaction of sex with age. Both studies found significant age differences but no sex differences and no sex-by-age interactions. Tuddenham, MacBride, & Zahn (1958) examined the role of the sex composition of the group in relation to the gender difference in conformity. They found that across situations, women tended to conform more than men. However, men in same-sex groups conformed more than men in mixed-sex groups, while women conformed more in mixed-sex groups. Other features have also been studied.

Another common design for conformity studies is the "fictitious norm group" situation. In these studies, the position to which subjects may conform (typically, an opinion) is again planned to be discrepant from that expected of each subject. There are usually no confererates or agents present to observe the subject's response or to espouse the preselected position. Instead, the subject's response is made privately and the position is usually indicated in written form on the outcome scale.

The fictitious norm group is the one to which the preselected position is attributed. For example, a response on a rating scale might be labeled "Chosen most often by 200 high school seniors." The fictitious group of high school students is the norm group.

Sistrunk and McDavid (1971) presented the same fictitious responses to two groups of subjects and described them as having been made by either a group of men or a group of women. Though the two-way interaction of sex of the norm group with sex of subject was not significant, the three-way interaction of those two factors with sex-relevance of the items was significant. All subjects tended to be more influenced by opposite-sex than by same-sex norm groups, though the most conformity occurred when women were presented with information about masculine topics by allegedly female norm groups.

Quantitative Research Synthesis Methods

In the research reviews I describe below, several quantitative summary methods are employed. The authors carefully employed the best methods available at the time the reviews were conducted. Since then more rigorous synthesis methods have become available. Before discussing the earlier reviews, I outline and discuss the quantitative summaries used in them.

Vote-counting

Eagly (1978) summarized the studies of persuasibility and conformity with the vote-counting technique. Also Maccoby and Jacklin used this technique informally in their 1974 review. In using this method, one counts the studies that have significant results in each direction (favoring and counter to the hypothesis) and those with nonsignificant results. The outcome (hypothesis favored, no difference, or hypothesis disfavored) receiving a plurality of "votes" or receiving at least some specified "large" proportion of them (e.g., half or more) is considered to be supported. Though this method is intuitively appealing and can be used when few statistics are reported, Hedges and Olkin (1980) have shown that it can be misleading and has especially low power to detect small effects. In fact, the power of the vote-counting procedure tends to zero (rather than one) in many cases, and especially when the number of studies is large.

P-value Summaries

Both Cooper (1979) and Eagly and Carli (1981) used summaries of significance values to comment on the studies of gender differences in conformity.

There are quite a few methods available for summarizing p-values, many of which were outlined by Rosenthal (1978). The methods are attractive because they require few assumptions and use only a significance value to represent each study outcome. Often studies that report insufficient information for calculation of mean differences do report p-values.

Unfortunately, the simplicity of the requirements for use of p-value summaries is accompanied by broadness in the kinds of conclusions that can be based on application of the methods. The null hypothesis tested by these summaries is "All studies are of populations that show no gender difference." The alternative is one-sided: "At least one study is of a population wherein women conform more than men." Thus there are many situations that can lead to rejection of the null hypothesis.

The combined null hypothesis is rejected when at least one study reflects a nonzero population effect. This is not well suited to the reviewer's purpose, which is usually to make an assessment of the strength of support for an effect across all studies. (Becker, 1982, discussed the hypotheses underlying p-value summaries in more detail.)

Both Cooper's and Eagly and Carli's conclusions based on p-value summaries are less conservative than their conclusions based on effect size data. It may be that many of the significant p-value summaries resulted from p-values representing large differences or large studies rather than because of moderate but consistent gender differences.

Effect Size Analyses

In earlier syntheses, reviewers often considered measures of the gender difference, usually effect sizes (standardized mean differences), as "typical" data and applied analyses based on standard normal distribution theory (e.g., t-tests, linear regression). They considered study features in attempting to find patterns among the results of the studies. For example, Eagly and Carli (1981) used correlations to relate effect size outcomes to features like date of publication of the study, as well as t-tests and analysis of covariance to examine variability in the size of the gender difference between groups of studies.

Hedges (1981) has shown the problems inherent in the application of such methods to effect size data. The main flaw is that they require that one make the assumption of homogeneity of residual or error variance for all observations (i.e., studies). Hedges showed that the variance of the effect size is proportional to the size of the sample for which it is calculated. Thus if studies vary in sample size, the variances for their effect sizes will differ accordingly.

Rarely will all of the studies in a review have the same sample size (Becker, 1985). Thus the necessary assumption underlying these most familiar analyses is violated for effect size data. Though analysis of variance (ANOVA) is thought to be robust to violations of the variance-homogeneity assumption, Hedges and I note (see chap. 2) that the consequences for the ANOVA of the kinds of violations most likely to occur in the meta-analysis context have not been investigated. Though there may be rare situations in which the homogeneity of variance assumption would not be violated, new methods proposed by Hedges (1982a, 1982b) have other distinct advantages that make them preferable to the ad hoc effect size analyses previously applied.

Reviews of Persuasion and Conformity

I now discuss four major reviews of the literature on gender and social influence: Cooper (1979); Eagly (1974); Eagly and Carli (1981), and Maccoby and Jacklin (1974). Though there may be others, these four are important because they all used (either formally or informally) quantitative summary techniques. I present the major conclusions of each review, qualified with a critical analysis of the summary methods upon which the conclusions were based.

Maccoby and Jacklin's Review

Maccoby and Jacklin briefly treated studies of persuasion and conformity in their chapter on power relationships in *The Psychology of Sex Differences* (1974). Using mainly a narrative review, they discussed 47 studies of subjects ranging in age from 3 to 21 years. They tabulated features of the studies and also summarized the results of the studies in terms of directions of significant differences.

Maccoby and Jacklin's inferences were based on an overall assessment of the results of the 47 studies—a kind of informal count of significant supporting versus nonsupporting studies. The studies reviewed in their book were selected from a particular set of journals (which they describe) from 1966 through spring 1973 and from lists given in *Psychological Abstracts*. They obtained more sources by inspecting references in the initially identified studies. They included unpublished reports and conference papers as well as published works, though they apparently located no unpublished papers on the topics of persuasion and conformity.

Their summary of the results of these studies led them to believe that in "the relatively impersonal situation that is involved in persuasive communications, neither sex is more suggestible than the other." They noted, however, that "In face-to-face encounters, when an individual must openly disagree with the opinion of others, . . . women somewhat more often conform to others' judgments, but inconsistency of the findings and the frequency of sex similarity are striking" (1974, p. 268).

Maccoby and Jacklin did not identify a common "theme" that clearly distinguished the studies finding a gender difference from those that found none. They called attention to the finding by Sistrunk and McDavid (1971) that conformity seemed to relate to knowledge of the topic for the conformity task (e.g., men conformed more on "feminine" tasks), suggesting that it might be a clue to the nature of the inconsistency of results.

The weakness and vagueness of Maccoby and Jacklin's conclusions is attributable to the fact that they are based on counts of significant findings. Though many of the studies reported nonsignificant gender differences, the magnitudes of those differences cannot be discerned. Additionally, the power of the vote-count procedure tends to zero for series of studies similar in number and size to these studies (Hedges & Olkin, 1980), thus Maccoby and Jacklin were not likely to detect differences simply because they employed this procedure.

Eagly's Review

In an award-winning *Psychological Bulletin* article (1978), Eagly reviewed in greater depth the research on gender differences in persuasion and conformity. Eagly's assessment was also that there were not large differences between the sexes across many kinds of studies.

A major innovative feature of Eagly's review was her consideration of contextual (setting-related) features of social influence studies and their relation to gender differences. She separately examined those studies employing different paradigms (persuasion, group pressure, and other conformity paradigms). She concluded that gender differences in influenceability were neither large nor consistent across paradigms. She reported that most of the differences could have been attributable to sex bias in the experimental tasks (they often concerned topics of little apparent interest to women). For group pressure studies, Eagly found more evidence of gender differences, though she noted that the conformity may have been only superficial (the result of the women agreeing "in order to preserve social harmony" rather than because of a real attitude change).

Though most of Eagly's review was narrative, she employed counts of significant gender differences to make some generalizations. Additionally, she used chi-square tests to assess differences in the percentages of significant differences within and between study paradigms. Eagly's conclusions largely agreed with those of Maccoby and Jacklin, but again, her conclusion that the gender differences were small may have resulted in part from her use of the vote-counting procedure.

Cooper's Review

In one of the earliest demonstrations of more complex meta-analysis methods, Cooper (1979) examined again the studies of social influence. Since his primary goal was to demonstrate the usefulness of quantitative reviewing methods versus the more subjective narrative review techniques traditionally used, Cooper used the same set of 47 studies that were reviewed by Maccoby and Jacklin. He did not add to or update the sample of studies from that earlier review, though he mentioned the possibility of bias in the sample, which included only published studies.

Cooper did eliminate some studies from those collected by Maccoby and Jacklin. He omitted three studies of foreign subjects, three correlational studies, and two studies of behavior under experimental conditions, as well as the 1971 study by Sistrunk and McDavid, which evidenced a sex by conformity-item-type interaction. He dropped this last study because of "its special place in the literature" (Sistrunk and McDavid were among the first to obtain such an interaction). This is the study that Maccoby and Jacklin suggested might give a clue to understanding the inconsistency of findings on the influence gender difference.

In order to compare the narrative and quantitative review methods more directly, Cooper examined the following three results of the summary by Maccoby and Jacklin:

1. Across all studies of social influence, the results are inconsistent and neither sex shows an overall tendency to be more conforming.
2. In face-to-face encounters, women tend to conform somewhat more, but findings are generally inconsistent and the performance of the two sexes is often similar.
3. Studies of persuasion consistently show no gender difference.

As indicators of the influenceability gender difference, Cooper used the effect size, or standardized mean difference (Glass, 1976), and the significance value (p-value). (All reviewers who have examined influenceability gender differences in terms of effect sizes have represented relatively more female influenceability as a positive mean difference.) Cooper used the summary methods advocated by Glass (1976) and those reviewed by Rosenthal (1978).

Using the Stouffer p-value summary to obtain a significant overall probability value for 46 of the 47 studies, Cooper failed to substantiate the first finding of Maccoby and Jacklin. This is not surprising considering the many diverse outcomes for which the Stouffer statistic and other p-value summaries reject the hypothesis of no effect (here, no gender difference) in any study (Becker, 1982). The summaries are meant to reject that hypothesis even if only one study is of a population with a true difference.

Cooper used a scheme similar to Eagly's to group the studies and make comparisons. His three classes of studies were Asch-type conformity studies, studies with fictitious norm groups, and persuasive communication (attitude change) studies. Nine of the 47 studies from Maccoby and Jacklin did not fit into Cooper's classes (see Cooper, 1979, p. 137, for his rationale for excluding studies).

Cooper analyzed both p-values and effect sizes in addressing the second and third conclusions of Maccoby and Jacklin. He corroborated their results, reporting larger Stouffer test values and a larger mean effect size for the Asch-type group pressure studies than for the fictitious norm group studies. These larger positive effects indicated even more female compliance in the Asch-type studies. Cooper inspected the effect sizes and calculated standard deviations as an ad hoc assessment of consistency of results.

He found small values for the mean effect size and for the Stouffer combined significance test for the persuasive communication studies. The smallness of these values was in part due to the fact that very few persuasion studies (only 2 of 14) had reported enough data to allow calculation of effect sizes or exact p-values. Cooper concluded that there was essentially no gender difference for these studies. However, the problem of reporting bias dramatically affects his results. The size of the gender difference calculated for the two studies for which effect sizes were available is almost one standard deviation, as opposed to 0.14 standard deviation units when the missing data are included as zeroes. Thus Cooper's conclusions about the magnitudes of gender differences in influenceability are probably overly conservative because of the methodology he used to analyze the effect size measures.

One problem with comparing Cooper's results to those of Maccoby and Jacklin relates to his use of the p-value summaries. The p-value methods answer the question "Is there a nonzero (population) gender difference in *any* of the studies?" The results of such tests will not always support inferences about overall strength or consistency of effect such as those made by Maccoby and Jacklin or Eagly on the basis of their narrative reviews. Also, whereas the vote-counting method has very little power to detect effects, the combined significance tests are relatively powerful at detecting even single unusual effects. Thus inferences based on vote-counts and combined significance tests may sometimes appear to disagree.

Eagly and Carli's Review

Realizing the limitations of Cooper's sample of studies, Eagly and Carli (1981) attempted a more thorough meta-analysis using the studies reviewed earlier by Eagly (1978). Again, concern with differences between experimental paradigms and with bias in conformity-task stimulus materials gave direction to the review.

Eagly and Carli represented the gender difference by the direction and significance of the difference and, where possible, by its one-tailed probability, effect size, and percentage of nonoverlap of distributions. They examined for each study the publication date, sample size, percentage of male authors, and sex of the first author, and for persuasion studies the degree of gender differences in *interest in* and *knowledge about* the topic of the persuasive message (as indicated by a group of undergraduates).

Using three summaries of probability values, Eagly and Carli found significant results indicating more female conformity for all three study paradigms and across all the studies combined. (Again this is not surprising, recalling that such summaries are designed to detect even a single truly non-null population effect.)

Eagly and Carli also examined effect sizes, and made t-test comparisons between the mean effect sizes for the three classes. They found that the mean gender difference for 43 group pressure studies, 0.32 standard deviation units, differed significantly from that for 33 persuasion studies, which was 0.16 standard deviations. The 11 "other"conformity studies showed an intermediate gender difference of 0.28 standard deviations.

Eagly and Carli then examined the studies within each paradigm and correlated their gender-difference outcomes with the study features listed above. The most notable findings were the low correlations between effect sizes and gender differences in knowledge of and interest in the persuasive message topic for persuasion studies, as well as the lack of sex bias in knowledge and interest across the topics. Women reported no less or more knowledge of the topics and significantly more interest in the 83 topics than did the men.

The percentage of male authors of each study correlated highly with the influence gender difference for studies in all three paradigm types. The relationship was strongest for the "other conformity studies" and, for all paradigms, indicated that studies with relatively more male authors found women to be more easily influenced than men.

Eagly and Carli concluded that their meta-analysis found stronger evidence for a gender difference in persuasion studies than did the 1978 Eagly review. This undoubtedly resulted in part because they used more powerful effect size analyses rather than vote-counting techniques. They noted that the similarity of their findings for the persuasion and group pressure studies "weakens the claim that processes unique to the group pressure setting contribute to the sex difference" (1981, p. 16).

Eagly and Carli expressed concern about the strong relationships between sex of author and study results. They noted similar findings for Hall's studies of gender differences (1978) in decoding nonverbal behavior. In both cases, the relationships indicated that "researchers portray their own gender more favorably than researchers of the opposite sex do" (Eagly & Carli, 1981, p. 17). Finally, Eagly and Carli discussed the possible sources of sex-linked biases in study design and the reporting of study results and how such biases may have been manifest in the social influence literature.

Eagly and Carli were able to make more informative statements about the magnitudes of gender differences in influenceability than did Eagly in her earlier study because they employed effect size estimates to represent study results. However, their inferences about the effect sizes were based on ad hoc analyses. Though the use of t-tests on effect size data is intuitively sensible, because the data are based on different-sized samples, such analyses involve violation of the basic assumption of homogeneity of variance. Thus, though the calculated average effect sizes probably represent typical magnitudes of the gender differences for the three paradigm types, the tests of differences between the averages may not be valid.

Similarly, though the correlations of the effect sizes with study features may represent interrelationships fairly well, the data points are measured with differing precision; therefore a weighted correlation would be more appropriate. This is discussed in detail in chapter 2.

Methods

Model-fitting Techniques

The techniques I use below are based on statistical distribution theory for the effect size (Hedges, 1981), an index first introduced by Glass (1976). I use this measure both because it is a better index of the effect than the p-value (it does not depend as much on the sample size of the study from which it is taken) and because there is a justifiable statistical theory that provides a way to examine explanatory models for effect sizes.

Glass's effect size, denoted g, is simply the difference between two sample means—in this case, the means (M) for females and males on an influenceability variable—divided by the pooled (within-sex) sample standard deviation (S_p). We write:

$$g = \frac{M_F - M_M}{S_p}.$$

There has been some controversy about the standard deviation that should be used in the calculation of g (McGaw & Glass, 1980). Using different standard deviation estimates implies that different effect size parameters are being estimated. If we are interested in gender differences alone, we should use the pooled within-sex standard deviation as S_p. I use this standard deviation in this review.

Hedges (1981) showed that the estimator g is biased for small samples, but that the bias can be corrected by multiplying g by a correction factor c. If the numbers of females and males are denoted as n_F and n_M, respectively, and m is defined as $n_F + n_M - 2$, then c is approximately $1 - (3/[4m - 1])$.

A table of values for this correction can be found in Glass, McGaw, and Smith (1981).

The effect size $d = cg$ is an unbiased sample estimate of the parameter δ, the population standardized mean difference. Here δ is the parameter represented by the substitution of the corresponding population mean and standard deviation parameters into the above formula for the sample estimate g. The analyses presented by Hedges allow the reviewer to test hypotheses about population values of δ for the k accumulated studies.

I use Hedges's methods (1982a, 1982b) for testing the homogeneity (consistency) of effect sizes and for estimating and testing categorical and continuous linear models for effect sizes when they are not homogeneous.

The Studies Reviewed

I examine the set of studies considered by Eagly (1978) and Eagly and Carli (1981). Eagly and Carli presented effect sizes for 90 of 148 independent comparisons, from 138 separate sources or articles. Their articles were located through a survey of all journals in social psychology and the earlier reviews by Maccoby (1966) and Maccoby and Jacklin (1974), as well as through citations from relevant social psychology texts. The studies were limited to those whose subjects were of high school age or older. The literature search is discussed in Eagly (1978).

From some source articles, I was able to extract several independent effect sizes that differed on relevant dimensions (e.g., age of the subjects). This augments the number of comparisons by four but does not change the overall number of subjects in the analysis, since it is simply a different partitioning of existing data. I eliminate from the original data set 15 studies that either provide insufficient data for calculating the effect size g or that use incorrect analyses. A total of 78 effect sizes remains.

The 78 effect sizes are recalculated using the standard deviation pooled only within sexes as S_p. Recalculation changes the values for over half of the (biased) effect sizes for the 74 samples common to this analysis and that of Eagly and Carli. Yet 60 percent of the new effect sizes differ from the original effect sizes by 0.05 (i.e., 0.05 standard deviation units) or less.

Ten effect sizes change by over a tenth of a standard deviation unit. Some of these large differences occur because the new effect sizes represent different subject groups (e.g., Tuddenham, MacBride & Zahn, 1958) or because the effect size for a specific single outcome is used to represent the gender difference rather than the mean of two available effect sizes (e.g., Vidulich & Stabene, 1965). However, some of the large differences are associated with change in S_p (e.g., Glinski, Glinski & Slatin, 1970).

Some studies presented nonparametric analyses, and the typical parametric measures (means and standard deviations) were not reported. In some of these cases, I use methods for transforming test statistics to effect sizes to calculate g (Glass, McGaw & Smith, 1981, pp. 130-147).

Studies without Effect Sizes

The exclusion of the 15 effect sizes previously examined by Eagly and Carli raises the number of sources without effect size estimates from 58 to 73. This is 49 percent of the total 148 studies accumulated by Eagly and Carli. Almost half of the available reports do not furnish enough data to allow estimation of an effect size. Some of these articles describe several experiments (e.g., Sistrunk & McDavid, 1971) and report enough information for estimating effect sizes for some samples but inadequate information for others.

The primary reason that studies are not included in this review is that they provide insufficient data for calculation of the effect size. This could have happened in two ways: either the data were simply not presented because the results of the test for gender differences were not statistically significant or the test did not examine the parameter of interest, which was the mean difference on influenceability standardized by the appropriate estimate of the standard deviation S_p described above.

For example, studies by Rotter (1967) and Crano (1970) are eliminated because they do not present enough data for calculation of the pooled-within-sex error term for S_p. A study by Patel and Gordon (1960) is deleted because it presented only an analysis of variance that used the within-subject variable of item difficulty as a between-subject factor. The error mean square (from which the S_p estimate is calculated) and the degrees of freedom for error are thus incorrect.

Some studies that examined hypotheses about gender differences and found significant results used more powerful (multifactor) ANOVA designs, and their data reporting did not allow repooling of the error terms (e.g., Endler, Wiesenthal & Geller, 1972). Other reports simply presented their data in a format that did not allow effect size computation (e.g., Johnson & MacDonnell, 1974, presented the proportions of the two sexes who conformed on individual stimulus items). Though Glass, McGaw, and Smith (1981) presented methods for obtaining effect sizes from some other metrics, the statistical properties of the transformations are not well understood.

Often meta-analysts include studies with insufficient data for calculation of exact effect sizes by considering missing effect sizes to be zero, assuming that all (or the average) of the studies with insufficient data find exactly no gender difference. I do not replace unreported data with zero effect sizes because I am not willing to make that assumption, and because I do not want to risk the possible distortion of results discussed in chapter 2. Because I omit these studies, however, my results are likely to reflect larger differences

Table 8.1 List of Coded Study Characteristics and Categories

Characteristic	Categories
Types of subjects	Americans of high school age
	Americans of college age or older
	Americans of both age groups (high school or older)
	Non-Americans
Type of outcome measure	Posttest on an opinion or performance scale
	Posttest count or percentage of errors made in conformity task
	Covariate-adjusted posttest
	Standardized posttest created by centering scores on control means
	Post-pre difference on opinion or performance scale
	Two- or three-state discrete outcome (change toward conformity response, no change, or change away from conformity response)
Number of agents (confederates)	
Number of items in outcome measure	

than if all data were included (because the bulk of the omitted results are not statistically significant).

Study Features

Essential to the model-fitting methods for meta-analysis is consideration of study characteristics. Ten features in addition to those examined by Eagly and Carli (1981) were coded for each study, though not all proved to be useful in examining variability in outcomes. Table 8.1 presents a list of the features used in the analyses and, where applicable, the categories for each.

Type of Subjects

The type of subjects examined in each study is included for several reasons. Cultural differences between American subjects and subjects from countries where women typically have a more traditional role might affect the amount of conformity for the sexes (Whittaker & Meade, 1967). Cooper acknowledged some cross-cultural differences by excluding such studies from his 1979 review. Similarly, the age of the subjects, though it could only be measured roughly for most studies, might be differently related to the amount of conformity expected for the two sexes. Two studies examined but did not find such an interaction (Costanzo & Shaw, 1966; Klein, 1972).

Type of Outcome Measure

Type of outcome measure is important for methodological reasons as well as substantive ones. All of the studies used some kind of measure to assess the amount each subject had conformed. However, some studies used measures that by definition differed in variability from the others.

Specifically, studies using both pretests and posttests did so in order to "equate" the initial performances of the two sexes, who might have actually started at different performance levels or with different attitudes. It is well known that when pretests and posttests are positively correlated, the variance of the change scores will be reduced. The same holds true for posttests adjusted for covariates (i.e., residual scores).

These two types of outcome would have smaller standard deviations than would posttest scores. Consequently, the mean difference in the effect size would be divided by a smaller standard deviation for these measures. Effect sizes from studies using covariate scores and change scores might be larger (in absolute magnitude) than those from studies using simple posttests.

Another consideration is whether posttest and difference-score scales have the same meaning. Amount of attitude change may not have the same interpretation as "position on an attitude scale." If the raw score interpretations differ, then special caution must be used in trying to combine or compare effect sizes for these two outcomes.

The variability of discrete outcomes also may differ from that for the simple posttests. Many of the effect sizes for these outcomes were estimated from nonparametric tests (e.g., chi-squares) rather than from actual mean differences. Some of these studies would perhaps be more sensibly considered to be examining the population parameters π_M and π_F, the proportions of men and women who conform, rather than the parameter δ.

Yet if we reflect upon the discrete outcome carefully, it can be considered a categorical version of the change scores discussed above. That is, a positive change score would be considered a "1," a zero score would be a "0," and a negative change score a "−1." It would not be surprising to find that studies using discrete outcomes had effect sizes comparable to those of studies using change scores.

The standardized posttest created by centering scores about control group means is used only in studies by Tuddenham (1958, 1961; Tuddenham, MacBride & Zahn, 1958) or others using his materials (Allen & Levine, 1969). This outcome is in fact a sum of three such standardized scores. The scores are centered about the means of different control groups for the two sexes. It is uncertain how the variability of these scores, and thus the magnitude of related effect size estimates, compares with that of the other outcome types.

Though there is no a priori reason to believe that the two types of posttest measures (opinion and performance scales versus percentage or number of conforming errors) have differing variances, this distinction (which relates more to type of task than type of outcome) is coded as well. Interactions between task type and sex of subject that have been found in single studies (e.g., Sistrunk & McDavid, 1971) may be evident across studies as well.

Number of Agents

The number of agents or confederates of the experimenter is coded because of its possible relation to the strength of the gender difference, especially in the group pressure studies. If women are more influenceable than men in a group situation (Eagly, 1978), then a larger group might produce a stronger gender difference and a larger effect size. Latané's theory of social impact (1981) highlights this variable.

Though a linear relationship between effect size and group size may not actually exist, there does seem to be at least a qualitative difference between the group pressure situation with only one confederate (a partner) and a situation with more than one. Researchers have specifically examined influence in dyads (Delin & Poo-Kong, 1974). In fact, in some of the studies using only one agent, that agent was known or even well known to the subject (e.g., Ex, 1960). In other of the single-agent studies, the subject was explicitly told to "attend to" the responses of his or her partner (Kanareff & Lanzetta, 1960a, 1960b, 1961). The number of agents ranged from 1 to 8 for the 35 group pressure studies with a mean of 3.1 agents and a standard deviation of 2.8.

In the fictitious norm group paradigm, the number-of-agents variable corresponds to the number of persons in the alleged norm group. Although the connection here is clearly more tenuous than that for the real group situations, one might wonder whether a larger fictitious norm group would convey a stronger message to conform. If, again, women are more likely to respond to such group pressure, the size of the gender difference should relate to the number of agents for ficitious norm group studies as well. The number of agents ranges from 5 to 400 for the other conformity studies ($M = 110$, $SD = 134$).

Number of Items

The number of items in the outcome measure is coded as a representation of the reliability of the outcome measure. Longer tests are more reliable measures of any construct. The numbers of items used in these studies range from 1 to 150, with a mean of 21 items ($SD = 26.5$).

Other Features

Other study characteristics coded are type of publication (e.g., unpublished matter, general psychology journal, speech and communication journal), importance of sex differences in the report (e.g., whether sex was mentioned in the title or only in the literature review or not at all), sex of agent(s) and experimenter, whether interactions between sex of subjects and other variables were considered, and how the effect sizes were calculated (e.g., from means and standard deviations or from t-tests). Though I attempted to fit several models that used the features not included in table 8.1, fit statistics for those models indicated that they did not explain a reasonable amount of the variability in outcomes.

Results

I first test the consistency (homogeneity) of the results of all the studies. The value of the homogeneity test H_T (Hedges, 1982a) is 183.78. H_T is a chi-square variable with $k - 1 = 77$ degrees of freedom (where k is the number of studies), so this value is quite large ($p < .001$). The effect sizes are not consistent across the studies. This inconsistency of study results is not surprising, because the studies are quite diverse, and the unbiased effect sizes range from -0.51 to 1.09.

I next group the studies, as Eagly and Carli did, into three classes: studies of persuasion, of group pressure, and of other conformity (fictitious norm group) situations. I use Hedges's methods (1982a) for fitting categorical models to calculate the statistics presented in table 8.2.

An overall test of the within-class homogeneity, H_W, is the sum of the homogeneity values for each class. The value 170.7 is highly significant compared to the chi-square distribution with $k - p = 75$ degrees of freedom (where p is the number of classes), indicating considerable heterogeneity

Table 8.2 Analysis of Outcome Variability for Three Classes of Studies

Source of Variation	df	Homogeneity Statistic	Probability	Mean Effect Size	Standard Error
Between Classes	2	13.71	< .005		
Within Classes	75	170.07	< .001		
Persuasion	32	66.71	< .001	0.11	0.02
Group pressure	34	76.75	< .001	0.28	0.04
Other conformity	9	26.61	< .001	0.13	0.06
Total	**77**	**183.78**	**< .001**		

within the three classes. The large H_{Wi} values indicate that within each class the effect sizes are still quite inconsistent.

The test for differences between mean effect sizes for the groups is given by H_B, which is also a chi-square variable, with $p - 1 = 2$ degrees of freedom. The hypothesis that the three sets of studies have one population effect size is rejected because the H_B value of 13.71 is significant. Thus the differences in effect size between these three categories of studies are significant.

The pooled effect size estimates given in table 8.2 can be compared by means of linear contrasts, which in this case are not post hoc. The average size of the gender difference for persuasion studies, 0.11, is essentially equal to that for other conformity studies, 0.13 ($z = -0.23, p > .50$). The mean gender difference for the group pressure studies seems to differ from the averages in the other two groups; the difference is significant according to another contrast ($z = 2.12, p < .03$).

Caution is needed in interpreting the average effect sizes given in table 8.2 because they do not represent adequately the outcomes of all studies in each class (e.g., all persuasion studies). They are average effects, not common effects.

I now examine each of the three classes of studies separately to see if the study features discussed above are associated with variation among the effect sizes.

Persuasion Studies

I estimated first a linear model for the 33 effect sizes, using the numbers of items and of agents and Eagly and Carli's (1981) predictors of gender differences in topic knowledge and in topic interest, percentage of male authors, and publication date. Though several of the predictors were significant, the model did not adequately explain the variability in outcomes. Since the continuous model did not explain the study results, several categorical models were next estimated.

An adequate model is obtained by classing the effect sizes according to subject type and type of outcome measure. None of the other categorical models attempted provided a model that fit the data as indicated by the model-specification tests.

I first dichotomize the persuasion studies according to whether or not the subjects were American. There are four studies of foreign subjects: (Chu (1966) studied Taiwanese, Feldman (1975) studied the Gusii of Kenya, Rosenberg (1965) examined Israelis, and Singh (1970) considered Indian subjects.

The studies of American and of foreign subjects are not internally homogeneous, as is shown in table 8.3 ($H_W = 61.01, df = 31$). This inconsistency is not surprising for the studies of foreign subjects because of the diversity of

Table 8.3 Analysis of Outcome Variability for Thirty-Three Persuasion Studies

Source of Variation	df	Homogeneity Statistic	Probability	Mean Effect Size	Standard Error
Between Subject Types	1	5.70	< .025		
Within Subject Types	31	61.01	< .005		
Foreign subjects	3	12.94	< .005	−0.04	0.07
American subjects	28	48.07	< .025	0.13	0.03
Total	**32**	**66.71**	**< .001**		

cultural settings examined. (Numerous other differences between the studies also exist; thus there are many possible explanations for the lack of homogeneity of results.) The results of the four foreign studies are inconsistent, and the average effect size of −0.04 does not differ significantly from zero ($z = 0.60$). I do not examine these four study outcomes further.

I next group the studies of American subjects according to type of outcome measure used. Five of the six measure types appear in these 29 studies; only standardized posttests do not. Table 8.4 shows the analysis of outcome variability for the studies, and figure 8.1 depicts 95 percent confidence intervals for the population effect sizes for the five groups.

The groups are all homogeneous, and there are significant differences among the groups as indicated by the homogeneity statistic of 22.53 ($p < .005$) for between-group variation. Admittedly, the numbers of studies in some of the groups are low. Thus a finding of consistent results may seem trivial at first glance. (A class consisting of one study will always be homogeneous.) However, because consistency depends more on the numbers of subjects in the groups (i.e., the variances of the effect sizes) than on the numbers of studies, it is actually fairly uncommon to obtain consistent results for groups of two or three studies when the studies are moderate to large in size.

Despite significant between-group differences, some sets of effects are quite similar. As figure 8.1 illustrates, the estimated effect sizes for studies using non-posttest outcomes and their confidence intervals are all positive and very close. Pooling together the 16 studies using covariate-adjusted, change-score, or discrete outcomes and testing for their homogeneity, we obtain a chi-square value of 12.13, which is not significant ($df = 15$, $p > .50$). The study results appear consistent, and the mean effect size estimate for these studies is 0.24, with a standard error of 0.04.

The mean effect size for the studies that used error posttests is also positive and resembles the non-posttest effect sizes more than the mean effect size for the 10 studies that used opinion or performance-scale posttests.

Table 8.4 Analysis of Outcome Variability for Twenty-Nine Persuasion Studies of American Subjects

Source of Variation	df	Homogeneity Statistic	Probability	Mean Effect Size	Standard Error
Between Measure Types	4	22.53	< .005		
Within Measure Types	24	25.55	> .25		
O,P posttest	9	9.27	> .25	−0.02	0.04
Error posttest	2	4.67	> .05	0.17	0.10
Covariate score	1	3.63	> .05	0.28	0.10
Change score	11	7.92	> .25	0.25	0.05
Discrete outcome	1	0.06	> .75	0.24	0.05
Total	**28**	**48.08**	**< .025**		

I use post hoc linear contrasts to investigate the magnitudes of the mean effect sizes for the two posttest groups and the pooled mean for the 16 non-posttest studies. The error posttest effect size and the non-posttest effect sizes are essentially equal ($z = -0.67, p > .05$). The effect size for the studies that used opinion or performance-scale posttests differs significantly from the average of the effect sizes based on error posttests and non-posttest

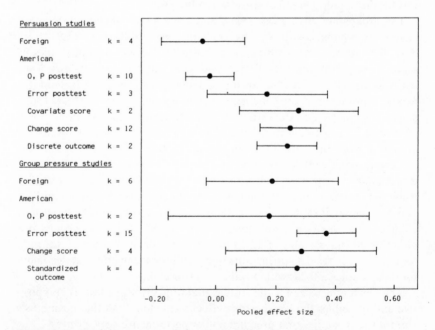

Figure 8.1 Confidence Intervals for Pooled Effect Sizes (95%)

outcomes ($z = -3.30$, $p < .01$), though it appears equal to the error post-test effect size ($z = -1.73$, $p > .05$).

The pattern of results is consistent with two dichotomizations of the American persuasion studies. One categorization separates studies using posttests from other studies. Yet this scheme does not acknowledge the similarities between error posttest and non-posttest measures.

The second scheme contrasts studies using posttests on opinion or performance scales with all other studies. This entails the combining of studies using error posttests with studies using covariate change or discrete outcomes. Though this scheme may initially seem illogical, consideration of the statistical and conceptual differences between error and performance-scale posttests and hypothetical pretests justifies it.

The error posttests measured counts or percentages of errors on a conformity task. One would assume that subjects of either sex who were not confronted with a persuasive message for that task would respond with equivalent skill. Thus all subjects would make either no errors or some average number or percentage of errors in an imaginary pretest situation. Essentially, we would expect no gender difference on a hypothetical error-score pretest.

The opinion and performance-scale posttest variables measured each subject's position on an attitude or performance variable (e.g., Eagly's 1974 scale concerning hours of sleep needed). Unlike the imagined error pretest, a pretest on an opinion or performance scale does not have an expected baseline score level. There is no a priori reason to believe that the two sexes should answer equivalently, though it would not be unreasonable for them to do so.

If males and females are not equivalent in skill (or are not in accordance of opinion) on the performance (or attitude) scales, then raw posttest outcomes cannot accurately represent any differential effects of the persuasive message. Because of this uncertainty about the prior levels of the sexes on performance and opinion posttests, such posttests should not be interpreted in the same way as the error posttests.

The error posttests, under the assumption of equivalent prior error levels, are in a sense more akin to change scores, and this is expressed in the results shown in table 8.4. The pooled effect size obtained by grouping the error-posttest effect sizes with the covariate, change-score and discrete-outcome effect sizes is 0.23, with a standard error of 0.03.

The effect size from the studies using hypothetical or actual adjustments for preexisting differences indicates that, on average, women conform one fourth of a standard deviation unit more than men. Studies that did not control preexisting differences show a negligible gender difference of 0.02 standard deviation units, with a standard error of 0.04. These results support earlier findings of relatively more female persuasibility.

Group Pressure Studies

The first step in analyzing the results of the group pressure studies is again to separate studies of American and non-American subjects. Table 8.5 shows this breakdown. The six studies of non-American subjects have a pooled effect size of 0.19 standard deviation units, which does not differ from zero ($z = 1.80$). The within-group fit statistic for the studies is not significant, indicating lack of a sex difference in *all* of these foreign studies. The subjects studied were from Britain (Beloff, 1958), Germany (Timaeus, 1968), Japan (Frager, 1970), the Netherlands (Ex, 1960), and New Zealand (Vaughan & Taylor, 1966).

Because of the central role of the "type of outcome" variable used to explain the outcomes of persuasion studies, I include that variable in the examination of the group pressure studies. Attempting to fit a model with outcome type as the single categorical factor to the studies of American subjects leads to findings of heterogeneity within some of the "outcome measure" subgroups. Thus the very simple model that accounts for essentially all variability in outcomes of the conformity studies does not explain the group pressure study outcomes.

Several of the studies using error posttests involved a single agent or confederate who was well known to the subject (Kanareff & Lanzetta, 1960*a*, 1960*b*, 1961). These studies seem qualitatively different from studies with an unfamiliar agent or with more than one agent. Also, a study involving the detection of lying in an experimental situation is in this set of very inconsistent effect sizes (Glinski, Glinski & Slatin, 1970). This study seems to differ considerably in design from the other group pressure studies in that it requires the subject to make a judgment of the character of another individual rather than a statement of personal attitude or an exhibition of skill.

The value of the homogeneity statistic for the 19 studies using error posttests is 37.94, which is highly significant ($df = 18$, $p < .005$). Removing the 4 studies described above reduces the homogeneity statistic to a nonsignificant value of 15.34, as shown in table 8.6. Similarly, the removal of these 4

Table 8.5 Analysis of Outcome Variability for Thirty-Five Group Pressure Studies

Source of Variation	df	Homogeneity Statistic	Probability	Mean Effect Size	Standard Error
Between Subject Types	1	0.77	> .25		
Within Subject Types	33	75.98			
Foreign subjects	5	10.81	> .05	0.19	0.11
American subjects	28	65.17	< .005	0.29	0.04
Total	**34**	**76.75**	**< .005**		

Table 8.6 Analysis of Outcome Variability for Twenty-Five Group Pressure Studies of American Subjects

Source of Variation	df	Homogeneity Statistic	Probability	Mean Effect Size	Standard Error
Between Measure Types	3	2.02	> .25		
Within Measure Types	21	41.94	< .005		
O,P posttest	1	1.78	> .10	0.18	0.17
Error posttest	14	15.34	> .25	0.37	0.05
Change score	4	2.02	> .25	0.29	0.13
Standard score	3	22.80	< .005	0.27	0.10
Total	**24**	**43.96**	**< .01**		

studies reduces the overall homogeneity statistic for the group pressure studies of American subjects from 65.17 for 29 studies (see table 8.5) to 43.97 for 25 studies. This is a considerable reduction in variability. (The "change in H" value of 21.20 can be compared to a chi-square statistic with 4 degrees of freedom to give $p < .005$. Removing these studies has significantly increased the consistency of the results.)

With these four omissions, the results are homogeneous within all of the measure-type groups except for one, the set of four effect sizes from studies that had used standardized scale scores. These studies were either authored by Tuddenham (1958, 1961; Tuddenham, MacBride & Zahn, 1958) or had utilized Tuddenham's measure as an outcome (Allen & Levine, 1969). Further partitioning did not create homogeneous subsets of studies. Table 8.6 presents the average effect size estimate for this heterogeneous subgroup of studies.

The mean effect sizes for the four types of outcome are all positive and do not differ from one another. As is true for the persuasion studies, gender differences are greater for the 20 group pressure studies using change-score and error posttests than for the 2 studies using opinion and performance-scale posttests, though, again, they are not significantly greater ($z = 0.84$).

Persuasion and Group Pressure Studies

Figure 8.1 depicts mean effect size estimates and 95 percent confidence bands for all subgroups of persuasion and group pressure studies. Most of the estimates and intervals lie on the positive side of the figure, indicating more female conformity.

Effects for the measure-type groups were similar for the studies using both the persuasion and group pressure paradigms. No differences were found in effect sizes between studies from the two paradigms using error posttests ($z = 1.75$), change scores ($z = 0.23$), or opinion and performance posttests ($z = 1.13$). The weighted average sizes for the studies using these three types of measure across the two paradigm types are -0.01 for the studies using opinion and performance posttests, 0.26 for studies using change-score outcomes, and 0.32 for the studies using error posttests.

On the basis of this analysis, differences between the outcomes used in the studies appear to be more powerful at explaining variability in gender differences than differences in paradigms used to study conformity. In fact, the gender difference for the persuasion studies shown in table 8.2 may be smaller than that for the group pressure studies because of differences in the kinds of outcomes used.

Ten persuasion studies (34 percent) used opinion or performance posttests and 19 (66 percent) used adjusted scores, whereas only 2 of the group pressure studies (4 percent) employed opinion or performance posttest scores versus 23 (96 percent) that used some kind of adjusted score. If studies that use adjusted scores find larger gender differences, then group pressure studies should find larger gender differences simply because more group pressure studies use such scores. Both Cooper (1979) and Eagly (1978) reported finding such a difference in their reviews. Paradigm type is somewhat confounded with outcome type in these studies because the proportions of studies using the different outcome types differ so drastically for the two paradigms.

Other Conformity Studies

Fitting a regression model to the 10 effect sizes for the other conformity studies, I found, as did Eagly and Carli (1981), that percentage of male authors was a significant predictor, with higher percentages corresponding to more female conformity. A linear model including only this variable explains a significant amount of the variability in the outcomes and also gives an adequate fit to the data.

However, percentage of male authors is an unusual predictor variable in the sense that it is difficult to understand the substantive implications of an increase or decrease in its value. It could be that this variable was acting as a "proxy" for some other processes (such as experimenter bias, if the authors were the experimenters or agents in the studies) or other study features. To account for these possible alternative explanations, I examine other variables that are correlated with the gender difference in conformity.

Several variables correlate with both percentage of male authors and effect size, including the number of items in the outcome measure and the number of "agents" in these studies, most of which involved fictitious norm groups. I incorporate each of those variables as a single predictor of effect size in a linear model.

Table 8.7 Intercorrelations for Predictors and Effect Sizes in Ten Other Conformity Studies

	Effect Size (d)	Agents (N)	Items (N)	Male Authors (%)
Effect size	1.00	0.46	0.80	0.72
N of agents		1.00	0.77	0.47
N of items			1.00	0.60

Note: The critical values for testing whether the Pearson product-moment correlation is zero for 10 pairs of observations are 0.63 for the .05 significance level and 0.77 for the .01 significance level.

The best fitting of the models predicts the size of the gender difference from the natural logarithm of the number of items (NITEMS) in the outcome measure. The model is

$$d = -0.29 + 0.20 \log (\text{NITEMS}) + e.$$

The test of significance for the model is $H_M = 20.16$, which as a chi-square with one degree of freedom is significant ($p < .001$). The fit (error) statistic for the model is 6.44, which as a chi-square with 8 degrees of freedom is not significant ($p > .25$). Thus the size of the gender difference in the other conformity studies is predicted quite successfully with knowledge of the length of the test used in each study.

As noted above, other correlates of the percentage of male authors for the studies are also satisfactory predictors of effect size. Table 8.7 presents the correlations among these predictors and their correlations with the unbiased effect size d. All of the values are quite high and differ significantly from zero (at the 0.05 level) in spite of the small number of cases. The implications of these interrelationships among the predictors are discussed below.

Discussion

Meta-analysis

The application of rigorous meta-analysis methods to the studies of social influence illustrates the kinds of inferences that are possible in quantitative reviews. The analysis of the "other conformity studies" exhibited both the strengths and limitations of the methods.

In most of the "other comformity studies," there is no distinct persuasive message, the subject is simply informed of a group's responses to each of the items on the outcome measure. Thus a longer test may convey a stronger message, as well as being more reliable. If estimates of the reliability of the tests used in the studies are available, the effect sizes can be adjusted for unreliability before doing the homogeneity analyses (Hedges, 1981). The relationship of test length to effect size indicates that when effect size estimates are not disattenuated, the unreliability of the measures may still influence the outcome of the analysis.

The fact that so many predictors "explain" variability in the sizes of the outcomes for the 10 studies indicates that no conclusive interpretation can consider only one predictor. In this case, the predominance of male authors is confounded with the reliability of the outcome, the size of the sample, and the size of the alleged norm group. Here any claims of simple experimenter bias or expectancy (e.g., women conform more when male investigators expect that they will) must be qualified: perhaps women conform more because the norm group is larger *or* the test was longer *or* the message was stronger.

Thus this note of caution must be made. There will not always be only one model that explains study outcomes. We must use care when we base substantive conclusions on the findings of a meta-analysis. In the "other conformity study" data, three study features relate to the size of the gender difference. Clearly the same could occur in other reviews. We probably cannot use the methods of meta-analysis to establish unique substantive or theoretical conclusions. However, without use of the model-fitting methods, we cannot make a valid investigation of whether the factors that we suspect relate to study outcomes explain an adequate amount of outcome variability.

Gender Differences in Influenceability

Gender differences in influenceability are not consistent across the studies reviewed, with results differing by study type, type of subject, and by type of outcome used. Consistent effects are found for the persuasion studies when the outcomes of studies of American subjects are grouped by type of outcome measure. Studies using measures of change show moderate gender differences, while those using only posttest measures evidence essentially no gender difference.

The "stable" gender difference for persuasion studies that had been noted by Maccoby and Jacklin (1974) seems to be substantiated. When position on the outcome variable (prior to being influenced) is equated for the sexes, women appear to change more from that position than do men.

Patterns of effects similar to those reported for persuasion studies are found for the group pressure studies. The similarity of the results for the persuasion and group pressure studies reaffirms Eagly and Carli's findings that the influenceability gender difference is not prevalent only in the group pressure situation. Gender differences are found in both types of influence situation and vary according to the type of outcome measure used to detect them. Because differences between the persuasion and group pressure paradigms are confounded with effects due to the use of different outcome measures, we cannot explain them solely in terms of psychological or group processes.

For the other conformity studies, percentage of male authors, test length, and size of the fictitious norm group all relate to effect size. Several methodological features as well as Eagly and Carli's percentage-of-male-authors variable (representing sex-related bias) adequately describe the results. One sensible model, which fits the data better than the other models tried, relates the size of the gender difference to test length. Larger differences occur for longer tests, with women conforming more than men.

This review indicates that studies that presented sufficient data for effect size estimation find a small to moderate difference indicating more female conformity. The size of the difference in persuasion and group pressure studies depends to some extent on the outcome measure used. In studies classed as "other" conformity studies, effects relate to a number of confounded predictors, and more male conformity is found for some configurations of study features. Effect sizes were not calculable for over half of the source articles originally identified by Eagly and Carli.

An oversimplification of these results is that women conform more. But this conclusion is based on just less than half of the available studies. Most often, results were unreported, and hence effect sizes not computed, because there was no finding of a significant gender difference. Since significance depends on effect size, we would suppose that large effects are not "hidden" in the other studies. It is unlikely that the true (population) gender difference is much larger than that reported above.

Even if a "real" gender difference of 0.25 or 0.30 standard deviation units exists for the population examined in these studies, its generalizability must be considered. The conformity gender difference has often been measured in experimental and hence somewhat artificial settings. Most samples are of college students and may not represent well the general populace.

Also, the external validity of some of the paradigms used may be low. For instance, the topics of the influence inductions do not bear great resemblance to the kinds of topics about which we are influenced in our daily lives. Rarely does one hear disagreement about whether football is played on a diamond-shaped field (Sistrunk, 1971) or about the number of dots in a visual display (Wyer, 1966).

Similarly, the agents in the studies of social influence may not resemble those we would expect to influence us in real life. Responses to conformity messages presented by "agents" who are familiar or well known may be different from responses to unknown agents. The few studies that used familiar agents showed inconsistent results, some showing much more female conformity (e.g., Kanareff & Lanzetta, 1960a; Whittaker, 1965), and others more male conformity (e.g., Kanareff & Lanzetta, 1960b; Vidulich & Bayley, 1966).

Finally, though it appears that in these studies women were more influenceable than men, the extent to which the opinions and performances of both sexes were modified is not addressed. It is possible that both groups were influenced very little. The permanence of the opinion or performance change is also uncertain.

It would be unwise to make broad-reaching decisions on policy on the basis of the findings reported above. At a minimum, it seems that women (and girls as well) could benefit more than males from encouragement to be independent thinkers, because it is sensible to be critical and analytical in any situation. However, whether the gender difference in influenceability is sizeable enough in real-life situations to be perceptible in differences in male and female behavior is another question.

Thus, as usual, we must keep the results of these experimental studies in a realistic framework. Though the studies of social influence reviewed indicate that under controlled circumstances women have been found to conform more than men, we might not expect to find that result in every situation, especially in our day-to-day experiences.

References

Allen, V. L., & Levine, J. M. (1969). Consensus and conformity. *Journal of Experimental Social Psychology, 5*, 389–399.

Asch, S. E. (1956). Studies of independence and conformity. Part 1: A minority of one against a unanimous majority. *Psychological Monographs, 70*, 9.

Becker, B. J. (1982). *Conceptual problems in the summarization of significance values*. Paper presented at the annual meeting of the American Educational Research Association, New York, March 1982.

Becker, B. J. (1985). *Applying tests of combined significance: Hypotheses and power considerations*. Doctoral dissertation, University of Chicago.

Beloff, H. (1958). Two forms of social conformity: Acquiescence and conventionality. *Journal of Abnormal and Social Psychology, 56*, 99–104.

Burgoon, M., Jones, S. B., & Stewart, D. (1975). Toward a message-centered theory of persuasion: Three empirical investigations of language intensity. *Human Communication Research, 3*, 240–256.

Chu, G. C. (1966). Culture, personality, and persuasibility. *Sociometry, 29*, 169–174.

Cooper, H. M. (1979). Statistically combining independent studies: A meta-analysis of sex differences in conformity research. *Journal of Personality and Social Psychology, 37*, 131–146.

Costanzo, P. R., & Shaw, M. E. (1966). Conformity as a function of age level. *Child Development, 37*, 967–975.

Crano, W. D. (1970). Effects of sex, response order, and expertise in conformity: A dispositional approach. *Sociometry, 33*, 239–252.

Crutchfield, R. S. (1955). Conformity and character. *American Psychologist, 10*, 191–198.

Delin, P. S., & Poo-Kong, K. (1974). The measurement of mutual conformity in a dyadic situation. *British Journal of Social and Clinical Psychology, 13*, 211–213.

Eagly, A. H. (1974). Comprehensibility of persuasive arguments as a determinant of opinion change. *Journal of Personality and Social Psychology, 29,* 758-773.

Eagly, A. H. (1978). Sex differences in influenceability. *Psychological Bulletin, 85,* 86-116.

Eagly, A. H., & Carli, L. L. (1981). Sex of researchers and sex-typed communications as determinants of sex differences in influenceability: A meta-analysis of social influence studies. *Psychological Bulletin, 90,* 1-20.

Endler, N. S., Wiesenthal, D. L., & Geller, S. H. (1972). The generalization of the effects of agreement and correctness on relative competence mediating conformity. *Canadian Journal of Behavioral Science, 4,* 322-329.

Ex, J. (1960). The nature of the relation between two persons and the degree of their influence on each other. *Acta Psychologica, 17,* 39-54.

Feldman, R. H. L. (1975). Changes in nutrition attitudes and knowledge as a function of similar and expert communication sources among the Gusii of Kenya (Doctoral dissertation, Syracuse University, 1974). *Dissertation Abstracts International, 35,* 5694B.

Frager, R. (1970). Conformity and anticonformity in Japan. *Journal of Personality and Social Psychology, 15,* 203-210.

Glass, G. V. (1976). Primary, secondary, and meta-analysis of research. *Educational Researcher, 5,* 3-8.

Glass, G. V., McGaw, B., & Smith, M. L. (1981). *Meta-analysis in social research.* Beverly Hills: Sage.

Glinski, R. J., Glinski, B. C., & Slatin, G. T. (1970). Non-naivety contamination in conformity experiments: Sources, effects, and implications for control. *Journal of Personality and Social Psychology, 16,* 478-485.

Hall, J. A. (1978). Gender differences in decoding nonverbal cues. *Psychological Bulletin, 85,* 845-857.

Hedges, L. V. (1981). Distribution theory for Glass's estimator of effect size and related estimators. *Journal of Educational Statistics, 6,* 107-128.

Hedges, L. V. (1982a). Fitting categorical models to effect sizes from a series of experiments. *Journal of Educational Statistics, 7,* 119-137.

Hedges, L. V. (1982b). Fitting continuous models to effect size data. *Journal of Educational Statistics, 7,* 245-270.

Hedges, L. V., & Olkin, I. (1980). Vote-counting methods in research synthesis. *Psychological Bulletin, 88,* 359-369.

Janis, I. L., & Field, P. B. (1959). Sex differences and personality factors related to persuasibility. In C. I. Hovland & I. L. Janis (eds.), *Personality and persuasibility.* New Haven: Yale University Press.

Johnson, R. W., & MacDonnell, J. (1974). The relationship between conformity and male and female attitudes toward women. *Journal of Social Psychology, 94,* 155-156.

Kanareff, V. T., & Lanzetta, J. T. (1960a). Effects of success-failure experiences and probability of reinforcement on the acquisition and extinction of an imitative response. *Psychological Reports, 7,* 151-166.

Kanareff, V. T., & Lanzetta, J. T. (1960b). Effects of task definition and probability of reinforcement upon the acquisition and extinction of imitative responses. *Journal of Experimental Psychology, 68,* 340-348.

Kanareff, V. T., & Lanzetta, J. T. (1961). Effects of congruent social and task reinforcement upon acquisition of imitative responses. *Psychological Reports, 8*, 47-57.

Kirkpatrick, C. (1936). An experimental study in the modification of social attitudes. *American Journal of Sociology, 41*, 649-656.

Klein, R. L. (1972). Age, sex, and task difficulty as predictors of social conformity. *Journal of Gerontology, 27*, 229-236.

Latané, B. (1981). The psychology of social impact. *American Psychologist, 36*, 343-356.

Leventhal, H., Jones, S., & Trembly, G. (1966). Sex differences in attitude and behavior change under conditions of fear and specific instructions. *Journal of Experimental Social Psychology, 2*, 387-399.

Maccoby, E. E. (1966). *The development of sex differences*. Stanford: Stanford University Press.

Maccoby, E. E., & Jacklin, C. N. (1974). *The psychology of sex differences*. Stanford: Stanford University Press.

McGaw, B., & Glass, G. V. (1980). Choice of the metric for effect size in meta-analysis. *American Educational Research Journal, 17*, 325-337.

Milgram, S. (1963). Behavioral study of obedience. *Journal of Abnormal and Social Psychology, 41*, 371-378.

Morelock, J. C. (1980). Sex differences in susceptibility to social influence. *Sex Roles, 6*, 537-548.

Patel, A. S., & Gordon, J. E. (1960). Some personal and situational determinants of yielding to influence. *Journal of Abnormal and Social Psychology, 61*, 411-418.

Rosenberg, J. J. (1965). Persuasibility in personality and culture (Doctoral dissertation, Columbia University, 1962). *Dissertation Abstracts, 26*, 2905-2906.

Rosenthal, R. (1978). Combining results of independent studies. *Psychological Bulletin, 85*, 185-193.

Rotter, G. S. (1967). An experimental evaluation of group attractiveness as a determinant of conformity. *Human Relations, 20*, 273-282.

Scheidel, T. M. (1963). Sex and persuasibility. *Speech Monographs, 30*, 353-358.

Singh, U. P. (1970). Sex and age differences in persuasibility. *Journal of Social Psychology, 82*, 269-270.

Sistrunk, F. (1971). Negro-white comparisons in social conformity. *Journal of Social Psychology, 85*, 77-85.

Sistrunk, F., & McDavid, J. W. (1971). Sex variable in conformity behavior. *Journal of Personality and Social Psychology, 17*, 200-207.

Timaeus, E. (1968). Untersuchungen zum sogenannten konformen Verhalten. *Zeitschrift für Experimentelle und Angewandte Psychologie, 15*, 176-194.

Tuddenham, R. D. (1958). The influence of a distorted group norm upon individual judgment. *Journal of Psychology, 46*, 227-241.

Tuddenham, R. D. (1961). The influence of a distorted group norm upon judgments of adults and children. *Journal of Psychology, 52*, 231-239.

Tuddenham, R. D., MacBride, P. D., & Zahn, V. (1958). The influence of the sex composition of the group upon yielding to a distorted norm. *Journal of Psychology, 46*, 243-251.

Vaughan, G. M., & Taylor, A. J. W. (1966). Clinical anxiety and conformity. *Perceptual and Motor Skills, 22,* 719-722.

Vidulich, R. N., & Bayley, G. A. (1966). A general field experiment technique for studying social influence. *Journal of Social Psychology, 69,* 253-263.

Vidulich, R. N., & Stabene, F. P. (1965). Source certainty as a variable in conformity behavior. *Journal of Social Psychology, 66,* 323-330.

Whittaker, J. O. (1965). Sex differences and susceptibility to interpersonal persuasion. *Journal of Social Psychology, 66,* 91-94.

Whittaker, J. O., & Meade, R. D. (1967). Sex and age as variables in persuasibility. *Journal of Social Psychology, 73,* 47-52.

Wyer, R. S., Jr. (1966). Effects of incentive to perform well, group attraction, and group acceptance as conformity in a judgmental task. *Journal of Personality and Social Psychology, 4,* 21-24.

Meta-analysis of Studies of Gender Differences: Implications and Future Directions
Marcia C. Linn

9

Abstract

In this chapter, first, the contributions of meta-analysis to research on gender differences are analyzed. In particular, the strengths and weaknesses of the homogeneity statistics are discussed and issues in validity are examined. The lack of homogeneity found in many of the studies of gender reported in this volume suggests that gender differences in tasks studied are moderated by factors such as task context, age of respondents, and task content.

The second section of the paper discusses the contributions of the chapters in this book to a psychology of gender. Looking at the history of explanations for gender differences reveals that views based on biological factors were generated to account for the observed differences in the intellectual accomplishments of men and women. Later researchers attempted to ascertain whether these differences reflected differential opportunities for schooling and employment. Recently, researchers have paid considerable attention to the factors likely to maximize or minimize gender differences.

In synthesizing studies of gender differences in a wide range of areas, contributors to this volume found that gender alone was not sufficient to account for the pattern of results. These findings support the position that an interactionist psychology of gender is needed. They are consistent with a steady decline in confidence in biological factors as the sole determiners of gender differences. They empower educators, legislators, and others to establish and support educational and social programs to create equal opportunities for all citizens.

Major advances in understanding differences between males and females are reported in this volume. Meta-analysis helps to establish the reliability and generalizability of these understandings. This, in turn, fosters clear thinking about the likely causes of the differences.

This volume includes chapters on issues in the psychology of gender seen as important in the last ten years. Researchers from a range of perspectives have each reviewed the findings and commented on each other's work to increase the validity of the conclusions. Taken together, the chapters in this volume synthesize over one thousand effect sizes from studies, including national assessments, involving close to half a million subjects. The quality of these syntheses reflects the opportunity for precise analysis gained from the use of a recently developed tool called meta-analysis. In this concluding chapter, the impact of meta-analysis is assessed.

Recent advances in meta-analytic techniques have helped to move the explanatory focus for gender differences from main effects to interactions between gender and other variables. For example, gender differences may arise in a laboratory setting but not in a naturalistic setting. Systematic interactions between gender and the context in which behavior is studied arise regularly. Rather than identifying consistent gender differences, the authors of this volume have identified conditions under which gender is related to performance and conditions under which the same sort of performance is not gender related. These results coincide with a variety of widely discussed feminist perspectives. They support the position articulated by Deaux (1984, 1985) that an interactionist view of the psychology of gender is needed.

Contribution of Meta-analysis

The statistical technique of meta-analysis provides two crucial types of information for those undertaking research synthesis, as discussed in detail by Hedges and Becker (chap. 2). First, current procedures allow the computation of effect sizes unbiased by sample size. Thus the magnitude of the influence of a variable (in this case, sex) on an outcome (such as spatial ability) can be represented in a uniform metric. For some time, researchers have been able to compute effect sizes and the percentage of variance accounted for by such effects. Current procedures, however, make these computations considerably more precise and comparable. In addition, use of a standard unit, d, for reporting results of single studies and for syntheses of studies allows comparability across investigations and aids interpretability by other researchers and practitioners.

Second, current procedures allow researchers to detect interactions between the variable of interest and the conditions under which performance is measured in the studies. This is done by assessing the homogeneity of the effect sizes. Investigation of homogeneity is essential for interpreting findings from research synthesis. An average effect size of zero is meaningless if it results from 30 studies with d's of 1.0 and 30 with d's of -1.0. Lumping such studies together introduces only confusion. To determine whether results are consistent across studies, homogeneity tests can be computed. Furthermore, if studies can be blocked into groups with similar characteristics, refinements of the homogeneity-testing technique can be used to assess whether the blocking variable accounts for significant amounts of variance.

Homogeneity tests assess whether each study in the meta-analysis is a replication of every other study. This stringent requirement is met when the homogeneity test is significant. Slight deviations from homogeneity indicate lack of perfect replication. Massive deviations, obviously, suggest that studies are not duplicates at all. A difficulty with this statistic is that it rests on the assumption that the studies are parallel to each other. Thus studies sampling systematically different populations may investigate the same question and may, taken together, represent the total population; yet they may not appear homogeneous. For this reason, users of homogeneity statistics partition the studies they analyze into groups with similar characteristics. Effect sizes from these groups of studies can appropriately be tested for homogeneity. Since meta-analysis is a relatively new statistical technique, many of the ramifications of homogeneity and lack of homogeneity remain unexplored.

Homogeneity in Meta-analysis

As the meta-analysis in this volume reveal, effect sizes for gender are rarely homogeneous. Essentially, this finding indicates that gender differences on the tasks studied are influenced by other factors. As a result, it is invalid to conclude that gender alone is the causal factor. Rather, the factors influencing the magnitude of gender differences and leading to lack of homogeneity require specification. The large number of meta-analyses reported here provide useful examples of variables that moderate gender differences in intellectual and psychosocial tasks.

Interpreting Homogeneity Statistics

Lack of homogeneity of the effect sizes in a meta-analysis indicates that studies thought to assess the same relationship differ in some systematic way. Hence, one cannot draw valid conclusions about the average effect size without taking the systematic effects into account. At least some of the studies in the meta-analysis are not true replicates of each other when effect sizes are heterogeneous.

Whereas heterogeneity of effect size signals some systematic influence, homogeneity says only that the studies *could* be replicates of each other. Homogeneity does not imply that all the studies measure the same relationship, since the same magnitude of effect could result from a number of different causes. Similarly, homogeneity does not imply validity, since the studies could all suffer from the same flaw.

Factors Leading to Heterogeneity of Effect Sizes

In meta-analysis, the problem of homogeneity is especially acute because there are at least two sources of difficulty: the single study and the group of studies. Single studies going into the analysis could individually be flawed. That is, they could each suffer from design flaws, making them poor studies and poor replicates of each other. Threats to validity of single studies are discussed extensively by Cook and Campbell (1979) and Campbell and Stanley (1963). Second, the group of studies selected for the meta-analysis could each be valid, but as a group, they could systematically sample different populations, result from different measurement biases, or in some other fashion fail to replicate each other. Campbell and Fiske (1959) discuss one way to separate out the effects of measurement methods. Alternatively, the group of studies could all be replicates of each other but not represent the universe to which the meta-analyst wishes to generalize.

Heterogeneity of effect sizes may result from a lack of consistency in the outcome measures used in the studies sampled. Studies that would be replicates of each other if they all used a highly reliable test to assess the factor under study and if all data were available may appear to lack homogeneity because the measures employed vary in reliability or because authors tend to report only some of the data from their studies.

One such source of heterogeneity is low test reliability for outcome measures in all studies. Outcome measures with low reliability fail to detect differences even when they exist. Low reliability of outcome measures will result in d's that underestimate the true difference between groups and may misrepresent the magnitude of effect or even fail to detect it.

Heterogeneity also results from differences in reliability of outcome measures across studies. Such differences will result in heterogeneity of effect sizes since more reliable outcome measures yield larger effect sizes. Suppose that some outcome measures had a reliability of 0.90 while others had a reliability of 0.25 and the same true d. Studies using these different outcome measures will yield different average d's. Thus a lack of similar reliability for outcome measures in the studies in the meta-analysis could lead to heterogeneity of effect sizes.

Many meta-analyses—including the social influence analysis reported by Becker (chap. 8) and the spatial ability analysis reported by Linn and Petersen (chap. 4)—report that partitioning groups of effect sizes by outcome measure explains some of the heterogeneity in the sample of studies. In chap. 4, the larger effect sizes for the Vandenberg-Metzler mental rotations test compared to the primary mental abilities–space test may, for example, be due in part to the lower reliability of the latter, which is the shorter of the two measures.

Another source of heterogeneity is the influence of experience with the outcome measure. Students who have more experience with an outcome measure are likely to do better. If the effects of practice are confounded with treatment group then spuriously high or low effect sizes could result. For example, boys who take physics classes more often than girls may practice items from physics achievement tests and perform better than females on that basis. Thus practice on items from the outcome measure used to assess effects of gender could be confounded with gender. Across studies, testing could also reduce homogeneity of effect sizes if some samples have more practice than others.

Another source of heterogeneity in outcome measures is developmental trends. As respondents age, they may develop skills that change what the outcome measure is assessing. They may have longer attention spans or greater processing capacities. These factors may result in larger or smaller effect sizes depending on how the change interacts with the outcome measure. For example, students younger than about 12 perform at the chance level on the Vandenberg-Metzler mental rotations test because they cannot follow the directions. A lack of gender difference for this group stems from random performance. Combining results for respondents under 12 with results for older respondents could result in heterogeneity of effect sizes.

Incomplete data is another source of heterogeneity of effect sizes. When meta-analysts lack complete information about the results of a study, they may over- or underestimate the effect size. Some researchers have, for example, used a d of zero to represent the effect size for a study reporting a non-significant effect. Such an approach will generally underestimate the effect and therefore introduce heterogeneity into the group of effect sizes. In contrast, excluding such effects will usually result in overestimates of the average effect size. Researchers can contribute to the ultimate effectiveness of their research by providing information to facilitate meta-analysis.

The meta-analyses reported in this volume illustrate how infrequently complete information is available. Often, fewer than 50 percent of the studies identified provided sufficient information for the computation of effect sizes. (see, e.g., chaps. 3 and 8). When research is not motivated by the study of gender and when no gender differences are found, authors may fail to report sufficient information for computing effect sizes. Just as a bias toward publishing only studies revealing significant differences may well contribute to inflated effect sizes when only published studies are used, so could a "data-reporting bias" contribute to inflated effect sizes when details are reported only when differences are significant.

The chapters in this volume reveal that homogeneity of effect sizes in studies of gender differences occurs infrequently. At least some sources of heterogeneity do not detract from conclusions. For example, lack of homogeneity due to heterogeneous test reliability is frustrating but may not detract from conclusions about the construct under investigation. In this new field, we need more experience in order to understand better the need for and actual limits on homogeneity.

Validity of Meta-analysis Results

Eagly, in her American Psychological Association presentation in 1983 and in chapter 7 of this volume, has made a landmark contribution to the understanding of issues in the validity of meta-analysis results. She articulates issues in construct and external validity that require the attention of those doing research synthesis. Several of the issues she identified are illustrated in the meta-analyses reported in other chapters in this volume and are discussed in this section.

In the area of construct validity the question is, What *is* in a name? Much of research interpretation rests on the assumption that constructs are properly named (e.g., Cronbach and Meehl, 1955). As Eagly discusses, in research synthesis, the problem is monumental. Synthesizers are often confronted with a multitude of studies involving similar tests, each named differently. Those conducting meta-analyses need to partition studies into groups that are replicates and to name constructs for homogeneous effects. They seek to capture the most valid information. Often no consensus among research studies contributing to the synthesis can be detected. The meta-analysis of spatial ability reported in chapter 4 is a good example: distinct forms of spatial ability fall on very different dimensions and several aspects of spatial ability were ultimately identified, each with a different average effect size.

As Eagly notes, external validity is threatened if the results of the meta-analysis do not generalize to new populations, settings, or times. An example of a threat to external validity occurs when students from several national groups are used. Cultural differences may introduce heterogeneity of effects. Frequently the number of studies from non-American cultural groups is small. To allow valid conclusions about cultural groups in the United States and about international populations, the pool of effects needs to be reasonably large. Thus, as several authors in this volume indicate, meta-analyses are often designed to generalize to all Americans or to a subset of Americans, and studies of other national groups are omitted. Meta-analysis must depend on the studies available. It is often the case that gender differences on a particular dimension vary across cultural groups but that the groups have not been studied extensively and are not adequately represented in the meta-analysis as a result.

Another source of lack of external validity is bias in selection of setting. This often occurs because of logistic difficulties in arranging field trials and may also occur because of experimenter bias toward a certain measurement technique. This volume illustrates the distinction between laboratory and naturalistic settings for several dimensions (aggression, nonverbal behavior). To accommodate setting differences, meta-analysis results have often been blocked on the naturalistic-laboratory dimension. Settings often prove to be sufficiently disparate that they cannot be meaningfully grouped.

Another example of a possible threat to external validity is biased selection of times. Historical time, seasonal time, and time of day are possible influences on results. Many meta-analyses of gender differences use the studies sampled by Maccoby and Jacklin (1974), the last of which was conducted in about 1973. Trends over time, such as changes in enrollment patterns for mathematics and science and changes in sports participation patterns may make these studies unrepresentative of the current situation. For example, Hyde (chap. 3) found a relationship between date of publication and outcome for studies of aggression.

Recommendations

Meta-analysis is a new and in many ways very exciting tool for research synthesis. Like any such tool, it has drawbacks. Slavin (1984a, 1984b) recently examined the use of meta-analysis in education and raised issues about the kinds of biases it might elicit. He suggested that the tool may "pull a veil of numbers" over complex and often contradictory findings (1984b, p. 26). The response to Slavin's article revealed that researchers using the technique were well aware of the complexities in the studies entered into their meta-analyses and had no intention of veiling their findings (Carlberg et al., 1984). All attempts at research synthesis emphasize some findings and reduce others to "noise." The criteria researchers use to make these decisions deserve scrutiny. Just as researchers carefully examine applications of statistical procedures to single studies to ensure that their conclusions are valid, so do they examine applications of meta-analysis to multiple studies to ensure that their conclusions are valid. Like any technique, meta-analysis can be used in both effective and incomplete research syntheses. Because meta-analysis is relatively new, researchers need experience in assessing results from syntheses using this tool.

The authors of each of the chapters in this book have been concerned about the validity of their meta-analysis procedures. Assessment of homogeneity has proved helpful. Such assessment motivates researchers to examine studies that yield aberrant effect sizes and to identify variables for partitioning groups studies with heterogeneous effect sizes.

As Eagly discusses (chap. 7), opportunities to conduct meta-analyses allow researchers to focus more precisely on issues of construct validity and external validity in assessing gender differences. This opportunity encourages refinement of the constructs and conditions under which gender differences occur. Lack of construct validity could result in invalid policy recommendations. For example, if mathematics tests involving only computation are used to assess sex differences, researchers might conclude that females are better mathematicians than males and recommend that males avoid math-related careers such as engineering and physics. Thus both experience and informed judgments are required to interpret meta-analyses, just as they are required to interpret all efforts at research synthesis.

Perhaps the most important conclusion concerning the application of meta-analysis to studies of gender differences is that homogeneity of effect sizes is difficult to achieve. Gender differences are moderated by a large number of factors. Rather than discovering well-defined constructs that differentiate males and females, we see that relatively weak effects that interact with many contextual variables emerge.

Results Reported in This Volume

Major findings in the area of gender differences have been refined and reinterpreted in many studies conducted since 1974. In this volume, meta-analysis has been used for reanalysis of gender differences in all the areas where Maccoby and Jacklin found consistent effects except verbal ability. In addition, some new areas, including nonverbal behavior, have been studied. More detailed understanding is now possible because researchers have followed up on themes identified by Maccoby and Jacklin (1974) and because meta-analysis techniques introduce greater precision.

This volume extends understanding of gender differences to include the relative magnitude of differences in the areas of aggression, mathematics, science, spatial ability, social influence, smiling and gazing, and helping behavior. In addition, it provides considerable refinement of our understanding of the conditions under which these differences occur.

Magnitude of Gender Differences

Gender differences in intellectual and psychosocial tasks are relatively small compared to the massive differences in participation of males and females in powerful, remunerative, satisfying, and secure careers. The differences in activities of males and females have changed dramatically over the years. Not so long ago, women were not deemed capable of benefiting from education, nor were they allowed to vote. Today growing numbers of women take advantage of all types of educational opportunities, and for the first time, a woman was selected by a national political party as part of the presidential ticket. Only recently, women were believed to be unable to develop the muscles required for athletic pursuits; there is now a rapidly diminishing gap between males and females in athletic records. Similarly, there has been a change from the view that women are not capable of understanding mathematics and science to an acknowledgment of their increasing participation in and contributions to those fields. We have seen the view that women have smaller brains give way to the realization that true brains of women are the same as the brains of men relative to their body sizes (Gould, 1981).

Magnitude of Effect Sizes

In contrast to larger differences in career experiences of males and females, the largest effect size for gender found in the meta-analyses in this volume was an average of about nine tenths of a standard deviation unit for mental rotations, one aspect of spatial ability (chap. 4). The next largest effect size was of about six tenths of a standard deviation unit found for gazing (chap. 6). Differences of about half a standard deviation unit were found for aggressive behavior and mathematics problems solving at age 17 but not at younger ages. The next largest findings were of about one third of a standard deviation reported for spatial perception (another aspect of spatial ability that involves ability to recognize the horizontal or vertical), smiling behavior, and aspects of social influence ability. Average effect sizes for attribution of success and failure to ability and effort, helping behavior, and acquisition of information about science were all under a quarter of a standard deviation. No differences between males or females were detected for measures of spatial visualization or for measures of scientific reasoning that did not involve mathematics knowledge or science information knowledge. Thus the largest effect sizes are found in the same areas in which Maccoby and Jacklin reported significant findings and in the nonverbal behavior of gazing, which was not studied previously.

Interactions of Gender Differences with Context, Knowledge Domain, and Developmental Level

Interactions between gender differences and other factors identified in this volume fall into three areas. First, researchers have identified the contextual factors under which gender differences occur. By context, we mean the situational conditions and the measurement conditions characterizing the research. Second, researchers have refined our understanding of the knowledge domain in which gender differences are found. Third, researchers have characterized developmental trends in the display of gender differences.

Context Influences

All the chapters in this book reported evidence for the influence of context on gender differences. In aggression, Hyde (chap. 3) reports that gender differences are larger in naturalistic than laboratory settings, larger for physical aggression than for verbal aggression, and larger when measured by direct observations or peer report than when measured by self-report. In spatial ability, Petersen and I (chap. 4) report that gender differences are larger for tasks involving mental rotation and detection of the vertical and horizontal and are nonexistent for tasks involving analytic combination of spatial strategies. For helping behavior, Eagly (chap. 7) reports heterogeneous gender differences, attributable to a variety of intercorrelated factors including perceived personal danger. For attributions, Whitley, McHugh, and Frieze (chap. 5) report larger gender differences for certain question wordings than for others, and for attributions of effort when failure occurs than for attributions of effort when success occurs. For smiling and gazing, Hall and Halberstadt (chap. 6) report larger gender differences in laboratory than in naturalistic settings, under conditions of warmth than under neutral conditions, and in a social context than in an impersonal context. Becker (chap. 8) reports that the magnitude of gender differences in influenceability reflects the type of scoring used, is larger in a group pressure context than in an individual context, and is larger for American subjects than for foreign subjects. These context effects indicate that gender differences are situational and multifaceted. Interactions between social, cultural, and situational context and gender differences are widespread.

Knowledge Domain Influences

The separation of the influence of knowledge of the subject matter from context influences is not always straightforward. In spatial ability, for example, the conditions of measurement influence gender differences. Moreover, refinement of the investigation suggests that there might be three different knowledge domains involved rather than a single dimension of spatial ability. Thus the context of measurement may indeed be confounded with the knowledge domain.

In mathematics, the knowledge domain is a component of gender differences, with females outperforming males in the area of computation and males outperforming females on problem solving. This result may reflect differential experience with courses emphasizing problem solving. Knowledge also influences performance in scientific reasoning. Scientific reasoning tasks involving proportional reasoning yield gender differences favoring males, but no similar differences are found for tasks without a proportional reasoning component.

In the area of scientific information, there is a definite influence of subject matter, with males outperforming females on items having to do with physical science knowledge and females outperforming males in the area of health knowledge. In attributions of success and failure, subject matter knowledge also appears to influence performance. Males are more likely to attribute success and failure to ability in traditional male domains such as mathematics and science than in other domains. Such a finding may be realistic. In areas where one does have more knowledge and ability, one is more likely to recognize the role of that knowledge in success and failure. Thus females may realistically attribute success and failure more to luck than to ability when their training and experience levels are lower than those for males. This finding is consistent with investigations that discuss attributions of success and failure in computer learning environments for males and females (Linn 1985, in press). In these studies, attribution patterns were consistent with the performance levels of males and females in that males had more experience than females in computer learning. Consistent with the conclusions of Whitley, McHugh, and Frieze (chap. 5), in these environments, females are more likely than males to attribute success to luck and males are more likely than females to attribute success to ability.

Thus subject matter knowledge is a factor in observed gender differences in a number of areas. It is hardly surprising to know that individuals with greater knowledge perform differently than those without that knowledge. In addition, since many research studies have demonstrated the ease with which subject matter knowledge levels can be modified, it follows that psychosocial gender differences in areas where there are large differences in subject matter knowledge may be more volatile than they are in other domains. Thus the decline in the magnitude of gender differences in mathematics reported in chapter 4 may reflect the influence of course enrollment, and the lack of clear evidence for gender differences in attribution may reflect interactions with subject matter knowledge.

Developmental Influences

Another factor that has an impact on gender differences is the age of the individuals measured. In aggression, Hyde (chap. 3) reports that there is a decrease in gender differences with age. For smiling and gazing, Hall and Halberstadt (chap. 6) report an increase with age up to college, and then a slight decrease consistent with other research in the field. For mathematical computation, Petersen and I (chap. 4) report a decrease in gender differences with age. Factors mediating these age-related changes require more clarification, but interactions between age and gender differences are well established.

Implications

Perhaps the major implication of the investigations reported in this volume is the strong evidence for an interactionist view of gender differences. Far from being well established and straightforward, gender differences are responsive to a large range of situational factors and background knowledge. There is strong evidence of interactions between what Maccoby and Jacklin found were "established" gender differences and the conditions under which these differences are measured. Thus conditions for performance can be selected to foster equality of opportunity for males and females or they can be selected to increase inequalities.

While gains in understanding of gender differences in intellectual and psychosocial variables have occurred, no general explanation for them has emerged. Relationships between gender differences in, say, aggression and spatial ability have not been detected. Even in areas where relationships have been hypothesized, such as between spatial ability and mathematics achievement, no such consistency has been observed. Links between gender differences in one area and those in another are difficult to establish.

Toward a Psychology of Gender Differences

To place the current results in perspective, a historical view is taken. It is helpful to briefly examine the history of explanations for differences between males and females. As this selective survey shows, the interactionist view that observed gender differences are strongly influenced by the experiences of males and females has only recently gained prominence. Historically, the primary view has been that observed gender differences result from biological differences that are only slightly moderated by environmental circumstances.

A Historical View

Views of gender differences in the intellectual and psychosocial domains have generally assumed that biological factors determine observed characteristics. These views typically suggest that the existing inequitable social circumstances of women result from their biological inferiority. Until the turn of the century, the stereotypes of male intellectual superiority and female nurturance, emotionality, and dependence were regarded as established, in spite of a total lack of empirical evidence.

Intellectual Ability

Shields (1982) provides insight into one biological argument for gender differences in mental ability—the variability hypothesis. The hypothesis stems from Darwin's assertion that males are more variable from one to another and are more highly evolved than females. Darwin's perspective is well illustrated in his comment that fortunately for women these processes are constrained by the fact that most inherited characteristics are transmitted equally for both male and female offspring, "otherwise, it is probable that man would have become as superior in mental endowment to women, as the peacock is in ornamental plumage to the peahen" (Darwin 1871, 1897; quoted by Shields, 1982, p. 772). Interestingly, Shields notes that Darwin first put these ideas forth tentatively in 1871 but by 1897 was asserting them forcefully, although the evidence had become no more persuasive.

Measurement of human abilities commenced with somewhat haphazard investigations of physical and motor skills. Galton (1879, 1883), for example, set up a booth at a fair and measured volunteers height, strength, reaction time, and the like. Generally, males are taller and stronger than females and, therefore, outperformed females. Encouraged by these results, Galton attempted to establish the role of heredity in the incidence of genius. He compiled lists of eminent individuals (who were mostly males) and examined their ancestors for genius. This tradition of compiling lists was continued by others, providing documentation for the belief that females were innately less likely than males to achieve genius. Few questioned this view at the time, and those who did were usually women. For example, in 1913 Cora Castle compiled a list of eminent women in history. Commenting on the small number, she notes, "Has innate inferiority been the reason for the small number of eminent women, or has civilization never yet allowed them an opportunity to develop their innate powers and possibilities" (Castle, 1913; quoted by Shields, 1982, p. 780). Thus Castle expressed concern about the interaction between opportunity and ability. An interactionist view is expressed, albeit with some uncertainty and limited impact.

The mental-testing movement began in response to evidence that the motor skills measured by Galton did not predict intellectual functioning. It was the first effort to measure mental ability empirically, and therefore it provided the first practical evidence of gender differences in these areas. Binet (Binet & Simon, 1905) developed individual tests of reasoning ability. Large-scale mental testing occurred during World War I when group tests starting with the Army alpha test were administered. Soon afterward, tests became commonplace in schools (Cronbach, 1975).

Mental tests of general ability failed to detect differences between males and females in the 1920s, just as they fail to detect such differences today (Maccoby, 1966; Maccoby & Jacklin, 1974). Nevertheless, the variability hypothesis (that females are less prone to genius) was put forth by male scholars to reconcile these findings with the prevailing view that males were superior (Shields, 1982).

Not surprisingly, female scholars, who were only first admitted to graduate schools in 1880 (Woody, 1929), vociferously argued for an interactionist perspective. For example, a literature survey conducted by Hollingsworth (1914) found no evidence for gender differences in mental ability, and systematically refuted other arguments for male superiority, such as the low incidence of eminent women, on the grounds of differences in early socialization and in expected social role.

In summary, females historically have been viewed as less intellectually able and less likely to achieve eminence as a result of biologically inherited factors. The primary explanation put forth has been the variability hypothesis. This view prevailed in spite of a lack of evidence: "Thus the variability hypothesis, though it has undergone some modifications and lost much of its social importance since its origins at the turn of the century, has survived to the present day with relatively little factual support" (Shields, 1982, p. 794).

Strong arguments for an interactionist view of gender differences in mental ability were also voiced during this period—primarily by women. These views influenced other women and ultimately were embraced by some men, for example, Terman, conducted longitudinal studies of the gifted (Terman, 1975). He was able to identify more gifted males than females, and he consequently embraced the variability hypothesis. But after reviewing the accomplishments of gifted males and females, he changed his views, and in 1974, he remarked:

> The woman who is a potential poet, novelist, lawyer, physician, or scientist usually gives up any professional ambition she may have had and devotes herself to home, husband, and children. The exclusive devotion to domestic pursuits robs the arts and sciences of a large fraction of the genius that might otherwise be dedicated to them. My data strongly suggest that this loss must be debited to motivational causes and limited opportunity rather than to lack of ability. (Terman, 1975, 225)

Psychosocial Characteristics

Historically, psychosocial differences between males and females were viewed as resulting from biological factors just as were intellectual differences. Recently an interactionist perspective has also permeated the psychosocial domain, and these differences are now seen by some as resulting from the interaction between biological factors and social experience. Freud's psychoanalytic theory placed strong emphasis on biological factors. Freud, basing his theory on anatomical differences, concluded that women were deprived by nature of resolving their developmental struggles satisfactorily and therefore experienced developmental failure in the early years and feelings of inferiority during adolescence (see Freud, 1961).

Chodorow (1974, 1978) counters this view with strong evidence for women's psychosocial development being shaped by their social roles. She focuses attention on early experience, following Freud's emphasis on this period. She argues that universally women are primarily responsible for early child care. Thus male and female children have different experiences and different social environments in their early years. Chodorow concludes that "in any given society, feminine personality comes to define itself in relation and connection to other people more than masculine personality does" (1974, p. 44).

Gilligan (1982), focusing on moral development, draws attention to the reliance of earlier theory on the characteristics of male behavior as the norm and the characteristics of female behavior as either "confused" or incompletely developed. Emphasizing the attention women pay to others, reflected in their role in child care, their responsible consideration of the views of others, and their supportive role in traditional families, Gilligan raises "a different voice" in the effort to understand the psychosocial development of women:

> As we have listened for centuries to the voices of men and the theories of development that their experience informs, so we have come more recently to notice not only the silence of women but the difficulty in hearing what they say when they speak. Yet in the different voice of women lies the truth of an ethic of care, the tie between relationship and responsibility, and the origins of aggression in the failure of connection. The failure to see the different reality of women's lives and to hear the differences in their voices stems in part from the assumption that there is a single mode of social experience and interpretation. (1982, p. 173)

Thus contemporary views of psychosocial development emphasize interactions of biological factors and social circumstances. Gilligan, by stressing the contributions that arise from the different perspectives of women, cautions us not to seek a single standard for psychosocial development. Recent views of psychosocial development also draw attention to early reliance of theorists on male behavior as a norm, and on biological factors as the justification for such a position. Choice of different norms will result in different views of the strengths and weaknesses of males and females.

Empirical Approaches

Until quite recently, gender differences were attributed to biological factors without benefit of empirical evidence. Growing dispute about the role of socialization in these differences led to a larger number of systematic studies. These studies raised many questions because of their inconsistent results, setting the stage for attempts at research synthesis.

The widely disparate views of the causes of intellectual and psychosocial differences in males and females were noted by Maccoby (1966) and effectively addressed by Maccoby and Jacklin (1974). Acknowledging that intense debate surrounded such questions, Maccoby and Jacklin, "proceeded on the assumption that before we can attempt to understand the 'why' and 'how' of psychological sex differentiation, we must have as accurate and detailed a knowledge as possible concerning the nature of existing differences" (1974, p. 1). Their volume synthesized results from over two thousand studies in order to characterize the existing gender differences.

Maccoby and Jacklin summarized gender differences in the intellectual and psychosocial areas and concluded that only four constructs yielded consistent findings. These were verbal ability favoring females, mathematics ability favoring males, spatial ability favoring males, and aggression found more frequently in males. Block (1976) subsequently offered both elaboration and criticism of these conclusions, but by and large they have guided investigators.

In assessing what their findings meant, Maccoby and Jacklin considered several hypotheses. They concluded that biological factors probably play a role in gender differences in aggression and might be implicated in spatial ability. They concluded that although parental socialization is important, its effects are not sufficient to explain all observed differences. Regarding imitation of the same-sex parent as a mechanism to account for gender differences, Maccoby and Jacklin were unconvinced. Finding these social-learning explanations insufficient, they introduced the process of "sub-socialization," adapted from Kohlberg (1966). In this process, children gradually acquire concepts of "masculinity" and "feminity" they eventually use to govern their own behavior. Such a process is influenced by the general level of cognitive development the child has achieved and progresses as cognitive skills become more sophisticated.

A Psychology of Gender: From Main Effect to Interaction

At the turn of the century, theorists had linked an "obvious" biological explanation to the observed societal differences between males and females. Today researchers document powerful interactions between changing societal circumstances and the performance of each sex. Views of the differences between males and females have changed dramatically. Darwin in 1897 felt justified in strengthening his statements about the biological basis for gender differences although the evidence had not changed. In contrast, two decades of extensive analysis of the evidence suggests that the role of biological processes in intellectual and psychosocial gender differences is small.

The evidence in this volume supports a highly interactive relationship between gender, social context, intellectual ability and psychosocial skills. This is hardly surprising given the interactive nature of human society. The human infant depends on interactions with others for survival, and some members of society take responsibility for that survival. Such relationships help shape the expectations and training experienced by men and women.

As social roles change, so do these expectations. For example, Jeanne Brooks-Gunn reports that "girls whose mothers work have higher self-esteem and career aspirations than girls whose mothers don't work" (quoted by Shreve, 1984, p. 43). Researchers report that these changing relationships are carried into play situations. Nancy Close reports an increasing incidence of preschool girls "packing up briefcases to go to the office just like mom," Mary Ann Weinberger reports that boys in nursery school "play in the kitchen more than they used to" (ibid., p. 54). The long-term implications of these recent changes have yet to be established, but the precedent of increased opportunities for women and increased preparation for those opportunities is apparent.

Changes in social roles have been slow, but they could not have been predicted by the stereotypic views of women, biologically based theories, and lack of concern for empirical evidence that characterized writings on gender differences prior to 1900. Creating a case for the interactionist view required extensive effort. Much of the effort came from women, who, of course, had a personal interest in the issues. Hollingsworth compiled extensive evidence in the early 1900s. Many women and some men conducted research that was ultimately synthesized by Maccoby (1966) and Maccoby and Jacklin (1974). These writers recognized the role of interaction, yet the view of a main biological effect remained strong, perhaps reinforced by stereotypic views of women as well as by some, but far from all, research results.

The appeal of the main effect of a biological factor is evident. Main effects are tidy. Scientists generally seek ultimate causes for things. Interactions can be elusive, effects of complex naturally occurring influences such as "experience" are not readily established. Keller (1982) argues this point convincingly for interactionist theories in the history of biology. The interactionist position has been taken more frequently by women than men in biology, Keller suggests, because women have favored different methodologies, different working styles, and different theoretical orientations than men. A primary example in biology is McClintock (1951), whose work was dismissed, reintroduced, and ultimately awarded the Nobel Prize long after the results and implications were established. Keller notes that McClintock "developed a paradigm that diverged as radically from the dominant paradigm of the field as did her methodological style" (1982, p. 601). Interactionist approaches have often been championed by women, perhaps because of their experience in nurturing roles, and have often been poorly received. Although we lack good understanding of the influences that lead to acceptance or rejection of theories, Keller and others raise our suspicions that some perspectives have been selected against in the past. Such selection processes must be modified, and what has been called the feminist voice brings a mechanism for this modification.

A feminist perspective is emerging in a range of disciplines. While not clearly defined nor unified, many examples of effective contributions from this perspective exist (e.g., McGaw, 1982). The views of Chodorow, Gilligan, Keller, Brooks-Gunn, and others cited in this chapter are examples. Carol Stack's ability to bring order to the reported chaos of life in urban black communities by her redefinition of the family unit (1974) is another example. To encourage responsible consideration of these perspectives, Kahn and Jean (1983), Boxer (1982), and others argue for strong programs of women's studies. Clearly, an intellectual environment that values and responds to the feminist perspective is needed. Under such circumstances, a thoughtful, feminist philosophy is likely to emerge.

Conclusions

Meta-analysis coupled with tests of homogeneity focuses our attention on what constitutes a "replication" of a finding. What allows generalizability from a research study to a naturally occurring situation or from one study to another? The meta-analyses reported in this book illustrate how infrequently we find true replications of gender-difference effects. Heterogeneity of effect size characterizes research on gender differences. Main effects for gender are small and they are readily moderated by the context of measurement.

Future Research

As the authors of each chapter have discussed, the current findings suggest many avenues for future investigation. Further refinement of dimensions that interact with frequently found gender differences is a primary motivation for such work. Meta-analysis techniques are likely to enhance the opportunities for validation of hypotheses about interactions.

One direction for research is a greater emphasis on naturally occurring situations. For example, Eagly notes that helping has mainly been studied in short-term contexts. In contrast, long-term opportunities for helping may yield a different pattern of findings. Hyde reports that aggression is more realistically studied in naturalistic situations yet is frequently studied in laboratories.

An area where there is lack of clear construct definition is attribution. As Whitley, McHugh, and Frieze point out, attribution may be a constellation of constructs, some of which deserve further scrutiny and perhaps reanalysis and others of which have not contributed to our understanding of gender differences and should be dropped from future study.

An area where research could make a major contribution is in longitudinal understanding of the factors contributing to observed gender differences. Several of the studies in this volume reported developmental trends. However, by and large, those trends were garnered from analysis of cross-sectional data. Longitudinal investigations are extremely important in order to establish the causal factors leading to the observed differences. Several longitudinal studies are currently under way and offer great opportunities for understanding these questions. (Petersen & Gitelson, in press; Block & Block, 1985.)

Especially important are questions relating one gender-related effect to another. The reported results do not fit a single explanation. Studies examining how gender effects are linked or illustrating a lack of linkage would clarify the nature of gender differences in intellectual and psychosocial domains.

Career Opportunities

Given the large differences in the distributions of males and females in positions of power and financial remuneration, and in positions of nurturance and support, the relatively small differences in psychological variables observed in the studies in this volume are, in fact, the surprising findings. One important question concerns the relationship between these discrepancies. After noting the small differences on variables considered to be important in the acquisition of positions of power and leadership, it is disheartening to observe how few females are represented in those positions. Similarly, after noting the small differences in psychosocial skills, it is discouraging to note how few males participate extensively in child rearing.

Changes in opportunities for the sexes have been dramatic in the last ten years. In particular, career opportunities for females have increased significantly. Admission of females to professional schools, especially medical schools, has increased. The number of female representatives in male-dominated professions such as carpentry and electronics has increased. Female participation in athletic pursuits has also undergone notable change.

These hard-won opportunities for females are likely to encourage increasing numbers of women to enroll in previously male-dominated programs. However, persistence is required in order to maintain and expand these opportunities. There are still large differences in the representation of females and males in careers such as engineering and computer science and in positions such as tenured professorships and corporate presidencies.

Changes in opportunities for men have also occurred. The presence of nurturing females in male-dominated professions has, at times, empowered men to take a more substantial role in child rearing and other forms of caring for others. These changes have profound and far-reaching implications for society. The acceptance of men as being nurturing, caring, and emotional increases the opportunities available to them. The presence of men in female-dominated professions such as nursery school teaching and homemaking has increased. Persistence is required to maintain and expand these opportunities.

Research that documents whether and when intellectual and psychosocial gender differences influence career opportunities and that describes the rewards of caring for others will help those designing career education programs for both sexes. Programs building on this research can lead to social change. Good examples of how this process can succeed are found in the *AERA Handbook for Achieving Sex Equity through Education* (Klein, 1985).

Implications

Historically, views of gender differences emphasized main effects. Results reported in this volume from over a thousand studies of close to half a million individuals show that gender differences can be moderated or potentiated by the context in which they are measured. These results warn us against unwarranted generalizations. They illustrate how widely held stereotypes can interact with small differences to make them appear larger. They demonstrate how well-chosen circumstances might serve to eliminate gender differences. They provide guidance for those designing educational programs to provide the greatest opportunities for both males and females and ensure equity in our society.

References

Binet, A., & Simon, T. (1905). Méthodes nouvelles pour le diagnostic du niveau intellectuel des anormaux. *Année psychologique, 11*, 191–224.

Block, J. H. (1976). Issues, problems, and pitfalls in assessing sex differences: A critical review of *The Psychology of Sex Differences. Merrill-Palmer Quarterly, 22*, 282–308.

Block, J. H., & Block, J. (1985). Ego control and ego resiliencies: A longitudinal study of gender differences. Manuscript.

Boxer, M. J. (1982). For and about women: The theory and practice of women's studies in the United States. *Signs: Journal of Women in Culture and Society, 7*, 661–695.

Campbell, D. T., & Fiske, D. W. (1959). Convergent and discriminant validation by the multitrait-multimethod matrix. *Psychological Bulletin, 56*, 81–105.

Campbell, D. T., & Stanley, J. C. (1963). Experimental and quasi-experimental designs for research on teaching. In N. L. Gage (ed.), *Handbook of research on teaching*. Chicago: Rand McNally.

Carlberg, C. G., et al. (1984). Meta-analysis in education: A reply to Slavin. *Educational Researcher, 13*, 16–23.

Castle, C. (1913). A statistical study of eminent women. *Columbia University Contributions in Philosophy and Psychology, 22,* 1–90.

Chodorow, N. (1974). Family structure and feminine personality. In M. Z. Rosaldo & L. Lamphere (eds.), *Women, culture, and society.* Stanford: Stanford University Press.

Chodorow, N. (1978). *The reproduction of mothering.* Berkeley: University of California Press.

Cook, T. D., & Campbell, D. T. (1979). *Quasi-experimentation: Design and analysis issues for field settings.* Chicago: Rand McNally.

Cronbach, L. J. (1975). Five decades of public controversy over mental testing. *American Psychologist, 30,* 1–14.

Cronbach, L. J., & Meehl, P. E. (1955). Construct validity in psychological tests. *Psychological Bulletin, 52,* 281–302.

Darwin, C. (1871). *The descent of man and selection in relation to sex.* London: John Murray.

Darwin, C. (1897). *The descent of man and selection in relation to sex* (2nd ed.). New York: D. Appleton.

Deaux, K. K. (1984). From individual differences to social categories. *American Psychologist, 39,* 105–116.

Deaux, K. K. (1985). Sex and gender. *Annual Review of Psychology, 36,* 49–81.

Eagly, A. H. (1983). Using meta-analysis to examine biases in gender-difference research. Paper presented at the annual meeting of the American Psychological Association, Los Angeles.

Freud, S. (1961). *The complete psychological works.* London: Hogarth Press.

Galton, F. (1879). Psychometric experiments. *Brain, 2,* 149–162.

Galton, F. (1883). *Inquiries into human faculty and its development.* London: Macmillan.

Gilligan, C. (1982). *In a different voice: Psychological theory and women's development.* Cambridge: Harvard University Press.

Gould, S. J. (1981). *The mismeasure of man.* New York: Norton.

Hollingsworth, L. S. (1914). Variability as related to sex differences in achievement. *American Journal of Sociology, 19,* 510–530.

Kahn, A. S., & Jean, P. J. (1983). Integration and elimination or separation and redefinition: The future of the psychology of women. *Signs: Journal of Women in Culture and Society, 8,* 659–671.

Keller, E. F. (1982). Feminism and science. *Signs: Journal of Women in Culture and Society, 7,* 589–602.

Klein, S. S. (Ed.). (1985) *Handbook for achieving sex equity through education.* Baltimore: Johns Hopkins University Press.

Kohlberg, L. (1966). Cognitive stages and preschool education. *Human Development, 9,* 6.

Linn, M. C. (1985). Gender equity in computer learning environments. *Computers and the Social Sciences, 1,* 19–27.

Linn, M. C. (1985). Fostering equitable consequences from learning environments. *Sex Roles, 13,* 229–240.

Maccoby, E. E. (1966). *The development of sex differences.* Stanford: Stanford University Press.

Maccoby, E. E., & Jacklin, C. N. (1974). *The psychology of sex differences.* Stanford: Stanford University Press.

McClintock, B. (1951). Chromosome organization and genic expression. *Cold Spring Harbor Symposium of Quantitative Biology, 16,* 13-44.

McGaw, J. A. (1982). Women and the history of American technology. *Signs: Journal of Women in Culture and Society, 7,* 798-828.

Petersen, A. C., & Gitelson, I. B. (in press). *Toward understanding sex-related differences in cognitive performance.* New York: Academic Press.

Shields, S. A. (1982). The variability hypothesis: The history of a biological model of sex differences in intelligence. *Signs: Journal of Women in Culture and Society, 7,* 769-797.

Shreve, A. (1984). The working mother as role model. *New York Times Magazine,* September 9.

Slavin, R. E. (1984a). Meta-analysis in education: How has it been used? *Educational Researcher, 13,* 6-15.

Slavin, R. E. (1984b). A rejoinder to Carlberg et al. *Educational Researcher, 13,* 24-27.

Stack, C. (1974). *All our kin.* New York: Harper & Row.

Terman, L. (1975). Human intelligence and achievement. In M. V. Seagoe (ed.). *Terman and the gifted.* Los Altos, Calif.: William Kaufmann.

Witkin, H. A., & Goodenough, D. R. (1981). *Cognitive styles: Essence and origins.* New York: International Universities Press.

Woody, T. (1929). *A history of women's education in the United States.* New York: Science Press.

Appendix A:
Studies Reviewed
in Aggression

Abramovitch, R., Corter, C., & Lando, B. (1979). Sibling interaction in the home. *Child Development, 50*, 997–1003

Ahmed, S. M. S. (1979) Visibility of the victim. *Journal of Social Psychology, 107*, 253–255

Allen, R. D. (1978). An analysis of the impact of two forms of short-term assertive training on aggressive behavior. *Dissertation Abstracts International, 39*, 2058A.

Arms, R. L., Russell, G. W., & Sandilands, M. L. (1979). Effects on the hostility of spectators of viewing aggressive sports. *Social Psychology Quarterly, 42*, 275–279.

Bakker, C. B., Bakker-Rabdau, M. K., & Breit, S. (1978). The measurement of assertiveness and aggressiveness. *Journal of Personality Assessment, 42*, 277–284.

Bandura, A., Grusec, J. E., & Menlove, F. L. (1966). Observational learning as a function of symbolization and incentive set. *Child Development, 37*, 499–506.

Bankart, C. P., & Anderson, C. C. (1979). Short-term effects of prosocial television viewing on play of preschool boys and girls. *Psychological Reports, 44*, 935–941.

Barclay, A. M. (1970). The effect of female aggressiveness on aggressive and sexual fantasies. *Journal of Projective Techniques and Personality Assessment, 34*, 19–26.

Barrett, D. E. (1979). A naturalistic study of sex differences in children's aggression. *Merrill-Palmer Quarterly, 25*, 193–203.

Baumrind, D. (1971). Current patterns of parental authority. *Developmental Psychology Monographs, 4*(1).

Baumrind, D., & Black, A. E. (1967). Socialization practices associated with dimensions of competence in preschool boys and girls. *Child Development, 38*, 291–327.

Berk, L. E. (1971). Effects of variations in the nursery school setting on environmental constraints and children's modes of adaptation. *Child Development, 42*, 839-869.

Brenner, O. C., & Tomikewicz, J. (1980). Relationship between aggression and managerial effectiveness. *Psychological Reports, 47*, 271-274.

Brion-Meisels, S. J. (1978). Helping, sharing, and cooperation: An intervention study of middle childhood. *Dissertation Abstracts International, 38*, 4081-4082.

Brissett, M., & Nowicki, S., Jr. (1973). Internal versus external control of reinforcement and reaction to frustration. *Journal of Personality and Social Psychology, 25*, 35-44.

Brodzinsky, D. M., Messer, S. B., & Tew, J. D. (1979). Sex differences in children's expression and control of fantasy and overt aggression. *Child Development, 50*, 372-379.

Bullock, D., & Merrill, L. (1980). The impact of personal preference on consistency through time: The case of childhood aggression. *Child Development, 51*, 808-814.

Buss, A. H. (1966). Instrumentality of aggression, feedback, and frustration as determinants of physical aggression. *Journal of Personality and Social Psychology, 3*, 153-162.

Ciccolella, M. E. (1978). Differences in aggression of male and female athletes. *Dissertation Abstracts International, 39*, 3447A.

Crain, W. C., & Smoke, L. (1981). Rorschach aggressive content in normal and problematic children. *Journal of Personality Assessment, 45*, 2-4.

Crowther, J. H., Bond, L. A., & Rolf, J. E. (1981). The incidence, prevalence, and severity of behavior disorders among preschool-aged children in day care. *Journal of Abnormal Child Psychology, 9*, 23-42.

Deaux, K. K. (1971). Honking at the intersection: A replication and extension. *Journal of Social Psychology, 84*, 159-160.

Deluty, R. H. (1979). Children's Action Tendency Scale: A self-report measure of aggressiveness, assertiveness, and submissiveness in children. *Journal of Consulting and Clinical Psychology, 47*, 1061-1071.

DiPietro, J. A. (1981). Rough-and-tumble play: A function of gender. *Developmental Psychology, 17*, 50-58.

Ditrichs, R., Simon, S., & Greene, B. (1967). Effect of vicarious scheduling on the verbal conditioning of hostility in children. *Journal of Personality and Social Psychology, 6*, 71-78.

Doob, A. N., & Gross, A. E. (1968). Status of frustrator as an inhibitor of horn-honking responses. *Journal of Social Psychology, 76*, 213-218.

Doolittle, J. C. (1980). Immunizing children against possible antisocial effects of viewing television violence: A curricular intervention. *Perceptual and Motor Skills, 51*, 498.

Eisenberg, G. J. (1980). Children and aggression after observed film aggression with sanctioning adults. *Annals of the New York Academy of Sciences, 347*, 304–318.

Emmerich, W. (1971). Structure and development of personal-social behaviors in preschool settings. *Educational Testing Service–Head Start Longitudinal Study*, PR-71-20. Princeton, N.J.: Educational Testing Service.

Epstein, R. (1965). Authoritarianism, displaced aggression, and social status of the target. *Journal of Personality and Social Psychology, 2*, 585–589.

Fagot, B. I., & Patterson, G. R. (1969). An in vivo analysis of reinforcing contingencies for sex-role behaviors in the preschool child. *Developmental Psychology, 1*, 563–568.

Ferguson, L. R., & Maccoby, E. E. (1966). Interpersonal correlates of differential abilities. *Child Development, 37*, 549–571.

Feshbach, N. D. (1969). Sex differences in children's modes of aggressive responses toward outsiders. *Merrill-Palmer Quarterly, 15*, 249–258.

Feshbach, N. D. (1972). Cross-cultural studies of teaching styles in four-year-olds and their mothers: Some educational implications of socialization. *Minnesota Symposium on Child Development*.

Feshbach, N. D., & Devor, G. (1969). Teaching styles in four-year-olds. *Child Development, 40*, 183–190.

Finchum, K. G., & Freitag, C. B. (1979). Achievement, aggression, and perceived adult age stages. *Journal of Psychology, 102*, 179–184.

Forman, S. G. (1980). Self-statements of aggressive and nonaggressive children. *Child Behavior Therapy, 2*, 49–57.

Foster, K. T. (1979). The effect of model consistency and sex on the subsequent aggressive behavior of male and female observers. *Dissertation Abstracts International, 39*, 4027B–4028B.

Franzini, L. R., Litrownik, A. J., & Blanchard, F. H. (1978). Modeling of sex-typed behaviors: Effects on boys and girls. *Developmental Psychology, 14*, 313–314

French, L. A., & Wailes, S. N. (1980). Regional comparisons of suicidal aggression. *Corrective and Social Psychiatry and Journal of Behavior Technology, Methods, and Therapy, 26*, 180–192.

Frodi, A. (1978). Experiential and physiological responses associated with anger and aggression in women and men. *Journal of Research in Personality, 12*, 335–349.

Grusec, J. E. (1972). Demand characteristics of the modeling experiment: Altruism as a function of age and aggression. *Journal of Personality and Social Psychology, 22*, 139–148.

Grusec, J. E. (1973). Effects of co-observer evaluations on imitation: A developmental study. *Developmental Psychology, 8*, 141.

Hanson, D. J. (1978). Drinking norms and aggression. *Psychology, 15*, 34.

Hapkiewicz, W. G., & Roden, A. H. (1971). The effect of aggressive cartoons on children's interpersonal play. *Child Development, 42*, 1583–1585.

Harden, R. R., & Jacob, S. H. (1978). Relationship between aggression of preschoolers and teachers' sex. *Psychological Reports, 43*, 1172–1174.

Harmatz, M. G. (1967). Verbal conditioning and change on personality measures. *Journal of Personality and Social Psychology, 5*, 175–185.

Hartup, W. W. (1974). Aggression in childhood: Developmental perspectives. *American Psychologist, 29*, 336–341.

Hatfield, J. S., Ferguson, L. R., & Alpert, R. (1967). Mother-child interaction and the socialization process. *Child Development, 38*, 365–414.

Hayes, S. C., Rincover, A., & Volosin, D. (1980). Variables influencing the acquisition and maintenance of aggressive behavior: Modeling versus sensory reinforcement, *Journal of Abnormal Psychology, 89*, 254–262.

Hess, R. D., & Camara, K. A. (1979). Post-divorce family relationships as mediating factors in the consequences of divorce for children. *Journal of Social Issues, 34*, 79–96.

Hicks, D. J. (1968). Effects of co-observer's sanctions and adult presence on imitative aggression. *Child Development, 39*, 303–309.

Hokanson, J. E., & Edelman, R. (1966). Effects of three social responses on vascular processes. *Journal of Personality and Social Psychology, 3*, 442–447.

Hoppe, C. M. (1979). Interpersonal aggression as a function of subject's sex-role identification, opponent's sex, and degree of provocation. *Journal of Personality, 47*, 317–329.

Hoving, K. L., LaForme, G. L., & Wallace, J. R. (1974). The development of children's interpersonal aggression in a competitive task. In J. deWit & W. W. Hartup (eds.). *Determinants and origins of aggressive behavior.* The Hague: Mouton.

Hoving, K. L., Wallace, J. R., & LaForme, G. L. (1979). Aggression during competition: Effects of age, sex, and amount and type of provocation. *Genetic Psychology Monographs, 99*, 251–289.

Huesmann, L. R., Lefkowitz, M. M., & Eron, L. D. (1978). Sum of MMPI Scales F, 4, and 9 as a measure of aggression. *Journal of Consulting and Clinical Psychology, 46*, 1071–1078.

Huston-Stein, A., Fox, S., Greer, D., Watkins, B. A., & Whitaker, J. (1981). The effects of TV action and violence on children's social behavior. *Journal of Genetic Psychology, 138*, 183–191.

Hyde, J. S. & Schuck, J. R. (1977). The development of sex differences in aggression: A revised model. Paper presented at the meeting of the American Psychological Association, San Francisco, August 1977.

Hynan, M.; Harper, S.; Wood, C.; & Kallas, C. (1980). Parametric effects of blocking and winning in a competition paradigm of human aggression. *Bulletin of the Psychonomic Society*, *16*, 295-298.

Jackson, W. L. (1978). Level of subject hostility and the effects of viewing filmed aggression. *Dissertations Abstracts International, 38*(12-B), 6241-6242.

Jersild, A. T., & Markey, F. V. (1935). Conflicts between preschool children. *Child Development Monographs*, no. 21.

Johnson, S. D. (1980). Reverse discrimination and aggressive behavior. *Journal of Psychology, 104*, 11-19.

Jones, J. W., & Bogat, G. A. (1978). Air pollution and human aggression. *Psychological Reports, 43*, 721-722.

Klaus, R. S., & Gray, S. W. (1968). The early training project for disadvantaged children: A report after five years. *Monographs of the Society for Research in Child Development, 33*(120).

Klesges, R. C., McGinley, H., Jurkovic, G. J., Morgan, T. J. (1979). The predictive validity of typical and maximal personality measures in self-reports and peer reports. *Bulletin of the Psychonomic Society, 13*, 401-404.

Knott, P. D., & Drost, B. A. (1970). Sex-role identification, interpersonal aggression, and anger. *Psychological Reports, 27*, 154.

Koerner, F. E. (1977). The effects of depression and sex on aggression affect and behavior toward the self and toward others. *Dissertation Abstracts International, 38*, 1887B-1888B.

Lando, H. A., & Donnerstein, E. I. (1978). The effects of a model's success or failure on subsequent aggressive behavior. *Journal of Research in Personality, 12*, 225-234.

Langlois, J. H., & Downs, A. C. (1979). Peer relations as a function of physical attractiveness: The eye of the beholder or behavioral reality? *Child Development, 50*, 409-418.

Langlois, J. H., Gottfried, N. W., & Seay, B. (1973). The influence of sex of peer on the social behavior of preschool children. *Developmental Psychology, 8*, 93-98.

Larder, D. L. (1962). Effect of aggressive story content on nonverbal play behavior. *Psychological Reports, 11*, 14.

Larsen, K. S., Coleman, D., Forbes, J., & Johnson, R. (1972). Is the subject's personality or the experimental situation a better prediction of a subject's willingness to administer shock to a victim? *Journal of Personality and Social Psychology, 22*, 287-295.

Laventure, R. O. (1978). The relationship between attitudes towards women and perceptions of aggression and resultant aggressive behavior. *Dissertation Abstracts International, 38*, 6015A.

Lefkowitz, M. M., Huesmann, L. R., & Eron, L. D. (1978). Parental punishment: A longitudinal analysis of effects. *Archives of General Psychiatry, 35*, 186–191.

Leventhal, D. B., Shemberg, K. M., & van Schoelandt, S. K. (1968). Effects of sex-role adjustment upon the expression of aggression. *Journal of Personality and Social Psychology, 8*, 393–396.

Liebert, R. M., & Baron, R. A. (1972). Some immediate effects of televised violence on children's behavior. *Developmental Psychology, 6*, 469–475.

Lindquist, C. U., Lindsay, J. S., & White, G. D. (1979). Assessment of assertiveness in drug abusers. *Journal of Clinical Psychology, 35*, 676–679.

Lockwood, J. L., & Roll, S. (1980). Effects of fantasy behavior, level of fantasy predisposition, age, and sex on direction of aggression in young children. *Journal of Genetic Psychology, 136*, 255–264.

Madsen, C. (1968). Nurturance and modeling in preschoolers. *Child Development, 39*, 221–236.

Mallick, S. K., & McCandless, B. R. (1966). A study of catharsis of aggression. *Journal of Personality and Social Psychology, 4*, 591–596.

Mandel, R. A. (1978). The relationship between approval or disapproval of filmed violence and aggression in children. *Dissertation Abstracts International, 38*, 3894B.

Manosevitz, M., Prentice, N. M., & Wilson, F. (1973). Individual and family correlates of imaginary companions in preschool children. *Developmental Psychology, 8*, 72–79.

Martin, M. F., Gelfand, D. M., Hartmann, D. P. (1971). Effect of adult and peer observers on boys' and girls' responses to an aggressive model. *Child Development, 42*, 1271–1275.

Matthews, K. A., & Angulo, J. (1980). Measurement of the Type A behavior pattern in children: Assessment of children's competitiveness, impatience-anger, and aggression. *Child Development, 51*, 466–475.

McCandless, B. R., Bilous, C. B., & Bennett, H. L. (1961). Peer popularity and dependence on adults in preschool age socialization. *Child Development, 32*, 511–518.

McCarthy, E. D., Langner, T. S., Gersten, J. C., Eisenberg, J. G., & Orczeck, L. (1975). Violence and behavior disorders. *Journal of Communication, 25*, 71–85.

McGuire, J. M. (1973). Aggression and sociometric status with preschool children. *Sociometry, 36*, 542–549.

McIntyre, A. (1972). Sex differences in children's aggression. *Proceedings of the Eightieth Annual Convention of the American Psychological Association, 7*, 93–94.

McKee, J. P., & Leader, F. B. (1955). The relationship of socioeconomic status and aggression to the competitive behavior of preschool children. *Child Development, 26*, 135-142.

Moore, M. (1966). Aggression themes in a binocular rivalry situation. *Journal of Personality and Social Psychology, 3*, 685-688.

Morissette, M. L. (1978). Some relationships among imaginative predisposition, empathy, and aggression in children. *Dissertation Abstracts International, 38*, 4692A-4693A.

Muste, M. J., & Sharpe, D. F. (1947). Some influential factors in the determination of aggressive behavior in preschool children. *Child Development, 18*, 11-28.

Nagelbush, J. L. (1978). An observational analysis of the relationship between dominance and selected social behaviors in nursery school children. *Dissertation Abstracts International, 39*, 1051B.

Nelson, J. D., Gelfand, D. M., & Hartmann, D. P. (1969). Children's aggression following competition and exposure to an aggression model. *Child Development, 40*, 1085-1097.

Newsom, M. W. (1979). Assertiveness, aggressiveness, dominance, and affiliation: Construct validation of the Interpersonal Behavior Survey using the Interpersonal Check List. *Dissertation Abstracts International, 39*, 4047B.

Omark, D. R., Omark, M., & Edelman, M. (1973). Dominance hierarchies in young children. In T. R. Williams (ed.). *Psychological Anthropology*. The Hague: Mouton.

Paolino, A. F. (1964). Sex differences in aggressive content. *Journal of Projective Techniques and Personality Assessment, 28*, 219-226.

Parton, D. A., & Geshuri, Y. (1971). Learning of aggression as a function of presence of a human model, response intensity, and target of the response. *Journal of Experimental Child Psychology, 11*, 491-504.

Pearce, J. W. (1978). Relationship of socioeconomic status and aggression in preschool children. *Psychological Reports, 43*, 379-382.

Pederson, F. A., & Bell, R. Q. (1970). Sex differences in preschool children without histories of complications in pregnancy and delivery. *Developmental Psychology, 3*, 10-15.

Prerost, F. J. (1976). Reduction of aggression as a function of related content in humor. *Psychological Reports, 38*, 771-777.

Propst, L. R. (1979). Effects of personality and loss of anonymity on aggression: A reevaluation of deindividuation. *Journal of Personality, 47*, 531-545.

Puleo, J. S. (1978). Acquisition of imitative aggression in children as a function of the amount of reinforcement given the model. *Social Behavior and Personality, 6*, 67-71.

Pytkowicz, A. R., Wagner, N. N., & Sarason, I. G. (1967). An experimental study of the reduction of hostility through fantasy. *Journal of Personality and Social Psychology, 5*, 295–303.

Raden, D. (1980). Authoritarianism and overt aggression. *Psychological Reports, 47*, 452–454.

Ratliff, C. D. (1978). A correlation of selected personality characteristics to behavior problems of students in an integrated secondary school. *Dissertation Abstracts International, 39*, 134A.

Rau, M., Stover, L., & Guerney, B. G., Jr. (1970). Relationship of socioeconomic status, sex, and age to aggression of emotionally disturbed children in mothers' presence. *Journal of Genetic Psychology, 116*, 95–100.

Rogers, R. W. (1980). Expressions of aggression: Aggression-inhibiting effects of anonymity to authority and threatened retaliation. *Personality and Social Psychology Bulletin, 6*, 315–320.

Rosekrans, M. A., & Hartup, W. W. (1967). Imitative influence of consistent and inconsistent response consequences to a model on aggressive behavior in children. *Journal of Personality and Social Psychology, 7*, 429–434.

Samek, W. R. (1978). Aggressive and sexual arousal as a function of the attribution of the type of arousal, the sex of the subject, and the sexual composition of the group. *Dissertation Abstracts International, 38*, 6126B.

Santrock, J. W. (1970). Paternal absence, sex typing, and identification. *Developmental Psychology, 2*, 264–272.

Scheier, M. F., Buss, A. H., & Buss, D. M. (1978). Self-consciousness, self-report of aggressiveness, and aggression. *Journal of Research in Personality, 12*, 133–140.

Schein, S. L. (1978). Anxiety, aggression, and familial attitudes of college nailbiters. *Dissertation Abstracts International, 38*, 4479B.

Schuck, S. Z., Schuck, A., Hallam, E., Mancini, F., & Wells, R. (1971). Sex differences in aggressive behavior subsequent to listening to a radio broadcast of violence. *Psychological Reports, 28*, 931–936.

Sears, R. R., Rau, L., & Alpert, R. (1965). *Identification and child rearing.* Stanford: Stanford University Press.

Segall, S. R. (1978). The effects of assertive training and defense preference on dream recall, pleasantness, and aggression. *Dissertation Abstracts International, 38*, 5043B.

Seibert, S. M., & Ramanaiah, N. V. (1978). On the convergent and discriminant validity of selected measures of aggression in children. *Child Development, 49*, 1274–1276.

Semler, I. J., & Eron, L. D. (1967). Replication report: Relationship of aggression in third-grade children to certain pupil characteristics. *Psychology in the Schools, 4*, 356–358.

Semler, I. J., Eron, L. D., Meyerson, L. J., & Williams, J. F. (1967). Relationship of aggression in third-grade children to certain pupil characteristics. *Psychology in the Schools, 4,* 85–88.

Serbin, L. A., O'Leary, K. D., Kent, R. N., & Tolnick, I. J. (1973). A comparison of teacher response to the pre-academic and problem behavior of boys and girls. *Child Development, 44,* 796–804.

Shomer, R. W., Davis, A. H., & Kelley, H. H. (1966). Threats and the development of coordination: Further studies of the Deutsch and Krauss trucking game. *Journal of Personality and Social Psychology, 4,* 119–126.

Shope, G. L., Hedrick, T. E., & Geen, R. G. (1978). Physical/verbal aggression: Sex differences in style. *Journal of Personality, 46,* 23–42.

Shortell, J. R., & Biller, H. B. (1970). Aggression in children as a function of sex of subject and sex of opponent. *Developmental Psychology, 3,* 143–144.

Siegel, A. E. (1956). Film-mediated fantasy aggression and strength of aggressive drive. *Child Development, 27,* 365–378.

Singer, J. L., Singer, D. G., & Sherrod, L. R. (1980). A factor analytic study of preschoolers' play behavior. *Academic Psychology Bulletin, 2,* 143–156.

Slaby, R. G. (1974). Verbal regulation of aggression and altruism. In J. deWit & W. W. Hartup (eds.). *Determinants and origins of aggressive behavior.* The Hague: Mouton.

Staats, S. R., Brockman, C.., & Gates, M. (1978). Associates by age, sex, and method to aggressive words with double meaning. *Psychological Reports, 43,* 151–155.

Strayer, J., & Strayer, F. F. (1978). Social aggression and power relations among preschool children. *Aggressive Behavior, 4,* 173–182.

Taylor, S. P., & Epstein, S. (1967). Aggression as a function of the interaction of the sex of the aggressor and the sex of the victim. *Journal of Personality, 35,* 474–496.

Titley, R. W., & Viney, W. (1969). Expression of aggression toward the physically handicapped. *Perceptual and Motor Skills, 29,* 51–56.

Tucker, P. T. (1978). The relationship between communication sensitivity and selected types of aggression. *Dissertation Abstracts International, 38,* 5127B.

Vasta, R., & Copitch, P. (1981). Simulating conditions of child abuse in the laboratory. *Child Development, 52,* 165–170.

Vaughn, B. E., & Waters, E. (1981). Attention structure, sociometric status, and dominance: Interrelations, behavioral correlates, and relationships to social competence. *Developmental Psychology, 17,* 275–288.

Vernon, D. T., Foley, J. M. & Schulman, J. L. (1967). Effect of mother-child separation and birth order on young children's responses to two potentially stressful experiences. *Journal of Personality and Social Psychology, 5*, 162–174.

Wagman, M. (1967). Sex differences in types of daydreams. *Journal of Personality and Social Psychology, 7*, 329–332.

Walker, R. N. (1967). Some temperament traits in children as viewed by their peers, their teachers, and themselves. *Monographs of the Society for Research in Child Development, 32*(6).

Whiting, B., & Edwards, C. P. (1973). Cross-cultural analysis of sex differences in the behavior of children aged three to eleven. *Journal of Social Psychology, 91*, 171–188.

Wohlford, P., Santrock, J. W., Berger, S. E., & Liberman, D. (1971). Older brothers' influence on sex-typed, aggressive, and dependent behavior in father-absent children. *Developmental Psychology, 4*, 124–134.

Youssef, Z. I. (1968). The role of race, sex, hostility, and verbal stimulus in inflicting punishment. *Psychonomic Science, 12*, 285–286.

Zillman, D., & Cantor, J. R. (1972). Directionality of transitory dominance as a communication variable affecting humor appreciation. *Journal of Personality and Social Psychology, 24*, 191–198.

Table A.1   Studies Used in Meta-analysis of Gender Differences in Aggression

Study	Effect Size d	N	Age of Subjects	Design	Method of Measure- ment	Kind of Aggres- sion	Sample
Abramovitch, Corter &	NA	34	4	2	1	1	1
Lando, 1979	NA					2	
Ahmed, 1979	NA	70	19	1	1	6	1
Allen, 1978	NA	21	19	1		2	1
Arms, Russell & Sandilands,							
1979	0.17	214	19	1	2	1 + 2	1
Bakker, Bakker-Rabdau &							
Breit, 1978	0.15	250	19	2	2	2	1
Bandura, Grusec & Menlove,							
1966	NA	72	7	1	1	7	1
Bankart & Anderson, 1979	1.68	22	4	1	1	1	1
Barclay, 1970	NA	55	19	1	4	9	1
Barrett, 1979	1.26	79	7	2	1	1	1
	0.86					2	
Baumrind, 1971	0.56	238	4	2	1	1 + 2	1
Baumrind & Black, 1967	0.62	103	4	1	1	8	3
Berk, 1971	0.15	72	4	2	1	1	1
Brenner & Tomkiewicz, 1980	NA	86	30	2	2		3
Brion-Meisels, 1978	NA	29	10	1	1		1
Brissett & Nowicki, 1973	NA	80	19	2	2	9	1
Brodzinsky, Messer & Tew,							
1979	NA	127	11	2	5	1	1
						2	
						3	
Bullock & Merrill, 1980	0.84	110	9	2	5	1 + 2	3
Buss, 1966	NA	240	19	1	1	6	1
Ciccolella, 1978			20	2	2	1 + 2	3
Crain & Smoke, 1981	0.21	42	9	2	4	3	3
Crowther, Bond & Rolf, 1981	−0.56	25	2	2	3	1	1
	0.41	106	3				
	0.71	212	4				
	0.47	136	5				
Deaux, 1971	0.26	123	30	1	1	9	1
Deluty, 1979	0.77	46	10	2	2	1 + 2	1
DiPietro, 1981	NA	52	4	2	1	1	1
						4	
Ditrichs, Simon & Greere,							
1967	NA	150	14	1	1	2	1
Doob & Gross, 1968	0.40	74	30	1	1	9	1
Doolittle, 1980	0.46	103	12	1	2	1 + 2	1
Eisenberg, 1980	−0.14	80	7	1	2	1	1
Emmerich, 1971	NA	596	4.5	2	1	1 + 2	3
Epstein, 1965	0.97	80	19	1	1	6	3
Fagot & Patterson, 1969	0	36	3.5	2	1	1	1
Ferguson & Maccoby, 1966	0.39	239	10	2	5	1	3
Feshbach, 1969	NA	84	6	1	1	9	1
Feshbach, 1972	NA	104	4	1	1	6	1
Feshbach & Devor, 1969	NA	204	4	1	1	2	1
Finchum & Freitag, 1979	0.33	173	19	2	2	1 + 2	1
Forman, 1980	0.41	60	9	2	3	1 + 2	3

Table A.1 Studies Used in Meta-analysis of Gender Differences in Aggression (cont.)

Study	Effect Size d	N	Age of Subjects	Design	Method of Measurement	Kind of Aggression	Sample
Foster, 1979	NA		19	1	1	6	1
Franzini, Litrownik & Blanchard, 1978	−0.28	80	4	1	1	7	3
French & Wailes, 1980	1.72	2,904	30	2	6	1	3
Frodi, 1978	NA	48	19	1	1	6	1
Grusec, 1972	NA	54	9	1	1	7	1
						1	
Grusec, 1973	0	30	5	1	1	7	1
	0.36	30	10				
Hanson, 1978	NA	2,636	19	2	2	1 + 2	1
Hapkiewicz & Roden, 1971	0.23	60	7	1	1	7	1
	1.05					1	
Harden & Jacob, 1978	1.84	16	5	2	1	1	1
Harmatz, 1967	NA	50	19	2	2	8	1
Hartup, 1974	NA	102	5	2	1	1 + 2	1
Hatfield, Ferguson & Alpert, 1967	NA	40	4	1	1	1	3
Hayes, Rincover & Volosin, 1980	NA	48	4	1	1	1	1
Hess & Camara, 1979	NA	32	10	2	2 + 3	1 + 2	3
Hicks, 1968	NA	84	7	1	1	7	1
Hokanson & Edelman, 1966	NA	28	19	1	1	6	1
Hoppe, 1979	0.005	96	19	1	1	6	1
Hoving, LaForme & Wallace, 1974	NA	142	7	1	1	6	1
	NA	142					
Hoving, Wallace & LaForme, 1979	NA	161	6	1	1	6, 9	1
			10				
Huesmann, Lefkowitz & Eron, 1978	0.33	425	19	2	2	1 + 2	1
Huston-Stein et al., 1981	NA	66	4	1	1	1 + 2	1
Hyde & Schuck, 1977	3.13	157	4	2	1	1	1
	0.91					2	
Hynan et al., 1980	0.31	60	19	1	1	6	1
Jacklin & Maccoby, 1979	0.17	48	3	2	1	1	1
	0.26	101					
	0.41	108					
Jackson, 1978	NA	172	17	1	2	8	1
Jersild & Markey, 1935	0.60	30	3	2	1	1	1
	−0.64					2	
Johnson, 1980	0.05	32	19	1	1	9	1
Jones & Bogat, 1978	NA	48	19	1	1	6	1
Klaus & Gray, 1968	NA	88	6	2	5	1	3
Klesges et al., 1979	0.27	100	19	2	1	1	1
	0.17				2		
	0.18				5		
Knott & Drost, 1970	NA	80	19	1	1	6	1
Koerner, 1977	NA	120	19	1	1	6	1
Lando & Donnerstein, 1978	NA	50	19	1	1	7	1

Table A.1 Studies Used in Meta-analysis of Gender Differences in Aggression (cont.)

Study	Effect Size d	N	Age of Subjects	Design	Method of Measure- ment	Kind of Aggres- sion	Sample
Langlois & Downs, 1979	NA	64	4	1	1	1	3
Langlois, Gottfried & Seary, 1973	NA	32	3 5	1	1	1	1
Larder, 1962	NA	15	4	1	1	6	1
Larsen et al., 1972	0.00 0.27, 0.27 −0.09, −0.10, −0.16	213	19	1	1	6	1
Laventure, 1978	0.03	48	19	1	2	2	1
Lefkowitz, Huesmann & Eron, 1978	0.83 0.82	371	19	2	2 5	1	1
Leventhal, Shemberg & van Schoelandt, 1968	0.17	40	19	1	1	6	3
Liebert & Baron, 1972	NA NA	136	7	1	1	7	1
Lindquist, Lindsay & White, 1979	NA	37	22	2	2	NA	1
Lockwood & Roll, 1980	NA	57	6	1	6	1	1
Madsen, 1968	NA	40	4	1	1	7 2 1	1
Mallick & McCandless, 1966	NA	48	9	1	1	6	1
Mandel, 1978	NA	80	4	1	1	1 + 2	1
Manosevitz, Prentice & Wilson, 1973	NA	222	5	2	3	1	1
Martin, Gelfand & Hartmann, 1971	0.83	100	6	1	1	7	1
Matthews & Angulo, 1980	0.35 0.68 0.48	67 99 82	6 8 10	2	3	1 + 2	1
McCandless, Bilous, & Bennett, 1961	NA	60	4	2	1	1 + 2	1
McCarthy et al., 1975	NA	732	14	2	3	1	1
McGuire, 1973	0.51 0.71	78 54	4	2	1	1 + 2	1
McIntyre, 1972	NA NA	27	3	2	1	1 2	1
McKee & Leader, 1955	−0.11	112	4	1	1	1 + 2	1
Moore, 1966	NA	180	13	1	1	9	1
Morisette, 1978	NA	59	10	2	3	1 + 2	1
Muste & Sharpe, 1947	NA	30	4	1	1	1 + 2	1
Nagelbush, 1978	NA		4	2	1	1, 2	1
Nelson, Gelfand & Hartmann	0.00 1.01	96	6	1	1 1 + 2	1+2+7	1
Newsom, 1979	NA	194	19	2	2	2	1
Omark, Omark & Edelman, 1973	NA	450	6	2	1	1	1
Paolino, 1964	0.83	84	19	2	4	9	1

Table A.1 Studies Used in Meta-analysis of Gender Differences in Aggression (cont.)

Study	Effect Size d	N	Age of Subjects	Design	Method of Measurement	Kind of Aggression	Sample
Parton & Geshuri, 1971	NA	112	5	1	1	7	1
Pearce, 1978	0.50	40	4	2	1	1	1
Pederson & Bell, 1970	0.54	55	2.5	2	1	9	1
Prerost, 1976	0.35 −0.31	144	19	1	2	8	1
Propst, 1979	NA	56	19	1	1	6	1
Puleo, 1978	0.59	40	5	1	1	7	1
Pytkowicz, Wagner & Sarason, 1967	NA	120	19	1	2	8	1
Raden, 1980	NA	71	19	1	1	6	1
Ratliff, 1978	NA	79	15	2	2	2	1
Rau, Stover & Guerney, 1970	0.82	79	8	1	1	1	2
Rogers, 1980	0.63	96	19	1	1	6	1
Rosekrans & Hartup, 1967	NA	64	4	1	1	7	1
Samek, 1978	NA NA	238	19	1 1	2 4	1 3	1
Santrock, 1970	1.28 1.59	60	5	2 4	3	1	3
Scheier, Buss & Buss, 1978	NA	63	19	2	1, 2	6, 1 + 2	3
Schein, 1978	NA	64	19	2	2	9	1
Schuck et al., 1971	1.31	40	19	1	1	6	1
Sears, Rau & Alpert, 1965	1.31 1.01	40	4	2	1	1 2	1
Segall, 1978	NA	72	19	1	2	3	1
Seibert & Ramanaiah, 1978	NA	204	9	2	2 3 5		1
Semler & Eron, 1967	0.54	863	9	2	5	1	1
Semler et al., 1967	0.72	567	9	2	5	1	1
Serbin et al., 1973	NA	225	4	2	1	1 + 2	1
Shomer, Davis & Kelley, 1966	NA	64	19	1	1	9	1
Shope, Hedrick & Geen, 1978	NA	171	19	1	1	2, 6	1
Shortell & Biller, 1970	NA	48	12	1	1	6	1
Siegel, 1956	NA	24	4	1	1	1	1
Singer, Singer & Sherrod, 1980	0.84	141	4	2	1	1	1
Slaby, 1974	0.62	60	10	1	1	6	1
Staats, Brockman & Gates, 1978	NA	172	35	2	6	2	1
Strayer & Strayer, 1978	1.43	36	4	2	1	1	1
Taylor & Epstein, 1967	NA	24	19	1	1	6	1
Titley & Viney, 1969	.84	40	18	1	1	6	1
Tucker, 1978	NA	703	19	2	2	1 2 9	1
Vasta & Copitch, 1981	NA	22	19	1	1	6	1
Vaughn & Waters, 1981	NA	22	4	2	1	1	1

Table A.1   Studies Used in Meta-analysis of Gender Differences in Aggression (cont.)

Study	Effect Size d	N	Age of Subjects	Design	Method of Measurement	Kind of Aggression	Sample
Vernon, Foley & Schulman, 1967	0.55	32	4	1	1	1	3
	0.15	32	4	1	3	8	3
Wagman, 1967	0.84	206	19	2	2	3	1
Walker, 1967	0.62	406	10	2	2	1 + 2	1
	0.43				3		
Whiting & Edwards, 1973	NA	24	5	2	1	1	1
						2	
						5	
Wohlford et al., 1971	NA	66	5	2	3	1	3
	0.57				4		
Youssef, 1968	NA	120	19	1	1	6	3
	NA	120	19	1	2	8	3
Zillman & Cantor, 1972	NA	40	19	1	2	9	1

Note: NA = not available (could not be computed from information in original article, and author did not respond to request for information or could not supply it).
Design: 1 = experimental; 2 = naturalistic, correlational; 3 = other.
Method of measurement: 1 = direct observation; 2 = self-report; 3 = parent or teacher report; 4 = projective; 5 = peer report.
Kind of aggression: 1 = physical; 2 = verbal; 3 = fantasy; 4 = rough-and-tumble play; 5 = counterattack; 6 = willingness to shock or otherwise hurt; 7 = imitative; 8 = hostility scale; 9 = other.
Kind of sample: 1 = general, classroom; 2 = families seeking therapy; 3 = other.

Appendix B: Studies Reviewed in Spatial Ability

Abravanel, E., & Gingold, H. (1977). Perceiving and representing orientation: Effects of the spatial framework. *Merrill-Palmer Quarterly, 23,* 265–278.

Allen, M., & Wittig, M. (1982). Measurement of adult performance on Piaget's water horizontality task, *Intelligence, 8,* 305–313.

Block, J., & Block, J. (1982). Cognitive development from childhood to adolescence. NIMA research grant MH16080. Manuscript.

Bouchard, T. J., Jr., & McGee, M. G. (1977). Sex differences in human spatial ability: Not an X-linked recessive gene effect. *Social Biology, 24,* 332–335.

Connor, J. M., Schackman, M., & Serbin, L. A. (1978). Sex-related differences in response to practice on a visual-spatial test and generalization to a related test. *Child Development, 49,* 24–29.

DeAvila, E. A., Havassy, B., with Pascual-Leone, J. (1976). *Mexican-American school children: A neo-Piagetian analysis.* Washington, D.C.: Georgetown University Press.

Erdos, G. (1979). Sex differences in feedback: Effects on rod-and-frame performance. *Perceptual and Motor Skills, 48,* 1279–1285.

Fennema, E., & Sherman, J. (1977). Sex-related differences in mathematics achievement, spatial visualization, and affective factors. *American Educational Research Journal, 14,* 51–71.

Geiringer, E. R., & Hyde, J. S. (1976). Sex differences on Piaget's water-level task: Spatial ability incognito. *Perceptual and Motor Skills, 42,* 1323–1328.

Guay, R. B., & McDaniel, E. D. (1977). The relationship of mathematical achievement and spatial abilities among elementary school children. *Journal of Research in Mathematics Education, 8,* 211–215.

Harris, L. F., Hanley, C., & Best, D. T. (1978). Conservation of horizontality: Sex differences in sixth graders and college students. In M. C. Smart & P. C. Smart (eds.), *Adolescents' development and relationships.* New York: Macmillan.

Hughes, R. N. (1978). Sex differences in field dependence: Effects of unlimited time on group embedded-figures test performance. *Perceptual and Motor Skills, 47,* 1246.

Hyde, J. S., Geiringer, E. R., & Yen, W. M. (1975). On the empirical relation between spatial ability and sex differences in other aspects of cognitive performance. *Multivariate Behavioral Research, 10,* 289–310.

Jamison, W., & Signorella, M. L. (1980). Sex-typing and spatial ability: The association between masculinity and success on Piaget's water-level task. *Sex Roles, 6,* 345–353.

Karplus, R., Pulos, S., & Stage, E. (1983). Proportional reasoning of early adolescents. In R. Lesh & M. Landau (eds.), *Acquisitions of mathematics concepts and processes.* New York: Academic Press.

Kelly, J. T., & Kelly, G. N. (1977). Perception of horizontality by male and female college students. *Perceptual and Motor Skills, 44,* 724–726.

Liben, L. S. (1974). Operative understanding of horizontality and its relation to long-term memory. *Child Development, 45,* 416–424.

Liben, L. S. (1978). Performance on Piagetian spatial tasks as a function of sex, field dependence, and training. *Merrill-Palmer Quarterly, 24,* 97–110.

Liben, L. S., & Golbeck, S. L. (1980). Sex differences in performance on Piagetian spatial tasks: Differences in competence or performance. *Child Development, 51,* 594–597.

Linn, M. C. (1984). *Adolescent reasoning project: Annual report 1984.* Berkeley: Lawrence Hall of Science, University of California.

Linn, M. C., Clement, C., Pulos, S. M., & Sullivan, P. (1982). Logical vs. sensible reasoning: An instruction based investigation. Adolescent Reasoning Project, Berkeley: Lawrence Hall of Science, University of California.

Linn, M. C., de Benedictis, T., & Delucchi, K. (1982). Adolescent reasoning about advertisements: Preliminary investigations. *Child Development, 53,* 1599, 1613.

Linn, M. C., & Pulos, S. (1983). Male-female differences in predicting displaced volume: Strategy usage, aptitude relationships, and experience influences. *Journal of Educational Psychology, 75,* 86–96.

McGee, M. G. (1978). Effects of training and practice on sex differences in mental rotation test scores. *Journal of Psychology, 100,* 87–90.

Petersen, A. C. (1982). Biological correlates of spatial ability and mathematical performance. Presentation at the annual meeting of the American Association for the Advancement of Science, Washington, D.C., January, 1982.

Peterson, A. C., & Gitelson, I. B. (in press). *Toward Understanding sex-related differences in cognitive performance.* New York: Academic Press.

Pitblado, C. (1976). Superior performance by women in a visual orienting task: A limit on the concept of field dependence. *Perceptual and Motor Skills, 42,* 1195–1200

Pulos, S. M., Stage, E. K., & Karplus, R. (1983). *Cognitive correlates of proportional reasoning in early adolescence.* Berkeley: Lawrence Hall of Science, University of California.

Richmond, P. G. (1980). A limited sex difference in spatial test scores with a preadolescent sample. *Child Development, 51,* 601–602.

Sanders, B., Soares, M. P., & D'Aquila, J. M. (1982). The sex difference on one test of spatial visualization: A nontrivial difference. *Child Development, 53,* 1106–1110.

Sherman, J. (1980). Mathematics, spatial visualization and related factors: Changes in boys and girls, grades 8–11. *Journal of Educational Psychology, 72,* 476–482.

Signorella, M. L., & Jamison, W. (1978). Sex differences in the correlations among field dependence, spatial ability, sex-role orientation, and performance on Piaget's water-level task. *Developmental Psychology, 14,* 689–690.

Sneider, C., & Pulos, S. (1983). Children's cosmographies: Understanding the earth's shape and gravity. *Science Education, 67,* 205–221.

Strauch, A. B. (1979). Origins of sex differences in high school mathematics achievement and participation. Paper presented at the annual meeting of the American Educational Research Association, San Francisco, April, 1979.

Taylor, L. J. (1977). Sex and psychological differentiation. *Psychological Reports, 41,* 192–194.

Van Leeuwen, M. A. (1978). A cross-cultural examination of psychological differentiation in males and females. *International Journal of Psychology, 13,* 87–122.

Walker, J. T., & Krasnoff, A. G. (1978). The horizontality principle in young men and women. *Perceptual and Motor Skills, 46,* 1055–1061.

Wilson, J. R., & Vandenberg, S. G. (1978). Sex differences in cognition: Evidence from the Hawaii family study. In T. E. McGill, D. A. Dewsbury & B. Sachs (eds.), *Sex and behavior: Status and prospectus.* New York: Plenum.

Table B.1 Meta-analysis of Spatial Perception Studies

Study	Effect Size	N Females	N Males	Age of Subjects
Abravanel & Gingold, 1977	0.42	24	26	10
	0.94	24	26	9
Allen & Wittig, 1982	0.57	121	74	20
	0.38	121	74	20
Block & Block, 1982	−0.27	60	60	4
	0.80	60	60	11
DeAvila, Havassy & Pascual-Leone, 1976	0.23	593	589	9
Erdos, 1979	0.63	40	40	20
Geiringer & Hyde (1976)	0.51	30	30	12
Harris, Hanley & Best, 1978	0.42	30	30	17
	0.81	28	33	17
	0.95	110	48	20
	0.86	105	53	20
	0.74	63	48	20
	0.33	65	45	20
Hyde, Geiringer & Yen, 1975	0.44	46	35	20
Jamison & Signorella, 1980	0.70	58	43	20
Karplus, Pulos & Stage, 1983	0.36	57	60	11
	0.21	74	62	13
Kelly & Kelly, 1977	0.99	191	123	20
Liben, 1974	0.68	96	99	10
Liben, 1978	0.62	33	33	16
	0.50	33	33	16
Liben & Golbeck, 1980	0.15	12	12	8
	−0.10	12	12	10
	0.95	12	12	12
	0.20	12	12	14
	0.30	12	12	16
	0.50	12	12	8
	1.00	12	12	10
	0.65	12	12	12
	0.85	12	12	14
	0.20	12	12	16
Linn, 1984	0.98	19	13	12
	0.77	11	12	12
	0.59	40	42	12
	0.86	17	15	13
	0.44	24	24	13
	0.73	30	30	13
	0.17	20	14	12
	0.86	17	14	13
Linn & Pulos, 1983	0.48	66	64	12
	0.43	46	42	12
	0.51	47	35	12
	0.21	25	29	14
	0.39	19	49	14
	0.14	26	42	14
	0.60	60	53	16
	−0.07	24	23	16
	0.61	43	31	16

Table B.1 Meta-analysis of Spatial Perception Studies (cont.)

Study	Effect Size	N Females	Males	Age of Subjects
Peterson, 1982	0.81	42	29	11
	0.53	71	58	11
	0.40	72	67	17
Pitblado, 1976	0.10	15	24	30
Pulos, Stage & Karplus, 1983	0.06	15	15	8
	0.28	210	228	13
Sherman, 1980	0.11	25	25	20
Signorella & Jamison, 1978	0.12	45	48	13
Snieder & Pulos, 1983	0.85	13	12	11
	0.76	16	10	12
	0.65	13	15	13
Walker & Krasnoff, 1978	0.44	49	44	20

Table B.2 Meta-analysis of Mental Rotation Studies

Study	Effect Size	N Females	Males	Age of Subjects
Bouchard & McGee, 1977	0.82	237	241	20
	0.86	168	155	48
Geiringer & Hyde, 1976	−0.08	30	30	12
	0.64	30	30	17
Guay & McDaniel, 1977	0.57	46	44	10
McGee, 1978	0.31	174	173	20
Petersen & Gitelson, in press	0.67	42	29	11
	0.47	71	58	11
	0.36	74	55	12
	0.07	77	59	13
	0.81	72	67	17
Richmond, 1980	0.03	237	232	10
Sanders, Soares & D'Aquila, 1982	0.29	658	354	21
Signorella & Jamison, 1978	0.10	45	48	13
Wilson & Vandenberg, 1978	0.83	191	201	14
	0.74	294	296	15
	0.90	249	244	16
	0.90	202	233	17
	1.12	138	130	18
	0.96	70	68	19
	1.00	54	56	20
	1.00	123	94	23
	1.11	23	28	28
	1.28	125	51	33
	1.06	418	370	38
	1.06	435	510	43
	0.91	241	424	48
	1.12	102	208	53
	0.70	22	95	58

Table B.3 Meta-analysis of Spatial Visualization Studies

Study	Effect Size	N Females	N Males	Age of Subjects
Block & Block, 1982	−0.49	60	60	4
	0.16	60	60	11
Connor, Schackman & Serbin, 1978	0.46	19	26	6
	0.04	19	26	6
Fennema & Sherman (1977)	−0.05	49	52	11
	0.09	60	62	11
	0.16	48	46	11
	0.32	46	43	11
	−0.21	59	57	12
	0.23	73	64	12
	−0.24	26	29	14
	0.10	20	49	14
	0.12	26	45	14
	0.33	60	54	16
	0.30	25	23	16
	0.26	45	31	16
Guay & McDaniel, 1977	0.45	46	44	10
Hyde, Geiringer & Yen, 1975	−0.05	46	35	20
	0.21	46	35	20
	0.32	46	35	20
Hughes, 1978	0.11	67	63	20
Linn, de Benedictis & Delucchi, 1983	0.30	19	13	12
	0.21	41	41	12
	−0.29	17	15	13
	0.05	21	22	13
	0.27	30	25	13
Linn, et al., 1983	0.17	66	64	12
	−0.10	46	44	12
	0.11	47	37	12
	−0.19	25	29	13
	−0.37	20	49	13
	−0.06	26	45	13
	0.04	52	42	12
	0.14	41	43	12
	−0.01	51	46	13
	0.05	103	78	13
	−0.21	56	51	13
	0.07	50	48	13
	−0.15	41	38	14
	0.05	45	44	14
	0.16	58	50	14
	0.25	75	62	14
	−0.02	38	47	15
	0.71	42	36	15
	−0.06	30	43	15
	0.36	59	55	15
	−0.16	47	41	16
	0.13	33	52	16
	0.13	46	49	16
	0.58	47	51	16
	−0.16	47	25	17

Table B.3 Meta-analysis of Spatial Visualization Studies (cont.)

| Study | Effect Size | N | | Age of Subjects |
		Females	Males	
Linn & Pulos, 1983	0.15	65	63	12
	0.16	45	44	12
	0.09	47	37	12
	0.47	60	54	14
	−0.37	24	23	14
	0.04	45	32	14
Petersen & Gitelson, in press	0.27	75	57	12
	0.05	89	71	13
	−0.02	72	67	17
	0.24	72	67	17
Pulos, Karplus, & Stage, 1980	0.26	82	84	13
Sherman, 1980	0.55	135	75	13
	0.23	135	75	16
	0.07	25	25	20
	0.20	25	25	20
Strauch, 1979	0.13	296	297	7
	0.23	299	298	10
	0.17	295	296	13
	0.15	198	198	16
Taylor, 1977	0.02	18	21	6
	0.50	17	18	6
	−0.18	18	20	7
	0.18	19	21	8
	−0.63	17	23	10
	−0.11	18	21	6
	−0.11	17	18	6
	−0.46	18	20	7
	0.50	19	21	8
	−0.91	17	23	10
Van Leeuwen, 1978	0.18	71	67	20

Appendix C:
Studies Reviewed
in Attributions

Bar-Tal, D., & Frieze, I. H. (1977). Achievement motivation for males and females as a determinant of attributions for success and failure. *Sex Roles, 3*, 301–313.

Berg, P. A., & Hyde, J. S. (1976). *Gender and race differences in causal attributions in achievement situations.* Bowling Green: Bowling Green State University (ERIC Document Reproduction Service No. ED 138 865).

Breen, L. J., Vulcano, B., & Dyck, D. G. (1979). Observational learning and sex roles in learned helplessness. *Psychological Reports, 44* 135–144.

Croke, J. H. (1973). Sex differences in causal attributions and expectancies for success as a function of the sex-role appropriateness of the task. Manuscript, Department of Psychology, University of California, Los Angeles.

Deaux, K. K., & Farris, E. (1977). Attributing causes for one's own performance: The effects of sex, norms, and outcomes. *Journal of Research in Personality, 11*, 59–72.

Feather, N. T., & Simon, J. G. (1972). Luck and the unexpected outcome: A field replication of laboratory findings. *Australian Journal of Psychology, 24*, 113–117.

Feather, N. T., & Simon, J. G. (1973). Fear of success and causal attributions for outcomes. *Journal of Personality, 41*, 525–542.

Forsythe, D. R., & Schlenker, B. R. (1977*a*). Attributing the causes of group performance: Effects of performance quality, task importance, and future testing. *Journal of Personality, 45*, 220–236.

Forsythe, D. R., & Schlenker, B. R. (1977*b*). Attributional egocentrism following performance of a competitive task. *Journal of Social Psychology, 102*, 215–222.

Goldberg, C., & Evenbeck, S. (1976). Causal attributions for success and failure as a function of authoritarianism and sex. *Perceptual and Motor Skills, 42*, 215–222.

Griffen, B. O., Combs, A. L., Land, M. L., & Combs, N. H. (1981). Attributions of achievement for academic achievement: A field study. Paper presented at the annual meeting of the Midwestern Psychological Association, Detroit, May 1981 (ERIC Document Reproduction Service No. ED 205 884).

Levine, R. (1980). High need for achievement, superego severity, and causal attributions for success and failure (Doctoral dissertation, New York University, 1979). *Dissertation Abstracts International, 48,* 5410B.

Levine, R., Gillman, M. G., & Reis, H. (1982). Individual differences for sex differences in achievement attributions? *Sex Roles, 8,* 455–466.

Luce, S. R. (1980). Sex differences in achievement attributions: Patterns and processes (Doctoral dissertation, Carlton University, 1979). *Dissertation Abstracts International, 40,* 5871B.

McHugh, M. C., Fisher, J. E., & Frieze, I. H. (1982). Effects of situational factors on the self-attributions of females and males. *Sex Roles, 8,* 389–394.

McMahan, I. D. (1971). Sex differences in causal attributions for success and failure. Paper presented at the annual meeting of the Eastern Psychological Association, New York, April 1971.

Meerdink, G. B. (1980). The effects of psychological androgyny on attributions for success and failure (Doctoral dissertation, University of Toledo, 1980). *Dissertation Abstracts International, 41,* 1118B.

Miller, D. T. (1976). Ego involvement and attributions for success and failure. *Journal of Personality and Social Psychology, 34,* 901–906.

O'Connell, A. N., & Perez, S. (1982). Fear of success and causal attributions of success and failure in high school and college students. *Journal of Psychology, 111,* 141–151.

Pasquella, M. J., Mednick, M. T., & Murray, S. R. (1981). Causal attributions of achievement outcomes: Sex-role identity, sex, and outcome comparisons. *Psychology of Women Quarterly, 5,* 586–590.

Sasfy, J. H. (1975). Some relationships between causality for task participation and the causal attribution of task outcome (Doctoral dissertation, Pennsylvania State University, 1974). *Dissertation Abstracts International, 35,* 7134A–7135A.

Simon, J. G., & Feather, N. T. (1973). Causal attributions for success and failure at university examinations. *Journal of Educational Psychology, 64,* 46–56.

Stephan, W. G., Rosenfield, D., & Stephan, C. (1976). Egotism in males and females. *Journal of Personality and Social Psychology, 34,* 1161–1167.

Sweeney, P. D., Moreland, R. L., & Gruber, K. L. (1982). Gender differences in external attributions for academic performance. *Sex Roles, 8*, 358-374.

Teglasi, H. (1977). Influence of situational factors on causal attributions of college females. *Psychological Reports, 41*, 495-502.

Viaene, N. (1979). The influence of expectancy for success androgyny and locus of control on sex differences in causal attributions for success and failure. Paper presented at the International Conference on Sex Role Stereotyping, Cardiff, July 1979.

Wiegers, R. M., & Frieze, I. H. (1977). Gender, female traditionality, achievement level, and cognitions of success and failure. *Psychology of Women Quarterly, 2*, 125-137.

Wong, P. T. P. (1982). Sex differences in performance attribution and contingency judgment. *Sex Roles, 8*, 381-388.

Table C.1 Effect Sizes for Sex Differences within Outcome in Studies of Attribution

Study	Ability Success	Ability Failure	Effort Success	Effort Failure	Task Success	Task Failure	Luck Success	Luck Failure
Informational Wording								
Bar-Tal & Frieze, 1977	0.19	−0.24	−0.21	0.45	0.00	0.03	−0.43	−0.76
*Croke, 1973	0.00	0.00	0.00	0.00	0.00	0.00	0.00	0.00
*Deaux & Farris, 1977 (Study 1)	0.07	0.89	0.00	0.00	0.18	−0.20	−0.62	1.08
(Study 2)	0.21	0.50	−0.40	0.33	−0.56	−0.35	−0.67	0.36
*Forsythe & Schlenker, 1977b	0.68	0.68	0.00	0.00	0.00	0.00	−0.76	0.63
McHugh, Fisher & Frieze, 1982	0.01	0.27	−0.04	0.00	0.20	0.00	0.25	0.07
*Miller, 1976	0.00	0.00	0.00	0.00	0.00	0.00	0.00	0.00
Pasquella, Mednick & Murray, 1981	0.23	0.45	0.03	0.83	0.36	0.16	1.74	−0.01
Causal Wording								
*Berg & Hyde, 1976	0.00	0.00	0.00	0.00	0.00	0.00	0.00	0.00
Breen, Vulcano & Dyck, 1979	0.29	0.04	0.11	−0.14	−0.16	0.66	−0.59	−0.76
*Feather & Simon, 1972	0.00	0.00	0.00	0.00	0.00	0.00	0.00	0.00
*Feather & Simon, 1973	0.13	0.00	0.12	0.00	0.21	0.00	−0.15	0.00
*Forsythe & Schlenker, 1977a	0.00	0.00	0.00	0.00	0.00	0.00	0.00	0.00
*Goldberg & Evenbeck, 1976	0.00	0.00	0.00	0.00	0.00	0.00	0.00	0.00
*Griffin et al., 1981	0.00	0.00	0.00	0.00	0.00	0.00	0.00	0.00
Levine, 1980	0.33	−0.26	0.30	−0.19	0.40	−0.49	0.21	−0.10
*Levine, Gilman & Reis, 1982	0.59	0.89	−0.50	−0.44	0.00	0.00	−0.56	−0.37
*Luce, 1980	0.00	0.00	0.00	0.00	0.00	0.00	0.00	0.00
McMahan, 1971	0.85	0.49	0.04	0.24	0.46	−0.31	0.40	−0.30
Meerdink, 1980	0.49	0.69	−0.22	−0.51	−0.14	−0.15	−0.09	−0.25
O'Connell & Perez, 1982	0.61	0.26	0.61	0.26	−0.61	−0.26	−0.61	−0.26
*Sasfy, 1975	0.00	0.00	0.00	0.00	0.00	0.00	0.00	0.00
Simon & Feather, 1973	0.25	−0.12	−0.25	1.11	0.05	−1.21	−0.13	−1.24
*Stephan, Rosenfield & Stephan, 1976	0.00	0.00	0.00	0.00	0.00	0.00	0.00	0.00
Sweeney, Moreland & Gruber, 1982	−0.19	0.36	−0.17	0.47	0.02	−0.08	0.00	−0.79
Teglasi, 1977	−0.08	0.24	−0.07	0.24	−0.65	0.15	−0.14	−0.33
Viaene, 1979	0.07	0.00	−0.15	0.00	−0.18	0.25	−0.39	−0.36
*Weigers & Frieze, 1977	−0.12	−0.17	−0.30	1.16	0.08	−0.36	−0.66	−0.13
*Wong, 1982	0.00	0.00	0.00	0.00	0.00	0.00	−0.82	−0.82

Note: A positive effect size indicates a stronger attribution by men; a negative sign indicates a stronger attribution by women.
*Effect size of zero was assigned based on a report of a nonsignificant difference.

Table C.2 Effect Sizes for Outcome Differences within Sex in Studies of Attribution

Study	Ability Women	Ability Men	Effort Women	Effort Men	Task Women	Task Men	Luck Women	Luck Men
Informational Wording								
Bar-Tal & Frieze, 1977	2.14	2.57	0.87	0.20	-2.88	-2.92	0.94	1.27
*Croke, 1973	0.78	0.78	0.61	0.61	0.00	0.00	0.78	0.78
*Deaux & Farris, 1977 (Study 1)	2.10	1.36	0.00	0.00	-2.11	-1.57	2.94	1.34
(Study 2)	2.34	2.14	0.56	-0.02	-2.39	-2.81	2.58	1.67
*Forsythe & Schlenker, 1977b	1.71	0.74	1.64	0.71	0.00	0.00	1.47	-0.12
McHugh, Fisher & Frieze, 1982	3.58	3.23	0.27	0.22	-0.64	0.35	1.86	2.12
Miller, 1976	2.28	2.28	0.88	0.88	-0.67	-0.67	-1.28	-1.28
Pasquella, Mednick & Murray, 1981	0.89	0.75	0.74	0.03	-0.30	-0.02	-0.14	1.90
Causal Wording								
*Berg & Hyde, 1976	0.22	0.22	0.00	0.00	0.00	0.00	-0.22	-0.22
Breen, Vulcano & Dyck, 1979	-0.49	-0.29	0.59	1.09	0.42	-0.37	-0.61	-0.42
*Feather & Simon, 1972	0.45	0.45	0.00	0.00	0.00	0.00	0.00	0.00
Feather & Simon, 1972	0.15	0.14	0.54	0.51	-0.10	-0.10	0.40	0.38
Forsythe & Schlenker, 1977a	0.75	0.75	0.09	0.09	-0.70	-0.70	0.04	0.04
*Goldberg & Evenbeck, 1976	0.58	0.58	0.00	0.00	0.00	0.00	0.00	0.00
Griffin et al., 1981	0.38	0.37	0.44	0.44	-0.24	-0.23	0.02	0.02
Levine, 1980	-0.82	-0.16	0.78	0.81	-0.79	0.18	0.00	0.35
*Levine, Gilman & Reis, 1982	0.12	-0.18	0.44	0.43	0.00	0.00	-0.14	-0.37
Luce, 1980	0.73	0.73	0.96	0.96	0.44	0.44	0.21	0.21
McMahan, 1971	1.64	1.48	0.52	0.34	-0.14	0.59	0.58	0.85
Meerdink, 1980	0.17	-0.39	0.54	1.37	0.05	0.11	-0.68	-0.50
O'Connell & Perez, 1982	0.74	1.12	0.74	1.12	-0.74	-1.12	-0.74	-1.12
Sasfy, 1975	0.93	0.93	2.11	2.11	-1.60	-1.60	0.67	0.67
Simon & Feather, 1973	1.40	1.50	0.92	-0.46	-1.24	0.10	-1.03	0.14
*Stephan, Rosenfield & Stephan, 1976	0.43	0.43	0.43	0.43	0.00	0.00	-0.44	-0.44
Sweeney, Moreland & Gruber, 1982	1.09	0.50	0.84	0.33	-1.09	-0.61	-0.65	0.07
Teglasi, 1977	1.01	0.73	1.42	1.10	0.73	0.01	0.08	0.55
Viaene, 1979	0.31	0.43	0.80	0.71	-0.34	0.08	-0.02	0.04
Weigers & Frieze, 1977	0.55	0.55	-0.16	-1.52	0.17	-0.57	0.63	0.07
*Wong, 1982	0.00	0.00	0.66	0.66	1.03	1.03	1.18	1.18

Note: A positive effect size indicates a stronger success attribution; a negative effect size indicates a stronger failure attribution.

*Effect size of zero was assigned based on a report of a nonsignificant difference.

Appendix D:
Studies Reviewed in
Smiling and Gazing

Studies that contributed results to tables 6.1 and 6.2 are indicated as follows: C = children; A = adults; S = smiling; G = gazing. For example, "ASG" means that the study contributed adult gender-difference data for both smiling and gazing.

Achenbach, T. M., & Weisz, J. R. (1975). A longitudinal study of relations between outer-directedness and IQ changes in preschoolers. *Child Development, 46*, 650–657. CG

Aiello, J. R. (1972). A test of equilibrium theory: Visual interaction in relation to orientation, distance and sex of interactants. *Psychonomic Science, 27*, 335–336. AG

Aiello, J. R. (1977a). A further look at equilibrium theory: Visual interaction as a function of interpersonal distance. *Environmental Psychology and Nonverbal Behavior, 1*, 122–140. AG

Aiello, J. R. (1977b). Visual interaction at extended distances. *Personality and Social Psychology Bulletin, 3*, 83–86. AG

Ames, L. B. (1949). Development of interpersonal smiling responses in the preschool child. *Journal of Genetic Psychology, 74*, 273–291. CS

Anderson, F. J., & Willis, F. N. (1976). Glancing at others in preschool children in relation to dominance. *Psychological Record, 26*, 467–472. CG

Archer, J., & Westeman, K. (1981). Sex differences in the aggressive behaviour of schoolchildren. *British Journal of Social Psychology, 20*, 31–36. CS

Argyle, M., & Dean, J. (1965). Eye-contact, distance, and affiliation. *Sociometry, 28*, 289–304. AG

Argyle, M., & Ingham, R. (1972). Gaze, mutual gaze, and proximity. *Semiotica, 6*, 32–49. AG

Argyle, M., Ingham, R., Alkema, F., & McCallin, M. (1973). The different functions of gaze. *Semiotica, 7*, 19–32. AG

Ashear, V., & Snortum, J. R. (1971). Eye contact in children as a function of age, sex, social, and intellective variables. *Developmental Psychology, 4*, 479. CG

Bates, J. E. (1976). Effects of children's nonverbal behavior upon adults. *Child Development, 47*, 1079-1088. ASG

Baum, A., & Greenberg, C. I. (1975). Waiting for a crowd: The behavioral and perceptual effects of anticipated crowding. *Journal of Personality and Social Psychology, 32*, 671-679. AG

Beach, D. R., & Sokoloff, M. J. (1974). Spatially dominated nonverbal communication of children: A methodological study. *Perceptual and Motor Skills, 38*, 1303-1310. CG

Beier, E. G., & Sternberg, D. P. (1977). Marital communication: Subtle cues between newlyweds. *Journal of Communication, 27*, 92-97. AG

Bond, M. H., & Shiraishi, D. (1974). The effect of body lean and status of an interviewer on the non-verbal behavior of Japanese interviewees. *International Journal of Psychology, 9*, 117-128. AS

Cary, M. S. (1978). Does civil inattention exist in pedestrian passing? *Journal of Personality and Social Psychology, 36*, 1185-1193. AG

Chaiken, S. (1979). Communicator physical attractiveness and persuasion. *Journal of Personality and Social Psychology, 37*, 1387-1397. ASG

Chaikin, A. L., & Derlega, V. J. (1978). Nonverbal mediators of expectancy effects in black and white children. *Journal of Applied Social Psychology, 8*, 117-125. ASG

Chaikin, A. L., Sigler, E., & Derlega, V. J. (1974). Nonverbal mediators of teacher expectancy effects. *Journal of Personality and Social Psychology, 30*, 144-149. AS

Chapman, A. J. (1973). Social facilitation of laughter in children. *Journal of Experimental Social Psychology, 9*, 528-541. CS

Chapman, A. J. (1974). An experimental study of socially facilitated "humorous laughter." *Psychological Reports, 35*, 727-734. CS

Chapman, A. J. (1975). Humorous laughter in children. *Journal of Personality and Social Psychology, 31*, 42-49. CSG

Chapman, A. J., & Chapman, W. A. (1974). Responsiveness to humor: Its dependency upon a companion's humorous smiling and laughter. *Journal of Psychology, 88*, 245-252. CSG

Cherulnik, P. D. (1979). Sex differences in the expression of emotion in a structured social encounter. *Sex Roles, 5*, 413-424. AG

Cherulnik, P. D., Neely, W. T., Flanagan, M., & Zachau, M. (1978). Social skill and visual interaction. *Journal of Social Psychology, 104*, 263-270. AG

Coutts, L. M., & Schneider, F. W. (1975). Visual behavior in an unfocused interaction as a function of sex and distance. *Journal of Experimental Social Psychology, 11*, 64-77. AG

Dabbs, J. M., Jr., Evans, M. S., Hopper, C. H., & Purvis, J. A. (1980).

Self-monitors in conversation: What do they monitor? *Journal of Personality and Social Psychology, 39*, 278-284. AG

Davis, M., & Weitz, S. (1981). Sex differences in body movements and positions. In C. Mayo & N. M. Henley (eds.), *Gender and nonverbal behavior.* New York: Springer-Verlag, AS

Ding, G. F., & Jersild, A. T. (1932). A study of the laughing and smiling of preschool children. *Journal of Genetic Psychology, 40*, 452-472. CS

Exline, R. V. (1963). Explorations in the process of person perception: Visual interaction in relation to competition, sex, and need for affiliation. *Journal of Personality, 31*, 1-20. AG

Exline, R., Gray, D., & Schuette, D. (1965). Visual behavior in a dyad as affected by interview content and sex of respondent. *Journal of Personality and Social Psychology, 1,* 201-209. AG

Exline, R. V., & Winters, L. C. (1965). Affective relations and mutual glances in dyads. In S. S. Tomkins & C. E. Izard (eds.), *Affect, cognition, and personality: Empirical studies.* New York: Springer-Verlag. AG

Feldman, S. S., & Ingham, M. E. (1975). Attachment behavior: A validation study in two age groups. *Child Development, 46*, 319-330. CG

Finley, G. E., & Layne, O., Jr. (1971). Play behavior in young children: A cross-cultural study. *Journal of Genetic Psychology, 119*, 203-210. CG

Foddy, M. (1978). Patterns of gaze in cooperative and competitive negotiation. *Human Relations, 31*, 925-938. AG

Foot, H. C., Chapman, A. J., & Smith, J. R. (1977). Friendship and social responsiveness in boys and girls. *Journal of Personality and Social Psychology, 35*, 401-411. CSG

Foot, H. C., Smith, J. R., & Chapman, A. J. (1979). Non-verbal expressions of intimacy in children. In M. Cook & G. Wilson (eds.), *Love and attraction.* Oxford: Pergamon. CSG

Frances, S. J. (1979). Sex differences in nonverbal behavior. *Sex Roles, 5*, 519-535. ASG

Fromme, D. K. & Beam, D. C. (1974). Dominance and sex differences in nonverbal responses to differential eye contact. *Journal of Research in Personality, 8*, 76-87. AG

Galassi, J. P., Galassi, M. D., & Litz, M. C. (1974). Assertive training in groups using video feedback. *Journal of Counseling Psychology, 21*, 390-394. AG

Griffith, W., May, J., & Veitch, R. (1974). Sexual stimulation and interpersonal behavior: Heterosexual evaluation responses, visual behavior, and physical proximity. *Journal of Personality and Social Psychology, 30*, 367-377. AG

Hammen, C. L., & Peplau, L. A. (1978). Brief encounters: Impact of gender, sex-role attitudes, and partner's gender on interaction and cognition. *Sex Roles, 4,* 75-90. AG

Harris, L. (1968). Looks by preschoolers at the experimenter in a choice-of-toys game: Effects of experimenter and age of child. *Journal of Experimental Child Psychology, 6,* 493-500. CG

Ickes, W., & Barnes, R. D. (1977). The role of sex and self-monitoring in unstructured dyadic interactions. *Journal of Personality and Social Psychology, 35,* 315-330. AG

Ickes, W., & Barnes, R. D. (1978). Boys and girls together—and alienated: On enacting stereotyped sex roles in mixed-sex dyads. *Journal of Personality and Social Psychology, 36,* 669-683. ASG

Ickes, W., Schermer, B., & Steeno, J. (1979). Sex and sex-role influences in same-sex dyads. *Social Psychology Quarterly, 42,* 373-385. ASG

Jorgenson, D. O. (1978). Nonverbal assessment of attitudinal affect with the smile-return technique. *Journal of Social Psychology, 106,* 173-179. AS

Justin, F. (1932). A genetic study of laughter provoking stimuli. *Child Development, 3,* 114-136. CS

Kendon, A. (1967). Some functions of gaze-direction in social interaction. *Acta Psychologica, 26,* 22-63. AG

Kendon, A., & Cook, M. (1969). The consistency of gaze patterns in social interaction. *British Journal of Psychology, 60,* 481-494. AG

Kleinke, C. L., Desautels, M. S., & Knapp, B. E. (1977). Adult gaze and affective and visual responses of preschool children. *Journal of Genetic Psychology, 131,* 321-322. CG

LaFrance, M., & Carmen, B. (1980). The nonverbal display of psychological androgyny. *Journal of Personality and Social Psychology, 38,* 36-49. ASG

LaFrance, M., & Mayo, C. (1976). Racial differences in gaze behavior during conversations: Two systematic observational studies. *Journal of Personality and Social Psychology, 33,* 547-552. AG

Langlois, J. H., Gottfried, N. W., & Seay, B. (1973). The influence of sex of peer on the social behavior of preschool children. *Developmental Psychology, 8,* 93-98. CS

Levine, M. H., & Sutton-Smith, B. (1973). Effects of age, sex, and task on visual behavior during dyadic interaction. *Developmental Psychology, 9,* 400-405. CAG

Libby, W. L., Jr. (1970). Eye contact and direction of looking as stable individual differences. *Journal of Experimental Research in Personality, 4,* 303-312. AG

Libby, W. L., Jr., & Yaklevich, D. (1973). Personality determinants of eye contact and direction of gaze aversion. *Journal of Personality and Social Psychology, 27,* 197-206. AG

Lochman, J. E., & Allen, G. (1981). Nonverbal communication of couples in conflict. *Journal of Research in Personality, 15*, 253-269. ASG

Lott, B. (1978). Behavioral concordance with sex role ideology related to play areas, creativity, and parental sex typing of children. *Journal of Personality and Social Psychology, 36*, 1087-1110. CS

Maccoby, E. E., & Feldman, S. S. (1972). *Mother-attachment and stranger-reactions in the third year of life.* Monographs of the Society for Research in Child Development, vol. 37, no. 146. Chicago. CG

Mackey, W. C. (1976). Parameters of the smile as a social signal. *Journal of Genetic Psychology, 129*, 125-130. AS

McClintock, C. C., & Hunt, R. G. (1975). Nonverbal indicators of affect and deception in an interview setting. *Journal of Applied Social Psychology, 5*, 54-67. ASG

McDowell, K. V. (1972). Violations of personal space. *Canadian Journal of Behavioural Science, 4*, 210-217. AG

Mehrabian. A. (1971a). Nonverbal betrayal of feeling. *Journal of Experimental Research in Personality, 5*, 64-73. ASG

Mehrabian. A. (1971b). Verbal and nonverbal interaction of strangers in a waiting situation. *Journal of Experimental Research in Personality, 5*, 127-138. ASG

Mehrabian. A., & Williams, M. (1969). Nonverbal concomitants of perceived and intended persuasiveness. *Journal of Personality and Social Psychology, 13*, 37-58. AS

Moskowitz, D. S., Schwarz, J. C., & Corsini, D. A. (1977). Initiating day care at three years of age: Effects on attachment. *Child Development, 48*, 1271-1276. CSG

Nevill, D. (1974). Experimental manipulation of dependency motivation and its effects on eye contact and measures of field dependency. *Journal of Personality and Social Psychology, 29*, 72-79. AG

Noller, P. (1980). Cross-gender effect in two-child families. *Developmental Psychology, 16*, 159-160. AG

Patterson, M. L. (1973). Stability of nonverbal immediacy behaviors. *Journal of Experimental Social Psychology, 9*, 97-109. AG

Patterson, M. L. (1977). Interpersonal distance, affect, and equilibrium theory. *Journal of Social Psychology, 101*, 205-214. AG

Pedersen, F. A., & Bell, R. Q. (1970). Sex differences in preschool children without histories of complications of pregnancy and delivery. *Developmental Psychology, 3*, 10-15. CSG

Pilkonis, P. A. (1977). The behavioral consequences of shyness. *Journal of Personality, 45*, 596-611. ASG

Rosenfeld, H. M. (1966). Approval-seeking and approval-inducing functions of verbal and nonverbal responses in the dyad. *Journal of Personality and Social Psychology, 4*, 597-605. AS

Rosenthal, R. (1976). *Experimenter effects in behavioral research* (enlarged ed.). New York: Irvington. AS

Ross, M., Layton, B., Erickson, B., & Schopler, J. (1973). Affect, facial regard, and reactions to crowding. *Journal of Personality and Social Psychology, 28*, 69–76. AG

Rubin, Z. (1970). Measurement of romantic love. *Journal of Personality and Social Psychology, 16*, 265–273. AG

Ruble, D. N. (1975). Visual orientation and self-perceptions of children in an external-cue-relevant or cue-irrelevant task situation. *Child Development, 46*, 669–676. CG

Ruble, D. N., & Nakamura, C. Y. (1972). Task orientation versus social orientation in young children and their attention to relevant social cues. *Child Development, 43*, 471–480. CG

Ruble, D. N., & Nakamura, C. Y. (1973). Outerdirectedness as a problem-solving approach in relation to developmental level and selected task variables. *Child Development, 44*, 519–528. CG

Russo, N. F. (1975). Eye contact, interpersonal distance, and the equilibrium theory. *Journal of Personality and Social Psychology, 31*, 497–502. CG

Rutter, D. R., Morley, I. E., & Graham, J. C. (1972). Visual interaction in a group of introverts and extraverts. *European Journal of Social Psychology, 2*, 371–384. AG

Sarason, I. G., & Winkel, G. H. (1966). Individual differences among subjects and experimenters and subjects' self-descriptions. *Journal of Personality and Social Psychology, 3*, 448–457. ASG

Scheman, J. D., & Lockard, J. S. (1979). Development of gaze aversion in children. *Child Development, 50*, 594–596. CG

Schneider, F. W., Coutts, L. M., & Garrett, W. A. (1977). Interpersonal gaze in a triad as a function of sex. *Perceptual and Motor Skills, 44*, 184. AG

Schwarz, J. C. (1972). Effects of peer familiarity on the behavior of preschoolers in a novel situation. *Journal of Personality and Social Psychology, 24*, 276–284. CG

Slane, S., Dragan, W., Crandall, C. J., & Payne, P. (1980). Stress effects on the nonverbal behavior of repressors and sensitizers. *Journal of Psychology, 106*, 101–109. AG

Stern, D. N., & Bender, E. P. (1974). An ethological study of children approaching a strange adult: Sex differences. In R. C. Friedman, R. M. Richart, & R. L. Vande Wiele (eds.), *Sex differences in behavior.* New York: Wiley. CS

Strongman, K. T., & Champness, B. G. (1968). Dominance hierarchies and conflict in eye contact. *Acta Psychologica, 28*, 376–386. AG

Tauber, M. A. (1979). Parental socialization techniques and sex differences in children's play. *Child Development, 50*, 225-234. CG

Tidd, K. L., & Lockard, J. S. (1978). Monetary significance of the affiliative smile: A case for reported altruism. *Bulletin of the Psychonomic Society, 11*, 344-346. AS

Wittig, M. A., & Skolnick, P. (1978). Status versus warmth as determinants of sex differences in personal space. *Sex Roles, 4*, 493-503. AG

Table D.1 Effect Sizes and Predictor Variables for Studies of Gender Differences in Smiling and Gazing

| Study | Effect Sizes | | Predictor Variables | | | | | | | | | | | | | | | |
	Smiling	Gazing	1	2	3	4	5	6	7	8	9	10	11	12	13	14	15	16
Aiello, 1972		0.55*	4	54	51	2	2	2	1	6.0	3	2	4.0	2.0	7.0	5.5	7.0	4.5
Aiello, 1977a		0.54*	4	65	66	2	2	1	1	7.0	3	2	5.5	2.0	6.0	2.0	7.5	5.0
Aiello, 1977b		1.48*	4	20	20	2	2	1	1	6.5	3	2	4.0	3.0	5.0	2.0	8.0	7.5
		1.13*	4	20	20	2	2	1	1	6.5	3	2	4.0	3.0	5.0	2.0	8.0	7.5
		−0.49	4	20	20	2	2	2	1	6.5	3	2	4.0	3.0	5.0	2.0	8.0	7.5
Argyle & Dean, 1965		0.89	5	12	12	2	1	2	1	3.5	2	2	3.5	1.5	7.5	5.5	8.5	7.5
Ashear & Snortum, 1971		0.51*	2	45	45	2	1	1	1	3.5	3	2	3.5	2.0	6.5	8.5	5.5	6.5
Bates, 1976	0.53		4	32	32	2	2	3	1	2.5	3	2	2.0	2.0	7.5	1.5	9.0	8.5
Beier & Sternberg, 1977		−0.04	5	51	51	1	5	2	1	2.0	2	2	2.0	4.5	8.0	9.0	1.5	8.0
Bond & Shiraishi, 1974	0.74		4	16	16	2	2			3.5	2	2	2.5	1.5	7.0	5.0	5.0	7.0
Cary, 1978		−0.52*	4	40	40	2	2	2	2	8.5	5	1	8.5	5.0	5.0	2.0	1.0	1.0
Chaiken, 1979	0.65*		4	34	34	1	1	2	1	3.0	2	1	2.5	4.0	6.0	4.0	7.0	8.0
Chaikin & Derlega, 1978	0.56*		4	38	34	2	2	3	1	1.5	3	2	1.5	3.5	7.0	1.5	8.5	4.5
Chaikin, Sigler & Derlega, 1974	0.90*		4	21	21	2	2	3	1	3.0	2	2	3.0	3.0	7.0	2.5	8.5	4.5
Chapman, 1975		0.37	2	50	50	2	2	2	2	5.0	3	1	5.5	3.5	7.5	7.0	4.5	5.0
Coutts & Schneider, 1975		0.62	4	40	40	1		2	1	2.5	4	1	3.0	4.5	6.0			1.0
Dabbs et al., 1980		1.11*	4	24	24	1	2	2	1	5.0	2	2	3.0	2.5	6.5	7.5	2.0	2.5
Davis & Weitz, 1981	0.84*		5	24	24	1	1	2	1	4.0	2	2	3.0	3.0	6.0	7.5	3.5	2.5
Exline, 1963		1.00*	4	48	48	1	1	2	1	4.0	3	2	2.5	7.0	6.0	4.5	8.5	5.5
Exline, Gray & Schuette, 1965		0.74*	4	40	40	2	2	1	1	2.5	3	2	2.5	5.0	5.0	8.5	5.5	7.0
Feldman & Ingham, 1975		0.61*	1	18	21	1	5		1	1.5	5	2	1.5	1.0	9.0	9.0	2.5	5.0
Foddy, 1978		0.86*	4	28	28	1	2	2	1	2.5	3	2	4.5	5.0	5.0	1.5	9.0	9.0
Frances, 1979	0.54*	0.62*	5	44	44	1	1	2	1	3.0	2	2	2.5	4.5	7.5	8.0	3.0	4.0
Fromme & Beam, 1974		−1.09*	4	16	16	2	1	1	1	1.0	2	1	1.0	3.5	4.5	4.5	3.5	2.0
Harris, 1968		−0.19	1	20	20	2	3	1	1	1.5	5	1	5.5	3.0	7.0	2.5	8.5	3.5
Ickes & Barnes, 1977	0.45*	1.33*	4	60	60	1	1	2	1	4.0	4	2	4.5	4.5	6.0	4.0	3.5	1.5
Ickes & Barnes, 1978	0.69*	1.06*	4	40	40	1	1	2	1	4.0	4	2	4.5	4.0	6.0	4.0	3.5	1.5
Kleinke, Desautels & Knapp, 1977		0.78*	1	24	24	2	2	1	1	3.0	5	2	4.5	3.0	6.0	2.0	8.0	5.5

Table D.1 Effect Sizes and Predictor Variables for Studies of Gender Differences in Smiling and Gazing (cont.)

Study	Effect Sizes		Predictor Variables															
	Smiling	Gazing	1	2	3	4	5	6	7	8	9	10	11	12	13	14	15	16
LaFrance & Carmen, 1980	1.02*	1.12*	4	36	36	1	2	2	1	4.0	3	2	3.5	5.0	5.0	7.0	7.0	5.5
LaFrance & Mayo, 1976		0.72*	5	90	90	1	4		2	9.0	5	2	8.0	3.5	8.0			
Levine & Sutton-Smith, 1973		0.17	1	12	12	1	3	2	1	4.0	2	2	5.0	2.5	8.0	8.5	2.0	4.0
		0.56	2	12	12	1	3	2	1	4.0	2	2	5.0	2.5	8.0	8.5	2.0	4.0
		0.57	2	12	12	1	3	2	1	4.0	2	2	5.0	2.5	8.0	8.5	2.0	4.0
		0.87	4	12	12	1	2	2	1	4.0	2	2	5.0	2.5	8.0	8.5	2.0	4.0
Libby, 1970		0.87*	4	52	52	2	2	1	1	1.5	2	2	2.5	3.5	6.0	8.5	4.0	6.0
Libby & Yaklevich, 1973		1.08*	5	35	35	2	2	1	1	2.5	3	2	2.0	4.0	5.5	8.5	3.5	6.5
Mackey, 1976	0.23*		5	411	411	2			2	9.0	5	1	8.5	2.5	5.5	5.5	1.0	1.5
Mehrabian & Williams, 1969	0.48*		4	36	36	2	1	2	1	1.5	3	1	2.0	5.0	4.5	1.5	8.5	8.0
Nevill, 1974		0.47*	4	40	40	2	2	1	1	3.0	3	2	3.0	4.0	5.0	6.5	3.5	4.0
Patterson, 1973		1.17*	4	13	13	2	2	1	1	4.5	3	2	4.0	2.0	6.5	7.5	5.5	6.0
Patterson, 1977		0.39	4	24	24	2	2	1	1	2.0	2	2	2.0	4.0	5.5	4.5	6.0	5.0
Pilkonis, 1977	0.71*	0.79*	4	23	23	2	1	2	1	4.5	4	2	4.5	3.5	6.5	6.5	3.0	2.5
Rubin, 1970		0.64*	4	79	79	1		2	1	3.5	4	2	4.0	2.5	7.5	8.5	1.5	3.5
Ruble & Nakamura, 1972		0.14	4	28	28	2	2		1	1.5	3	1	2.0	6.5	4.5	1.5	9.0	9.0
Russo, 1975		0.87*	2	72	72	2	3	2	2	3.0	2	2	5.5	2.0	6.5	7.5	2.5	5.0
Rutter, Morley & Graham, 1972		0.52	4	10	10	1	2	2	1	3.0	2	2	4.5	2.0	7.0	7.5	2.5	5.5
Sarason & Winkel, 1966	1.07*	1.07*	4	8	8	1	2	3	1	2.0	5	2	5.5	3.0	7.0	5.5	5.0	6.5
Slane et al., 1980		0.91*	4	96	96	1	2	3	1	2.0	3	2	3.0	3.5	6.0	8.0	3.0	4.5
Tauber, 1979		0.36*	2	71	75	1	3	3	1	7.5	2	1	6.0	3.5	6.0	2.0	8.5	4.0
Tidd & Lockard, 1978	0.00		5	48	48	2	1	3	2	9.0	5	1	8.0	2.0	6.5	6.0	7.0	1.0

Note: Predictor variables are (1) subject age, (2) N of females, (3) N of males, (4) other's programming, (5) acquaintanceship, (6) subject status, (7) location, (8) naturalness, (9) unobtrusiveness, (10) interpersonal interaction, (11) comfort, (12) competition, (13) friendliness, (14) socioemotional emphasis, (15) goal orientation, (16) complexity. Effect sizes are d. All ratings are given as the mean of the two authors' ratings. See text for complete description of coding categories and rating scales. Blanks occur when effect sizes were not available and when predictors could not be coded. This table is based only on those effect sizes analyzed in tables 6.3 and 6.4.

* Significant result.

Appendix E:
Studies Reviewed
in Influenceability

Allen, V. L., & Levine, J. M. (1969). Consensus and conformity. *Journal of Experimental Social Psychology, 5,* 389-399.

Asch, S. E. (1956). Studies of independence and conformity. Part 1: A minority of one against a unanimous majority. *Psychological Monographs, 70,* no. 416.

Beloff, H. (1958). Two forms of social conformity: Acquiescence and conventionality. *Journal of Abnormal and Social Psychology, 56,* 99-104.

Bem, S. L. (1975). Sex-role adaptability: One consequence of psychological androgyny. *Journal of Personality and Social Psychology, 31,* 634-643.

Biondo, J., & MacDonald, A. P., Jr. (1971). Internal-external locus of control and response to influence attempts. *Journal of Personality, 39,* 407-419.

Burgoon, M., Jones, S. B., & Stewart, D. (1975). Toward a message-centered theory of persuasion: Three empirical investigations of language intensity. *Human Communication Research, 3,* 240-256.

Chaiken, S., & Eagly, A. H. (1976). Communication modality as a determinant of message persuasiveness and message comprehensibility. *Journal of Personality and Social Psychology, 34,* 605-614.

Chaiken, S., Eagly, A. H., Sejwacz, D., Gregory, W. L., & Christensen, D. (1979). Communicator physical attractiveness as a determinant of opinion change. *Catalog of Selected Documents in Psychology.* Journal Supplement Abstract Service.

Chandra, S. (1973). The effects of group pressure on perception. *International Journal of Psychology, 8,* 37-39.

Chu, G. C. (1966). Culture, personality, and persuasibility. *Sociometry, 29,* 169-174.

Coleman, J. F., Blake, R. R., & Mouton, J. S. (1958). Task difficulty and conformity pressures. *Journal of Abnormal and Social Psychology, 57,* 120-122.

Costanzo, P. R., & Shaw, M. E. (1966). Conformity as a function of age level. *Child Development, 37,* 967–975.

Crano, W. D. (1970). Effects of sex, response order, and expertise in conformity: A dispositional approach. *Sociometry, 33,* 239–252.

Crowne, D. P., & Liverant, S. (1963). Conformity under varying conditions of personal commitment. *Journal of Abnormal and Social Psychology, 66,* 547–555.

Crutchfield, R. S. (1955). Conformity and character. *American Psychologist, 10,* 191–198.

Delin, P. S., & Poo-Kong, K. (1974). The measurement of mutual conformity in a dyadic situation. *British Journal of Social and Clinical Psychology, 13,* 211–213.

DiVesta, F. J., & Cox, L. (1960). Some dispositional correlates of conformity behavior. *Journal of Social Psychology, 52,* 259–268.

Eagly, A. H. (1974). Comprehensibility of persuasive arguments as a determinant of opinion change. *Journal of Personality and Social Psychology, 29,* 758–773.

Eagly, A. H., & Telaak, K. (1972). Width of the latitude of acceptance as a determinant of attitude changes. *Journal of Personality and Social Psychology, 23,* 388–397.

Eagly, A. H., & Warren, R. (1976). Intelligence, comprehension, and opinion change. *Journal of Personality, 44,* 226–242.

Eagly, A. H., & Whitehead, G. I. (1972). Effect of choice as receptivity to favorable and unfavorable evaluations of oneself. *Journal of Personality and Social Psychology, 22,* 223–230.

Eagly, A. H., Wood, W., & Chaiken, S. (1978). Causal inferences about communicators and their effect on opinion change. *Journal of Personality and Social Psychology, 36,* 424–430.

Endler, N. S. (1965). The effects of verbal reinforcement on conformity and deviant behavior. *Journal of Social Psychology, 66,* 147–154.

Endler, N. S. (1966). Conformity as a function of different reinforcement schedules. *Journal of Personality and Social Psychology, 4,* 175–180.

Endler, N. S., Wiesenthal, D. L., Coward, T., Edwards, J., & Geller, S. H. (1975). Generalization of relative competence mediating conformity across differing tasks. *European Journal of Social Psychology, 5,* 281–287.

Endler, N. S., Wiesenthal, D. L., & Geller, S. H. (1972). The generalization of the effects of agreement and correctness on relative competence mediating conformity. *Canadian Journal of Behavioral Science, 4,* 322–329.

Ex, J. (1960). The nature of the relation between two persons and the degree of their influence on each other. *Acta Psychologica, 17,* 39–54.

Feldman, R. H. L. (1975). Changes in nutrition attitudes and knowledge as a function of similar and expert communication sources among the Gusii of Kenya (Doctoral dissertation, Syracuse University, 1974). *Dissertation Abstracts International, 35,* 5694B.

Feldman-Summers, S., Montano, D. E., Kaspryzyk, D., & Wagner, B. (1977). Influence attempts when competing views are gender related: Sex as credibility. Manuscript, University of Washington.

Frager, R. (1970). Conformity and anticonformity in Japan. *Journal of Personality and Social Psychology, 15,* 203-210.

Furbay, A. L. (1965). The influence of scattered versus compact seating on audience response. *Speech Monographs, 32,* 144-148.

Geller, S. H., Endler, N. S., & Wisenthal, D. L. (1973). Conformity as a function of task generalization and relative competence. *European Journal of Social Psychology, 3,* 53-62.

Gerard, H. B., Wilhelmy, R. A., & Conolley, E. S. (1968). Conformity and group size. *Journal of Personality and Social Psychology, 8,* 79-82.

Glinski, R. J., Glinski, B. C., & Slatin, G. T. (1970). Non-naivety contamination in conformity experiments: Sources, effects, and implications for control. Journal of Personality and Social Psychology, 16, 478-485.

Halperin, K., Snyder, C. R., Shenkel, R. J., & Houston, B. K. (1976). Effects on source status and message favorability on acceptance of personality feedback. *Journal of Applied Psychology, 61,* 85-88.

Hollander, E. P., Julian, J. W., & Haaland, G. A. (1965). Conformity process and prior group support. *Journal of Personality and Social Psychology, 2,* 852-858.

Insko, C. A., Arkoff, A., & Insko, V. M. (1965). Effects of high and low fear-arousing communications upon opinions toward smoking. *Journal of Experimental Social Psychology, 1,* 256-266.

Janis, I. L., & Field, P. B. (1959). Sex differences and personality factors related to persuasibility. In C. I. Hovland & I. L. Janis (eds.), *Personality and persuasibility.* New Haven: Yale University Press.

Julian, J. W., Regula, C. R., & Hollander, E. P. (1968). Effects of prior agreement by others on task confidence and conformity. *Journal of Personality and Social Psychology, 9,* 171-178.

Julian, J. W., Ryckman, R. M., & Hollander, E. P. (1969). Effects of prior group support on conformity: An extension. *Journal of Social Psychology, 77,* 189-196.

Kanareff, V. T., & Lanzetta, J. T. (1960a). Effects of success-failure experiences and probability of reinforcement on the acquisition and extinction of an imitative response. *Psychological Reports, 7,* 151-166.

Kanareff, V. T., & Lanzetta, J. T. (1960b). Effects of task definition and probability of reinforcement upon the acquisition and extinction of imitative response. *Journal of Experimental Psychology, 68,* 340-348.

Kanareff, V. T., & Lanzetta, J. T. (1961). Effects of congruent social and task reinforcement upon acquisition of imitative responses. *Psychological Reports, 8*, 47–57.

King, B. T. (1959). Relationships between susceptibility to opinion change and child-rearing practices. In C. I. Hovland & I. L. Janis (eds.), *Personality and persuasibility*. New Haven: Yale University Press.

Klein, R. L. (1972). Age, sex, and task difficulty as predictors of social conformity. *Journal of Gerontology, 27*, 229–236.

Landsbaum, J. B., & Willis, R. H. (1971). Conformity in early and late adolescence. *Developmental Psychology, 4*, 334–337.

Larsen, K. S. (1974). Conformity in the Asch experiment. *Journal of Social Psychology, 94*, 303–304.

Middleton, R. (1960). Ethnic prejudice and susceptibility to persuasion. *American Sociological Review, 25*, 679–686.

Morelock, J. C. (1980). Sex differences in susceptibility to social influence. *Sex Roles, 6*, 537–548.

Nakamura, C. Y. (1958). Conformity and problem solving. *Journal of Abnormal and Social Psychology, 56*, 315–320.

Paulson, S. F. (1954). The effects of the prestige of the speaker and acknowledgment of opposing arguments on audience retention and shift of opinion. *Speech Monographs, 21*, 267–271.

Reitan, H. T., & Shaw, M. E. (1964). Group membership, sex composition of the group, and conformity behavior. *Journal of Social Psychology, 64*, 45–51.

Rosenberg, J. J. (1965). *Persuasibility in personality and culture* (Doctoral dissertation, Columbia University, 1962). *Dissertation Abstracts, 26*, 2905–2906.

Sampson, E. E., & Hancock, F. T. (1967). An examination of the relationship between ordinal position, personality, and conformity. *Journal of Personality and Social Psychology, 5*, 398–407.

Scheidel, T. M. (1963). Sex and persuasibility. *Speech Monographs, 30*, 353–358.

Sikkink, D. E. (1956). An experimental study of the effects on the listener of anti-climax order and authority in an argumentative speech. *Southern Speech Journal, 22*, 73–78.

Silverman, I. (1968). Role-related behavior of subjects in laboratory studies of attitude change. *Journal of Personality and Social Psychology, 8*, 343–348.

Silverman, I., Ford, L. H., Jr., & Morganti, J. B. (1966). Inter-related effects of social desirability, sex, self-esteem, and complexity of argument on persuasibility. *Journal of Personality, 34*, 555–568.

Singh, U. P. (1970). Sex and age differences in persuasibility. *Journal of Social Psychology, 82*, 269–270.

Sistrunk, F. (1971). Negro-white comparisons in social conformity. *Journal of Social Psychology, 85*, 77–85.

Sistrunk, F. (1972). Masculinity-feminity and conformity. *Journal of Social Psychology, 87*, 161–162.

Sistrunk, F., & McDavid, J. W. (1971). Sex variable in conformity behavior. *Journal of Personality and Social Psychology, 17*, 200–207.

Steiner, I. D., & Rogers, E. D. (1963). Alternative responses to dissonance. *Journal of Abnormal and Social Psychology, 66*, 128–136.

Stone, W. F. (1973). Patterns of conformity in couples varying in intimacy. *Journal of Personality and Social Psychology, 27*, 413–418.

Timaeus, E. (1968). Untersuchungen zum sogenannten knoformen Verhalten. *Zeitschrift für Experimentelle und Angewandte Psychologie, 15*, 176–194.

Tuddenham, R. D. (1958). The influence of a distorted group norm upon individual judgment. *Journal of Psychology, 46*, 227–241.

Tuddenham, R. D. (1961). The influence of a distorted group norm upon judgments of adults and children. *Journal of Psychology, 52*, 231–239.

Tuddenham, R. D., MacBride, P. D., & Zahn, V. (1958). The influence of the sex composition of the group upon yielding to a distorted norm. *Journal of Psychology, 46*, 243–251.

Vaughan, G. M., & Taylor, A. J. W. (1966). Clinical anxiety and conformity. *Perceptual and Motor Skills, 22*, 719–722.

Vidulich, R. N., & Bayley, G. A. (1966). A general field experimental technique for studying social influence. *Journal of Social Psychology, 69*, 253–263.

Vidulich, R. N., & Stabene, F. P. (1965). Source certainty as a variable in conformity behavior. *Journal of Social Psychology, 66*, 323–330.

Whittaker, J. O. (1965a). Consistency of individual differences in persuasibility. *Journal of Communication, 15*, 28–34.

Whittaker, J. O. (1965b). Sex differences and susceptibility to interpersonal persuasion. *Journal of Social Psychology, 66*, 91–94.

Whittaker, J. O., & Meade, R. D. (1967). Sex and age as variables in persuasibility. *Journal of Social Psychology, 73*, 47–52.

Wyer, R. S., Jr. (1966). Effects of incentive to perform well, group attraction, and group acceptance as conformity in a judgmental task. *Journal of Personality and Social Psychology, 4*, 21–24.

Wyer, R. S., Jr. (1967). Behavioral correlates of academic achievement: Conformity under achievement, and affiliation-incentive conditions. *Journal of Personality and Social Psychology, 6*, 255–258.

Table E.1 Study Results and Study Features for Persuasion Studies

Study	Effect Size (g)	N Females	N Males	Male Authors (%)	Type of Subject	Type of Outcome
Burgoon, Jones & Stewart, 1975	0.54	68	77	67	College students	Covariate
Chaiken & Eagly, 1976	0.03	126	126	0	College students	O,P post
Chaiken et al., 1978	0.09	159	159	20	College students	O,P post
	0.09	103	104	20	College students	O,P post
Chu, 1966	0.04	90	92	100	Non-Americans	O,P post
Eagly, 1974	−0.20	127	126	0	College students	O,P post
	−0.11	98	95	0	College students	O,P post
	−0.15	183	176	0	College students	O,P post
Eagly & Telaak, 1972	0.17	59	65	0	College students	Change
Eagly & Warren, 1976	0.05	78	41	0	High school students	Change
Eagly & Whitehead, 1972	0.20	72	73	50	College students	Change
Eagly, Wood & Chaiken, 1978	0.05	107	107	0	College students	O,P post
Feldman, 1975	−0.30	166	165	100	Non-Americans	Unknown
Furbay, 1965	0.26	204	205	100	College students	Discrete
Halperin et al., 1976	−0.18	30	30	75	College students	O,P post

Study					
Insko, Arkoff & Insko, 1965	0.22	72	72	67	High school students	Change
Janis & Field, 1959	0.36	96	86	100	High school students	Change
Middleton, 1960	0.14	131	130	100	College students	Covariate
Morelock, 1980	−0.13	68	68	0	College students	O,P post
Paulson, 1954	0.20	399	579	100	College students	Discrete
Rosenberg, 1965	0.07	145	146	100	Non-Americans	Unknown
Scheidel, 1963	0.37	138	104	100	College students	Change
Sikkink, 1956	0.12	132	80	100	College students	Change
Silverman, 1968	0.16	139	191	100	College students	O,P post
Silverman, Ford & Morganti, 1966	−0.09	90	76	100	College students	Error post
	0.35	74	67	100	College students	Error post
	0.35	72	40	100	College students	Error post
Singh, 1970	0.63	30	30	100	Non-Americans	Change
Whittaker, 1965a	0.50	12	8	100	College students	Change
Whittaker & Meade, 1967	0.19	44	31	100	College students	Change
	0.82	18	29	100	High school students	Change
	0.18	35	21	100	College students	Change
	0.60	14	14	100	College students	Change

Note: Opinion or performance posttests are denoted "O,P post."

Table E.2 Study Results and Study Features for Conformity Studies

Study	Effect Size (g)	N Females	N Males	Male Authors (%)	Agents	Type of Subject	Type of Outcome
Allen & Levine, 1969	−0.20	78	79	100	4	College students	Change
Beloff, 1958	0.25	25	35	0	4	Non-Americans	Change
Bem, 1975	0.32	27	27	0	3	College students	Error post
Chandra, 1973	0.63	25	26	100	8	Non-Americans	Error post
Costanzo & Shaw, 1966	0.31	48	48	100	3	Americans	Error post
Crowne & Liverant, 1963	0.40	13	9	100	4	College students	Error post
DiVesta & Cox, 1960	0.48	35	35	100	4	College students	Error post
	0.35	135	42	100	4	College students	Error post
Endler, 1965	−0.22	35	40	100	3	College students	Error post
Endler, 1966	0.34	50	50	100	4	College students	Error post
Ex, 1960	0.05	32	32	100	1	Non-Americans	Change
Frager, 1970	−0.01	62	66	100	3	Non-Americans	Error post
Geller, Endler & Wiesenthal, 1973	0.74	31	30	100	4	College students	Error post
Gerard, Wilhelmy & Conolley, 1968	0.33	66	88	100	4	High school students	Error post
Glinski, Glinski & Slatin, 1970	−0.52	32	23	67	3	College students	Error post
Julian, Regula & Hollander, 1968	0.51	120	120	100	4	College students	Error post

Study							
Julian, Ryckman & Hollander, 1969	0.48	50	50	100	4	College students	Error post
Kanareff & Lanzetta, 1960a	0.57	24	24	50	1	College students	Error post
Kanareff & Lanzetta, 1960b	−0.02	24	24	50	1	College students	Error post
Kanareff & Lanzetta, 1961	−0.44	36	36	50	1	College students	Error post
Klein, 1972	0.24	36	36	100	3	College students	Change
Landsbaum & Willis, 1971	0.14	32	32	50	1	Mixed-age Americans	Error post
Nakamura, 1958	0.40	77	64	100	4	College students	Error post
Reitan & Shaw, 1964	0.42	48	48	100	3	College students	Error post
Steiner & Rogers, 1963	0.33	50	50	100	1	College students	O,P post
Stone, 1973	0.15	49	49	100	1	College students	Change
Timaeus, 1968	−0.04	13	22	100	7	Non-Americans	Error post
Tuddenham, 1958	0.48	48	49	100	4	College students	Standardized
	0.10	29	27	100	4	College students	Standardized
Tuddenham, 1961	0.50	33	32	100	4	College students	Error post
Tuddenham, MacBride & Zahn, 1958	1.10	40	48	100	4	College students	Standardized
Vaughn & Taylor, 1966	0.95	11	18	100	4	Non-Americans	Error post
Vidulich & Bayley, 1966	−0.14	24	24	100	1	College students	O,P post
Vidulich & Stabene, 1965	0.50	20	20	100	1	College students	Change
Whittaker, 1965b	0.81	10	10	100	1	College students	Change

Note: Opinion or performance posttests are denoted as "O,P post."

Table E.3 Study Results and Study Features for Other Conformity Studies

Study	Effect Size (g)	N Females	N Males	Male Authors (%)	Items (N)	Agents (N)	Type of Outcome
Feldman-Summers et al., 1977	-0.22	71	70	25	2	5	Stdzd
King, 1959	0.04	59	60	25	2	5	Stdzd
Sampson & Hancock, 1967	0.35	136	118	100	38	4 00	Change
Sistrunk, 1971	-0.30	114	77	50	2	50	Change
Sistrunk, 1972	0.63	32	32	100	30	20	O,P post
Sistrunk, 1972	0.81	10	10	100	45	200	O,P post
Sistrunk & McDavid, 1971	0.39	45	45	100	45	200	O,P post
	0.46	30	30	100	45	200	O,P post
Wyer, 1966	0.36	40	40	100	5	10	Change
Wyer, 1967	-0.06	64	61	100	5	8	Change

Note: Opinion or performance posttests are denoted as "O,P post."

Author Index

Abramovitch, R., 233
Abravanel, E., 248
Achenbach, T. M., 260
Adams, R. M., 148
Adler, T. F., 81, 94
Ahmed, S.M.S., 233
Aiello, J. R., 137, 154, 260
Alkema, F., 260
Allen, G., 264
Allen, M. J., 126, 248
Allen, R. D., 233
Allen, V. L., 193, 201, 269
Alpert, R., 236, 240
Ames, L. B., 260
Anderson, C. C., 233
Anderson, F. J., 260
Angrist, S. S., 128
Angulo, J., 238
Archer, J., 260
Argyle, M., 260
Arkes, H. R., 117
Arkin, R. M., 105
Arkoff, A., 271
Arms, R. L., 233
Armstrong, J. M., 78, 82
Aronson, E., 64, 106
Asch, S. E., 181, 269
Ashear, V., 260-261
Atkinson, R. C., 51
Atkinson, R. L., 51

Bakker, C. B., 233
Bakker-Rabdau, M. K., 233
Bandura, A., 61, 233
Bandura, M., 69, 76-77, 81
Bankart, C. P., 233

Barclay, A. M., 233
Barnes, R. D., 263
Baron, R. A., 166, 238
Barrett, D. E., 233
Bart, P. B., 118
Bar-Tal, D., 104, 124, 255
Bates, J. E., 261
Baum, A., 261
Baumrind, D., 233
Bayley, G. A., 205, 273
Beach, D. R., 261
Beam, D. C., 154, 262
Becker, B. J., 32, 35, 45, 183-184, 186, 211, 213, 219
Bell, R. Q., 239, 264
Beloff, H., 200, 269
Bem, S. L., 269
Benbow, C. P., 67, 79
Bender, E. P., 265
Ben Haim, D., 92
Bennett, H. L., 238
Berg, P. A., 255
Berger, S. E., 242
Berk, L. E., 233-234
Berkowitz, L., 163
Bernard, J., 160-161
Best, D. T., 70, 248
Bier, E. G., 261
Biller, H. B., 241
Bilous, C. B., 238
Binet, A., 222
Biondo, J., 269
Birg, L. D., 106
Black, A. E., 233
Blake, R. R., 269
Blanchard, F. H., 235
Block, J., 81, 86, 228, 248

Block, J., 81, 86, 248
Block, J. H., 160, 225, 228
Bock, R. D., 76-77
Bogat, G. A., 237
Bond, L. A., 234
Bond, M. H., 261
Bouchard, T. J., Jr., 248
Boxer, M. J., 227
Breen, L. J., 255
Breit, S., 233
Brenner, O. C., 234
Brion-Meisels, S. J., 234
Brissett, M., 234
Brockman, C., 241
Brodzinsky, D. M., 234
Brooks-Gunn, Jeanne, 226-227
Brown, J. S., 80
Brush, L., 68, 80-81, 86-87, 90
Buck, R., 156
Bullock, D., 234
Burger, J., 127
Burgoon, M., 180, 269
Burnett, S. A., 91
Burnett-Doering, J., 125
Buss, A. H., 63, 128, 164, 234, 240
Buss, D. M., 240
Byrne, D., 166

Camara, K. A., 236
Campbell, D. T., 163-164, 213
Campbell, R. E., 126
Cann, A., 122
Cantor, J. R., 242
Carey, S. E., 76
Carlberg, C. G., 216
Carli, L. L., 16, 140-141, 169, 171-172,
    182-184, 187-192, 195-196, 202,
    204-205
Carmen, B., 263
Carpenter, P. A., 71
Carpenter, T. P., 67, 79, 90-91
Carter, P., 75
Cary, M. S., 261
Castle, Cora, 222
Cattell, R. B., 71
Chaiken, S., 261, 269-270
Chaikin, A. L., 144, 261
Champness, B. G., 265
Chandra, S., 269
Chapman, A. J., 144, 261-262
Chapman, W. A., 144, 261

Cherulnik, P. D., 144, 261
Chipman, S. F., 68, 80-81, 86-87, 90
Chodorow, N., 224, 227
Christensen, D., 269
Chu, G. C., 196, 269
Ciccolella, M. E., 234
Clement, C., 249
Close, N., 226
Cohen, J., 109-111, 113, 127, 141, 154
Coleman, D., 237
Coleman, J. F., 269
Combs, A. L., 256
Combs, N. H., 256
Conger, J. J., 51-52
Connor, J. M., 90, 92, 248
Conolley, E. S., 271
Cook, M., 263
Cook, T. D., 127, 163-165, 213
Cooper, H. M., 15, 109-110, 127, 182-187,
    192, 202
Cooper, L. A., 71, 75, 91
Copitch, P., 241
Corely, R. P., 77
Corsini, D. A., 264
Corter, C., 233
Costanzo, P. R., 181, 192, 270
Coutts, L. M., 261, 265
Coward, T., 270
Cox, L., 270
Cox, P. W., 70
Crain, W. C., 234
Crandall, C. J., 265
Crandall, V. C., 107
Crane, D., 122
Crano, W. D., 191, 270
Crittenden, K. S., 106
Crockett, L., 76-77
Crockett, L. S., 90
Croke, J. H., 255
Cronbach, L. J., 128, 163, 215, 222
Crowley, M., 172-173
Crowne, D. P., 270
Crowther, J. H., 234
Crutchfield, R. S., 181, 270

Dabbs, J. M., Jr., 261-262
D'Aquila, J. M., 250
Darwin, C., 222, 225
Davis, A. H., 241
Davis, M., 262
Dayton, C. M., 77

Deaux, K. K., 81, 93-94, 104, 107, 109, 120, 123, 161, 211, 234, 255
DeAvila, E. A., 70, 248
de Benedictis, T., 83, 86, 91, 249
DeFries, J. C., 76
Delin, P. S., 194, 270
Delucchi, K., 83, 85, 249
Deluty, R. H., 234
DePaulo, B. M., 156
Derlaga, V. J., 144, 261
DerSimonian, R., 21
Desautels, M. S., 263
Detchon, C. S., 105
Devor, G., 235
Diamond, R., 76
Ding, G. F., 262
DiPietro, J. A., 234
Ditrichs, R., 234
DiVesta, F. J., 270
Donnerstein, E. I., 237
Doob, A. N., 234
Doolittle, J. C., 234
Dougherty, K., 79
Downs, A. C., 237
Dragan, W., 265
Dratt, L. M., 91
Drost, B. A., 237
Dwyer, C. A., 166
Dyck, D. G., 255
Dyk, R. B., 70

Eagly, A. H., 140-141, 166, 169, 171-173, 180-192, 194-196, 199, 202, 204-205, 215, 217, 219, 227, 269-270
Eagly, H. H., 16
Eakins, B. W., 137
Eakins, R. G., 137
Edelman, M., 239
Edelman, R., 236
Edenhurt-Pape, M., 79
Edwards, C. P., 242
Edwards, J., 270
Eisenberg, G. J., 234-235
Eisenberg, J. G., 238
Eisenberg-Berg, N., 64
Ekehammer, B., 124
Ekstrom, R. B., 71
Elig, T. W., 104, 118, 128
Eliot, J., 77
Emmerich, W., 235
Endler, N. S., 191, 270-271

Epstein, R., 235
Epstein, S., 124-125, 241
Epstein, Y. M., 166
Erdos, G., 248
Erickson, B., 265
Ericsson, K. A., 109
Eron, L. D., 236-238, 240-241
Evans, M. S., 261-262
Evenbeck, S., 124, 255
Ex, J., 200, 270
Exline, R. V., 144, 262
Eysenck, H. J., 47, 175

Fagot, B. I., 235
Farris, E., 104, 109, 123, 255
Feather, N. T., 105-106, 117-118, 255, 256
Feldman, R.H.L., 196, 270-271
Feldman, S. S., 262, 264
Feldman-Summers, S., 120, 271
Feng, C., 71
Fennema, E. H., 67, 79, 90-91, 248
Ferguson, L. R., 235-236
Feshback, N. D., 235
Field, P. B., 178, 180, 271
Finchum, K. G., 235
Finley, G. E., 262
Fisher, J. E., 107, 120, 128, 256
Fiske, D. W., 15, 109, 126, 163-164, 213
Fitch, G., 107
Flanagan, M., 261
Flannagan, M., 70
Fleming, M. L., 82, 84
Foddy, M., 144, 262
Foley, J. M., 241-242
Foot, H. C., 144, 262
Forbes, J., 237
Ford, L. H., Jr., 272
Forman, S. G., 235
Forsythe, D. R., 255
Foster, K. T., 235
Fox, S., 236
Frager, R., 200, 271
Fralley, J. S., 77
Frances, S. J., 139, 262
Francis, W. R., 122
Franzini, L. R., 235
Freitag, C. B., 235
French, J. W., 71
French, L. A., 235
Freud, S., 223

Frieze, I. H., 102–108, 117–118, 120–122,
    124–126, 128, 137, 219–229, 227,
    255–257
Frodi, A., 163, 235
Fromme, D. K., 154, 262
Furbay, A. L., 271

Galassi, J. P., 262
Galassi, M. D., 262
Galton, F., 222
Gandelman, R., 77
Garrett, W. A., 265
Garske, J. P., 117
Gates, M., 241
Geen, R. G., 241
Geiringer, E. R., 248–249
Gelfand, D. M., 238–239
Geller, S. H., 191, 270–271
Gentner, D. R., 92
Gerard, H. B., 271
Gersten, J. C., 238
Geshuri, Y., 239
Giaconia, R. M., 17
Gilligan, C., 64, 86, 160, 224, 227
Gillman, M. G., 124, 256
Gingold, H., 248
Gitelson, I. B., 81, 228, 250
Glass, G. V., 15–18, 20–21, 25–28, 43, 54,
    69, 127, 168–169, 186, 189–191
Glinski, B. C., 190, 200, 271
Glinski, R. J., 190, 200, 271
Golbeck, S. L., 249
Goldberg, C., 124, 255
Good, T., 127
Goodenough, D. R., 70, 77
Gordon, J. E., 191
Gottfried, N. W., 237, 263
Gould, S. J., 218
Grady, K. E., 160
Graham, J. C., 265
Gray, D., 144, 262
Gray, S. W., 237
Green, B. F., 170
Greenberg, C. I., 261
Greene, B., 234
Greeno, J. G., 80
Greenwald, A. G., 120
Greer, D., 236
Gregory, W. L., 269
Griffen, B. O., 256
Griffith, W., 262

Gross, A. E., 234
Gruber, K. L., 117–119, 256–257
Grusec, J. E., 233, 235
Guay, R. B., 71, 248
Guerney, B. G., Jr., 240

Haaland, G. A., 271
Halberstadt, A., 20, 87, 220
Hall, J. A., 20, 87, 137–138, 140, 142, 151,
    154, 156, 170–171, 220
Hallam, E., 240
Halperin, K., 271
Hammen, C. L., 262–263
Hancock, F. T., 272
Hanley, C., 70, 248
Hansen, R. D., 109
Hanson, D. J., 235
Hanusa, B. H., 117, 122–123, 128
Hapkiewicz, W. G., 236
Harden, R. R., 236
Harmatz, M. G., 236
Harper, S., 236–237
Harris, L., 263
Harris, A., 83
Harris, B., 86
Harris, L. F., 248
Harris, L. J., 70
Hartlage, L. C., 77
Hartmann, D. P., 238–239
Hartup, W. W., 236, 240
Hatfield, J. S., 236
Havassy, B., 70, 248
Hayes, S. C., 236
Healey, J. M., Jr., 128
Hedges, L. V., 17, 22–23, 29–30, 35, 53,
    56–57, 59–61, 69, 72, 90, 109–110, 127,
    169–170, 182–183, 185, 189–190, 195,
    203, 211
Hedrick, T. E., 241
Heilman, M. E., 107, 123
Heller, J. I., 80
Hendrick, C., 166
Henley, N. M., 137–138, 150
Herbert, M., 79
Hess, R. D., 236
Hicks, D. J., 236
Hilgard, E. R., 51
Hinde, R. A., 138
Hoffman, M. L., 86
Hokanson, J. E., 236
Hollander, E. P., 271

Hollingsworth, L. S., 161, 223, 226
Hoppe, C. M., 236
Hopper, C. H., 261-262
Houston, B. K., 271
Hoving, K. L., 236
Hueftle, S. J., 81-84, 86
Huesmann, L. R., 236-238
Hughes, R. N., 249
Hunt, R. G., 264
Hunter, J. E., 127
Huston, A. C., 51-52
Huston-Stein, A., 236
Hyde, J. S., 53, 55, 60-63, 79, 117, 161, 216, 236, 248-249, 255
Hynan, M., 236-237

Ickes, W., 107, 263
Ingham, M. E., 262
Ingham, R., 260
Inhelder, B., 70
Inkso, C. A., 271
Insko, V. M., 271

Jackaway, R., 107
Jacklin, C. N., 52-53, 56, 61-62, 68-69, 72, 74, 79, 91, 120, 161, 178, 182, 184-187, 190, 204, 216-217, 222, 225
Jackson, G. B., 15, 127
Jackson, T. T., 126
Jackson, W. L., 237
Jacob, S. H., 236
Jamison, W., 77, 249-250
Janis, I. L., 178, 180, 271
Janoff-Bulman, R., 118
Jean, P. J., 227
Jersild, A. T., 237, 262
Johnson, R. W., 191, 237
Johnson, S. D., 237
Jones, J. W., 237
Jones, R. A., 166
Jones, S., 180
Jones, S. B., 180, 269
Jorgenson, D. O., 263
Julian, J. W., 271
Jurkovic, G. J., 237
Just, M. A., 71
Justin, F., 263

Kaczala, C., 81, 94
Kagan, J., 51-52
Kahan, J., 122

Kahle, J. B., 86
Kahn, A. S., 227
Kail, R., 75
Kallas, C., 236-237
Kanareff, V. T., 194, 200, 205, 271-272
Kaplan, A. G., 160
Karplus, R., 249-250
Kaspryzyk, D., 271
Keller, E. F., 226
Kelley, H. H., 241
Kelly, G. N., 249
Kelly, J. T., 249
Kendon, A., 263
Kent, R. N., 241
Keolbl, S.L.M., 109
Kessler, S. J., 164
Kiesler, S. B., 120
King, B. T., 272
Kirkevold, B., 148
Kirkpatrick, C., 179
Klaus, R. S., 237
Klein, R. L., 181, 192, 272
Klein, S. S., 93, 229
Kleinke, C. L., 263
Klesges, R. C., 237
Knapp, B. E., 263
Knott, P. D., 237
Koerner, F. E., 237
Kohlberg, L., 225
Kolakowski, D., 76-77
Kram, K. E., 107, 123
Krasnoff, A. G., 77, 250
Kruglanski, A. W., 128
Kuse, A. R., 76
Kyllonen, P. C., 70

LaForme, G. L., 236
LaFrance, M., 263
Laird, N. M., 21
Lakes, M. K., 86
Land, M. L., 256
Lando, B., 233
Lando, H. A., 237
Landsbaum, J. B., 272
Lane, D. M., 91
Langlois, J. H., 237, 263
Langner, T. S., 238
Lanzetta, J. T., 194, 200, 205, 271-272
Larder, D. L., 237
Larsen, K. S., 237, 272
Laventure, R. O., 237

Layden, M. A., 107
Layne, O., Jr., 262
Layton, B., 265
Leader, F. B., 238-239
Lefkowitz, M. M., 236-238
Lenney, E., 107
Leventhal, D. B., 238
Leventhal, H., 180
Levine, J. M., 193, 201, 269
Levine, M. H., 144, 263
Levine, R., 124, 256
Leviton, L. C., 127, 165
Libby, W. L., Jr., 263
Liben, L. S., 70, 249
Liberman, D., 242
Liebert, R. M., 238
Light, R. J., 69, 170-171
Lindquist, C. U., 238
Lindsay, J. S., 238
Linn, M. C., 68-70, 73, 83, 85-86, 90, 92,
    213, 220, 249
Litrownik, A. J., 235
Litz, M. C., 262
Liverant, S., 270
Lochman, J. E., 264
Lockard, J. S., 265-266
Lockwood, J. L., 238
Loevinger, J., 128
Lohman, D. F., 75, 89, 91
Lott, B., 264
Lowe, C. A., 122
Luce, S. R., 256
Luginbuhl, J., 122

Macaulay, J., 163
MacBride, P. D., 181, 190, 193, 201, 273
McCallin, M., 260
McCandless, B. R., 238
McCarthy, E. D., 238
McClintock, B., 226
McClintock, C. C., 264
Maccoby, E. E., 52-53, 56, 61-62, 68-69,
    72, 74, 79, 91, 120, 161, 178, 182,
    184-187, 190, 204, 216-217, 222,
    224-226, 235, 264
McDaniel, E. D., 71, 248
McDavid, J. W., 172, 182, 185-186, 191,
    194, 273
MacDonald, A. P., Jr., 269
MacDonnell, J., 191
McDowell, K. V., 264

McGarvey, W. E., 122
McGaw, B., 17-18, 20-21, 25, 54, 127,
    168-169, 189-191
McGaw, J. A., 227
McGee, M. G., 77, 248
McGinley, H., 237
McGuire, J. M., 238
McGuire, W. J., 120
McHugh, M. C., 117-118, 120, 123,
    128-129, 219-220, 227, 256
McIntyre, A., 238
McKee, J. P., 238-239
McKenna, W., 164
Mackey, W. C., 144, 264
McMahan, I. D., 256
Madsen, C., 238
Maehr, M. L., 16, 82, 84, 89
Magnusson, D., 124
Mallick, S. K., 238
Malone, M. R., 82, 84
Mancini, F., 240
Mandel, R. A., 238
Manosevitz, M., 238
Markey, F. V., 237
Marshall, S. P., 79-81
Martin, M. F., 238
Maruyama, G. M., 105
Matthews, K. A., 238
May, J., 262
Mayo, C., 138, 263
Meade, R. D., 192, 273
Mednick, M.T.S., 104, 160, 124, 256
Meece, J. L., 80-81
Meehan, A. M., 67, 82, 84-86
Meehl, P. E., 128, 163, 215
Meerdink, G. B., 256
Mehrabian, A., 144, 264
Menlove, F. L., 233
Merrill, L., 234
Messer, S. B., 234
Mettee, D., 106
Metzler, J., 71
Meyer, J. P., 109
Meyerson, L. J., 241
Middleton, R., 272
Milgram, S., 179
Miller, D. T., 122, 256
Mischel, W., 124
Mitchell, M. E., 122
Montano, D. E., 271
Moore, M., 239

Moreland, R. L., 117-119, 256-257
Morelock, J. C., 180, 272
Morely, I. E., 265
Morgan, T. J., 237
Morganti, J. B., 272
Morissette, M. L., 239
Moskowitz, D. S., 264
Moutons, J. S., 269
Murray, S. R., 104, 124, 256
Mussen, P. H., 51-52, 64
Muste, M. J., 239

Nagelbush, J. L., 239
Nakamura, C. Y., 265, 272
Neely, W. T., 261
Nelson, J. D., 239
Nevill, D., 144, 264
Newcombe, N., 69, 76-77, 81
Newsom, M. W., 239
Nicholls, J. G., 106, 122
Noller, P., 264
Norman, D. A., 92
Nowicki, S., Jr., 234

O'Connell, A. N., 124, 256
Oetzel, R. M., 52
O'Leary, K. D., 241
O'Leary, V. E., 109
Olkin, I., 23, 69, 90, 127, 182, 185
Oltman, P. K., 70
Omark, D. R., 239
Omark, M., 239
Oresick, R. J., 128
Orezeck, L., 238

Paolino, A. F., 239
Parlee, M. R., 159-160, 171, 175
Parsons, J. E., 81, 94, 103, 106-107, 118,
   122
Parton, D. A., 239
Pascual-Leone, J., 70, 248
Pasquella, M. J., 104, 124, 256
Patel, A. S., 191
Paterson, H. F., 70
Patterson, G. R., 235
Patterson, M. L., 264
Paulson, S. F., 272
Payne, P., 265
Peaco, D., 77
Pearce, J. W., 239
Pearce, L., 122
Peckham, P. D., 27-28

Pedersen, F. A., 264
Pederson, F. A., 239
Pellegrino, J., 75
Peplau, L. A., 262-263
Perez, S., 124, 256
Peskin, J., 85
Petersen, A. C., 68-69, 73, 76-77, 81, 90,
   213, 219-220, 228, 249, 250
Phares, E. J., 104
Piaget, J., 70
Pilkonis, P. A., 264
Pillemar, D. B., 69, 170-171
Pitblado, C., 250
Poo-Kong, K., 194, 270
Prentice, N. M., 238
Prerost, F. J., 239
Presby, S., 26, 47
Price, L. A., 71
Propst, L. R., 239
Puleo, J. S., 239
Pulos, S., 86, 90, 249
Pulos, S. M., 249-250
Purvis, J. A., 261-262
Pylysyshyn, Z. W., 71
Pytkowicz, A. R., 239-240

Raden, D., 240
Rakow, S. J., 81-84, 86
Ramanaiah, N. V., 240
Ramsey, S. J., 137
Ratliff, C. D., 240
Rau, L., 240
Rau, M., 240
Raven, 75
Read, S. J., 106
Regula, C. R., 271
Reid, P. T., 125
Reinisch, J. M., 77
Reis, H., 124, 256
Reitan, H. T., 272
Rensberger, B., 64
Richmond, P. G., 250
Riley, M. S., 80
Rincover, A., 236
Roden, A. H., 236
Rogers, E. D., 273
Rogers, R. W., 240
Rolf, J. E., 234
Roll, S., 238
Ronis, D. L., 109
Rosekrans, M. A., 240

Rosenberg, B. G., 117
Rosenberg, J. J., 196, 272
Rosenberg, R., 161
Rosenfeld, H. M., 264
Rosenfield, D., 123, 256
Rosenthal, H. M., 142
Rosenthal, R., 23, 34, 51–52, 56, 62, 127, 147, 156, 170, 183, 186, 265
Rosnow, R. L., 147
Ross, M., 265
Rotter, G. S., 191
Rubin, D. B., 34, 56, 62, 170
Rubin, Z., 265
Ruble, D. N., 265
Russell, G. W., 233
Russo, N. F., 144, 265
Rutter, D. R., 265
Ryckman, R. M., 271

Samek, W. R., 240
Sampson, E. E., 272
Sanders, B., 250
Sanders, J. R., 27–28
Sandilands, M. L., 233
Santrock, J. W., 240, 242
Sarason, I. G., 239–240, 265
Sasfy, J. H., 256
Schackman, M., 92, 248
Scheidel, T. M., 180, 272
Scheier, M. F., 240
Schein, S. L., 240
Scheman, J. D., 265
Scheppele, K. L., 118
Schermer, B., 263
Schlenker, B. R., 255
Schmidt, F. L., 127
Schneider, F. W., 261, 265
Schopler, J., 265
Schuck, A., 240
Schuck, J. R., 60, 236
Schuck, S. Z., 240
Schuette, D., 144, 262
Schulman, J. L., 241–242
Schwartz, J. C., 264
Schwarz, J. C., 265
Sears, R. R., 240
Seay, B., 237, 263
Sedney, M. A., 160
Segall, S. R., 240
Seibert, S. M., 240
Sejwacz, D., 269

Semler, I. J., 240–241
Serbin, L. A., 90, 92, 241, 248
Sharpe, D. F., 239
Shaw, M. E., 181, 192, 270, 272
Shemberg, K. M., 238
Shenkel, R. J., 271
Shepard, R. N., 71
Sherif, Carolyn, 159–160, 175
Sherman, J., 248, 250
Sherrod, L. R., 241
Shields, S. A., 160–161, 221–223
Shiraishi, D., 261
Shomer, R. W., 241
Shope, G. L., 241
Shortell, J. R., 241
Shreve, A., 226
Siegel, A. E., 241
Sigler, E., 144, 261
Sigman, E., 70
Signorella, M. L., 249–250
Sikkink, D. E., 272
Silverman, I., 272
Simon, H. H., 109
Simon, J. G., 105–106, 117–118, 255–256
Simon, S., 234
Simon, T., 222
Singer, D. G., 241
Singer, J. L., 241
Singh, U. P., 196, 272
Sinnott, J. D., 85
Sistrunk, F., 172, 182, 185–186, 191, 194, 205, 273
Skolnick, P., 144, 266
Slaby, R. G., 241
Slane, S., 144, 265
Slatin, G. T., 190, 200, 271
Slavin, R. E., 216
Small, A., 79
Smith, J. R., 144, 262
Smith, M. L., 17–18, 20, 25, 43, 54, 127, 168–169, 190–191
Smoke, L., 234
Sneider, C., 250
Snortum, J. R., 260–261
Snow, R. E., 75. 91
Snyder, C. R., 271
Snyder, H. N., 104, 122, 125
Soares, M. P., 250
Sohn, D., 117, 120
Sokol, M., 128
Sokoloff, M. J., 261

Spiegel, F. S., 77
Spuhler, K. P., 76
Staats, S. R., 241
Stabene, F. P., 190, 273
Stafford, R. E., 77
Stage, E. K., 81, 83, 90, 249–250
Stanley, J. C., 67, 79, 163, 213
Steel, L., 78
Steeno, J., 263
Steiner, I. D., 273
Steinkamp, M. W., 16, 82, 84, 89
Stephan, C., 256
Stephan, W. G., 123, 256
Stern, D. N., 265
Sternberg, D. P., 261
Stewart, D., 180, 269
Stier, D. S., 171
Stock, W. A., 169
Stone, W. F., 273
Stover, L., 240
Strauch, A. B., 250
Strayer, F. F., 241
Strayer, J., 241
Strongman, K. T., 265
Sullivan, P., 249
Sutton-Smith, B., 144, 263
Swann, W. B., 106
Sweeney, P. D., 117–119, 256–257

Tanner, N. M., 64
Tauber, M. A., 266
Taylor, A.J.W., 200, 273
Taylor, D. G., 69, 76–77, 81
Taylor, L. J., 250
Taylor, S. P., 241
Teglasi, H., 124, 257
Telaak, K., 270
Terman, L. M., 52, 223
Tew, J. D., 234
Thier, H. D., 92
Thomas, H., 77
Thomas, S. J., 76, 85
Thome, P. R., 163
Thompson, Helen Bradford, 161
Thurstone, L. L., 71
Thurstone, T. G., 71
Tidd, K. L., 266
Tieger, T., 52
Timaeus, E., 200, 273
Titley, R. W., 241
Tobin-Richards, M. H., 77

Tolnick, I. J., 241
Tomikewicz, J., 234
Travis, C. B., 125
Trembly, G., 180
Tucker, P. T., 241
Tuddenham, R. D., 178, 181, 190, 193, 201, 273
Tyler, L. E., 52

Uleman, J., 124

Valle, V. A., 107
Vandenberg, S. G., 71, 73, 76, 250
Van Leeuwen, M. A., 250
Van Lehn, K., 80
van Schoelandt, S. K., 238
Vasta, R., 241
Vaughan, G. M., 200, 273
Vaughn, B. E., 241
Vaughter, R. M., 160
Veitch, R., 262
Vernon, D. T., 241–242
Vetter, B., 88
Viaene, N., 124, 257
Vidulich, R. N., 190, 205, 273
Viney, W., 241
Volosin, D., 236
Vulcano, B., 255

Waber, D. P., 76
Wagman, M., 242
Wagner, B., 271
Wagner, N. N., 239–240
Wailes, S. N., 235
Walker, J. T., 77, 250
Walker, R. N., 242
Wallace, J. R., 236
Warren, R., 270
Waters, E., 241
Watkins, B. A., 236
Weinberger, M. A., 226
Weiner, B., 102–104, 118
Weisz, J. R., 260
Weitz, S., 262
Welch, W. W., 78, 81–84, 86
Wells, R., 240
Westeman, K., 260
Wheeler, R., 86
Whitaker, J., 236
White, G. D., 238
White, K. B., 60

Whitehead, G. I., 270
Whiting, B., 242
Whitley, B. E., Jr., 105, 117, 121-122,
  126, 219-220, 227
Whittaker, J. O., 192, 205, 273
Wiegers, R. M., 124, 257
Wiesenthal, D. L., 191, 270
Wiley, M. G., 106
Wilhelmy, R. A., 271
Williams, J. F., 241
Williams, M., 264
Willis, F. N., 260
Willis, R. H., 272
Wilson, D., 68, 80-81, 86-87, 90
Wilson, F., 238
Wilson, J. R., 250
Winkel, G. H., 265
Winters, L. C., 262
Wise, L., 78, 90
Wisenthal, D. L., 271
Witkin, H. A., 70

Wittig, M. A., 76, 144, 248, 266
Wohlford, P., 242
Woltz, D. J., 75
Wong, P.T.P., 118-119, 257
Wood, C., 236
Wood, W., 270
Woods, B., 76
Woody, T., 223
Wortman, P. M., 168
Wyer, R. S., Jr., 205, 273

Yaklevich, D., 263
Yen, W. M., 77, 126, 249
Youssef, Z. I., 242

Zaccaro, S. J., 122
Zachau, M., 261
Zahn, V., 181, 190, 193, 201, 273
Zillman, D., 242
Zuckerman, M., 156

Subject Index

Achievement attributions. *See*
    Success-failure attributions
Aggression, types of
    imitative, 62
    physical versus verbal, 61-62
Aggression studies, 51-66, 233-247
    age trends in, 52, 56, 62
    biological factors in, 52
    coding of, 54
    construct underrepresentation in,
        163-164
    effect size in, 54-55, 61
    homogeneity tests of, 56-59, 60-61, 62
    interpretation of, 63-65
    meta-analysis contributions to, 62-65
    model specifications in, 59-60
    outlier study elimination, 60
    sample of, 53-54
    sources on, 51-52
ANOVA (Analysis of Variance), 19-20,
        35-39, 183-184
Attributional disposition, 125
Attributions. *See* Success-failure
        attributions

Biases, consequences of, 160-162
Biology, ability in, 82, 83
Buss paradigm, 163

Cognitive research perspective, 70
Combinatorial reasoning, 84-85
Computation ability, 78
Conformity studies. *See also* Persuasion
        studies; Social influence
    Asch-type, 186
    characteristics of, 181-182
    designs for, 181-182

effect size analysis of, 33, 186-187, 188
experimental paradigms and biases in,
        187-189
p-value summaries for, 186-187
reviews of, 184-189
studies in, 269-278
t-test comparisons of, 188
Construct irrelevancies, surplus, 164
Construct underrepresentation, 163-164,
        166
Construct validity
    classifying studies by, 168-169
    meta-analysis and, 165-166, 215, 217
    nature of, 163-164
    threat to, 166
Context influences, 219
Conventional analysis, problems with,
        25-28
    conceptual, 26-27
    statistical, 27-28
Correlations, effect size calculation from,
        20-21

Developmental influences, 220
Differential research perspective, 70
Dominance-status hypothesis, 138,
        150-151, 152-153
d-values
    analysis of variations in, 7
    in meta-analysis, 6-7

Earth science, ability in, 82, 83
Effect size(s), 16-49
    calculation of, 18-21
        from ANOVA statistics, 19-20, 35-39
        from correlations, 20-21

Effect size(s) *(continued)*
from means and standard deviations, 18-19
comparisons of, among groups, 39-46
a priori, 42
post hoc, 42
conventional analysis for, 25-28
conceptual problems with, 26-27
statistical problems with, 27-28
in correlational studies, 7-9
estimation of, 16-18
problems with, 21-23
from series of studies, 32-34
homogeneity tests of, 34-35, 46-48, 69, 211-215
model specification for, 46-49
modern methods for analysis of, 28-49
properties of, 28-31
regression analysis of, 42-46
Embedded figures test, 74
Empathy, 64, 86
External validity
classifying studies by, 168-169
generalizability and, 164-165
meta-analysis and, 167, 215-216, 217
nature of, 164-165

Failure attributions. *See* Success-failure attributions
Fictitious norm group, 181-182, 186-187, 194, 195
File drawer problem, 5-6
Fluid ability, 75-76
F-tests, 24, 28

Gazing studies, 260-267. *See also* Nonverbal skills and behaviors; Smiling, social
age factor in, 143, 144, 148-149, 150, 153
correlates of differences in, 143-145
interpersonal interaction in, 150-151, 153
methodological issues in, 145-147
data set, 145
dependent variables, 147
independent variables, 145-147
regression analysis of, 151-154
bivariate, 151-153
multiple, 153-154
research context of, 142-143

situational variables in, 144-145, 147
dominance-status, 150-153
social tension-nervousness, 150, 152, 154
warmth-affiliation, 147-152
General fluid ability, 75-76
Generalizability, replication and, 126, 127
Geometry tasks, ability in, 78, 90
Group pressure paradigm, 181
Group pressure studies, 181-182, 194. *See also* Conformity studies; Persuasion studies; Social influence
confidence intervals in, 198, 201-202
outcome variability in, 200-201
Groups, effect size comparisons among, 39-42

Helping behavior meta-analysis, validity of, 173-175
Homogeneity tests, 34-35, 69
difficulties with, 213-215
importance of, 46-48, 211-212
interpretation of, 212-213

Influenceability. *See* Conformity studies; Persuasion studies; Social influence
Integrative reviews, 14-15
Intellectual differences, 221-223, 224-225. *See also* Spatial ability differences
Interactionist perspective, 225-227

Knowledge domain influences, 219-220. *See also* Spatial ability differences

Latane's theory of social impact, 194
Laughing, social, 140. *See also* Smiling, social

Mathematics performance, 77-82. *See also* Science achievement; Spatial ability differences
age trends in, 78, 80, 89
in computation, 78, 79-80, 87-88
data sources for, 77-78, 79, 81
experience hypothesis on, 80-81, 92-93
in geometry, 78, 79
magnitude of differences in, 78-79, 88-89
nature of, 77-78, 87-88
in problem solving, 78, 79-80, 87-88
process analysis of, 79-80

societal expectations and, 81–82, 93–94
spatial ability and, 80–82, 87–94
Means, calculating effect sizes from, 18–19
Mental rotation performance, 71, 73, 74, 75–76, 90
Mental-testing movement, 222
Meta-analysis
advances in, 3–9, 69
contributions of, 211–217
definition of, 3
future directions for, 227–228
recommendations for, 218–219
validity of, 215–216
Model specification, 46–49
importance of, 46–48
problems in obtaining, 48–49
Moral development perspective, 224

Narrative reviews, problems with, 2–3
Nonverbal skills and behaviors. *See also*
Gazing studies; Smiling, social
factors limiting, 137
situational determinants of, 137–140
dominance-status, 138, 150–153
social tension-nervousness, 139, 150, 152, 154, 156
warmth-affiliation, 138, 147–152, 156
studies on, 137

Outcome measures, 193–194
effect size heterogeneity and, 213–215

Persuasion studies. *See also* Conformity
studies; Social influence
characteristics of, 181–182
confidence intervals in, 198, 201–202
outcome variability in, 196–199
p-value summaries of, 187
reviews of, 184–189
sex of author and, 188
studies in, 269–278
Physical science, ability in, 82, 83
Posttests, 193–194, 198–199, 200
Pretests, 193–194
Primary Mental Abilities Test, 73
Probability-combining techniques, 5–6, 62
Problem-solving ability, 78. *See also*
Mathematics performance
Problem-solving processes, 75–76
Proportional reasoning, 84–85, 91
Propositional reasoning, 84–85

Psychoanalytical perspective, 223
Psychology of gender difference, perspectives on, 221–227
biological, 221–224
empirical, 224–225
interactionist, 225–227
Psychometric research perspective, 70
Psychosocial differences, 223–225
Psychosocial perspective, 224
p-value summaries, 182–183, 186, 187

Regression analysis, 42–46, 151–154
Reliability, replication and, 126, 127. *See also* Validity
Replication, 126–129
Research perspectives, 70

Science achievement, 82–85. *See also*
Mathematics performance; Spatial ability differences
affective hypothesis on, 86–87, 93–94
age trends in, 82, 83, 84, 89
effect sizes estimation in, 84–85
experience hypothesis on, 86, 92–93
magnitude of difference in, 82, 83–85, 88–89
nature of, 82–83, 87–88
spatial ability and, 86, 87–94
Science information tasks, ability for, 82, 83, 88, 90
Scientific reasoning
ability for, 82–83, 84, 88, 90
types of, 84–85
Sex typing, 124, 154, 169, 178
Shepard-Metzler mental rotation test, 73, 74, 88
Smiling, social, 140–142. *See also* Gazing
studies; Nonverbal skills and behaviors
age factor in, 141, 142, 148–149, 150, 153
correlates of differences in, 143–145
effect size estimation of, 141–142
homogeneity test for, 142
interpersonal interaction and, 150–151, 153
methodological issues
data set, 145
dependent variables, 147
independent variables, 145–147
nature of, 142

Smiling, social *(continued)*
  regression analysis, 151–154
    bivariate, 151–153
    multiple, 153–154
  situational variables in, 144, 147
    dominance-status, 150–153
    social tension-nervousness, 150, 152,
      154, 156
    warmth-affiliation, 147–152, 156
  studies on, 140, 260–267
Social influence. *See also* Conformity
      studies; Persuasion studies
  attitudinal change and, 179
  generalizability in, 205
  homogeneity tests for, 195–196, 200
  intercorrelations among studies, 202–203
  meta-analysis results in, 203–206
  methodological issues in, 189–195
    effect sizes estimation, 190–192
    model-fitting techniques, 189–190
    study selection and features, 192–195
  quantitative summary methods for
    effect size analyses, 183–184, 186–187
    p-values, 182–183
    vote-counting, 182
  reviews of, 184–189
  studies in, 269–278
  study features, 192–195
    agents, 194
    experimenter sex, 195
    items, 194
    outcome measures, 192, 193–194
    publication types, 195
    subject types, 192
  types of studies on, 179–180
Social influence meta-analysis, validity of,
      172–173
Social-role perspective, 226, 228–229
Social tension-nervousness hypothesis, 139,
      150, 152, 154, 156
Spatial ability sex differences, 67–101. *See
      also* Mathematics performance;
      Science achievement
  age trends in, 68–69, 72, 73, 74, 89
  ambiguity of measures of, 68
  analysis procedure for, 72
  explanation of
    biological, 76–77, 94
    process-based, 75–76
  homogeneity tests of, 73–74

  magnitude of, 73–74, 88–89
  mathematics performance and, 80–82,
      87–94
  nature of, 70–71, 73–74, 87–88
  research perspectives on, 70
  scientific achievement and, 86, 87–94
  studies in, 248–254
  study selection for, 72
  symbolic information and, 73–74
Spatial perception, 70–71, 73, 74, 77,
      91–92
Spatial visualization, 71, 74, 75, 77, 89
Spearman-Brown prophecy formula, 147
Standard deviations, effect size calculation
      from, 18–19
Statistical methods, 14–50. *See also* Effect
      size
  goals of, 14–16, 23–25
Stouffer combined significance test, 187
Strategic research perspective, 70
Success-failure attributions, 102–135
  causal categories, 103
    ability, 103, 110–111, 113, 114, 115
    effort, 103, 110–111, 112, 113, 114,
      115–116
    luck, 103, 110–111, 112, 113, 115,
      116, 117–119
    task ease/difficulty, 103, 110–111,
      112, 113, 115, 116, 119
  effect sizes, 110–116
    within outcomes, 110–113
    within sex, 113–116
  future research on, 122, 128–129
  meta-analysis contributions to, 127
  methodological issues in
    effect size measures, 109–110
    measurement, 127–128
    personality and motivation, 124–125
    question wording, 104–105, 116–117,
      128
    replication, 126–129
    research context, 121–122
    selection of studies, 108–109
    social context, 123–124
    statistical analysis, 110
    task domains, 122–123
  models of, 102, 105–107
    controllability, 103
    externality, 105–106, 117–119
    internality, 103

low expectancy, 106, 107, 119–120
self-derogation, 106–107, 119
stability, 103, 119
situational variables in, 104
studies in, 255–259
Surplus construct irrelevancies, 164
Symbolic information, 73–74

Threshold effect, 155
t-test comparisons, 188

Validity, 159–177
bias and, 159–162

construct
definition of, 163–164
meta-analysis and, 167
definition of, 162
of meta-analysis, 215–216, 217
meta-analytic tests of, 172–175
in helping behavior studies, 173–175
in social influence studies, 172–173
replication and, 126, 127
threats to, 162–165, 167–171
Vote-counting, 3–5, 69, 182

Warmth-affiliation hypothesis, 138, 139,
147–150, 151–152, 156

The Johns Hopkins University Press

The Psychology of Gender

This book was set in English 49 text and Futura Book and Futura Bold display type by Action Comp Co., Inc., from a design by Chris L. Smith. It was printed on 50-lb. Sebago Eggshell Cream Offset paper and bound in Arrestox A by BookCrafters, Inc.